# The Hunt for Unicorns

# The Hunt for Unicorns

## HOW SOVEREIGN FUNDS ARE RESHAPING INVESTMENT IN THE DIGITAL ECONOMY

Winston Ma and Paul Downs

### FOREWORD by

**Margaret Franklin, CFA** President and CEO, CFA Institute
**Russell Read** former CIO, CalPERS, GIC-Kuwait, and APFC
**Ajay Royan** Co-founder with Peter Thiel of Mithril VC Funds

## WILEY

*Registered Office*
John Wiley & Sons, Ltd., The Atrium, Southern Gate, Chichester, West Sussex, PO19 8SQ, United Kingdom

For details of our global editorial offices, customer services, and more information about Wiley products visit us at www.wiley.com.

Wiley also publishes its books in a variety of electronic formats and by print-on-demand. Some content that appears in standard print versions of this book may not be available in other formats.

*Library of Congress Cataloging-in-Publication Data is Available:*

9781119746607 (paperback); 9781119746614 (ePDF); 9781119746621 (epub)

Cover Design: Wiley
Cover Image: © metamorworks/Getty Images

Set in 12/14pt, NewBaskervilleStd by SPi Global, Chennai, India.

Printed in Great Britain by CPI Antony Rowe.

10  9  8  7  6  5  4  3  2  1

"State-owned investment funds are the new frontier investors, larger in size, influence, and power than the traditional Wall Street of investment banks, asset managers, and hedge funds. They are the "unicorn-makers" behind the scene. Offering a series of in-depth case studies that combine broad perspectives on the tech investment world with specific national examples, this highly original book examines a vital and increasingly important relationship between governments and globalizing VC tech markets."

— **Anthony Scaramucci**, Founder & Managing
Partner of SkyBridge

"Ma and Downs' clear and expansive insights into these disproportion-ately important and yet little-known institutions will prove critical, both to practitioners in the field of investing as well as to the general public seeking answers to the big picture questions of why the new unicorns transforming their lives arose from the modern financial system."

— **Russell Read**, CFA, Ph.D, former CIO for
CalPERS, GIC-Kuwait, and APFC

"The private sector doesn't have the answers to a growing list of the world 's problems. It is the State, working through powerful institu-tions such as sovereign wealth funds, that has taken a key economic and investment role. Investors need to understand these state-controlled wealth funds - what they do and how they do it – and this book provides a timely update that fills a gap in the literature on global finance."

— **Dato' Seri Cheah Cheng Hye**, Co-Founder and Co-Chairman,
Value Partners and Non-Executive Director, Hong Kong
Exchanges and Clearing Ltd

"Sovereign Wealth Funds (SWFs) lie at the intersection of finance, politics, macroeconomics, international relations. This book not only constitutes perhaps the most in-depth and insightful investigation of sovereign investors to date, but the book starts a broader debate over globalization and state economic intervention in the context of world digital revolution. Invaluable to European governments and businesses, in particular, as the EU strives to become the third tech pillar of the world next to the US and China."

— **Pierre-Yves Lucas**, Head of Cooperation Mongolia,
European Union and former Adviser to the CEO
of the SWF of Kazakhstan

"A book that, against the backdrop of the world-altering coronavirus epidemic, provides a thoughtful guide to the role sovereign investors play in the world-changing digital transformation – and how one accelerates the other."

– **Margaret Franklin, CFA**, President and CEO, CFA Institute

"This is a story about Time Machines."

– **Ajay Royan**, Co-founder with Peter Thiel of Mithril VC Funds

*To Angela – I love you dearly*
– Winston Ma

*To Rebecca, whose support has been invaluable.*
– Paul Downs

# Contents

Foreword      xi

    It is Time to Build the Greatest of Time Machines     —Ajay Royan    xi

    The Investment Partners of Choice     —Russell Read, CFA, Ph.D    xviii

    Into the Vanguard of the Digital Transformation     —Margaret Franklin, CFA    xx

Authors' Notes and Acknowledgments      xxiii

Acknowledgements      xxvii

About the Authors      xxix

Preface      xxxi

Chapter 1    **Sovereign Investors Rising in Crisis**      1

Chapter 2    **From Passive Allocators to Active Investors**      33

Chapter 3    **Global Hunt for Unicorns (Decacorns)**      65

Chapter 4    **Long-term Capital into Digital Infrastructure**      103

Chapter 5    **Spurring Domestic Digital Transformation**      137

Chapter 6    **Go Early, Go Nimble**      175

Chapter 7    **The Hunt for the Hunting Party**      205

Chapter 8    **Overseas Expansion and National Security Collide**      241

Chapter 9    **Tech Transactions Snared by Geotech Tension**      275

Chapter 10    **Super Asset Owners**      313

Appendix: Table of Abbreviations                           343

Bibliography                                               347

Index                                                      359

# Foreword

# It is Time to Build the Greatest of Time Machines

This is a story about Time Machines.

No, dear reader, you did not stumble upon the science fiction aisle at the bookstore. You are, however, holding a chronicle of the hunt for their closest earthly cousins.

In this timely book, Winston Ma and Paul Downs bring to light the oft mysterious world of transformative technology startups and the burgeoning sovereign wealth funds who invest in them. Together, these constitute a group of builders and investors who have emerged as two of the biggest forces reshaping the world as we know it. Their origins are diverse, but their evolution has many parallels. And their future, and ours, is intertwined in more ways than anyone anticipated.

Over a nearly two-decade career in tech and investing, I have come to appreciate that every great technology startup is in fact a Time Machine, the fruit of a tribe of mad-genius progenitors intent on hurtling us into the future. Most fail, and almost all are unprecedented by popular opinion. When they succeed, however, they famously remake whole industries for a generation or two.

As this book goes to press, seven of the ten largest companies on earth by market capitalization are tech giants domiciled in the United States and China: Apple, Microsoft, Amazon, Alphabet, Facebook, Alibaba, and Tencent. Even a decade ago, that list would have been significantly varied to include energy, financial, and industrial leaders such as Exxon, ICBC, GE, and Citi. Today, the only *non-tech* companies in the top-ten are Berkshire Hathaway, Visa, and Johnson & Johnson.

Largely ignored by Wall Street after the 2000 Dotcom Bust, these startups managed to thrive with the quiet backing of a new generation of investors, themselves often startup founders who took pride in being founder centric. There was, and is, a strong element of community spirit among the best founders and their funding partners — you paid the favor forward, and in turn found yourself working with kindred spirits conspiring to brilliantly pull forward the future. There exists an equal measure of what one might call constructive paranoia, that no matter how successful one's enterprise might become, there is always lurking a competitor that mustn't be underestimated. After all, the venerable Microsoft and Apple had to be completely reinvented before they could take their spots on that list. Amazon, for its part, is famously obsessed with "Day 1". As founder Jeff Bezos emphasized in his 2016 shareholder letter, "Day 2 is stasis. Followed by irrelevance. Followed by excruciating, painful decline. Followed by death. And that is why it is always Day 1."

Much has changed already for those who would build to last.

As Peter Thiel pithily outlined in *Zero to One*, today's tech markets are defined above all by a winner-take-all dynamic. Victory belongs to the "last-mover", the first company to innovate and get something "just right", which almost never is the first company to enter the category. At the zenith, the sum of the value of all the competitors in a given category often adds up to less than that of the dominant leader. And what's more, it takes at least a decade to incubate and mature such winners.

As a result, today's winners are seemingly more mature, definitely much larger, and yet imbued with an awkward, permanent adolescence that belies their power. Gone are the shotgun IPOs and retail market boomlets. They've been replaced by vast sums of private capital fleeing depressed interest rates for the promise of enduring growth. And once successful, each of these champions begets well-funded corporate treasuries and large cohorts of successful employees, both of which become engines to fund yet another generation of transformative ideas.

Today's tech leaders are also more global, both in their reach and in their origins. Silicon Valley might host an outsized proportion of startups, but it is increasingly a state of mind divorced from location. And here lies a bigger story. For tech startups are scarcely the only time machines in this chronicle.

Before a teenaged immigrant journey that took me to Canada, and eventually to Silicon Valley, I grew up in what felt very much like a Time Machine. 1980s Abu Dhabi was at its core a startup city on a single-minded mission to pull the future forward as fast as humanly possible; where nothing was constant save rapid change and growth. As the best founders will attest, progress cannot happen without taking risk. Success depends on the unlikely combination of vision, focus, skill, drive, and endurance. And on being right. It was so for Abu Dhabi.

Once a small oasis dependent on pearling, Abu Dhabi transformed in the span of just a few decades into one of the world's most modern city-states. Hailing from India, I found myself living between two very different worlds: An ancient, deeply spiritual native land whose industrious people champed at the bit of the License Raj; and a bustling metropolis that seemed to arise from nowhere, its own economy the marriage of nature's gifts, global talent, and its leader's vision.

Similar dynamics unfolded elsewhere, both presaging and following Abu Dhabi's journey: Post-War Japan and South Korea, Lee Kuan Yew's Singapore and its neighboring Asian Tigers, and of course China under Deng Xiaoping. Each was rebooted into a startup mode designed to inspire a whole society to pull the future forward. As with startups, there were spectacular successes among the countries who tried; and yet many more failures. At the peak of their transformative journeys, each of these successes were defined by a strong sense of mission and competent execution that transcended governments and led to widespread prosperity. And once successful, each of these economic champions begot well-funded national treasuries and large pools of sovereign capital designated to sustain that prosperity for generations.

But more prosperity comes with a price. The cost of short-term incremental growth is rising due to greater competition within well-established industries; and low-hanging yields have been obliterated by a decade-long program of financial repression across the developed world. The economies who worked so hard to "arrive" into the developed world have found that they, and those whom they joined, are both faced with the Sisyphean paradox of constant and disruptive change. Further, as a country or company evolves into "developed" status, it becomes inured to set ways of doing things, comfortable in its newfound financial prowess and shockingly vulnerable to insurgents better able to harness the next generation of competitive innovations.

Meanwhile, even as low-hanging yields disappear, competitive pressures within tech mean that the next generation of blue water innovation often involves the transformation of healthcare or materials science, or of physical goods and services employing software and automation. These concepts embody a higher level of risk and complexity, and an intrinsically longer gestational period than traditional software or consumer Internet companies. An investor cannot harness these innovations and their associated equity premia unless it develops a capability to assess novel ideas from first principles *and* is able to underwrite productive risk capital with the time horizon appropriate to each project. This is what classic venture capital firms like mine are designed to do, mainly because they are small and nimble.

But, as Winston and Paul ably show, it is this reality that has caused the sovereign funds — large, long-term, and naturally defensive organizations — to remarkably evolve into some of the most prolific and capable investors in transformative technologies.

The underlying irony, unsurprising to my venture investor's gaze, is that several of the most capable funds are themselves startups, often mirroring the national developmental dynamic that begat them. Some, like Mubadala of Abu Dhabi or CIC of China, are young, dynamic organizations that simply didn't exist before 2002. Others, like Temasek of Singapore or CDPQ of Quebec, date from the 1960s and 70s but, much like the Microsoft and Apple of recent years, have been imbued with a progressive leadership that "gets it". The net result is that my peers in venture capital, who fifteen years ago would likely not have recognized any of the major sovereign funds save a few who made passive fund investments, find themselves happily partnered with them in everything from cancer therapy to cybersecurity, microsatellite constellations to nuclear fusion.

It would seem, therefore, that we are at an "End of History" moment in the growth of tech champions and sovereign investing, the categories and winners declared and enthroned.

But history is unkind to the complacent monarch.

In February 2020, the novel coronavirus pandemic definitively ended the remarkably smooth bull market that started in March 2009. Finance ministries and central banks worldwide unleashed a formidable fiscal and monetary fusillade. These acute measures can help in the near-term and potentially stanch bleeding in the *financial* economy. But the virus has exploded an economic neutron bomb across the *real* economy. Infrastructure is seemingly intact, but there are few humans in sight. Because of lag effects from the shock, widespread human suffering, continued epidemiological risk, and the general inability of supply chains to easily bounce back, this book will appear in a year where there is nary a prospect for a quick- V or W shaped recovery.

Several constructs that we have become comfortable with in recent decades have suddenly become open to debate. And startups and sovereigns alike will play critical roles in determining the outcomes.

Here are just two such questions:

*Deglobalization vs. Globalization.* The virus has closed even the most open borders, such as between Western European countries, and reopened what was thought to be a debate long settled in favor of more free trade and common standards. It is likely that economies become increasingly autarkic, both for reasons of political belief and physical need. As such, investors and founders alike must plan for a form of deglobalization. This calls for an openminded approach to unique approaches that originate from outside the ideas-bubble that spans Silicon Valley and its mimetic global proxies. Equally, the effort to universally vaccinate against or cure the virus might lead to more, not less, global cooperation; and more of an impetus for common approaches to shared resilience.

*Decentralization vs. Centralization.* The virus has disrupted the powerful, vital networks that animate modern life, creating an instant preference for technologies that increase local choice and push power to the edge of the network, thus reducing concentrated points of failure. Examples include distributed power generation and storage, efficient micro-factories, portable digital medical devices, and distributed trust applications like Bitcoin. One might think of this as a form of autarky expressed in product design. But there is also an argument to be made for even more *centralization;* that economies of scale for critical safety and productivity goods cannot be achieved without *more,* not *less,* coordination among countries and companies.

In sum, the world must plan for the worst and work, determinedly and deterministically, for the best. Here, past is *not* prologue. From Singapore to New York, governments and companies are running multiple experiments in real-time. All we know is that it will be a Long Recovery.

We will need to catch up to, and surpass, our former rate of growth. And to do so in a way that brings prosperity to billions of people. This will be impossible without a tsunami of technology-driven transformation, of entire industries and of the infrastructure needed to sustain them. Never have the protagonists described in this book had a more important mission, for the coming decade will become a live experiment in "super-productivity" that they are uniquely suited to foresee, finance, and prosecute.

The time has come to build the greatest of Time Machines.

Ajay Royan

*Ajay Royan cofounded and runs Mithril, a family of long-term investment funds for transformative and durable technology companies. Together with cofounder Peter Thiel, Ajay invests Mithril's funds in companies that encompass, among other areas, cybersecurity, nuclear energy, next generation finance, medical robotics, industrial automation, advanced antibody discovery, metabolic disease therapies, and specialized data integration, visualization, and analysis.*

# The Investment Partners of Choice

'Well, now that we have seen each other,' said the unicorn, 'if you'll believe in me, I'll believe in you.'"
– *Lewis Carroll; Through the Looking Glass*

This timely and important book by Winston Ma and Paul Downs turns a long-standing prevailing orthodoxy entirely on its head, and for good reasons! Not so long ago, particularly prior to the onset of the Global Financial Crisis of 2008-2009, the most sophisticated and successful pools of institutional capital were managed by pension funds, insurance companies, and university endowments largely in OECD countries which allocated their capital to investment fund managers in stocks, bonds, and to some degree also in the private markets for real estate and private equity.

Large scale was viewed largely as an impediment for achieving investment success because smaller funds were viewed as more nimble and less likely to move a market while it was securing disproportionate benefits (e.g., by investing in small cap stocks). Sovereign investment funds were few in number, lightly staffed, and seemingly one step behind their more adventurous institutional fund peers.

Today, the impact of these same sovereign funds cannot be understated both in terms of their impact on the global investment markets and economic development but also on modern life generally. Indeed, the significant changes we are seeing worldwide in ride-sharing versus taxis, away from motor-fueled cars and towards electric ones, and towards sharing office and home spaces can all be attributed in large measure to the actions of these sovereign investors. Rather than being rogue actors, which was greatly feared prior to 2008-2009, these sovereign investors have become a stabilizing force in the global capital markets for stocks and bonds because of their long investment time horizons and acceptance of long-term risk.

Moreover, rather than large scale being a disadvantage, these sovereign funds have also demonstrated that large size can become an advantage in terms of their ability to access new opportunities and their heightened credibility among project managers around the world who increasingly view them as the Investment Partners of Choice for international investing.

It is this now firmly established role as the Investment Partners of Choice for international investing that will enable the sovereign funds to have a disproportionately strong impact on modern life for many decades to come. Ma and Downs' clear and expansive insights into these disproportionately important and yet little-known institutions will prove critical both to practitioners in the field of investing as well as to the general public seeking answers to the big picture questions of why the new unicorns transforming their lives arose from the modern financial system.

Russell Read, CFA, Ph.D., London

*Russell Read, CFA, Ph.D. is the former Chief Investment Officer for the California Public Employees' Retirement System (CalPERS), the Gulf Investment Corporation (GIC-Kuwait), and the Alaska Permanent Fund Corporation (APFC)*

# Into the Vanguard of the Digital Transformation

Sometimes a book sheds light on a little known but powerful force. Sometimes it is timely because it catches the world at an inflection point. Rarely does a book accomplish both.

With the arrival of *Sovereign Investment Funds: The Hunt for Tech Unicorns* from Winston Ma and Paul Downs, we have that rare beast: a book that, against the backdrop of the world-altering coronavirus epidemic, provides a thoughtful guide to the role sovereign investors play in the world-changing digital transformation – and how one accelerates the other. The authors capture in a fast-paced, engaging format the way in which the world's largest pools of capital have again come to the fore, both as economic superheroes of the developing world and the comic-book villains of the developed markets.

Sovereign investors have gone from strength to strength as they navigated the first Gulf War, the Global Financial Crisis, and now the coronavirus pandemic. It is no wonder that they have been called upon in times of crisis. The resources at their command are staggering: $30 trillion, which may be on the conservative end. Simple, mechanical portfolio rebalancing at one of the larger funds can alter the course of the world's currency markets. Norway's fund holds, on average, 1.5 percent of every listed company on earth. And as they pivot from Wall Street to rescue their home economies, the resultant departure and arrival of their cash hoards will surely be felt as much in the corridors of investment banks as in their home governments' budgets and stimulus packages.

Meanwhile, the advent of stay-at-home orders and social distancing have only accelerated the trend toward the digitalization of everything. This digital transformation has been driven increasingly by massive pools of sovereign capital. Tracing the dramatic rise and recent fall of some unicorns – private companies with valuations of more than $1 billion — the book reveals in case studies how the Sovereign Investment Funds of its title have fueled the rise of this once-rare breed, backing the likes of Alibaba, AirBnb, JD.com, Tesla, Uber, WeWork, and the well-known unicorn-maker, the Softbank Vision Fund. And similarly, how they are themselves integrating AI and blockchain into their own operations – and into their thinking about mitigating digital disruption to their portfolios.

The book profiles a diverse cast of characters from the Middle East to Canada, from Southeast Asia to Africa, from Europe to Australia and from Latin America to East Asia as they invest in the digital transformation and are they themselves digitally transformed. The focus moves on from the tech hubs of Silicon Valley and Beijing to capture emerging hubs in India, Europe and the Middle East as well as Africa, a continent now entering the digital economy.

Geography also contributes to a growing digital divide: China and the US, homes to the authors, each envision a different digital future, forcing other nations to pick sides on such developments as the emerging 5G digital technology and the Internet of Things. The activities of sovereign investors are increasingly perceived as presenting risks as well but also, paradoxically, as the very means to counter those perceived risks. Against this backdrop, new funds are being launched and existing funds are being repurposed.

The sovereign investors are also becoming key arbiters of ESG and SDG principles. As major holders of equities, they have weighed in on sustainability, governance, climate change and more. In doing so, they have united across continents, giving one voice to their trillions as they speak to the companies with whose management they engage.

The authors' extensive, hands-on involvement in the deals and operations of this little-known world lends vibrancy as they recount practical, illustrative examples in a non-pedantic style. The book benefits from the contrasting backgrounds of its authors. Ma is a Chinese-born Wall Street veteran and was most recently the North America office head of China Investment Corporation (CIC), one of the world's largest sovereign wealth funds. He brings a depth of insight from his background as a lawyer, as a dealmaker, and as an institutional investor. Downs is American, formerly a partner in global law firm Hogan Lovells and has long acted as outside counsel for many sovereign funds across continents, bringing to bear on this book his decades of experience working on deals, governance and training. Together, their unique perspectives and differing approaches have produced a nuanced roadmap to the little known past and exciting prospects of these giants.

The book's timely message is clarion clear: the world's sovereign investors, the "trillion dollar club" in the authors' parlance, have shaken off their traditional, passive investor roles and stepped into the vanguard of the digital transformation we are all living through. No longer simply channeling their trillions through Wall Street handlers, these super asset owners have instead become active ESG guardians, fintech powerhouses, sustainability champions and – the authors propose a new leading role – digital diplomats. Thanks to the authors, we are now able to see clearly the perceived threat and – hopefully – the opportunity they present.

Margaret Franklin, CFA
President and CEO
CFA Institute
Charlottesville, Virginia

# Authors' Notes and Acknowledgments

## Winston Ma

At the early days of the global financial crisis 2007-2008, I was an investment banker and equity-linked products trader on Wall Street in New York, and China Investment Corporation (CIC), the sovereign wealth fund (SWF) of China, was established in Beijing to manage a part of China's trillion dollar foreign reserve. At that time, SWF was a new entrant to the global capital markets. I was among the first group of overseas hires by CIC, so I moved to Beijing and started the exciting journey with the sovereign investors, in China as well in all continents of Asia, Africa, Australia/Oceania, Europe, North America, and South America.

After 10 years with CIC, in 2019 I moved back home to New York and private capital markets. By then the sovereign funds were already recognized as important participants in the international monetary and financial system. In fact, it was hard to avoid the headlines their activities attract. As such, I have become an adjunct professor at New York University (NYU) School of Law, teaching a course on sovereign investors, capital markets, and regulatory challenges. When I was finalizing the script of this book in the spring of 2020, the coronavirus pandemic broke out, and the sovereign funds, with their massive portfolios of financial assets, were active (again) at the front line of capital markets turmoil and global financial crisis.

Therefore, this book of sovereign investment funds and their global tech investments is added with a new context – world economy downturn and international tensions. A book on such a complex and fast-moving topic would not have been possible if I had not been blessed to partner with an industry leader like Paul, who has practiced international law for more than four decades, and learn from an amazing group of mentors in finance/investments, law and tech.

＊　　＊　　＊　　＊　　＊　　＊　　＊　　＊　　＊

My deepest thanks go to Dr. Rita and Gus Hauser, the New York University (NYU) School of Law, and John Sexton, the legendary Dean of NYU Law School when I was pursuing my LL.M degree in Comparative Law. My PE/VC investing, investment banking, and practicing attorney experiences all started with the generous Hauser scholarship in 1997. During his decade-long tenure as the President of NYU, John kindly engaged me at his inaugural President's Global Council as he developed the world's first and only GNU – the "global network university." My NYU experience was the base for my future career as a global professional working in the cross-border business world.

My sincere appreciation to Mr. Lou Jiwei and Dr. Gao Xi-qing, the inaugural Chairman and President of China Investment Corporation (CIC), for recruiting me at the inception of CIC. One of the most gratifying aspects of being part of CIC is the opportunity to be exposed to a wide range of global financial markets' new developments. The unique platform has brought me to the movers and shakers everywhere in the world, including Silicon Valley projects that linked global tech innovation with the China market.

The same thanks go to Chairman Ding Xue-dong, President Li Ke-ping, and Supervisory Chairman Jing Liqun who I reported to at CIC in recent years. Chairman Jing is now the President of Asian Infrastructure Investment Bank (AIIB). He educated me about the works of Shakespeare, as well as guiding me professionally. The readings of Hamlet, Macbeth, and King Lear improved my English writing skills, and hopefully the writing style of this book is more interesting and engaging than my previous finance textbook "Investing in China."

For such a dynamic book topic, I benefited from the best market intelligence from a distinctive group of institutional investors, tech entrepreneurs, and business leaders at the World Economic Forum (WEF), especially the fellows at the Council on Long-Term Investing, the Council for Digital Economy and Society, and the Young Global Leaders (YGL) community. Professor Klaus Schwab, founder and executive Chairman of the World Economic Forum, has a tremendous vision of a sustainable, shared digital future for the world, which is an important theme of this book.

The WEF Council on Long-Term Investing has gathered the most forward-thinking leadership from major SWFs and public pensions, and I learned so much from the dynamic discussions with them, including Alison Tarditi (CIO of CSC, Australia), Adrian Orr (CEO of NZ Super, New Zealand), Gert Dijkstra (Chief Strategy of APG, Netherlands), Hiromichi Mizuno (CIO of GPIF, Japan), Jagdeep Singh Bachher (CIO of UC Regents, USA), Jean-Paul Villain (Director of ADIA, UAE), Lars Rohde (CEO of ATP, Denmark), Lim Chow Kiat (CEO of GIC, Singapore), Reuben Jeffery (CEO of Rockefeller & Co., USA), and Scott E. Kalb (CIO of KIC, Korea).

I have a special friendship with the leadership figures at major Canadian pensions, because for a few years I was the Head of CIC North America office based out of Toronto, Canada. Blake Hutcheson (CEO of OMERS/Oxford Properties) was the landlord of my office on the Bay Street. Michael Sabia (CEO of CDPQ), Ron Mock (CEO of OTPP), Andre Bourbonnais (CEO of PSP), and I were together for the investment panel of Bloomberg 2015 Canada Summit. Mark Machin and Mark Wiseman, the current and former CEO of CPPIB, have been friends of long standing and kindly supported my NYU program on SWFs, pensions and other asset owners, for which I am enormously grateful.

My gratitude goes to many other outstanding friends, colleagues, practitioners and academics, who provided expert opinions, feedback, insights and suggestions for improvement. For anecdotes, pointers, and constant reality checks, I turned to them because they were at the front line of industry and business practices. I would particularly like to thank the friends at the West Summit Fund, which I set up at CIC in 2009 for cross-border investments between Silicon Valley and China. For the past 10 years, we had a fun journey together.

Special thanks to Frank Guarini (NYU'50, LL.M.'55), the seven-term New Jersey congressman and a long-term friend from the NYU law school community. With incredible vision and generosity, he continues to give me invaluable guidance, even when he is in his 90s. The time with this admirable leader has reshaped my way of thinking as well as me as a person. He has been a tremendous mentor and I thank him for continuously being a great cheerleader.

On its journey from a collection of ideas and themes to a coherent book, the manuscript went through multiple iterations and a meticulous editorial and review process by the John Wiley team led by the book commissioning editor Gemma Valler. Our long-term collaboration started with my 2016 book China's *Mobile Economy* (among "best 2016 business books for CIOs" by i-CIO.com), and we are working together on another new book "*The Digital Woe*" as a sequel (forthcoming December 2020). The managing editor Purvi Patel and copyeditor Caroline McPherson contributed substantially to the final shape of the book. Special thanks to Gladys Ganaden for her design of the book cover and figures.

And last in the lineup but first in my heart, I thank my wife, Angela Ju-hsin Pan, who gave me love and support. You are a true partner in helping me frame and create this work. Thank you for the patience you had while I wrecked our weekends and evenings working on this book.

# Acknowledgements

## *Paul Downs*

Aglobal pandemic puts much in perspective, summoning gratitude to the fore. As I write this in quarantine, the only sounds punctuating the odd, pervasive silence of Manhattan are the sirens of the first responders. It is to them I must first acknowledge gratitude. Together with those who are keeping the logistics of food, medical care and basic services functioning as I sit safely at my laptop living the digital transformation that is the focus of this work.

Many others have been instrumental in bringing this book to fruition. My colleagues in the practice of law have imparted the knowledge on this topic that is not to be found in the server racks of the internet. Two, in particular, aided my understanding of the world portrayed in this book: Brett Dick, who authored the go-to book on the US tax treatment of sovereign investors and his successor in that role, Babak Nikravesh, who also accompanied me on countless visits to many of the sovereign investors who fill these pages, always offering insight and good company.

Thanks are due as well to Hogan Lovells who made possible the annual Sovereign Investor Conference that brought together thought leaders from the sovereign investors featured in this book. The panel participants and keynote speakers provided valuable, empirical insights to the themes of this book.

Reaching back in time, I must also recognize the contribution of two professors who contributed to my appreciation of international business transactions: Hal Scott, whose course at Harvard Law School provided the building blocks for a career in international business law; and the late Sergio Le Pera, Faculty of Law, University of Buenos Aires, whose mentorship in comparative law has stood the test of time.

In the present, no one has been more valuable than my co-author, Winston, whose insight, skilled editing and good natured collaboration have powered this book.

My family deserve my greatest thanks for indulging me in this project– as well as in the preceding decades of travel and late night conference calls that laid the foundation of experience upon which this book is built. My daughters Lex and Liv, both of whom provided great support (while occupied full time respectively at a unicorn and at college). And most fundamentally, my remarkable spouse, Rebecca Downs, who was my reality check and patient source of sanity as this project absorbed me.

# About the Authors

**Winston Wenyan Ma, CFA & Esq.**
Winston Ma is an investor, attorney, author, and adjunct professor in the global digital economy. He is one of a small number of native Chinese who have worked as investment professionals and practicing capital markets attorneys in both the United States and China. Most recently for 10 years, he was Managing Director and Head of North America Office for China Investment Corporation (CIC), China's sovereign wealth fund.

At CIC's inception in 2007, he was among the first group of overseas hires by CIC, where he was a founding member of both CIC's Private Equity Department and later the Special Investment Department for direct investing (Head of CIC North America office 2014-2015). He had leadership roles in global investments involving financial services, technology (TMT), energy and natural resources sectors, including the setup of West Summit (Huashan) Capital, a cross-border growth capital fund in Silicon Valley, which was CIC's first overseas tech investment.

Prior to that, Mr. Ma served as the deputy head of equity capital markets at Barclays Capital, a vice president at J.P. Morgan investment banking, and a corporate lawyer at Davis Polk & Wardwell LLP. Nationally certified Software Programmer as early as 1994, Mr. Ma is the book author of *China's Mobile Economy* (Wiley 2016, among "best 2016 business books for CIOs"), *Digital Economy 2.0* (2017 Chinese), *The Digital Silk Road* (2018 German), *China's AI Big Bang* (2019 Japanese), and *Investing in China* (Risk Books, 2006).

Mr. Ma has served on the boards of multinational listed and private companies. He was selected a 2013 Young Global Leader at the World Economic Forum (WEF) and has been a member of the Council for Long-Term Investing and Council for Digital Economy and Society. He is a member of New York University (NYU) President's Global Council since inception, and in 2014 he received the NYU Distinguished Alumni Award.

**Paul Downs Esq.**

Paul Downs practiced international law for more than four decades, most recently as a partner at Hogan Lovells in New York, where he co-founded the Sovereign Investor Practice and initiated its annual Sovereign Investor Conference. He has represented sovereign investors transacting in assets globally, has spoken and published on the topic and guest lectured at Columbia and New York University law schools.

Mr. Downs served as President of the American Foreign Law Association, is a member of the Association of the Bar of the City of New York, the International Bar Association and the American Bar Association.

He is a current or past director of international companies and not-for-profit organizations, including International House, New York, The Council for the United States and Italy, and the China US Business Alliance. Paul is a graduate of Princeton University and Harvard Law School.

\*    \*    \*    \*    \*    \*    \*    \*    \*

The authors can be reached on LinkedIn for comments and feedback on *The Hunt for Unicorns: How Sovereign Funds Are Reshaping Investment in the Digital Economy.*

# Preface

Who holds the power in financial markets? For many, the answer will probably be the large investment banks, big asset managers, and hedge funds that are often in the media's spotlight. But increasingly a new group of sovereign investors, which includes some of the world's largest sovereign wealth funds, government pension funds, central bank reserve funds, state-owned enterprises, and other sovereign capital-enabled entities, have emerged to become the most influential capital markets players and investment firms, with $30 trillion in assets under management (**"super asset owners"**).

Importantly, the rise of sovereign investors is reflected not only in the increase in the size of assets under their management but also in the proliferation of new funds established over the past decade and the anticipated establishment of new funds in countries with recent resource wealth (such as African countries), as well as in regions striving for government-driven economic transformation (e.g., the EU).

Their ample resources, preference for lower profile, passive investing, their long time horizon and adherence to sustainability, as well as their need to diversify globally and by sector, have helped to transform the investment world and, in particular, private markets for digital companies. They have helped create and sustain an environment that has fostered the rise of the likes of Uber, Alibaba, Spotify, and other transformative players in the digital economy, while providing their founders and business models the benefit of long-term capital.

Despite this increasingly important impact, sovereign investors remain mostly unknown, often maintaining a low profile in global markets. For the same reason, they're also among the most widely misunderstood investors, as many view investments made by sovereign investors as purely driven by political aims. The general perception is that most sovereign investors lack transparency and have questionable governance controls, causing an investee nation to fear exposure to risks of unfair competition, data security, corruption, and non-financially or non-economically motivated investments.

As this book goes to press, the pandemic raging around the globe has brought them again to the front pages. Sometimes it's their key role in fostering the rise of the tech unicorns of artificial intelligence (AI) and big data and their big bets on biotech startups searching for treatments and vaccines. More frequently, it's coverage of their role as economic superheroes called upon to rescue the global economy or as comic book villains scooping up Western champions the pandemic has made vulnerable. These simple caricatures do not reflect reality, of course. Revealing the complex reality behind these simplistic depictions is the task of this book.

The current global tensions around the AI race and tech competition – and now the corona virus pandemic – have exacerbated such misperceptions, spawning controversies around sovereign investors and capital markets, governments, new technologies, cross-border investments, and related laws and regulations (**see the chart below**):

As such, sovereign capital and the global digital economy are undergoing an unprecedented, contentious moment. This book maps the global footprints of these super asset owners; in particular, the three intersecting aspects of their pursuit of digital revolution: their strategy and institutional setup, their investments and impact, and regulatory policy responses.

This book is organized as follows.

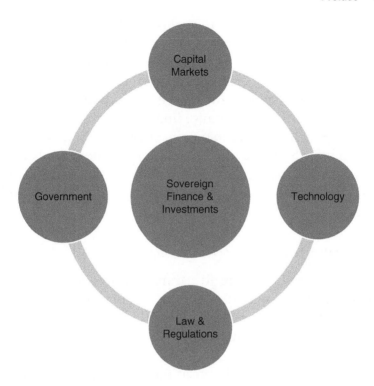

## Part I: The Trillion-Dollar Club

The two chapters in Part I lay the foundation for the rest of book by identifying key characteristics of the sovereign investors, such as capital size, investment policies, and governance structures. Many of the sovereign investment funds are transforming themselves to better invest into the new digital economy.

### Chapter 1: Sovereign Investors Rising in Crisis

This chapter surveys the universe of sovereign investors and analyzes the origin of different Sovereign Investment Funds (SIFs) from a comparative political economy perspective.

It reveals how sovereign investors perform a wide-ranging set of functions, which are not mutually exclusive – in fact most funds, today, perform more than one of the functions outlined in this chapter. It also introduces their little-known enormous capital power for global investments, highlighting that role in times of pandemic, financial crisis, and conflict as well as their global leadership in environmental, social, and governance (ESG) and sustainable development goals (SDG). Finally, it will focus on the factors behind the current rise in states' participation in high-tech markets – domestic as well as overseas.

### Chapter 2: From Passive Allocators to Active Investors

Chapter 2 recounts the funds' transition to active investment from their traditional function of simply allocating capital to external fund managers (which left them passive and little-known in the capital markets). The chapter goes on to highlight how they are increasingly active and direct in digital economy investments, collaborating among themselves as they become mature investors. Also in view is their cause/effect impact on the markets, their role in the rise of the unicorns, and the shrinkage of the public equities markets.

## Part II: In Pursuit of the Digital Revolution

These chapters cover in detail sovereign investors' pursuit of digital revolution.

### Chapter 3: The Global Hunt for Unicorns (Decacorns)

Chapter 3 turns its attention to the hunt for unicorns. Increasingly, sovereign investors are going direct into transactions in the tech industry and digital economy sectors, on par with private equity (PE) and venture capital (VC) funds. They are active globally, due to both overseas investments (global portfolio) and overseas presence (global offices).

The chapter chronicles high-profile investments in disruptive technology giants, such as e-commerce giants like Alibaba and JD.com, as well as sharing economy leading players like Airbnb, Uber, and WeWork, and AI/mobility pioneers GM Cruise, Tesla, and Waymo; their growing appetite to develop their own internal investment capabilities; and the close relationship between sovereign investors and national governments.

### Chapter 4: Long-term Capital into the Digital Infrastructure

Chapter 4 highlights how, for the sovereign investors, the digital economy infrastructure – and the much broader digital ecosystem – has become another frontier asset class as a proxy to invest in technology. Digital infrastructure investment also provides an avenue to foster development goals and green initiatives, consistent with global government initiatives such as China's Belt & Road and Blue Dot of the US.

This combination has attracted large pools of sovereign capital into data centers, global digital logistics systems, digital satellite networks, and smart cities. The next big thing is the Internet of Things, and fintech, paytech, and digital health all form part of the future digital infrastructure that the sovereign investors are keen to invest in.

### Chapter 5: Spurring Domestic Digital Transformation

Chapter 5 focuses on how, with such powerful positions, SIFs are being seen by their stakeholders not simply as vehicles for financial returns from digital infrastructure. They also enjoy significant leverage to serve multiple purposes for long-term investment strategies, solving countless needs from political pressures to domestic technology-infrastructure shortages.

New sovereign funds are being created to this end and existing funds are repurposed. Africa provides innovative examples of resource-based funds that foster the domestic digital ecosystem. This chapter describes the increase in collaboration among sovereign investors seeking to accelerate development of the domestic digital ecosystem from Italy to the UAE, from China to Russia, from Saudi Arabia to Egypt.

### Chapter 6: Go Early, Go Nimble

Chapter 6 reveals that little could have prepared these investors for the world of earlier stage venture capital where their hunt now took them. It recounts the ways in which sovereign investors have needed to fundamentally reinvent themselves as early stage venture investors and their spectacular successes and humbling failures in this new realm.

Shifting their investment process to support digital startups requires different key performance indicators, revenue standards, business models, growth potential, government relations, and more. To evolve in the changing landscape, they must strive to master early stage investing techniques, a field historically occupied exclusively by VC funds, to capture growth from emerging tech startups.

### Chapter 7: The Hunt for the Hunting Party

This chapter reviews the operational challenges that sovereign investors encounter as they seek to participate in the digital economy by recruiting larger, tech-savvy, local teams and moving close to the innovation source. The chapter contrasts successful strategies with those that have not worked as well, highlighting the unique advantages – and disadvantages – of sovereign investors as team builders. It concludes with a look at alternative routes to engage in the digital ecosystem, most notably the $100 billion Vision Fund, but also the seeding of new managers and fostering startup interaction among portfolio companies.

## Part III: Global Expansion, Regulatory Responses, and International Policies

These chapters address the regulatory response to the pursuit of the digital revolution by sovereign investors. All these tensions, currently highlighted by the China–US tech war, are playing out across the globe, from UK to Australia, from Germany to Canada, from Israel to Japan.

### Chapter 8: Overseas Expansion and National Security Collide

This chapter examines the national security implications in home and host states as a result of sovereign investors' activities – both overseas investments (global portfolio) and overseas presence (global offices). We explore how national security legislation has adjusted to the rise of sovereign investors with their ties to foreign governments. The Committee on Foreign Investment in the United States (CFIUS) mechanism and the related US–China tensions serve as one case study, as well as similar regulations in Australia, Canada, EU member states, and Israel. Finally, the chapter traces the evolution of the concept of "national security" from weaponry to critical infrastructure to data, where it inevitably collides with the ambitions of sovereign investors in the digital economy.

### Chapter 9: Tech Transactions Snared by Geotech Tensions

This chapter focuses on sovereign investors' direct investments into the AI and digital technology sectors. These activities have contributed to geopolitical tensions and tightened cross-border regulations. Deal blockings are on the rise under the US CFIUS and similar regimes of the EU, Israel, and Australia. Meanwhile, also on the rise, this time for US institutions, are restrictions on investments into foreign jurisdictions like China.

Such developments will profoundly impact venture capital and the startup ecosystem in the US, China, and elsewhere, because sovereign capital, whether foreign SIF funds or US pension funds, has been a major source of funds for the latest tech boom. The chapter concludes with an exploration of tactics available to sovereign investors investing overseas into digital technology in this ring-fenced environment.

## Closing Chapter: Super Asset Owners

Chapter 10 provides a portrait of sovereign investors as super asset owners and their growing impact and influence in four key roles (**see chart below**).

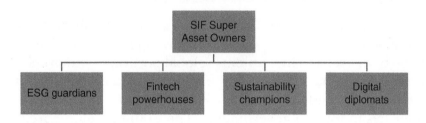

First, **ESG guardians.** They lead in ESG and SDG in the digital economy, uniting to counter live-streamed shootings, relying on AI to monitor the conduct of portfolio companies, chiding the management of others, and rebalancing their portfolios to de-risk them for climate change and technological disruption.

Second, **fintech powerhouses.** They have, by necessity, evolved into fintech hotbeds, creating internal teams focused on the risks, opportunities, and operational implications of the digitalization of everything. AI and blockchain are deployed internally and seeded in startups, as they are poised to be the leaders, instead of the clients, of the asset management industry.

Third, **Sustainability champions.** Sovereign investors are putting long-term capital to cutting-edge technologies, fostering innovation hubs out of traditional centers like the US and Germany. Consequently, emerging economies are becoming smarter and more competitive. Even those who view the digital future as a zero-sum game have come to recognize the utility of these super asset owners.

Finally, **digital diplomats.** Sovereign investors are confronting an increasingly fractured tech world. The collaboration among the SIFs, however, provides a path whereby the US, China, EU, Japan, and many other parts of the world could reach a new equilibrium and collectively drive innovation. Viewed for what they truly are, these super asset owners of the future can become opportunities for mutual prosperity.

# 1

# Sovereign Investors Rising in Crisis

*Passing through the understory of lounge chairs and low tables, you approach the bar with a view of televisions carrying the major international news channels. The suited barista serves up the coffee of your choice and you relax briefly as you scan your emails on the free wifi, glance at a few of the international papers and periodicals, and recover from the constant bustle just outside the lounge – business professionals from a multitude of lands clearing security and taking elevators from the towering atrium.*

*No, you are not in the first-class lounge at an international hub airport (although it might well be one from all appearances). You have arrived, instead, at the visitor lounge in the hometown high-rise offices of Abu Dhabi Investment Authority, one of the world's largest and lowest profile sovereign wealth funds. ADIA manages its vast $700 billion plus global portfolio from this edifice where it employs investment professionals from around the world in a gleaming glass tower that would not look out of place in any world city. And ADIA is but one of the growing number of large sovereign wealth funds that remain below the radar but have an increasing impact on global markets.*

Their low profile is in contrast to the better known deal-makers in the centers of finance. But their checkbooks and influence on the world at large outweigh the erstwhile titans of finance.

And as the number and size of such operations continue to surge, their influence does as well. Large as they are, in crises they have an even larger role to play. As this book went to press, the world was facing a pandemic, an inflection point where two themes of this book converged in sharp relief: the power of these massive funds in times of crisis and the world's now urgent march to the digital economy.

## Trillion-Dollar Club

The global economy has witnessed the emergence of a new set of key actors over the last two decades – the Sovereign Investors. In this group we include Sovereign Wealth Funds (SWFs) and the very large Public Pension Funds (PPFs), which are active in the global marketplace and have many of the characteristics of SWFs. The concept of SWFs also includes sovereign development ment funds (SDFs), government established investment vehicles with development objectives.

These Sovereign Investors have become pivotal players in global financial markets thanks to their enormous capital base, and they continue to increase in number, size, variety, and scope. This group of highly heterogeneous funds has different backgrounds, structures, and missions, but they share one ultimate goal: to preserve capital and maximize the return on investments. As such, in this book they are collectively referred to as the **Sovereign Investment Funds (SIF)**.

How much money are we talking about? Tens of trillions of dollars sit in these funds. **Table 1.1** shows the top ten sovereign wealth funds ranked by assets under management (AUM). The very top funds manage monies exceeding the GDP of

Table 1.1    Top Ten Sovereign Wealth Funds

| | |
|---|---|
| 1. | **Government Pension Fund of Norway,** Europe, $1,108,170,000,000 |
| 2. | **China Investment Corporation (CIC),** Asia, $940,604,000,000 |
| 3. | **Abu Dhabi Investment Authority (ADIA),** Middle East, $696,660,000,000 |
| 4. | **Kuwait Investment Authority (KIA),** Middle East, $592,000,000,000 |
| 5. | **Hong Kong Monetary Authority,** Asia, $509,353,000,000 |
| 6. | **GIC Private Limited,** Asia, $440,000,000,000 |
| 7. | **National Council for Social Security Fund,** Asia, $437,900,000,000 |
| 8. | **SAFE Investment Company,** Asia, $417,844,700,460 |
| 9. | **Temasek Holdings,** Asia, $375,383,000,000 |
| 10. | **Qatar Investment Authority (QIA),** Middle East, $328,000,000,000 |

Data Source: Sovereign Wealth Fund Institute, March 2020.

good-sized European countries. If AUM were GDP, they would rank among the top 20 nations.

As is discussed in more detail below, these sovereign investors are derived from different sources and serve different ends. But a common factor is their growth in size and geographic spread. Commonly thought of as a Middle Eastern phenomenon, broadly viewed, the funds are based in much of the developed world and include very large funds from North America, East Asia, and Europe as well as the Gulf. Increased growth is expected to come from other regions, most notably, sub-Saharan Africa, where natural resources may be the source and domestic economic development the objective.

Currently, according to the Sovereign Wealth Fund Institute's (SWFI's) "Top 86 Largest Sovereign Wealth Fund Rankings by Total Assets," the top ten largest sovereign wealth funds ranked by total assets are as shown in **Table 1.1**.

Public Pension Funds are important members of the SIF tribe. They are even larger, as the table below indicates; they are global and they are innovative, increasingly focused on tech innovation. GPIF (Japan), NPS (Korea), CPPIB (Canada), and CalPERS (US) are well known in the capital markets for their active investments (see **Table 1.2**). This combination of

Table 1.2  Top Ten Public Pension Funds

1. **Social Security Trust Funds,** North America $2,925,789,929,172
2. **Government Pension Investment Fund Japan (GPIF),** Asia $1,490,240,000,000
3. **Military Retirement Fund,** North America $813,555,000,000
4. **Federal Employees Retirement System,** North America $687,000,000,000
5. **National Pension Service of Korea (NPS),** Asia $593,192,000,000
6. **Federal Retirement Thrift Investment Board,** North America $572,370,000,000
7. **Zenkyoren Pension Japan,** Asia $523,463,576,000
8. **Stichting Pensioenfonds ABP,** Europe $476,000,000,000
9. **Canadian Pension Plan Investment Board (CPPIB),** North America $385,634,000,000
10. **California Public Employees Retirement System (CalPERS),** North America $370,300,000,000

Data Source: Sovereign Wealth Fund Institute, March 2020.

characteristics reinforces the perception of SIFs as savvy, silent heavyweights in the world's private and public markets.

Given this enormous concentration of wealth, it is no surprise that these giants have been viewed as **economic superheroes,** repeatedly turned to in times of crisis: in war, in the global financial crisis, and now in pandemic. Like superheroes, each has a role to play and some have even morphed to encompass additional roles, particularly when, as now, a new crisis arrives on the scene.

And their ranks continue to swell at an increasing pace. Assets under management continue their relentless rise while new funds emerge. The establishment of new funds is not a region-specific trend, as can be illustrated by funds being set up across the globe, including the Hong Kong Future Fund, Holdings Equatorial Guinea 2020, and West Virginia Future Fund. Europe is especially interesting, because Europe traditionally is not a significant player when it comes to sovereign wealth. (The **Norway Government Pension Fund** (also known as the Oil Fund), managed by Norges Bank Investment Management (**NBIM**), is considered the world's largest SWF, but it sits outside the European Union.)

There is now a Luxembourg entrant into the SWF world: Fonds soverain intergenerational du Luxembourg, which will invest for many generations to come. Also in Europe, the French, Italian, and Spanish funds, among other nations, emerged as a solution to attract other foreign players to co-invest with them in their respective domestic economies. Even a UK Citizens Wealth Fund has been proposed. But look to sub-Saharan Africa for the next surge of sovereign investors. While Nigeria and Kenya are highlighted in case studies later in this chapter, there are also sovereign funds in Algeria, Angola, Botswana, Ghana, Libya, Morocco, Nambia, and Rwanda. Not to be left behind, others, such as Japan and India, have also joined their ranks.

## Talk vs. Walk

There are two main approaches that institutional investors deploy when they seek to influence the strategies of their portfolio companies. To achieve environmental, social, and governance (ESG) aims, for example, they may remain as shareholders and engage with the top management and boards of such companies in order to reduce emissions (the "talk" channel). Or, they can "vote with their feet," by divesting polluting companies from their portfolio (the "walk" channel).

NBIM is well positioned for active engagement with public companies' management. By most accounts, its $1 trillion plus portfolio holds, on average, 1.5% of every listed company on Earth. NBIM's latest report on responsible investing released in March 2020, covering its 2019 voting, engagement with management, and follow up, runs to over 100 pages. Of the more than 9,000 companies in which it holds voting shares, NBIM cast votes in more than 97%, and it was not shy about voting against management even in its top holdings, such as Google, Amazon, and Facebook.

For climate change, NBIM has exercised both options: on the one hand engaging with companies developing strong decarbonization strategies; and on the other hand, divesting from heavy polluters like coal and fossil fuel companies. An ongoing and intriguing debate among SIF investors is whether it is better to divest, or better to engage. In practice, many SIFs use both channels and typically start with "talk."

Arguably, both strategies can be effective, and they can interact with each other, as the threat of "walk" can reinforce the influence of "talk." And sometimes the line is quite nebulous. "It's easy to have a slogan," said Raphael Arndt, the **Australia Future Fund**'s Chief Investment Officer. "But if someone says, 'Get rid of fossil fuel companies', do I sell AGL? That's also my biggest exposure to renewables."

**Their size alone** means that their actions, collectively and even individually, can have material impacts even when the intent is simply prudent management. For example, Norway's fund holds, on average, 1.5% of every listed company on earth, making it an investor that boards around the globe must heed (see **Box: Talk vs. Walk**). Japan's **GPIF,** the world's largest pension fund, was fingered by financial journalists as the mover behind an unexpected drop in the value of the yen. The action by GPIF to rebalance its portfolio in favor of more non-Japanese investments was enough to change the course of the $6 trillion daily volume of the foreign exchange markets. Wherever these giants turn their gaze, the impact is felt.

Their rise is taking place at a time when governments become ever more active players in markets across the board. This chapter surveys the universe of sovereign investors from a comparative political economy perspective. We will introduce their little-known enormous capital power for global investments, looking at how each is cast in a role, and how many have responded to the crisis of today, those of the past, and are anticipating those of the future.

## Follow the Money

Understanding how these actors of gargantuan proportions are funded and assigned their missions is key to grasping the unique nature of their power in the world. It is important to understand that the funding source and motivation for creating a sovereign investment fund varies widely and has an impact on its operations, structure, and investment profile. Most funds, with increasingly broadened mandates from their home states, perform more than one of the functions outlined here; in countries like Nigeria, multiple sovereign funds are established for different policy objectives of savings, stabilization, and development (see **Figure 1.2**).

**First,** the most widely known SWF is the **long-term savings fund** for the country's future generations (as such, also known as **"intergenerational funds"**). Savings funds are often set up by commodity-rich countries to save a portion of their resource wealth for the future. (As the cases below illustrate, sometimes the future arrives sooner than expected. And in unexpected ways.) Oil, gas, and precious metal reserves are finite: one day they will run out. There is also a risk that these resources will become stranded assets as climate-change regulation and green-energy alternatives may render hydrocarbon extraction uneconomic.

Using their SWFs to convert today's resource wealth into renewable financial assets, governments can hope to share the windfalls of today with the generations of tomorrow. The world's oldest SWF, the **Kuwait Investment Authority (KIA)**, is a good example, dating back to 1953. According to its website, it invests financial reserves to "[provide] an alternative to oil reserves, which would enable Kuwait's future generations to face the uncertainties ahead with greater confidence … ". Such uncertainties did arrive, with war and pandemics.

The fund for future generations of Kuwaitis did not have to wait for the oil to run out before it was called upon. After Kuwait had been sacked during the seven-month long Iraqi occupation in 1990, KIA provided over $85 billion (nearly $169 billion in 2020 dollars) to rebuild the Emirate. Its oilfields set ablaze by retreating Iraqi forces, the country was devastated in the wake of the occupation. With funds invested abroad for nearly four decades, the fund was at the ready to reconstruct its economy and physical infrastructure. And now, as recounted in **Chapter 4,** Kuwait sovereign funds are building, snug against the Iraqi border, a smart city of the future featuring a planned kilometer-high skyscraper.

The long-term savings funds of the oil-laden Gulf States also got the call to save the world a scant two decades later as the global financial crisis of 2008–2009 threatened to kill off the world's largest financial institutions and take the global economy with them. As we will explore in **Chapter 8,** KIA and **ADIA** of UAE in short order poured more than $10 billion into Citibank alone. And the Gulf States were not alone in riding to the rescue: **CIC** of China put nearly $10 billion in Morgan Stanley, and Singapore's twin SIFs, **GIC** and **Temasek,** dropped nearly $24 billion into Merrill Lynch, UBS, and (yes, again) Citibank (see **Figure 1.1**).

And now, as the coronavirus pandemic has rocked the world's financial markets, these economic superheroes are at it again. Amid the stock market turmoil, by early April 2020, **Saudi Arabia's PIF** had spent well over $7 billion to pick up stakes in the battered oil majors of Europe, ENI, Equinor, and Royal Dutch Shell as well as others. The moves provoked a

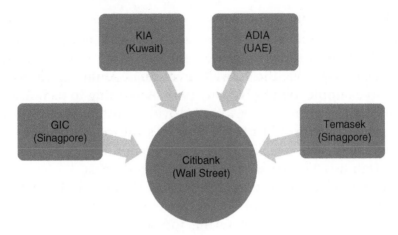

Figure 1.1    **SIFs to the Rescue of Citibank**

tightening of foreign investment restrictions in Italy, Germany, and Spain, exacerbating the tensions explored in **Chapters 8 and 9** (hugely different from the "white knight" cheers received during the previous global crisis).

Interestingly, PIF also laid out nearly $370 million to scoop over 8% of Carnival Cruises after the company's shares had plummeted over 75% due to the coronavirus pandemic and then over $500 million on a nearly 6% stake in similarly depressed live entertainment giant, LiveNation. Filling its pandemic shopping cart, PIF abandoned a £300 million purchase of English football club Newcastle United. As we will see in later chapters, PIF is instrumental in weaning the Kingdom's economy from its dependence on oil, with tourism as a focus. What looks like an opportunistic (or, from another viewpoint, perhaps even altruistic) move, is just as likely a move to serve the economic transformation.

Meanwhile, in the **US,** the economic dislocation has positioned the US to enact a $2 trillion stimulus package in 2020 known as the CARES Act. The legislation contemplates the US government owning shares in companies as a result of its bailout cash injections, a switch from its loan-based bailouts of the global financial crisis. Apparently anticipating voter demands that the taxpayers enjoy the potential corporate upside of the $2 trillion stimulus package, the Act mandates that, this time, loans include warrants, equity or participating senior debt. Only seen to a limited extent in the past (for example in the bailout of the US auto industry), the equity requirement is across all sectors and could result in the US government creating what is, in effect, a sovereign wealth fund.

Alaska already enjoys a SIF. In the pandemic, it is expected to disburse from its oil-funded coffers $3.1 billion, about 5% of its assets.

In addition, in a parallel to sovereign funds in many nations, the **Federal Reserve,** the US central bank, has been given a role as equity investor of last resort. The CARES Act provides for $454 billion fund for investment by the Federal Reserve. Within that fund is a facility specifically authorizing the Fed to purchase new security issuances in its efforts to maintain liquidity in markets. In this new age, Congress has not limited the facility to purchases of debt obligations. Yet, Janet Yellen, former Chair of the Federal Reserve, has argued for increasing the role of the Federal Reserve in capital markets even more, citing examples of other central banks like Japan that have broader authority to buy equity securities in the open market. When the world is facing down a global pandemic, the utility of sovereign investment funds becomes evident to the most seasoned observers.

## Dutch Disease

The Dutch Disease was first diagnosed by *The Economist* in 1977, in reference to the economic conditions burdening the Netherlands after the discovery of large offshore natural gas deposits in the 1950s which were blamed for loss of competitiveness.

In connection with natural resource windfalls, currency appreciation can distort the local production economy, as exports become less competitive and labor shifts into the extractive industry. In the case of the Netherlands, unemployment soared from 1.1% to over 5% in the 1970s and investment moved abroad while gas exports surged.

Studies have since examined the other detrimental effects of commodity dependence and ways to mitigate its effects. Moving the commodity cash to a sovereign investment fund is one approach, which may save some of the natural resource wealth for the benefit of future generations while promoting a diverse and sustainable economy after the resources are exhausted. By investing strategically in the domestic economy, a sovereign investment fund can encourage a more diversified export sector.

Sovereign wealth funds have also long been deployed to fight more metaphorical health risks. By investing overseas, savings funds in commodity-rich countries can also help prevent Dutch Disease, whereby a surge in commodity exports leads to a sharp rise in foreign exchange inflows, generating inflationary pressures and damaging the competitiveness of other economic sectors (see **Box: Dutch Disease**). With natural gas reserves dwarfing those of the Netherlands and a much smaller economy, Qatar has followed this approach and invests its massive surpluses abroad.

In 2019, the **Qatar Investment Authority (QIA)** reportedly acquired the stately St. Regis Hotel, steps from the Trump Tower on New York City's Fifth Avenue, one in a string of trophy hotel properties snapped up with funds from abundant natural gas exports of the lightly populated sheikdom. This is clearly a move that fits well within the accepted paradigm: a prime property in a global city functioning as a store of wealth for a small country in an unstable region. It also demonstrates that being a global investor when a pandemic hits may have its downside. Unlike the more recent move by PIF on Carnival Cruises, however, the timing of the move into hospitality could have been better. But a long-term investor will not worry. In fact, Qatar has reportedly borrowed £10 billion in anticipation of pursuing foreign assets at bargain prices.

Another source of savings in trade-based economies like **China,** is foreign exchange reserves accumulated from import and export. The "made in China" companies sell their goods overseas – shoes and jeans, or assembled iPhones and laptops – to American and European buyers, bringing back dollars or other foreign currencies. Then the central bank intervenes by printing local currency and buying the dollars for cash from the exporting companies. Traditionally, the central bank, through its investment arm **SAFE (State Administration of Foreign Exchange)**, mostly invested the dollars in the US government treasuries for safety and liquidity. As China's reserve reached trillions of dollars (at its peak, an astounding $4 trillion), the second sovereign fund, China Investment Corp (CIC), was established in 2007 to seek better risk-adjusted returns.

**Second, fiscal stabilization funds.** SWFs in this category aim to facilitate the fiscal stability of their country's economy, as well as stabilize its exchange rate in certain cases, in the event of an external shock. Often, commodity-rich nations create these funds to manage revenue streams; when commodity prices are high, money goes in, and when commodity prices are low, money goes out – to stabilize the budget. By helping to smooth out commodity revenues, stabilization funds can help governments avoid extreme peaks and troughs in the cycle. These funds are also used to help stabilize the value of the country's currency during macroeconomic shocks.

To fulfil this objective, these funds have short investment time-horizons and tend to hold a large proportion of their assets in liquid investments (and fewer private market investments). This largely limits them to fixed income products, as high exposure to equities and alternatives investments could result in more volatility and less liquidity, putting their ability to intervene on behalf of their economy at risk. **The Economic and Social Stabilization Fund (ESSF)** of **Chile,** the copper-rich country in Latin America, is the classic example. Founded in 2007 to repay public debt and fund fiscal deficits, ESSF is not a return-oriented fund, and it has kept its original objective over the years.

This can be seen in action in the 2020 coronavirus pandemic. One of the functions that the oil funds of the Middle

East have come to provide is budget stabilization, and they are called back from their day jobs to sustain their home economies. Suffering the double whammy of record low oil prices and the economic shock of the coronavirus, the Gulf states are expected to draw down from their enormous funds to cover government deficits and to fund stimulus spending.

In April 2020, Bloomberg News estimated that bankrolling their governments' stimulus packages, coupled with the decline in asset values and loss of oil surplus inflows, would cause a $300 billion drop in the assets of the funds of Abu Dhabi, Kuwait, Qatar, and Saudi Arabia. With over $2 trillion in assets going into the crisis, they are up to the task. Of course, Wall Street feared that much of the needed cash would be derived from liquidating the funds' massive investments, sending the money managers scrambling to replace the capital on which they have become reliant. In fact, the Gulf SIFs generated even more fees for the money managers by borrowing billions instead of selling at depressed prices. These giants have impacts that reverberate globally.

On the Gulf's frontline in the pandemic battle, the **UAE's Mubadala Investment Company (Mubadala)** was reported to be in discussions to invest in a rescue package for a troubled local healthcare company, NMC Health, the UAE's largest healthcare provider. While the AI and biotech companies in the portfolios of Mubadala and other SIFs search for cures and preventatives around the world, Mubadala is being called upon to keep the healthcare system afloat at home. In Southeast Asia, oil producer **Malaysia** is also turning to its sovereign fund, **Khazanah,** to aid the discount airline Air Asia. Khazanah has been called upon to guarantee loans to the discount airline, which is suffering from the dire effects of the coronavirus on the travel industry.

**Norway's Oil Fund,** the world's largest sovereign fund, is also at the ready to stabilize its domestic economy. Started in 1996 as a budget stabilization vehicle, the fund has grown to well over twice the country's GDP, hence it is viewed more as an intergenerational savings fund (see **Box: Transparency at**

**its Core**). However, to cover the massive costs to Norway of coronavirus-induced shock, the fund will be called upon to provide cash directly to fund its government – anywhere from $13 billion to as much as $25 billion or more, as the price of oil, its sole funding source, drops to record lows in 2020.

## Transparency at its Core

Norway's Oil Fund could be the dictionary definition of "transparent." It even once displayed on its website a constantly changing calculation of its market value, spinning like the numbers on a gas pump – or a slot machine. With population statistics, each Norwegian could immediately calculate his or her "share." And that share is not insignificant. At $1.1 trillion, for a country Norway's size, that works out to over $200,000 per person.

Its dedication to transparency has limited it largely to public markets, unlike its more opaque peers that allocate heavily to private markets for better returns. Initially, bonds comprised the entire portfolio, with the fund moving into a 60/40 allocation in favor of equities just at the dawn of the global financial crisis a decade ago. It promptly lost 23% of its value. During the crisis, the fund doubled down on its equities bet, buying $175 billion of listed shares, representing 0.5% of the world market (and enjoyed a long bull market run). The same tactic may not work in 2020, as the fund will be called upon to perform its budget stabilization function amid the coronavirus pandemic and record low oil prices. The government will call upon 4.8% of the fund's assets to fund pandemic costs.

Despite the nickname, the fund has also long been a leader in ESG principles. As an oil-based fund, that may seem odd. But there is a prudent rationale behind the bias. Norway's wealth is derived from oil and an intergenerational or budget stabilization fund has a mandate to mitigate the risk of that concentration. Looked at that way, the focus on sustainability makes for prudent investment management for a fund destined to support future generations even after the oil runs out.

ESG leadership and dedication to transparency nonetheless did not prevent an embarrassing misjudgment. The fund's retiring head failed to disclose his accepting a ride home from the United States in a private jet belonging to the hedge fund manager who was then a candidate to replace him. The succession remained in question for the scheduled September 1, 2020 start date over conflicts of interest. Living in a glass house is not easy.

But even this heightened Nordic obsession with transparency does not prevent some window dressing: also known as the Government Pension Fund of Norway, the fund name misleads with the inclusion of the term "pension," since the fund has no obligations to any pensioners. But it apparently could not forgo the friendly, easily marketed, and non-threatening nature of the term. In practice, nonetheless, it is commonly called "the oil fund."

**Third, development funds.** For a world economy frequently in and out of recession, this SIF group is expanding rapidly. Instead of prioritizing the fund's growth with international investments, development funds – like **Irish Strategic Investment Fund (ISIF)** or Russia's RDIF – focus on boosting a country's long-term productivity. They do so by investing in physical infrastructure (roads, railways, etc.), social infrastructure (education, healthcare, etc.), and, increasingly, digital infrastructure (telecom networks, data centers, etc.). They also promote strategic industries to diversify their domestic economies, often partnering with outside institutions (for example, peer SIFs) to attract foreign capital.

During the global financial crisis of 2008–2009, ISIF's core function was suspended, another example we see again and again when a crisis hits. The same fund was drafted in to play an out-of-character superhero role, as the bulk of the fund assets were morphed into the source of funding to bail out the Irish banking sector. Once it had saved the day and dropped off its pot of gold in the banks' coffers, it started to focus on economic development. By 2019, ISIF was credited for spurring over $3.5 billion inward investment into the Republic of Ireland through co-investments.

Also within the EU, **Spain** has taken an interesting approach with its "cooperation" sovereign fund model. The Spain–Oman Private Equity Fund (SOPEF) was created in 2018 as a 50/50 venture of **Oman's State General Reserve Fund (SGRF)** and Spanish state entities Compania Espanola de Financiacional al Desarrollo (Cofides) and its Fund for **Foreign Investment (FIEX)**. Each country contributed €100 million and they jointly selected a private sector PE manager to run the new fund.

The fund's focus is developmental: to support and enhance the overseas expansion of Spanish firms with a focus not only on Gulf countries but also on the wider region, including the Gulf, portions of Africa, India, and even Latin America. The arrangement contemplates investments in the €15 million range, with Oman the source of capital and Spain providing deal flow. Oman expects to benefit domestically, as well, from Spanish expertise in infrastructure, logistics, healthcare, and tourism. Later chapters will include more instances of this interesting "cooperation" fund trend in Europe, including France, Ireland, and Italy.

The "cooperation" trend has legs and is not unique to Europe. **Indonesia** and the UAE have announced a $23 billion commitment by the UAE to invest in Indonesia. The investment is to be made through Indonesia's new sovereign fund (set to be launched in mid-2020) which is designed to support local startups and boost growth. Indonesia's fund is reportedly modelled on Singapore's sovereign funds, Temasek and GIC. Indonesia lacks the foreign reserves of Singapore; the UAE funding appears to overcome that impediment and should enable Indonesia to foster further its already vibrant startup market, on which both the Singapore giants have placed multiple large bets. Indonesia itself, and the UAE, will now be joining Temasek and GIC in the hunt for tech unicorns (private startups with $1 billion valuation) in the archipelago nation.

Some SIFs are both a global investor and a domestic development fund. For example, **Mubadala** has a tech investment focus, maintaining offices in Silicon Valley and London; however, the stated objective of the fund is to "accelerate economic growth for the long-term benefit of Abu Dhabi." This is achieved by simultaneously investing in domestic infrastructure and tech sectors, such as the innovation accelerator program Hub71 launched in early 2019. The Hub71 initiative includes both a fund of funds component as well as a direct investment portfolio, aiming to drive the economic development of Abu Dhabi and the Middle East by stimulating tech innovation. Chapter 5 delves into Hub71 in detail.

In a context very different from the wealthy Gulf, Africa has been fertile ground for sovereign investment funds. There's the Rwanda Research and Innovation Fund which targets startups, for example, but more common are resource-based funds. In addition to multiple oil-based funds (including **Angola, Gabon, Ghana, Nigeria, Mauritania, and Uganda**), there's a diamonds-based fund (**Botswana's Pula Fund**) and a minerals-based fund (**Namibia's Minerals Development Fund**). More on these emerging funds in **Chapter 5,** which share the common policy objective to promote their respective economic development.

In Africa, the Kenya and Nigeria sovereign wealth funds are interesting case studies. The government of **Kenya** introduced legislation in early 2019 to establish a sovereign wealth fund – apparently as a result of the discovery of significant oil fields in 2012. The aim of the legislation is to create a sovereign wealth fund to ensure effective management of the proceeds from oil and other mineral exports. It is early days for the Kenya oil sector and the future of the proposal remains to be seen. Its appearance, nonetheless, reinforces the trend in sub-Saharan Africa – so evident elsewhere – to create sovereign funds to manage resource windfalls and diversify the economy.

**Nigeria** is the largest economy in Africa, and the **Nigerian Sovereign Investment Authority (NSIA)**, established in 2011, is favorably cited by the IMF as seeking to comply with the Santiago Principles on transparency, good governance, accountability, and prudent investment practices. NSIA consists of three separate, ring-fenced funds representing the three different functions of savings, stabilization, and development (see **Figure 1.2**), namely: (a) the Fiscal Stabilization Fund, to provide relief to the economy in times of financial stress; (b) the Future Generations Fund, which undertakes growth investments; and (c) the Nigeria Infrastructure Fund, which undertakes investment in domestic infrastructure projects.

Figure 1.2    **NSIA Divided into three Ring-fenced Sub-Funds**

**Finally, the public pension funds (PPFs).** As illustrated by the name of the Norwegian fund, the term "pension" could mean multiple things. There are mainly two types of PPFs. **For one,** pension reserve funds, which can be understood as pension-fund-type sovereign wealth funds. These funds, such as **Australia's Future Fund,** the **New Zealand Superannuation Fund (NZ super)**, and **Chile's Pension Reserve Fund,** typically invest budget surpluses in global markets to help defray their sponsoring government's future pension obligations.

Unlike orthodox pension funds, the assets they manage remain the property of the government and no individual has any claim on them. The liability stream goes to the government and then the government deploys the capital on behalf of the people. As a result, these funds can remain long-term investors even as they are drawn upon. Proceeds from a government privatization may conveniently be parked in a fund to provide funds for specified future needs or simply to keep them out of the hands of the politicians. They can feature among the most transparent funds.

**For two,** sovereign pension funds. The difference from the former is the liability stream. With a sovereign pension fund, the liability flows directly to the constituents of the fund. The Canadian government employee pension funds like **CPPIB** are good examples of the latter. They seek a rate of return that will enable them to meet their pension obligations to their members. They balance outflows to fund pension payouts with employer and employee contributions supplemented by their returns from investments. While longer term investors than private equity or venture capital funds, they must take into account actuarial liabilities, hence are often more limited than the intergenerational or pension guarantee funds such as NZ Super or Future Fund.

In North America, one sovereign fund with the management of pensions assets among its assigned tasks has taken on its superhero rescue mission. Dealing with the impact of the pandemic on the local economy, Quebec's **Caisse de Depot et Placement du Quebec (CDPQ)** in early 2020 created a C$4 billion fund to support Quebec companies adversely affected by the corona virus, whether or not they are in its portfolio. This program was quickly introduced to enable the recipient companies to survive the pandemic and underpin the recovery of the local economy. Before that, CDPQ was already deeply involved in Quebec's development; one major project is a C$6 billion high-speed, light-rail network in Montreal connecting with existing transport.

Such innovation – here seen in response to the coronavirus pandemic – is not out of character for public pension funds. Despite being increasingly subject to governance and regulatory obligations – like the global sovereign wealth funds (SWF) – public pension funds (PPF) have constantly braved new territories. Canadian funds are often acknowledged to be among the leaders in new asset classes, such as infrastructure and venture capital, in growing in-house capabilities rather than relying on outside managers, in opening outposts abroad, and in paying competitive compensation to attract talent.

Adding to the rapid ferment of ideas in the world of sovereign investors, PPFs frequently actively co-invest with the sovereign wealth funds. Sovereign Wealth Funds 2018, the report of the IE Foundation, provides a representative sampling of recent PPF/SWF co-investments of $1 billion or more (see **Table 1.3**).

Four Canadian PPFs, **CPPIB, British Columbia Investment Management Company (BCI), Ontario Teachers' Pension Plan (OTPP), and Public Sector Pension (PSP)** rank high on the league table of sovereign wealth fund co-investors, ahead of others such as Morgan Stanley and Macquarie (the banks

Table 1.3    Representative Volume of PPF/SWF Co-investments

| Pension Fund | Co-investments with SWFs |
| --- | --- |
| CPPIB | 6 |
| OTPP | 3 |
| BCI | 3 |
| PSP | 3 |
| (deal size $1 billion minimum) | |

Data Source: IE Sovereign Wealth Research 2019.

having rated only three each). Kuwait's sovereign investor teamed with OTPP and AIMCo (also Canadian) to acquire London's City airport; CPPIB has joint ventured with GIC to acquire and manage student housing; with Temasek, CPPIB also joined in the investment into South Korea's Home-plus, just to name a few. Therefore, this book will cover the sovereign wealth funds (SWF) and public pension funds (PPF) together as "sovereign investment funds" (SIF) and "sovereign investors."

## Big Spenders, ESG Promoters

For decades, sovereign investment funds preferred to remain in the shadows. Little was known about them and their nature as long-term passive investors helped keep it this way. In recent years, however, the nature of sovereign investors has begun to evolve. Alongside accumulating a large and growing pool of capital, once very passive holders of government wealth, sovereign investors have transformed operations in three critical ways: attracting better talent, adding more asset classes, and expanding into active investment strategies.

The Canadian pension funds, for example, have rebalanced to favor direct investments into alternative assets, including tech startups traditionally viewed as out of SIF's comfort zone. For example, at the end of the 1990s, **CPPIB** invested close to 100% in Canada; today, that figure is only 15%. The fund is global in its pursuit, placing tech bets in India from its office in Mumbai, among overseas offices in multiple continents. Also headquartered in Toronto, **Ontario Municipal Employees Retirement System (OMERS)** has established a ventures arm that directly invests in early stage tech companies and has dedicated venture teams in Silicon Valley as well as London. Notably, the Canadians have been savvy players in Washington, successfully lobbying for tax treatment on an equal footing to US pension plans.

Combining big spending on direct investments with promotion of ESG goals, a pair of deep pocketed SIFs, **GIC** and **ADIA,** have teamed up to back green, sustainable energy in the developing world. Both participated in 2019 in a nearly $500 million equity round to back a pair of green energy projects totaling $2 billion in India. This brings their aggregate investment to $2.2 billion in the issuer, Greenko Holding. With the latest round, Greenko Holding will be developing the two (2.4 GW total) projects, each with wind and solar generation and hydro energy storage. GIC is majority shareholder of Greenko, which holds the record for Asia's largest green bond issuance at $1 billion.

---

### Politics, Ethics, and International Diversification

In a country with a total equity market capitalization of $1.9 trillion (2018), South Korea's nearly $600 billion national pension fund has announced its intention to rebalance its portfolio from about 45% domestic fixed income and 18% domestic equities to 30% and 15%, respectively, while raising overseas equities from 20% to 30%.

Asset managers of the fund – which reports to the cabinet and South Korean parliament – will now have to deal increasingly with the politically charged determination of which Japanese issuers may have engaged in war crimes during the Japanese occupation of Korea. In the face of proposed South Korean legislation that would ban South Korean pension funds from investing in "war crime companies," the sovereign pension fund has announced a review of its portfolio of more than $1 billion in Japanese equities, the *Financial Times* has reported.

Of course, cross-border activity is not without baggage. In **South Korea,** the **National Pension Service (NPS)** has grown so large that the local markets are simply not deep and wide enough to absorb its moves. When expanding its overseas portfolio, however, the pension fund has faced difficult investment choices due to rising political tensions with Japan (see **Box: Politics, Ethics, and International Diversification**). In extreme cases, sovereign investors may turn into rogue traders themselves like those in the urban legends of the Wall Street (see **Box: 1MDB the Outlier**).

## 1MDB the Outlier

No survey of the sovereign investor playing field would be complete without a shout out to fugitive Malaysian financier Jho Low and **1Malaysia Development Berhad (1MDB),** founded by former Malaysian Prime Minister Najib Razak. The fund was created to finance infrastructure and other development projects in Malaysia; instead the funds ended up "invested" in Hollywood films ("Dumb and Dumber," "The Wolf of Wall Street"), a mega yacht, a private jet, a van Gogh, a Picasso, and luxury real estate.

Mr. Low, who remains at large and the subject of criminal charges for his alleged central role in defrauding up to $4.5 billion from 1MDB, recently agreed to forfeit over $700 million in assets to settle accusations of fraud involving the fund. That included a $125 million yacht, a $35 million jet, a $51 million New York City penthouse, the $139 million Park Lane Hotel in New York City, and, literally, a settlement from the producers of the "Wolf of Wall Street," a movie that was partly financed with 1MDB-embezzled funds.

A former Malaysian prime minister has been sentenced to prison in the scandal. And the Malaysian government reached a $3.9 billion settlement with Goldman Sachs in the same affair, after a Goldman Sachs partner pled guilty in August 2018 to bribery and money laundering. Even a failed sovereign fund has a big impact on Wall Street.

It is far from clear what transpired with all the monies transferred to the fund by the Malaysian government and further funds borrowed by it from investors. What is clear is that controls and governance were sorely lacking and that in the sovereign investor leagues, the numbers are big – even in the worst case.

Given their typically global mandate and long-term invest-ment horizon, sovereign investors increasingly **build their portfolios based on major future trends,** rather than on short-term market movements. Furthermore, they are not just passive actors affected by global megatrends, instead they actively influence the megatrends by their investments. For example, Temasek of Singapore has identified six structural trends, which collectively define the direction of its investment strategy: "Investing for a Better, Smarter, More Sustainable World" (see **Figure 1.3**):

Tech revolution essentially is the common denominator of all megatrends. Amid disruptions from new technologies, the sustainability of the world economy is critical for SIFs that seek long-term, sustainable returns from their investments. Consequently, most SIFs make global tech investments, either through external funds or directly; at the same time that they are integrating ESG factors into their investment process, leveraging tech capabilities for data analysis.

Take **APG,** the pension manager for **ABP** and a few other Dutch pension schemes, as an example. APG expresses its com-mitment to responsible investing by codifying such investing within one of its nine headline investment beliefs, and it has used digital tech for implementation. For instance, relating to the ESG/sustainable development goals (SDG) discussions in the previous section, whereas some asset owners say they are waiting for standardized data or more academic proof to imple-ment ESG strategies, APG has used artificial intelligence (AI)

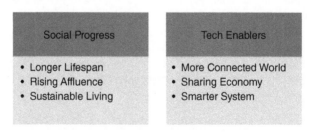

**Figure 1.3    Temasek Identified Six Structural Trends**
Source: Temasek.

to select companies that contribute sufficiently to the UN Sustainable Development Goals. ENTIS, the data analysis team of APG, uses smart algorithms to assess SDG-oriented investments, based on criteria that APG formulated itself.

On climate change, the most significant movement is the **One Planet** SWF Working Group formed by five hydrocarbon wealth powers (Norway and four Middle East funds) and the NZ Super (see **Figure 1.4**). Representing several trillions of assets under management, the six funds held the One Planet Summit on December 12, 2017, which was followed by the Climate Finance Day (building upon the success of the 2015 Paris Agreement to collectively mitigate the effects of climate change), and the working group was established at the event.

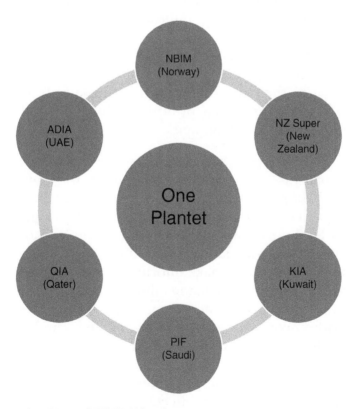

Figure 1.4    **One Planet SWF Working Group**

For sovereign investors, climate change is both a financial risk for long-term portfolios, and an opportunity, as the development of technology and changes in government policy create new avenues for investments. During the transition to a lower-carbon economy, SIFs have embraced opportunities ranging from solar and wind energy infrastructure in both developed and emerging markets, to early stage venture investments in the battery and mobility sectors. In July 2018, One Planet published an Investment Framework designed to accelerate efforts to integrate financial risks and opportunities related to climate change in the management of large, long-term asset pools like those of SIFs, including the following aims:

- foster a shared understanding of the key principles, methodologies, and indicators related to climate change;
- identify climate-related risks and opportunities in their investments; and
- enhance their investment decision-making frameworks to better inform their priorities as investors and participants in financial markets.

One Planet hopes that more SIFs and then the general institutional investors industry will adopt the Investment Framework. Its success, interestingly, is dependent on data and technology. That's because across the industry, high-quality company-level environmental data – for example, those relating to carbon emissions and environmental impact – is still not readily available. To make informed investment decisions, institutional investors demand timely, relevant, accurate, and complete climate-related data. As such, the Investment Framework encourages SIFs to adopt agreed standards that promote the disclosure of material climate-related data. With the help of big data technology, the SIFs collectively would improve the volume, quality, and consistency of financial data to promote ESG investments effectively.

Besides being the only non-oil SWF fund in the One Planet, NZ Super also signed onto a broader grouping launched at the same time which is more favored by pension funds. Characterized by Bloomberg Business Week as "the biggest, richest, and possibly the most benevolent bully the corporate world has ever seen," **Climate Action 100+** has been signed by more than 450 investors from across dozens of countries, who collectively control more than $40 trillion in assets, including aforementioned prominent pension funds such as **ABP, BCI, CDPQ, CalPERS, GPIF, ISIF, and OTPP**. They have pledged to work with their investee companies to ensure that they are minimizing (and disclosing) the risks and maximizing the opportunities presented by climate change.

Now the tech revolution is presenting the same mix of opportunities and risks for sovereign investors. On the one hand, investing into the high-growth tech sector can diversify their portfolios and generate superior financial returns. Given both their capital power and long-term investment horizons, they are best positioned for digital infrastructure (such as smart cities) that's critical for a sustainable global economy. On the other hand, major technological and disruptive innovations are disrupting traditional industries, putting SIFs' existing portfolio companies at risk. SIFs must act to "future-proof" their portfolios, as well as their own operating models. As will be seen in the next section, SIFs are all rushing into the digital economy revolution.

## Rush into the Digital Revolution

The overall trend of the sovereign investor world is to invest in the digital future – whether existing funds seeking to facilitate a digital transformation, or new funds established with that goal from the beginning. What's interesting is that this is not a new phenomenon: the states have (always) been active in tech investments. Silicon Valley and Tel Aviv were largely the creation of the US and Israeli states. Many of the innovations we take for granted today – such as the Internet, cloud computing, and virtual reality – were fostered by state seed capital or driven by government agencies.

And this continues to be partly the case: in 2014, the Pentagon, the US Defense Ministry, teamed up with the CIA to invest in cybersecurity startups. The CIA has been running its Q-Telventure capital fund since 1999, with extensive investments in tech companies. This state–military link is particularly important for understanding the rise of startups in Israel and its famous Yozma program, which unleashed the technical miracle Start-up Nation. Not to mention that space, initially the sole preserve of governments, now hosts Blue Origin (Jeff Bezos), SpaceX (Elon Musk), and Virgin Galactic (Richard Branson), backed in part by sovereign investor cash.

---

### The IPO to end all IPOs

One notable change in equity markets around the world can be laid at the feet of the patient, cash-rich sovereign investors: the dramatic decline in IPOs. The *Financial Times* headlined 2019's 10% drop from 2018 in capital raised in public listings, with the fewest flotations for three years. The massive investments by sovereign investors, eager to gain exposure to the digital economy, have enabled these tech stars to remain private far longer than would have been possible in the past (see the detailed discussion in the next chapter).

One result has been a dramatic drop off in IPOs; another, hefty pre-IPO valuations that are challenging for the tech giants to sustain in public markets. In the absence of patient, massive equity inflows from the sovereign investors, things may have played out quite differently. Others speculate that it was the arrival of SIFs into the market for late stage growth companies that enabled them to put off SEC scrutiny and meddlesome public shareholders, thereby shrinking public markets. Others see the mirror image, with the SIFs not as enablers but as driven to unicorns by the shrinking public markets.

Ironically, the largest IPO of 2019 was Saudi Aramco, which topped $2 trillion in market cap briefly after its listing. Nearly $30 billion in proceeds will largely fund PIF, which has as a goal the digital transformation of the economy and has heavily funded (via Vision Fund and directly) late stage tech stars such as Uber. In 2020, the oil price war with Russia and the economic impact of the coronavirus on the Saudi economy may cause PIF to redirect more proceeds to stimulus and funding deficits. But Vision 2030, the transformative digital future, remains in its sights.

---

The rest of this book will cover the tech investments of SIFs in detail. **The most prominent example of this trend is Saudi**

**Arabia and its Public Investment Fund (PIF)**, whose exceptionally large capital contribution to the **Vision Fund** has consequently had a profound impact on the global tech startups and capital markets. PIF is the beneficiary of the country's oil wealth and, most notably, the beneficiary of proceeds from the flotation of Aramco, briefly the most valuable company on Earth (see **Box: The IPO to end all IPOs**).

Saudi Arabia has successfully leveraged its resource-based capital in PIF to raise its profile as a major player in venture capital for tech companies. PIF committed $45 billion to the first Vision Fund's total raise of $100 billion (see **Figure 1.5**), at the time an unheard of fund size for venture capital – nearly double the amount raised by all other VC funds in a good year. Reportedly, PIF was contemplating a similar commitment to the second Vision Fund. The Fund also committed to a $500 million investment in Neom, the future oriented (flying taxis, robot dinosaurs) city Saudi Arabia is planning for its Red Sea coast.

Using its sovereign fund, Saudi Arabia has succeeded in drawing tech thought leaders to its "Davos in the Desert," despite talk that its domestic policies were anathema to the Silicon Valley ethos. The link to Neom city is of note as well. It is possible that the reciprocal investment promised by Softbank, Vision Fund's sponsor, in Neom will elevate its chances of

### Vision Fund's LP Investors (Billions)

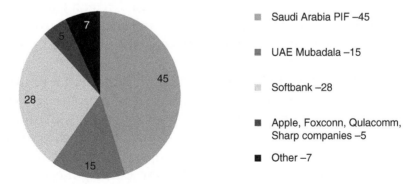

- Saudi Arabia PIF –45
- UAE Mubadala –15
- Softbank –28
- Apple, Foxconn, Qulacomm, Sharp companies –5
- Other –7

Figure 1.5    **SIFs Lead $100 billion Vision Fund**
Data Source: FT Research 2017.

attracting additional tech sector players to the country. Such a result would mean that PIF had also indirectly propelled the digital transformation of the Saudi economy by securing an anchor investor in its show piece of the digital future (see the more detailed discussion in Chapter 5).

**Another case in point is the European Union,** which is a late-comer to the world of sovereign investment funds and digital economy investments. With the rest of the world aggressively investing into tech ventures domestically and internationally, Europe has actually looked more like a net seller. Chinese buyers have acquired large robotics firms in Germany and Italy; in the UK, SoftBank bought the chip-maker ARM and one of its affiliates is set to bid on the UK's upcoming 5G auction. The UK's DeepMind, the AI pioneer that built the Alphago algorithm to beat the best human player in Go Chess, was sold to US Internet giant Google's parent company, Alphabet.

For Europeans, Apple of the US (and Samsung, from South Korea) are the most popular phones. Similarly, US companies dominate digital platforms in Europe: Facebook operates the most widely used social networks, Google rules online search and advertising, and Amazon reigns over e-commerce. Cloud infrastructure from Amazon and Microsoft is indispensable to Europe's companies. Meanwhile, China's Huawei produces the physical equipment on which Europe's digital economy runs. Driving home the extent of foreign digital dominance, EU officials had to call Los Gatos, California to ask US tech giant Netflix to lower its video streaming quality to prevent a European system crash during the coronavirus-induced surge in Internet traffic.

Things are set to change in 2020 and beyond. The European Union in February 2020 unveiled a plan to restore what officials called "technological sovereignty," with more public spending for the European tech sector. With the global economy becoming ever more reliant upon digital technology, European leaders are concerned that the European economy is overly dependent on technology developed and controlled elsewhere. As Ursula von der Leyen, the president of the

European Commission, the executive branch of the EU, said at a news conference: "We want to find European solutions in the digital age." Hence new sovereign investment funds in Europe.

According to media reports in August 2019, EU staff have drafted a plan to launch a €100 billion ($110 billion) sovereign wealth fund, to be called the "European Future Fund." The main goal of this proposed fund will be to invest into future "European tech champions," which could potentially compete in the same league as China's BAT (Baidu, Alibaba, and Tencent) or the US GAFA (Google, Apple, Facebook, and Amazon). Due to the complex EU politics, it is not clear that the fund will ever be realized; but the determination to compete with American and Chinese dominance, using a sovereign fund, in the future digital economy is clear.

**The third example is China** and its endeavor to reduce its semiconductor dependency on US technology. According to the *Wall Street Journal,* even after the creation in 2014 of its initial fund specifically targeted at fostering its domestic semiconductor industry, in 2018 alone China imported $312.1 billion in semiconductors well more than the year's $240.3 billion in oil imports. China has stepped up the effort to bolster its own chip industry through various means, including the acquisition of foreign technology companies, but the effort encountered push back by the US Committee on Foreign Investment in the United States (CFIUS), the agency that screens foreign direct investment for national security risks.

With an eye to further constraining foreign incursions in the sensitive tech sector, in 2018 (effective from early 2020) the Trump administration developed new CFIUS rules to scrutinize Chinese and other foreign investments more carefully, especially in high-tech fields. The new rule emphasizes national security review of transactions involving "TID" technologies – critical technology, critical infrastructure, and sensitive personal data (see **Figure 1.6**). While the rules would apply to any foreign investment, the effort is likely aimed at preventing China from gaining access to sensitive American

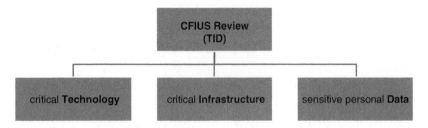

Figure 1.6    **The TID Focus of CFIUS**

technology and other valuable assets – after years of Chinese sovereign capital's activities in the Silicon Valley.

Still, China is not deterred from its determination to become more independent from US technology and keep pursuing global technology leadership. In October 2019, China set up a new national semiconductor fund (its second in less than five years) with 204 billion yuan ($28.9 billion) – its predecessor was capitalized with $20 billion in 2014. The fund's registered capital comes mainly from state organizations, according to company registration information, which include China's Ministry of Finance (22.5 billion yuan) and the policy bank China Development Bank (22 billion yuan), as well as state-owned enterprises such as China Tobacco Co. The new fund has an ambitious goal to cultivate China's complete semiconductor supply chain, from chip design to manufacturing, from processors to storage chips.

What's next for the US? Its own sovereign funds to develop 5G network technology (see **Figure 1.7**), a field in which Chinese company Huawei is the global leader. Whereas Europe's Ericsson and Nokia companies are close competitors to Huawei, the US has no 5G champions. In January 2020, a bipartisan group of US senators introduced legislation that the Federal Communications Commission (**FCC**) would create a research and development fund for Western alternatives to Huawei. Further, the newly created US **International Development Finance Corporation (DFC)**, with $60 billion in funding, would also invest in the development of mobile networks. More recently, one US government official suggested that the

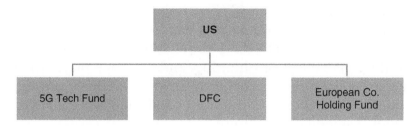

Figure 1.7    **New US SIFs for 5G**

US may consider a fund to take controlling stakes in the two European telecoms firms.

Meanwhile, the investment power of US federal, state, and local pension funds has not gone unnoticed in the corridors of the US Congress. Like their sovereign wealth fund cousins, cross-border tech investments are for them both attractive and politically charged. No longer passive allocators, they, too, live with the heightened scrutiny their profile and investment choices now attract.

In November 2019, a bill was introduced, notably with joint Republican and Democratic sponsors, that would limit the ability of the $600 billion federal **Thrift Savings Plan** to pivot its index investing to include Chinese equities, a reflection of the ongoing US–China battle over determining the future of technology. And there were reports of the White House contemplating a general ban on US pension funds (federal, state, and local) investing in technology plays in China. As US–China tensions continue, there is mounting talk of restricting the ability of US domestic pension funds to invest in Chinese tech companies. In fact, in August, 2020, the US State Department asked university endowments to divest Chinese equities, warning of more burdensome measures to come.

In summary, sovereign investors are throwing their considerable heft and influence into keenly investing in digital technology in domestic and foreign markets. Along with rising SIF activities, there is a sharp rise in global tensions, because the power of innovation is now viewed by all nations not only as an economic growth engine, but also as the key to future geopolitical dominance.

As a result, more countries are building up regulatory barriers around tech know-how and data resources as if they are "national treasures." The following chapters will follow the SIFs into their global unicorn hunting, and the hope that through the economic independence created by the SIFs of different nations, the world may find a new equilibrium and collectively develop a shared digital future.

*As you step out from the bustling, air-conditioned comfort of the ADIA tower into the Gulf heat, it strikes you that you are far from the financial centers of traditional finance or the tech hubs of the digital economy. But you will see, as you continue your journey through this book, that you have come to the doorstep of a force that will help determine their position in the post-pandemic world order. Next stop: the global village.*

CHAPTER 2

# From Passive Allocators to Active Investors

*The sovereign investment funds' (SIFs) community we cover is a highly hetero-geneous village of inhabitants from more than 100 nationalities, of differing backgrounds, age, and wealth. The North American villagers are rather boring. Mostly pensioners, above average wealth, age above average, and with moderate appetite for risk-taking in investments.*

*However, overall this is an extremely young village, where Gen Z and Mil-lennials (1980–1999) make up the majority of inhabitants. The Africans are especially young – most of them were born after 2000. No surprise after Chapter 1: Middle Easterners are wealthier than the rest. Together with Europeans, Asians, Latin Americans, and Oceanians (mostly from Australia), they form a very diverse settlement.*

*No two funds are the same though. The source of capital, the macroeconomic purpose, the government policies, the return objective, the target markets, the risk tolerance, the governance, and not the least the accountability, are only some of the factors affecting the final mix. They exhibit very different characteristics, as will be elaborated in the rest of this book, but they do share one thing in common: they are now grown-ups. They are more experienced, more sophisticated, and more active. In the global capital markets, the younger funds are sharing the platform with the most established and significant larger funds. The visit to this global village will teach us a lot.*

## Behind-the-Scene Asset Owners

In recent years, sovereign investment funds (SIFs) have wit-nessed a rise in their importance among institutional investors, thanks to their high AUM (assets under management) and increasingly sophisticated investment strategies. Historically, SIFs tended to allocate their portfolios mostly into fixed income and equities in the public markets. Due to the low interest rate environment over the past decade, they began to search for better yields in the private markets, such as private equity, venture capital, real estate, and infrastructure. This move to private markets led to the strengthening and increasing sophistication of SIF workforces, which eventually enabled SIFs to establish focused teams for the tech investments of late.

Before they become direct investors, SIFs approached private markets through private equity (PE) funds. Traditionally, the sovereign investors' main function for private market investing was to allocate capital to external fund managers. At the very beginning, they would invest into a fund of funds (**FOF**) arrangement (see **Figure 2.1**), which rendered the sovereign investors passive and little known in the capital markets. Doing so minimized the need for an in-house team to conduct diligence on, and maintain relationships with, many PE firms. Instead, the FOF manager served as the limited partnership (LP) investor of those PE funds, and in turn, delivered a diversified return to the SIF investor from the returns of a portfolio of LP investments.

But sovereign investment funds are not built simply to be outsourcing institutions. They manage large, scalable assets

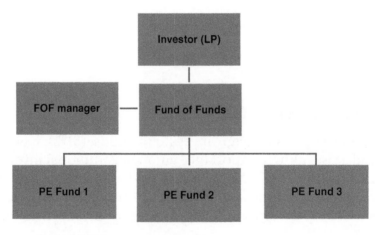

Figure 2.1   **Typical FOF Investment Structure**

and have a mandate to develop investment expertise and capability; thus, it's only natural that they would not continue investing in the same old way as smaller institutions (such as a small university endowment). Soon they realized that they really didn't need the FOF managers. For one, they were not interested in paying the second layer management fee (to the FOF managers, on top of the PE level management fee); for another, they preferred to directly interact with PE funds' general partner (GP) managers to learn about investment strategies and to acquire industry know-how. Essentially, SIFs are becoming FOF managers themselves (see **Figure 2.2**) by directly investing into PE funds as active LPs.

After years of being LP investors of external funds, SIFs have increasingly questioned high management fees and the heterogeneity of fund performance, and thus the validity of this investment model as well. This trend has been driven, in part, by a perceived misalignment of interests between fund managers and capital source (the classic "principal–agent" issue). In some cases, it is simply that SIFs have invested in too many external fund managers. For diversification purposes, a SIF may invest in many funds with different PE fund managers. More often than before, one portfolio fund may acquire an asset from another portfolio fund, and the net result for the LP investor

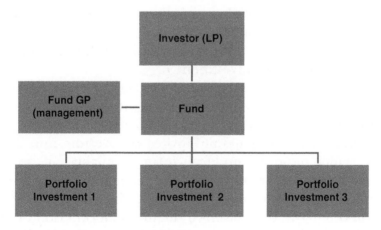

Figure 2.2    **Conventional LP Investing into Fund**

SIF is owning the same asset at a higher cost and incurring substantial fees for the privilege of doing so.

Second, the SIFs' rising profile as mature investors meant that deals also came directly to them (rather than via fund managers), a development that further called into question outside managers' value in sourcing deals. Third, SIFs considered the shorter investment horizons of external funds as not consistent with the long-term nature of their capital (a misalignment of timeframe). Therefore, the SIFs looked to reduce the number of outside managers and go direct into market deals themselves. They placed more focus on developing in-house capabilities, where they could replace high fees (to external funds) with annual salaries and operating costs (to internal staff).

The best start to their exposure to direct private equity deals, interestingly, was from their existing relationships with GP fund managers. Before going direct fully, co-investments – where the LP investor co-invests alongside fund managers in deals (see **Figure 2.3,** co-investing into portfolio investment 3 of the fund) – greatly helped the SIFs build up their knowledge of the deals process in the private markets. It's a good way to extract value from their private equity portfolios, because, first, the deal sourcing is provided, second, they can learn about due diligence practice from the GP manager reviewing the deal, and, finally, after the investment they can participate in the direct supervision of the investee company through market cycles. (Moreover, the technique often allows the LP to average down the management fees on the overall LP investment.)

The SIFs can accumulate valuable deal-making experience through co-investing before they step into full-fledged direct equity investment strategies. Co-investments, however, have downsides. The GP generally invites co-investors into larger deals, which tend to underperform (arguably, an adverse selection problem exists where fund managers may offer only lower-quality deals for co-investments). More importantly, the GP will often give the LP only a relatively short period of time to undertake due diligence; hence, the co-investor has limited visibility on the investment.

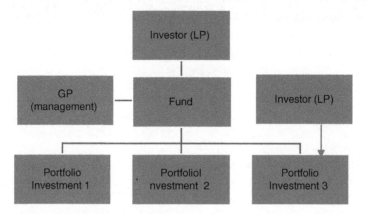

Figure 2.3    **LP Co-investing with Fund GP**

Furthermore, GP managers sometimes consider co-investments an onerous task due to the multiple downsides of offering co-investment rights to LPs:

- slows/delays the deal process;
- negative impact on relationships with LPs that are not offered co-investment rights;
- generally increasing transaction costs;
- management fee reductions;
- co-investors may have more control over the investment (e.g., exits, approvals);
- the LP investor may compete with the GP for deals in the future.

As a result, the actual volume of co-investments from the GPs is quite limited. To deepen relationships with fund managers and potentially gain more access to co-investments, the SIF even made direct investments into the PE firms to become their shareholders (but such a strategy's success also seemed limited, see **Box: Invest into the Professional Investors**). After mixed experiences from committing capital to PE and VC funds through a traditional LP model, various conflicts of interest surfaced. SIFs have since moved towards a combination of the LP/GP model and direct investment model, i.e., acquisition of equity stakes in target firms without any layer of external intermediation.

## Invest into the Professional Investors

It looked like a savvy move on the part of the SIFs and the big PE fund managers. The SIF would invest directly in the fund manager, providing liquidity to its investment professionals and an "anchor investor" in any potential IPO (initial public offering) of the fund manager. The SIF would get a piece of the "carry" and management fees its large investments (and those of other LPs) generated and, perhaps, an inside look at co-investment deals. And maybe some respect. Owning a piece of the big PE fund manager would seem likely to move you to the top of the LP charts.

In 2007, the **China Investment Corporation (CIC)** as its very first investment made a $3 billion pre-IPO direct investment in Blackstone, ultimately resulting in peak ownership of more than 9% of the publicly traded asset manager. Steve Schwartzman, head of Blackstone and already PE royalty, was catapulted into global circles, subsequently funding the "Schwartzman Scholars" a US–China program portrayed as the 21st century equivalent of the Rhodes Scholars. It is less evident what CIC got when it exited the stock position after more than a decade (Blackstone, on the other hand, has had CIC as LP investors in its PE and real estate funds).

The year 2007, the peak of the trend, also reportedly saw **ADIA** stump up for 9% of Apollo's fund management entity – which had its IPO a few years later. The same year **Mubadala** acquired 7.5% of Carlyle for a reported $1.35 billion. The SIFs were undoubtedly familiar with the mega PE fund managers, having entrusted billions to them over the preceding years, and may have viewed direct investing into these known quantities as not only a potential boost to co-investment deal flow but also as a straightforward sell of a known quantity to the SIF's investment committees.

Whatever the reason, the trend persisted for a while, despite the lack of evidence that the PE fund managers delivered more to the LPs who had invested directly in them than other more quotidian LPs who paid full fees and did not aspire to own a piece of the manager. The trend still had legs in 2009, when **GIC of Singapore** and **Australia's Future Fund** teamed up to acquire around 10% of Apax Partners, in which CIC was also a stakeholder. And GIC kept the flame alive by acquiring 4.5% of TPG in a joint venture with **KIA of Kuwait** in 2011. Finally, Mubadala also reportedly increased its stake in Carlyle in 2010.

A fruitful endeavor or a dead end? With opaque accounting on the part of both parties to these deals it is hard to know. What is clear is that the listed shares of the PE fund managers were hit hard by the global financial crisis and the early adopters suffered. CIC unceremoniously exited Blackstone in 2018. It is not evident to the observers, what, if anything, these strategic investments achieved for the SIFs: they seem to have moved on and left the trend behind with their Blackberries.

## Going Direct: Real Estate to Infrastructure

The last stage in the evolution of the SIFs' approach to private markets is fully fledged direct equity investing. In a direct solo investment, the SIF sources and executes the transactions on its own, bypassing the GP, and thus pays no fees or carried interest to external managers (see **Figure 2.4**). Sometimes in direct investments, it forms partnerships with a strategic partner (such as a tech company or infrastructure operator), or like-minded investors (peer SIFs or VC funds), or a combination of both, to jointly sponsor the deals.

The benefits of direct investing are aptly summarized in a Q&A posted in January 2020 by the **Dutch** pension **APG** on its website. Patrick Kanters, Managing Director Global Real Assets, explains what makes direct investments so attractive to SIFs: "First of all, we are able to save significantly on costs. When investing in funds, a lot of money is charged for fund management. And besides that, direct investments provide more control over the type of investment we make. Does it fit within the return and risk profile we envisage? Does the investment meet our investment beliefs? It also provides us with an opportunity to have a greater say in strategic decisions. How much borrowed capital will be allocated to underlying investments, what sustainability requirements do we impose?"

However, every opportunity comes with a challenge. In the old world of private equity, the SIFs' main task as an LP was manager selection. In the game of direct equity investing, new competencies are needed. Covering different industries requires a diverse range of deal professionals with different

Figure 2.4    **Direct Investing (Traditional LP Becoming the GP Itself)**

skills and backgrounds. The internal staff – not only the investment team, but also the middle and back offices – must be trained and experienced in transaction-related activities, including due diligence, risk management, operational and monitoring capabilities that are outside the traditional LP skill set.

The natural start, not at all surprisingly, is the real estate market. Even **Norway**'s conservatively run fund has sought and obtained a mandate to invest in alternative assets – so far limited to direct investing in real estate assets. **Qatar** has acquired trophy properties such as, most recently, New York City's St. Regis Hotel. **GIC of Singapore** formerly ran and managed its large real estate portfolio, including office towers and luxury hotels, relying on a dedicated team, but now outsources such management. Its joint venture with Global Student Accommodations is one noteworthy example of this approach, with 1900 beds acquired in Germany in 2018 alone.

**Canada's OMERS** has stuck with the captive management approach, having acquired Oxford Properties, a real estate business, which is now the OMERS' real estate arm (see the detailed case study in Chapter 7). It develops and manages real estate assets globally, most notably as a partner in the largest private mixed-use real estate project in the United States, Hudson Yards, rising over Manhattan's far west side to cover 28 acres of offices, residences, shopping, and public space.

## When Going Direct, Go Big

In November 2017, **CIC** acquired European warehouse firm Logicor from private equity group Blackstone for €12.25 billion ($13.8 billion). At the deal closing, the Logicor deal was the biggest private equity real estate deal in Europe on record, as well as CIC's largest direct investment in asset value.

At deal time, the company owned more than 600 logistics facilities in Europe that spanned 17 countries in seven major regions: the United Kingdom, Germany, France, Southern Europe, the Nordic countries, Central and Eastern

Europe, and Benelux. Thanks to the e-commerce boom, which requires a network of locations to store goods to ensure fast delivery, Logicor counted Amazon among its clients, and it has become the largest owner of European logistics and distribution properties.

After the CIC investment, Logicor expanded in European markets for digital economy businesses. In the UK, its two Amazon warehouses have employed thousands of new workers. In Poland, its sites in Lodz and Gorzow have supported growth in the high-tech manufacturing and automotive industries, providing warehouse space to companies like US electronics manufacturer Flex.

Not surprisingly, the leading competitors bidding on the investment were also sovereign investment funds – CIC fought off competition from another consortium led by Singapore sovereign investor **Temasek Holdings** and its real estate affiliate Mapletree Investments. CIC's close working relationship with Blackstone (as recounted in the previous **Box: Invest into the Professional Investors**) was reportedly an advantage.

After real estate, a less traditionally mainstream asset class is often the next target for SIFs: infrastructure – including ports, bridges, airports, water systems, pipelines, and the like. Blessed with large, regulated, income-producing assets, the asset class also suited the long-term hold strategy of SIFs. This meant that SIFs were – and are – frequently among the leading bidders for governments seeking to privatize airports, toll roads, and other assets. For **CIC,** one recent real estate transaction is its largest direct investment in asset value to date (see **Box: When Going Direct, Go Big**).

As with real estate, the SIFs recruited and developed teams to source, target, and manage these assets. As traditional infrastructure assets became a favored asset class, competition for them increased and returns flagged (the opaque nature of infrastructure assets brings extra challenges). But the infrastructure teams were ensconced and expanded their mandate to encompass "infra-like" assets, including lotteries, logistics, and data centers. It was not a big step into direct investing into tech. Meanwhile, they collaborate with like-minded investors (increasingly peer SIFs) to assess deal opportunities together and share transaction experiences, as illustrated by examples below and the case study of Global Strategic Investment Alliance (GSIA).

For example, in a 2016 deal, **Australia's Future Fund and Queensland Investment Corporation (QIC), OMERS, CIC, and NPS of Korea** were all investors in the $7.3 billion privatization of the Port of Melbourne. Similarly, **UAE's ADIA and Canada's CPPIB** participated in the $6.7 billion Transurban-led deal for the Sydney toll roads. Most recently, Generate Capital, a San Francisco-based renewable energy startup, has avoided VC funds and secured direct funding from the **Alaska Permanent Fund, QIC, and AustralianSuper,** raising $1 billion in a round reported in February 2020. Generate, an "infrastructure as a service" startup, funds and collaborates in infrastructure projects focused on sustainable technologies which are sold on to public and private customers.

It's worth noting that a distinction should be made between (a) co-investment, an option given to LP investors by fund GP managers to invest alongside a fund investment (see **Figure 2.3**) and (b) joint investment, a direct investment developed by a SIF in collaboration with like-minded investors. The like-minded investors may include PE or VC funds as well, but typically they don't have a GP–LP relationship with the SIF (see **Figure 2.5**). While the co-investments alongside PE/VC funds are a step in the right direction for sovereign investors "going direct," this book focuses more on the innovative models of collaboration among SIFs.

Along this path towards enhanced cooperation, the case of GSIA demonstrates the synergies among the SIFs. The Global Strategic Investment Alliance (GSIA) was established by OMERS Strategic Investments, an affiliate of the Ontario Municipal Employees Retirement System (**OMERS**), a Canadian pension fund with over C$70 billion in equity. In this case, OMERS, with decades of direct investment experience in infrastructure, teamed with peer institutions to form a co-investment platform with OMERS as its GP. The unusual arrangement came together in 2014 with the addition of

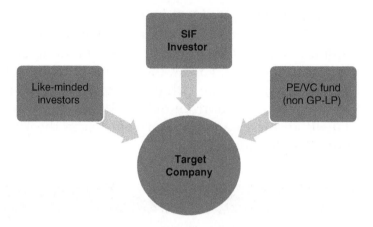

Figure 2.5    Joint Investment by SIF and PE/VC Fund

Table 2.1    GSIA Overview

| | |
|---|---|
| "GP": | OMERS, as lead investor, originates and manages investments |
| Size: | $12.5 billion, $5 billion from OMERS |
| Target: | "Whales" among core North American and European infrastructure assets ($2 billion threshold) |
| Structure: | "Opt-in" on a deal-by-deal basis, 15-year term; no carry or sponsor's fees |
| "LPs": | Development Bank of Japan, Japan Bank for International Cooperation, GPIF, Mizuho Bank, Pension Fund Assn (Japan), US pensions |

**Japan's Government Pension Investment Fund (GPIF)** to other Japanese and US institutions (see **Table 2.1**).

As infrastructure has become a more established asset class for large institutional investors, particularly for SIFs, competition for assets has increased and some investors have adapted by focusing on larger assets, the value of which may exceed their single asset risk limits if acquired 100%. This is reflected in the focus on "whales." The structure is "opt-in" without mandatory calls unless the participant commits to a specific deal. All are free to compete for deals falling below the "whale" threshold.

GSIA presents several novel aspects in collaboration among SIFs. For one, GPIF had not previously invested in infrastructure – either directly or via funds with private sector GPs, the more common entry point. For another, OMERS, as GP, generally contributes more than half of the capital required for every GSIA investment (much larger than the typical GP contribution percentage in PE funds, ensuring an alignment of interests with the LPs). Finally, there's the 15-year duration of the alliance, longer than private sector funds and more suited to the investment horizon of SIFs. In another twist, the GP sustained an increased regulatory burden in the US (see **Box: Other People's Money**).

### Other People's Money

The GSIA platform carries with it a side effect of the move to lead a network of SIFs: a regulatory line may be crossed when one SIF takes the lead and others add their funds to the pool.

The SEC subjects investment funds and investment advisers to registration and regulatory review. However, prior to the global financial crisis, market-moving hedge funds, as well as the juggernaut PE houses and sought after VCs, were not subject to the requirements of the Investment Advisers Act of 1940 (Advisers Act), due to the so-called "private adviser" exemption. Those who limited the number of their clients and did not advertise avoided SEC scrutiny. SIFs benefited from the same treatment when they opened offices in the US.

In the wake of the global financial crisis, the US Congress subjected the private advisers to the same regime of registration and regulation. This has led to the trend to shut down tremendously successful hedge funds and refashion them as family offices dedicated solely to managing the wealth of the founder. Even under its newly expanded mandate, the SEC does not oversee those who manage their own money, only other people's money.

When the legislative reform was adopted in response to the global financial crisis, scant attention was paid to sovereign investors. In what was probably an unintended consequence – the SEC staff did not see the regulation of the investment activities of foreign governments fitting with its primary mission of protecting American investors – SIFs were swept up in the regulatory net. The result was the GSIA-related SEC registration of the OMERS GP (due to the US presence of members of the OMERS infrastructure team), OMERS has also registered with the SEC its OMERS Ventures arm, whose presence in Silicon Valley evidently has made it subject to registration as well.

The GSIA provides a good example of how a network of investors can facilitate the establishment of an aligned co-investment platform. As noted earlier, the benefit of collaborating is that it not only allows for a better alignment of interests between investors, but also enables a critical mass to be achieved so that the GSIA is able to access the projects that previously were restricted mainly to large fund managers. Such an alignment provides other smaller institutional investors, without the ability to invest directly, with the opportunity to access infrastructure assets on more aligned terms and conditions than their default fund managers.

While the GSIA features PPFs, there is a marked trend towards SWFs partnering with other, often government-owned asset owners in both innovative new platforms and traditional private-equity-style transactions, which allow the partners to pool their networks and expertise for mutual benefit (see **Table 2.2** and see also in Chapter 1 **Table 1.3 PPF/SWF Co-investments**). The Chinese and Singaporean SIFs had the most SWF–SWF deals, which included collaboration among themselves: CIC, GIC, and Temasek all participated in a $1 billion co-investment in Cheniere Energy, a US natural gas export facility, and GIC and Temasek co-invested $1.53 billion with Khazanah in Alibaba Logistics. Of course, the $100 billion Vision Fund sponsored by **Saudi Arabia's PIF and UAE's Mubadala** is an exceptional arrangement in the tech world, which will be discussed in later chapters.

## Active Investors Taking Actions

Many SIFs, such as **NPS of Korea,** took years to become successful direct investors through a gradual evolution of the type described in previous sections; from being an investor in funds, to partnering in co-investments, and on to direct solo investor, with further levels of sophistication around different types of direct investing (early or growth stage versus late stage buyout of target companies). Having strong LP–GP relationships with

Table 2.2   SWF–SWF Co-investments as of 2018

| SWF | Total Co-Investments | SWF–SWF % |
| --- | --- | --- |
| Russian Direct Investment Fund (RDIF) | 8 | 100% |
| Kuwait Investment Authority (KIA) | 12 | 75% |
| Abu Dhabi Investment Council (ADIC) | 5 | 60% |
| Temasek Holdings | 21 | 57% |
| China Investment Corporation (CIC) | 27 | 56% |
| Mubadala Investment Company | 6 | 50% |
| Qatar Investment Authority (QIA) | 24 | 46% |
| GIC of Singapore | 35 | 46% |
| Abu Dhabi Investment Authority (ADIA) | 12 | 42% |

Source: IE Sovereign Wealth Research 2018.

major private equity funds is of critical importance for ongoing co-investment volume and knowledge exposure to emerging areas. At the same time, strategies gradually evolve to include a broader global reach as the fund strengthens its internal capabilities.

Along with becoming increasingly active in direct *investing*, sovereign investors also develop a more active style of *managing* their portfolio. For example, NPS was not known to actively engage the listed companies they invested in. In fact, it used to have a nickname, "yes man," since during shareholder meetings it agreed (voted "yes") with the management most of the time. The corporate structure of many Korean companies makes it difficult for outsiders to challenge the incumbent management, even in the event of management wrongdoing. Since NPS holds about 7% of the market cap of all public Korean stocks, its voting rights could have a significant impact at shareholder meetings, and polls show that the majority of its beneficiaries want NPS to take an active role in voting on corporate issues.

In 2015, the Fund Management Committee of NPS formulated the Guidelines for Exercise of Voting Rights. The

Table 2.3  NPS Voting Results 2016–2018

| Year | Against (%) | For (%) | Neutral/Abstain (%) |
|------|-------------|---------|---------------------|
| 2016 | 10.07% | 89.43% | 0.50% |
| 2017 | 12.87% | 86.89% | 0.24% |
| 2018 | 18.52% | 80.62% | 0.56% |

Data Source: NPS 2019.

rationale is that NPS as a long-term investor should have an active dialogue with its portfolio companies (shareholder engagement) to enhance corporate value and ultimately increase return for NPS. In the subsequent years of 2016–2018, NPS dealt with similar numbers of companies and agenda items at shareholder meetings, but NPS said "no" increasingly frequently (see **Table 2.3**).

The more comprehensive upgrade of voting activity, however, came in 2018, after a national outcry over incidents of abuse of power by the Korean "*chaebol*" (family-run conglomerate). In South Korea, a *chaebol* often consists of many industrial sectors and diversified affiliates, and the group is run and controlled by a powerful family. Members of the founding families of giant *chaebols* often include the second or third generations, who are treated as "emperors" (see **Box: "Nut Rage" and "Water Rage" Sisters**).

### "Nut Rage" and "Water Rage" Sisters

In 2014, Cho Hyun-ah, daughter of the Korean Air Lines Chairman, achieved worldwide fame after her anger over the way nuts should be served on an airplane. Korean Air Lines is owned by Hanjin Group, a top 15 biggest *chaebol* in Korea that also owns Jin Air Lines, Hanjin Transportation, and many other companies. Korean Air Chairman Cho Yang-ho is also the big boss of parent Hanjin Group.

The Chairman's daughter was angry that her macadamia nuts were served in a bag, not on a plate, and the taxiing flight was forced to return to the gate. The plane was grounded, causing substantial delay. More than 56,000 South Koreans signed a petition submitted to the presidential office asking the government to stop Korean Air from using a logo resembling the national flag, because foreigners may assume "Korean air is part of South Korea's national image" with the word "Korea" in its name.

In 2018, her sister, Cho Hyun-min, also known as Emily Cho, similarly generated major headlines. Emily Cho was a Senior Vice President overseeing the carrier's marketing and commercials, and during a meeting with an advertising agency, she verbally abused an advertising agent (her verbal abuse was recorded and leaked) and allegedly hurled a cup of water at him. She later apologized on Facebook, explaining that her outsized anger was sparked by her passion for business development.

To make matters worse, the recordings of another member of the Hanjin Group verbally abusing her private driver were also leaked at the same time. Afterwards, more than ten additional cases including smuggling, attacking an employee, and abusing their nannies were alleged against the members of Hanjin Group. These incidents were seen as abuses of power by elite business families that exercise outsized influence over publicly listed companies in South Korea, even though the families are not majority shareholders.

People were furious at the arrogance of the *chaebol* family members. They also questioned whether the family members were really suitable to manage their group and portfolio companies as CEO or board members. At the 2019 shareholders meeting, Chairman Cho Yang-ho became the first *chaebol* chief to lose a board seat at a portfolio company in a shareholder vote, for which NPS voting was crucial. Cho stayed on as Chairman of Korean Air, but has no involvement on the board.

To curb abuse of power by industry conglomerate owners, the Korean public demanded that NPS as the major shareholder play a more active role in corporate management. As a result, NPS (together with **Korea Investment Corporation (KIC)**, another major sovereign fund of South Korea) adopted seven stewardship principles for more active engagement with management of their portfolio companies.

These principles led to more active voting by NPS (as well as KIC) and the once "yes man" is now casting a "no" vote more often (see **Table 2.4**). The most notable case was the Korean Air board of directors election in early 2019, not only because it was the first *chaebol* put to the test after NPS adopted its seven stewardship principles, but also because the family of Chairman

Table 2.4    NPS Before vs. After the Adoption of Stewardship Principles

| Activity | Before | After |
|---|---|---|
| Voting | Mostly "yes" | More "no" |
| Shareholder-Engagement Focus List | Request for reasonable dividend payout policy | Focus list expands to cover<br>• legal violations<br>• executive compensation<br>• follow up on matters after a repeated vote-against |
| Litigation | litigation for seeking damages | shareholder class action; litigation for seeking damages |

Data Source: NPS 2019.

and Director Cho had become the leading symbol of "*gabjil*," where those with higher business status abuse their power over inferiors and create risks for their companies' operation and stock price.

At the March 2019 Korean Air's annual meeting, shareholders voted against the airline's proposal to extend Cho's term as a Board Director. The voting result was 64.1% in favor and 35.9% against, which fell just short of the two-thirds supermajority he needed to secure re-election. NPS, which was the second-largest shareholder of Korean Air with a stake of 12%, played a pivotal role in the dismissal of Cho as a Board Director. The pension service voted against extending Cho's term on grounds that he had a record "of undermining corporate value and infringing upon shareholder rights."

There are about 300 companies – including Samsung Electronics, Hyundai Motor, SK hynix, Naver, and Posco – in which NPS holds more than 5% of the shares and has influential power. To enhance independence in voting, NPS set up an independent committee, composed of external experts, to review and set the direction of shareholder activities. Going forward, NPS has determined to actively participate in broader corporate governance issues beyond voting for responsible investing (see **Table 2.4**).

## Rarity of Unicorns: In the Public Market

After building internal capabilities and a mindset to be active investors, the third factor driving SIFs into direct tech investments is the "shrinking" of the public stock market, especially for the technology sector in the US. In almost all markets throughout the world, the number of listed companies has fallen in recent years. This was probably the unexpected reason that attracted the major SIFs into venture investments, including the largest sovereign wealth fund in the world **Norway's Oil Fund,** which was always cautious about investing in unlisted companies for transparency reasons.

The public market of listed companies is getting smaller, and the reasons for the decline in the number of listed companies in the US from its peak in 1996 are – as will be discussed below and in the next chapter – complex. Even companies going for a public listing may not sell new shares through a public offering. Two famous tech unicorns, Swedish music streaming company Spotify (**AP6 of Sweden** and **ADIC, now part of Mubadala,** were backers) and US enterprise software company Slack (Vision Fund), have chosen to list their shares through a direct listing. In contrast to a conventional initial public offering (IPO), the companies issued no new shares and raised no new capital from investors. In many ways, the "direct listing" is a modified form of the auction model used by Google when it went public two decades ago (see **Box: DL vs. IPO**).

---

### Direct listing (DL) vs. Initial Public Offering (IPO)

A direct listing is an innovative structure that provides companies with an alternative to a traditional IPO as the path to going public. Here are the basics: just like an IPO, a company files its registration statement with the SEC and its outstanding shares are listed on a stock exchange. The company does not issue new shares (as in the case of an IPO) but starts trading on the stock exchange, where existing shareholders, such as employees and early stage investors, become free to sell their shares directly to the public market buyers.

Swedish music streaming company **Spotify**'s direct listing on the New York Stock Exchange in April 2018 was the first of its kind. Then in June 2019, **Slack,** the workplace messaging software popular in tech and media circles, became the second large tech company go public in the same fashion. "It's moronic," said Barry McCarthy, the Spotify CEO who led the pioneering deal, as he observed that traditional IPO process had not evolved in decades.

Besides no new share issuance, the main difference between a traditional IPO and a direct listing is the lack of the Wall Street banks serving as "underwriters" (see **Figure 2.6**). In a traditional initial public offering, investment banks act as "underwriters" to travel with aspiring public companies in a "roadshow" to potential institutional buyers, build up a "book" of confirmed IPO buyers, and set an offering price before trading starts on the stock exchange.

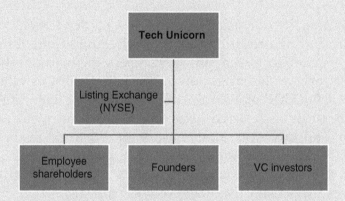

Figure 2.6    **Direct Listing – No Underwriters or New Share Issuance**

Since there is no underwritten offering, a direct listing does not require the participation of underwriters. Nor the institutional investors who traditionally are courted by the company to invest into the IPO companies when they go public. Therefore, there is no need for a roadshow either. In the spirit of digital economy, Slack hosted an "investor day" to distribute its corporate information, and the broadcast was live-streamed to anyone interested in buying the stock.

Spotify and Slack's success have challenged the Wall Street model: in a direct listing, companies may still hire the investment banks as financial advisers to help the process, which is far less expensive than the underwriting fee (traditionally 7% of the IPO proceeds). This raised questions about whether tech companies need the traditional support of big banks for going public. Skeptics from Wall Street have responded that direct listings only make sense for a very particular set of companies: those that are profitable and can afford to list shares without raising cash, or those that have well-known brands and a public following.

Only the market will tell. Conditions can change rapidly, closing market windows. Until early 2020, the apartment sharing unicorn **Airbnb** reportedly had been closely studying a direct listing, as apparently the company was profitable – which means it did not need to raise capital when going public – and it enjoys a global consumer brand. Until the coronavirus epidemic ravaged its business. Instead, it quickly raised $1 billion in fresh equity and debt from a round led by PE firm Silverlake, hoping to ride out the epidemic. It had looked likely to become the third Silicon Valley company to win in the tug-of-war with Wall Street. Instead, it remains a unicorn with an uncertain future.

For a variety of reasons outlined in Chapter 1, tech companies are staying private for longer and getting funded longer. Just a decade ago, a company such as Airbnb, the room-sharing application, would have gone public long before its valuation reached the GDP of a European country. Most likely, it would have been publicly listed before it reached unicorn status at a $1 billion valuation. Many have seen this trend in the light of the cost of being listed (and ongoing compliance requirements thereafter) having increased as a result of regulatory changes – especially for smaller companies.

The most important reason, however, is the simplest: private capital these days is more available than ever. The venture investment world used to be managed by venture capital (VC) funds exclusively, but recently it has been crowded by alternative providers of long-term risk capital; not only the sovereign funds but also institutional investors, mutual funds, and private equity (PE) funds (see **Figure 2.7**). Per PitchBook data, the value of VC deals in the US has risen to more than five times the 2009 volume. Furthermore, the securities law regulatory system has also evolved to permit more private capital in favor of startups staying private longer. For example, in August 2020 the SEC updated the definition of "Accredited Investor" to expand the group that is eligible to participate in private offerings of company shares (see **Box: More Accredited Investors**).

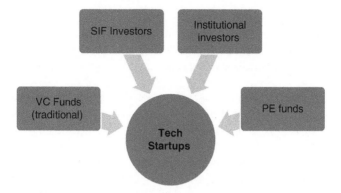

Figure 2.7    **The Entry of Non-Conventional Venture Investors**

In other words, a startup today has more alternative channels to raise capital privately from a larger swatch of investors than existed a decade ago. If I can stay private, continue raising rounds of cash, maintain near-total corporate control, and avoid the scrutiny of public shareholders and regulators, why bother with the trouble of an IPO? That seems to be the logical reasoning in the minds of unicorn founders. (The spring 2020 coronavirus crisis has led to a correction in the financial markets. However, the US Federal Reserve has launched a rescue policy of unlimited quantitative easing, pumping trillions of dollars into the monetary system. Therefore, it remains unclear when, or if, this logic will be challenged anytime soon, particularly with the volatility in capital markets effectively ruling out IPOs and direct listings.)

## More Accredited Investors

The US Securities Act of 1933 requires that every offer and sale of company securities be registered with the Securities and Exchange Commission (the "SEC"), unless an exemption is available (in which case, companies could sell equity and raise funding in a "private offering"). The purpose of registration is to provide investors with full and fair disclosure of material information so that they are able to make their own informed investment and voting decisions.

Regulation D under the Securities Act permits companies seeking financing to issue securities in a private offering limited to "accredited investors." Accredited investors are financially sophisticated and able to fend for themselves or sustain the risk of loss, thus rendering unnecessary the protections that come from a registered offering. In August 2020, the SEC finalized amendments to simplify the tests for who is eligible to participate in private offerings, which will:

- allow natural persons to qualify as accredited investors based on certain professional certifications and designations, such as a Series 7, 65, or 82 license, or other credentials issued by an accredited educational institution;
- with respect to investments in a private fund, add a new category based on the person's status as a "knowledgeable employee" of the fund;
- add limited liability companies (LLC) and certain other entity types to the current list of entities that may qualify, as well as a new catch-all for any entity owning investments in excess of $5 million and that was not formed for the specific purpose of investing in the securities offered; and
- add "family offices" with at least $5 million in assets under management and their "family clients," as each term is defined under the Investment Advisers Act.

Interestingly, these expansive amendments are based on the SEC observation that the advances in technology over the years have led to broader availability of information about issuers and other participants in the exempt private markets. (And the SEC also noted that more capital was raised in the Regulation D private market in 2018 than from registered offerings in the public market). No doubt, the revised "accredited investor" definition would further facilitate capital raising by early growth-stage tech companies.

The influx of money from non-traditional venture investors – again, not only the SIFs but also institutional investors and equity funds – has led to an odd phenomenon: the unicorns are not rare anymore. Market data firm CB Insights in 2019 counted more than 400 unicorns, about a tenfold increase from 2013. The matchup of unicorn and investor remains unsullied by market checks as the sovereigns can take a longer term view and founders can focus on growing the top line with abundant capital. How long will this fusion last? That's what the rest of the book will study and discuss. Nevertheless, the sovereign funds have undoubtedly become the new growth engine of the tech world.

## New Milestone for Grown-up SIFs

There are three powerful drivers causing sovereign funds to focus on tech investments (see **Figure 2.8**). **First of all,** technology has been the sector of choice for global SIFs in the second part of the last decade for growth and returns. *In fact, what is a technology company?* It used to be the concept of the "information technology" (IT) sector, comprising software and services, computer hardware and telecom equipment, and semiconductor chips and equipment. However, with technology disrupting all kinds of traditional industries and spawning new businesses, it is increasingly difficult to delineate a pure technology company. In this book, "technology" refers to all companies that sell mostly information technology products and services as well as those that are intensive users of technology in their business models – a huge universe that the SIF investors cover, with examples throughout this book.

**Second,** tech investments enable the SIF executives to gain insight and manage the impact of advances in technology across their portfolios. For the SIFs, technological advances

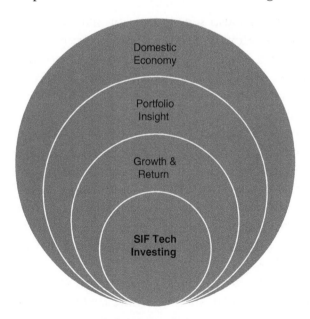

Domestic
Economy

Portfolio
Insight

Growth &
Return

SIF Tech
Investing

Figure 2.8     **Three Main Objectives of SIFs' Tech Investing**

present both investment opportunities and disruption risks to their asset portfolios. For example, investments in parking garages may not be sustainable for the long term in the future world of driverless cars. The knowledge they gain from new investments can help them to protect their existing portfolio investments as they face disruption. They can engage these companies to make sure they are conscious of the risks and preparing for them, and to encourage the innovative culture within companies.

For example, take **Malaysia's Khazanah.** A major part of its portfolio consists of infrastructure and legacy state-owned companies, such as power sector and consumer-facing businesses like banking, healthcare, and telecommunications. The Khazanah team makes new tech investments, and at the same time helps those legacy firms reinvent themselves to stay competitive. As the team becomes more sophisticated in the ways of the new economy, it works with industry partners (some from new investments) to explore how to bring in new services like digital payment systems or mobile healthcare to its legacy investee companies.

**Third,** the SIFs also see strong opportunities to accelerate their domestic development agendas from overseas tech investments. Many sovereign funds today have domestic and strategic objectives, and they seek tech investments to support economic activity and job creation at home, while simultaneously achieving commercial returns. They rush to Silicon Valley, China, and other innovation hubs of the world to join the unicorn hunt, with the intention of introducing globally competitive elements into their home economies. They motivate the investee companies to expand into the fund's own back yards to promote national economic advancement. (Many of them are also investing in their domestic markets, building up the digital infrastructure and venture capital ecosystem.)

For example, the Middle East sovereign investors are compelled to follow a domestic economic diversification program to "future-proof" their economies, accelerating their digital transformation in the face of potential "peak oil." **Saudi Arabia PIF**'s investments in Tesla, Cloud Kitchens, and, together with the **Mubadala,** in space port ventures, are emblematic of this. And anyone who has glimpsed the ambitions for Neom, Saudi Arabia's planned city of the future, or Abu Dhabi and Dubai, the smart cities of UAE, will recognize the contemplated destination of those petrodollars (see the more detailed discussion in **Chapter 5**).

As a result, from digital health to cloud software, fintech to artificial intelligence, semiconductors to e-commerce, sovereign investors are participating in the digital era in a myriad of ways, including limited partnership (LP) investments in VC funds and co-investments, as well as co-sponsorships (club deals) and sole direct investments.

For the smaller SIFs, club deals and direct investment structures are unavailable to, or impractical for, their investment strategy. The size of commitments required in those deals limits their ability to diversify their portfolios. Their exposure to the tech sector tends to be through LP positions in established VC funds. Indirect participation yields diversified (and often higher quality) deal flow, specialized technology expertise during origination and due diligence, and access to a deep network of industry executives through the external fund managers.

But the indirect approach has drawbacks, some relating to traditional fund investments and some specific to the tech sector (see **Figure 2.9**). First, there is significant fee exposure (management fee plus carry – with fund-of-funds structures, there may be additional fees). Second, getting access to the best-performing and "brand-name "managers is exceptionally difficult in this market, because the VC funds (relating to early stage investments) are much smaller than PE funds, while at the same time the market is experiencing unprecedented allocations of capital from LPs in this field. Third, for SIFs looking for tech insight, it is hard to crystallize and codify knowledge resulting from fund LP exposure – there is a ceiling to what can be learned through an arm's length relationship.

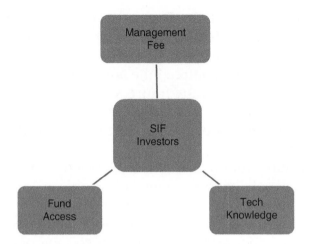

Figure 2.9    **Issues with VC Fund Investments**

As a result, larger sovereigns have sought to collaborate with other investors of similar scale at the asset level. Many sovereign investment funds have skipped the conventional evolution from LP investments into funds (VC funds), to co-investing with the fund GPs, and gradually going into direct investments in tech companies themselves. Instead, they have jumped straight into direct transactions and club deal partnerships (with the obvious exception of the Vision Fund, which requires separate treatment).

With the power of direct investing comes the responsibility of direct investing. In addition to the need to source deals, perform due diligence, and possibly attract fellow SIFs, the deal structuring and regulatory interface aspects that are served up by the GP in a typical PE or VC fund fall to the direct investor. Board representation may carry with it reputational, regulatory, and tax consequences which can impact returns. (It is worth noting that OMERS has not one, but two, units that have registered with the SEC as investment advisers, not only in connection with the GSIA above but also the OMERS Ventures discussed in later chapters, see **Box: Eyes on the Feet on the Ground.**)

### Eyes on the Feet on the Ground

Moving the SIF's portfolio into direct tech investing is often accompanied by moving a team into place in the tech hub. Besides managing other people's money, the structure of the SIF itself creates another way that having a team on the ground in the US can cause the SIF to fall within the purview of the SEC.

The structural reasons for this are multiple. Each SIF exists by virtue of its home country laws and customs. It is not uncommon for a SIF to be structured so that the assets are held in one entity while the investment professionals are employed by another. Accordingly, when the SIF's structure is reviewed by US securities counsel, it may be challenging to position the SIF as managing its own money for SEC purposes.

As much as the SEC staff is reluctant to exercise the responsibility to oversee management by a foreign government-affiliated entity of what are essentially its home country's assets, the staff is equally disinclined to open wide an exemption that could be used by any of the intended targets of the Advisers Act to avoid its clutches.

Falling within the oversight of SEC registration and disclosure is one possible consequence of the on-the-ground presence necessary to participate directly in the local venture ecosystem. The recruiting of local teams to enable direct investing in tech startups is the subject of **Chapter 7.**

Therefore, going direct into tech investments is a new milestone for the sovereign funds "growing up." Besides the external barriers listed above, they also need to develop a singular mindset to undertake this type of complex investing, re-calibrating internal operating models to accommodate the nuances of unicorn hunting (see **Figure 2.10**). These challenges are briefly mentioned below, and they will play out through this book. The most sophisticated SIFs, such as the Singaporean SWFs and Canadian pensions, have moved decidedly into this direction, and more are following.

**First, new team building.** To compete for deal sources, numerous SIFs have opened offices in the places where innovation flourishes. But attracting and retaining the right team in the right geography can be an obstacle for sovereign investors that have compensation arrangements that are not competitive in the industry, especially in developed markets

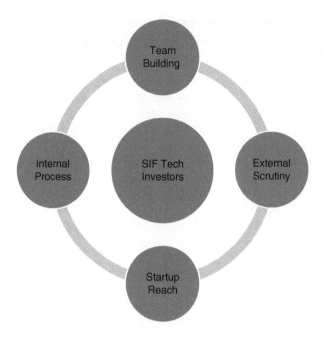

Figure 2.10 **SIFs Needs to Reorganize Themselves**

where investment professionals have other, potentially more lucrative, opportunities (see **Chapter 7** for detailed discussion). The increased office costs and salary costs (due to workforce expansion) and training costs (for existing internal staff to gain new skills) are significant investments that may take a long time to pay off.

Dealing with the startup ecosystem and tech industries in the target jurisdiction requires additional expertise and growing staff simply to source and execute the transactions. Further investment in local staff is often needed to provide oversight of the investment itself. And ranks of compliance staff will also swell to avoid (or mitigate) regulatory footfalls. Attracting and retaining talented staff in places like Silicon Valley, New York, and Singapore is a task unto itself, often not met by internal reposting and requiring local hires in a competitive market.

**Second, new organizational efforts.** Often, the internal review committee acts on a schedule which effectively precludes the sovereign investor from participating in deals in competition with VCs or PE funds. Hence the need to streamline the investment approval process and make prompt decisions on the opportunity. Meanwhile, given the uncertain and rapid nature of technological disruption, the SIF investors must remain cautious and selective. To achieve a good balance, the SIFs need specifically to design a new process.

For example, to access venture deals, both **Temasek and GIC of Singapore** have developed strong in-house capabilities and reconfigured their organizations, setting up specialized teams and dedicated subsidiaries (see **Chapter 6** for detailed discussion). They are more active in the VC sphere than many other SIFs who have not undertaken the same kind of organizational and developmental change process. The latter are still figuring out their way, either too passionate about unicorn growth opportunities to adhere to strict pricing discipline, or rigidly applying the traditional risk–reward calculus to startups and unable to make investment decisions.

**Third, rising regulatory scrutiny.** No longer passive limited partners in locally managed venture capital funds, their presence in board rooms and A rounds generates a higher profile and, with it, higher scrutiny by the local regulators. In addition, the new trend of sovereign investors turning their attention to the key technologies of the future (beyond pure e-commerce and Internet-enabled new business models) leads to national security concerns of the host countries (see **Chapters 8** and **9** for a detailed discussion). Government relations efforts must expand accordingly. For example, Temasek opened a Washington, DC office as it increased direct investment in the US.

As is discussed in later chapters, national security review has become a major investment evaluation consideration, especially in the direct investment sector. The SIF's bid may be disregarded, even though its terms are better, as a result of the seller's perception of deal risk – failure or delay – due to the national security review process. Similarly, SIFs may avoid bidding on, or even considering, potential deals out of an unwillingness to subject themselves to scrutiny and possible political backlash from the host country.

**Finally, and probably most problematically, the engagement with unicorns.** Establishing a profile as a startup-friendly source of capital is important in obtaining access to deal flow that is adequate to support a dedicated team and office. SIFs often have greater regard for reputational risk, something that falls more squarely upon them when investing directly. As a passive investor, it is easier for the SIF to distance itself from the startup's workplace scandals, perceived exploitation of "gig" workers, and privacy issues arising from governance or security failures. When the SIF has board representation and a sizeable equity position, it may be seen as neglectful or even complicit.

As classically passive investors, the sovereigns have tended not to challenge ensconced founders. In fact, being "passive" as active investors is an approach that holds appeal for startup founders. The comfortable sovereign investor approach of quietly backing founders worked well in the case of Jack Ma (Alibaba) and Mark Zuckerberg (Facebook). Alibaba has matured and grown successfully in China and global markets, and Facebook, while attracting a great deal of negative press, has performed like a blue chip public company – the SIFs have largely gone along for the ride and prospered (see **Figure 2.11**).

The same hands off approach has not produced similarly strong returns in the case of WeWork, whose failure even to

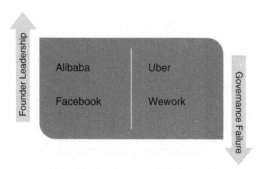

Figure 2.11    **Mixed Results from "Passive" Active Investors**

reach the public markets (IPO) led to a massive write down of value, the forcing out of the founder, legal actions by the WeWork parent's board, and substantial negative publicity for its main investor, the **SIF-backed Softbank Vision Fund.** Much has been written about WeWork. Its fall has dramatized the hazard of the increased availability of open checkbooks of passive investors seeking outsize returns without the scrutiny and attendant discipline of public markets. It is a story that may have been told even without the rise of the SIFs and their entry into the hunt for the unicorns. But it is nonetheless a cautionary tale.

Ultimately, the sovereign investment funds have been passive investors much longer than they have been active shareholders. They are still in the process of learning to deal with the muddy startup world directly. When the **PIF** fund invested in the San Francisco-based ride-hailing company Uber, it probably never imagined that it would ride into a maelstrom of controversies with the colorful startup founder: former employees published allegations of sexual harassment; founder and CEO Travis Kalanick got caught berating an Uber driver in a viral video; and, after Donald Trump was elected US president, hundreds of thousands of users staged a boycott over Kalanick's support of the controversial President. Giving money to a unicorn is easy, but it is only the start of the game.

In summary, the sovereign investment funds have transformed themselves from remote passive allocators to local, direct, active investors fostering the unicorns and displacing public markets as sources of capital. The shift in the risk profile of their investments, from safe, real assets to the frontiers of tech innovation, suggest that across the board SIFs are "grown-up" investors that will play a leading role in the forthcoming digital economy. The desire to participate in the tech revolution must be very strong, then, to overcome the obstacles outlined above. As we will see in the next chapter, it is. In their hunt for unicorns, they are taking a stance towards sophisticated and established VC and PE funds that dominated this space up to now. The race is on.

> *During your visit to the global village, you will have learned much about life in this unique setting: how its inhabitants organize themselves, how they cooperate… and compete. You now get to accompany them as they join in the hunt that will shatter the illusion that village life is predictable and backward. You will get to join them in the hunt for unicorns.*

# CHAPTER 3

# Global Hunt for Unicorns (Decacorns)

*Emerging from New York's Grand Central Terminal onto Park Avenue, you confront the gleaming ranks of skyscrapers that once bore the names of now extinct titans of finance – Bear Stearns, Chemical Bank, Manufacturers Hanover – names now faded into prehistory. You may wonder who has taken their places – as you stroll past the fleece vests exiting the towers. Some of those streaming past are doubtless coming from the trading desks or the alternate assets teams of the sovereign investors who now have boots on the ground in midtown Manhattan. And, in many cases, own the ground and the trophy properties atop it.*

*You could repeat your tour – admittedly not on foot but in your Tesla – on the roadways of Silicon Valley. Sovereigns have teams at work there, too. And London. And Singapore. Sovereign investors have planted teams across oceans to deploy their vast resources.*

Geography provides an interesting viewpoint. Sovereign investors have been growing their internal staff and shifting from being passive allocators selecting outside funds managers for some time. The more recent development has been their focus on establishing a presence in tech hubs. They continue to open offices in New York City, the global finance center, but, increasingly, the new choice in the US is Northern California, the precinct of Silicon Valley, the tech sector and home of the unicorns (see **Table 3.1**): sovereign investors are putting their teams where their money wants to be.

Table 3.1    Representative Sampling of US Offices of Sovereign Investors

| New York City | | |
| --- | --- | --- |
| Sovereign Investors | Country | Opened |
| APG | Netherlands | 1998 |
| CDPQ | Canada | 2014 |
| CIC | China | 2017 |
| CPPIB | Canada | 2014 |
| GIC | Singapore | 2010 |
| HKMA | Hong Kong | 1996 |
| KIA/Wafra | Kuwait | 1985 |
| KIC | South Korea | 2010 |
| Mubadala | UAE | 2019 |
| NBIM | Norway | 2010 |
| NPS | South Korea | 2011 |
| OMERS | Canada | 2011 |
| PIF | Saudi Arabia | 2019 |
| PSP | Canada | 2015 |
| QIA | Qatar | 2015 |
| SAFE | China | 2013 |
| Temasek | Singapore | 2013 |

| San Francisco | | |
| --- | --- | --- |
| Sovereign Investor | Country | Opened |
| CPPIB | Canada | 2019 |
| GIC | Singapore | 1986 |
| Khazanah | Malaysia | 2013 |
| Mubadala | UAE | 2019 |
| OMERS | Canada | 2019 |
| QIA | Qatar | 2019 |
| Temasek | Singapore | 2013 |

Sovereign wealth funds (SWFs) continue to bet on innovation and technology, a new trend that is becoming more firmly established over time. Investments are multiplying, spreading beyond major tech companies listed on Nasdaq and other stock markets. As described in previous chapters, increasingly sovereign investors are going direct into transactions, on par with PE and VC funds, targeting key emerging technologies (see **Table 3.2**). They are active globally, due both to overseas investments (global portfolio) and overseas presence (global office network). As a result, their mounting and ever-increasing presence is felt globally.

## Trillion Dollar Club – SIFs and Unicorns

Its reputation one of disruption and constant change, Silicon Valley's innovation ecosystem has long had its establishment of seasoned venture capital (VC) firms, serial entrepreneurs, leading research universities, and an established pecking order. The arrival of sovereign investors at first did not alter that, as the new kids, like other investors, sought coveted LP allocations at all the big names on Sand Hill Road. As the previous chapter showed, sovereign investors are no longer content to be passive allocators to fund managers. They are going direct into more asset classes, including high growth potential startups. That has, in turn, changed the face of venture capital in Silicon Valley.

Table 3.2    Top Five Sectors for SWF Investments (2018–2019)

| Sector | Deal Numbers | Deal Size % |
|---|---|---|
| Technology | 81 | 31.4 |
| Life Sciences | 45 | 13.4 |
| Real Estate | 43 | 15.9 |
| Services | 36 | 7.6 |
| Infrastructure | 19 | 11.2 |

Data Source: IE Center for the Governance of Change; SovereigNET (Fletcher School, Tufts University). (The 2019 data for the nine-month period January to September.)

Digital and technology businesses used to view SIFs as an option of last resort – a view arising from what was perceived to be SIFs' lack of understanding of those sectors, inexperience in high growth scaling, and limited global reach. But that perception has completely changed. With few exceptions, young technology and digital businesses now consider SWFs to be on a par with the world's leading global VC and technology-focused PE funds. The disruption in the Silicon Valley ecosystem shows in the numbers.

According to the International Forum of Sovereign Wealth Funds (**IFSWF**) Annual Report, a clear trend among SWFs is their preference for direct investments in unlisted companies, increasing their share of 50.6% (and 49.4% of listed companies) in 2015 gradually to 65.2% in 2018, a trend that continues powering ahead. As previously with real estate and infrastructure, sovereign investors have developed dedicated teams and vehicles to focus on venture capital as an asset class.

"The number of SWFs [sovereign investors] participating in investment rounds [directly] with other venture capital (VC) investors has grown exponentially over the last five years," noted the 2018 Sovereign Wealth Funds report from IE Sovereign Wealth Fund Research. The trend continued in 2019. According to the *Wall Street Journal,* as of October 2019, over the prior six years $550 billion has been invested by VC investors, easily outstripping the $320 billion from IPOs. The trend is clear: sovereign investors participated in only 14 VC rounds from 2009–2013 but the pace rocketed to 220 from 2014–2018.

Given the dominance of tech companies over the last few years in terms of contribution to equity returns and capital raising, it is little surprise that sovereign investors have placed such emphasis on the sector. Overall, the sovereign funds are a good match for startups, being long-term, non-intrusive investors with patient capital. They allow the unicorns to avoid the volatility and costs of transparency associated with a public listing while at the same time affording liquidity to their option holders, often key employees. The influx of "non-traditional" venture capital – including the SIF money – has, in turn, changed the way that startups are born and bred.

The design and manufacture of unicorns has been industrialized, with the central ingredient being online service, supported by mobile apps and marketed by social media. The private markets – not only in Silicon Valley, but also in emerging innovation hubs like China and India – have all tailored themselves to churning out such beasts, using the same ingredients and adding in local characteristics. When the term "unicorn" was coined in 2013, only 38 unicorns were identified; yet in 2019 the market data firm CB Insights counted more than 400 of them (see **Box: Unicorn, Decacorn, and Hectocorn**).

---

### Unicorn, Decacorn, and Hectocorn

In medieval lore, the unicorn was a strong, fierce creature – a beast with a single large, pointed, spiraling horn projecting from its forehead – that could be captured only by a virgin maiden. In the myth, the unicorn leaps into the virgin's lap and she suckles it. It is tempting to state that something similar is happening with tech unicorns and virginal sovereign investors.

In the context of tech investments, a **unicorn** is a privately held startup company valued at over $1 billion. By referring to the mythical animal, the term was used by venture capitalists to represent the statistical rarity of such successful venture investments. With the same logic, **decacorn** is used for those startup companies over $10 billion, while **hectocorn** is used for such a company valued over $100 billion.

By 2019, the search-engine giant Google's parent company, Alphabet Inc., together with its peers Apple Inc., Amazon.com Inc., and Microsoft Corp., have become the only four companies ever to reach $1 trillion market valuation during intraday trading. The biggest tech companies have soared to heights once unimaginable, and for now there is no "X-corn" term developed for the $1 trillion threshold.

In 2013, Aileen Lee, the founder of Cowboy Ventures, coined the word for 38 exceptional startups. Currently there are more than 400 unicorns globally (among them many decacorns and hectocorns). The rapid increase in the number of unicorns has led to many questioning whether the valuation of tech startups is sustainable. A close inspection of the herd in the stable is truly worrisome: some seem bred for show, not for labor; some have gathered too much fat to win their races; even worse, some are sick from their own behavior problems. Above all, the 2020 spring coronavirus pandemic is starting to ravage the herd. In the end, the word "unicorn" betokens something both rare and wonderful.

These large enough private startups are precisely the types of companies in which SIFs are looking to invest, especially the mature unicorns close to an IPO (the "pre-IPO" round). At the late phase of the unicorn growth cycle, the magical beasts become so highly valued that only the major players can write large enough equity checks to feed their hunger for more capital. While many of these investments have been made via fund vehicles – most notably Vision Fund, sometimes called the "supersized poster child" of the unicorn investor trend – many have also been direct, often as co-investments. Because sovereign investors tend to invest into a startup at its growth phase with a larger equity check than the VC firms (which mostly invest at the earliest stages), the SIFs are often the "unicorn-makers."

As outlined in the next section, SIFs bring varying levels of sophistication to the table. Less experienced funds typically seek to invest jointly with established players (and/or PE and VC funds) in order to obtain an entrée to venture opportunities. According to IFSWF's database, sovereign funds' involvement in consortium deals in technology companies has more than tripled since 2016. In 2019, the trend of sovereign funds investing as part of consortia reached its highest level ever, particularly in sectors such as healthcare and technology: 83 deals in healthcare and technology were completed as part of a consortium, against 16 as solo investors.

Along with increasing investments, the sovereign investors have also deepened their engagements with unicorns. The SIFs are now genuinely participating in, and setting the strategic agenda of, their portfolio tech companies through different

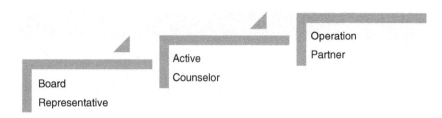

Figure 3.1    Three Layers of SIF/Unicorn Engagements

levels of participation (see **Figure 3.1**), which further drives their international expansion and overseas offices.

- Board representative: involved with investee company's development, but less direct involvement in decision making.
- Active counselor: provides strategic guidance, governance suggestions, inputs for value creation plans.
- Operation partner: uses their domestic and global influence to drive corporate performance, including defining long-term strategy providing market resources, and implementing value creation.

For example, **CIC** has been actively exploring investment opportunism with "China Factors" (see **Box: Preferred Investor – China Factors**), by making full use of the advantage of its local knowledge and partners in the Chinese market. This strategy focuses on overseas investments that have a strong potential synergy with the Chinese market from a commercial perspective. Post-investment, CIC offers its domestic political and business networks to support the growth ambitions of investee companies, which creates a win–win situation for both CIC and the investee companies. In return, this makes CIC a preferred investor for tech companies that seek to expand in the world's largest mobile market – more than 800 million users unified by the same language, culture, and mobile payments (a factor which is especially valuable for competitive deal sourcing).

## Preferred Investor – China Factors

As Mr. Lou Jiwei, the first term Chairman of the China Investment Corp. (CIC), commented at the 2011 Boao Forum for Asia, the rapid growth of China's economy was CIC's advantage – "We're trying to look for investment opportunities with a China angle or a China factor."

What he meant was that CIC was looking for investment opportunities that might be driven by China's market growth – synergies between China and world markets ("Global Investments, China Factors"). For foreign company investments, CIC could help the companies to design and execute innovative value-enhancing strategies in China. For Chinese portfolio companies seeking to globalize, CIC assists them to achieve their international objectives with CIC's global footprints – connecting them with foreign companies and facilitating investment cooperation.

CIC capital went into Silicon Valley at a time when China's economy started a digital transformation: China's mobile economy. CIC was sought after in Silicon Valley because CIC could provide a bridge to China's e-commerce market, where more than 800 million Internet users are integrated by the same language, culture, and mobile payments. For example, through its affiliated US–China tech growth investment platform West Summit Fund (see the detailed discussion in **Chapter 7**), CIC invested in the video platform company Twitch before it was acquired by Amazon in 2014.

Twitch was one of the leading video platforms and communities for gamers. Its video platform was the backbone of live and on-demand distribution for leading video game broadcasters, including casual gamers, pro players, tournaments, leagues, developers, and gaming media organizations. China is one of the larger and more innovative markets for live-streaming entertainment, and Twitch was scaling up in China to compete with Chinese domestic live-streaming platforms like NASDAQ-listed Chinese company YY. CIC got in on the Twitch deal precisely because of the opportunity for the US-based startup to expand its live streaming of games to mainland China and to expand its user base, as observed by West Summit executives during media interviews.

West Summit spotted the potential for Twitch to move beyond gaming to a live broadcasting social media platform – following the model of YY in aggregating and engaging users around a common platform. After the investment, CIC worked together with the company to formulate its China entry strategy and bridged the C-Level talks with the potential strategic local partners. The investment was made in September 2013 during Twitch's third round fundraising, and soon, in late 2014, Twitch was acquired by Amazon for $970 million.

Generally speaking, sovereign investors' entry into the tech startups and venture capital world is a win–win situation for all parties involved. The matchup of sovereign capital and startup founders essentially creates a trillion-dollar club: the sovereigns can take a longer term view on their investments, and the innovation companies can focus on growing their businesses with abundant capital. As such, the SIFs as the new venture capitalists have become a primary source of capital in the digital market.

## New Venture Capitalists at Silicon Valley

It's helpful to consider SIFs' arrival on the scene in Silicon Valley in three waves. First, we start with the South-east Asian first movers. Second, the arrival of the Middle Eastern sovereigns and their seismically active Vision Fund. Finally, we will look at the savvy tech investors, like pensions in Canada and Europe, either on the ground or visiting, who may not measure on the Richter scale of publicity but are leading the transformation, deal after deal.

**First, the Singapore pair, Temasek and GIC, have been pioneers. Khazanah, too.** Long considered a trailblazer and role model in the sovereign community for direct investing, Singapore's sovereign wealth fund GIC, which is estimated to hold assets of more than $300 billion, has emphasized the opportunities arising from technological adoption and innovation across all sectors for years. The same is true for another Singapore government fund, Temasek: its portfolio of TMT (telecommunications, media, and technology) sector investments reached 25% as early as 2016, overtaking financials as the largest sector in Temasek's portfolio.

According to Sovereign Wealth Center data, the two Singaporean institutions, GIC and Temasek, accounted for about two-thirds of sovereign investors' direct technology equity investments ($25.7 billion), committing $7 billion and $10.2 billion, respectively, from 2006 to 2017. In fact, until the SoftBank Vision Fund occupied the headlines from 2017, the

Table 3.3     Singapore's Direct Deals in Tech 2015–2016 (Sample)

| Year | Investor | Firm | Tech Sector |
|------|----------|------|-------------|
| 2016 | Temasek | Sprinkir | Social technology, New York |
| 2016 | Temasek | FNIS | Payment service provider, Florida |
| 2016 | Temasek | Homology Medicines | Gene therapy, Massachusetts |
| 2016 | Temasek | Illumina | Genetics analysis, California |
| 2016 | Temasek | Regneron | Biopharmaceuticals, New York |
| 2015 | Temasek | Flux Factory | Collaborative software, California |
| 2015 | Temasek | Makesense | Software, California |
| 2015 | Temasek | EMC | Data storage, Massachusetts |
| 2015 | Temasek | Hello | Sleep sense monitor, California |
| 2015 | GIC | Veritas | Data storage, California |
| 2015 | GIC | Matterpot | Imaging technology, California |

Source: Sovereign Wealth Center.

two Singaporeans were the most active SIFs in Silicon Valley (see **Table 3.3**).

To some extent, Temasek is an even more natural tech investor than GIC. Temasek's tech DNA dates back to 1974, when the government of Singapore established Temasek as a holding company to manage state-owned enterprises, including Singapore Telecommunications. GIC was set up in 1981, with the mission of preserving and growing the long-term value of the national reserves placed under its management. On technology investing, GIC likes to say it started from Day One, first by investing in technology companies listed on major stock markets, and then quickly expanding into venture capital.

GIC was on the ground in Northern California well ahead of the pack. It has maintained a presence in Northern California since the 1980s. Its early arrival – its San Francisco office was opened in 1986 – took place not long after its 1981 formation. At the time, the fund had not yet initiated the transformation from passive allocator to direct investor. However, GIC had a mandate to invest abroad and the US markets represented an even larger share of its potential investable universe in the 1980s. A California presence gave it an eye on US markets from a less inconvenient time zone than New York.

Choosing Northern California carried another benefit. Lim Chow Kiat, GIC's CIO, remarked on this in 2019. "Being there, you have more natural exposure to technology investment. It is not all smooth sailing, it goes up and down; right after the dot.com bubble there was a winter. But even during those times we learned: how do you pick the right startup, the right entrepreneur, the right business model?" When unicorns presented the opportunity for direct investing at a scale suitable for sovereign investors, GIC benefited from an established reputation as a reliable venture fund investor in Silicon Valley. Roughly 20 years after planting its flag there, it formed its own technology investment group that invests in startups as well as mega deals.

Temasek, Singapore's other SIF, only arrived in Silicon Valley in 2013. With its origin as a holding company, unlike GIC, it had long engaged in direct investing, first in Singapore and then in the wider South-east Asia markets, as we will see in the later sections of this chapter. After the global economic crisis, its direct investing focus moved increasingly to tech. Temasek describes its Enterprise Development Group, launched in 2014 as "a development engine, going beyond investing for growth to building for growth. The group focuses on mapping our future business value chain; staying abreast with innovation and macro business trends; and identifying and developing new business enterprises that have the potential to be global, regional or domestic champions."

The Singapore investor's team has clearly been busy. A roster of representative worldwide tech investments appears in Chapter 7, along with its ten plus offices expanding into almost all continents (see **Table 7.4**). A partial list of US unicorns recently added to Temasek's portfolio includes Amazon, Airbnb, Impossible Foods, and DoorDash. "We've been stepping up investments in tech, life sciences and healthcare, and having a presence in San Francisco helps us get closer to the companies in these sectors," Paul Ewing-Chow, an associate director at Temasek, told Reuters in 2017.

And step things up it did. Biotechnology is a sector where its activity has risen since 2016 (see **Table 3.3**), partly because of the commercial opportunities arising from developments in innovative FDA-approved gene-editing technologies. It is a good fit for large sovereign wealth funds like Temasek, because the lab work involved often requires a larger amount of capital up front for risky experiments than startups in other industries typically need. In January 2017, Temasek, through its office in San Francisco, bought an $800 million minority stake in Silicon Valley-based medical technology company Verily Life Sciences (formerly Google Life Sciences) from its parent company Alphabet.

Some of those investments are getting a big shot in their valuation these days from the global coronavirus outbreak (COVID-19) of early 2020. For example, Silicon Valley-based Vir Biotechnology has Temasek and two major SIFs, **ADIA** and **Alaska Permanent Fund Corp. (APFC)**, as its backers (see **Figure 3.2**). The company focuses on combining immunologic insights with cutting-edge technologies to treat and prevent serious infectious disease. In the spring of 2020, the stock of this previously obscure Nasdaq-listed startup surged after its announcement that the company had teamed with other major pharmaceutical groups for a research collaboration and made progress with clinical experiments. In April, GlaxoSmithKline invested – at a 10% premium to the market – $250 million for 6% of the company for strategic cooperation, sending its share price yet higher.

This movement into the venture capital ecosystem is not unique to Temasek or its stablemate, GIC. Also hailing from the Malay peninsula, **Malaysia**'s **Khazanah Nasional** has also joined them in the vanguard of the early stage investment trend. Khazanah, which means "treasure" in Malay, made its first foray into unicorn investment in China's Alibaba Group, over $400 million in 2012 and 2013. The investment became a huge success after the Chinese company's initial public offering in 2014. Today, Khazanah is among the most active tech-investing SIFs in

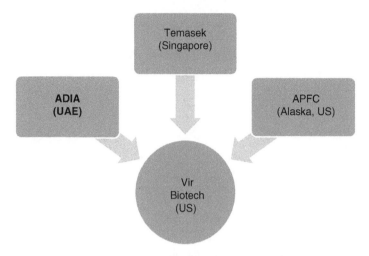

Figure 3.2    **SIF-backed Vir Searching COVID-19 Solution**

the world, which is a big transformation from just ten years ago, when close to 90% of Khazanah's holdings and investments were in Malaysian companies.

In the US, while following its mandate of investing in digital transformational companies that have the potential to bene-fit the Malaysian economy, Khazanah, too, adopted many of the characteristics of a classic Silicon Valley VC, mentoring its portfolio companies and leading rounds. An example of this adaptation are its investments in Fractal Analytics, a leading AI (artificial intelligence) analytics startup based in both the US and India which provides AI-based solutions to Fortune 500 companies. Khazanah partially exited the investment in 2019. At the time of sell down, it was the largest shareholder.

Furthermore, in another VC-style move, Khazanah has even set aside a portion of its portfolio for what it calls "Portfolio X," betting on long-shot, world-changing technology. In 2015, Khazanah took the lead investor role in a $27 million invest-ment round in General Fusion, a Vancouver-based startup pursuing commercial nuclear fusion power, the so-called Holy Grail of clean energy production. It is a risky investment because such efforts for emission-free, near-limitless electricity

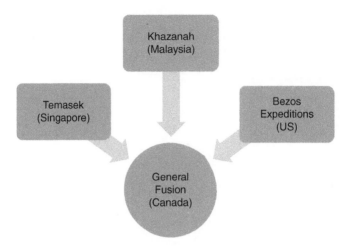

Figure 3.3    **Moon Shooting for Fusion Power**

have been going on for decades, but its success would overturn a market worth trillions. In 2019, the torch was handed off to Temasek which led a $65 million round. Khazanah participated again, but not as lead, alongside Bezos Expeditions and other venture capital firms (see **Figure 3.3**).

**Second, from the Middle East with Vision.** While the sovereign investors from Singapore and Malaysia jockey for leads, the Middle East has been garnering all the press in Silicon Valley. The region is home to three of the top ten wealth funds in tech – **Kuwait Investment Authority (KIA)**, **Qatar Investment Authority (QIA),** and **Public Investment Fund of Saudi Arabia (PIF)**. Not to mention Abu Dhabi's **Mubadala** with its Mubadala Ventures unit focused on tech investments, which we will return to after the saga of PIF and Vision Fund.

Saudi Arabia is no doubt the most prominent sovereign investor in Silicon Valley. In 2016, PIF cut a $3.5 billion check to Uber Technologies, breaking the record for the all-time biggest single investment in a venture-backed company. Déjà vu? Just two years before PIF, the QIA shook the Silicon Valley when it wrote a nine-digit check to Uber in 2014 (see **Figure 3.4**). Before its foray into the tech sector in 2011 with small stakes in US e-commerce player Coupons.com and

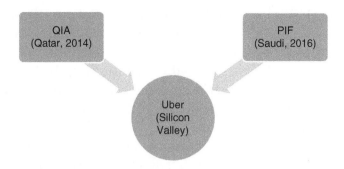

Figure 3.4    **Middle East SIFs Taking Uber**

French chip maker Altis Semiconductor SNC, QIA was well known for accumulating glamorous hotels and luxury brands.

Even for Saudi, the size of that Uber investment was no small change for its portfolio at the time: the PIF fund was established in 1971, and the fund managed $157 billion in assets as of June 2016 (after the 2019 IPO of Aramco, its AUM is expected to increase substantially). Prior to the Uber transaction, PIF had little or no international visibility, as most of its capital was invested in domestic stocks and loans to local businesses. Direct investing plays an important but not exclusive role in tech investing by the Saudi investor. PIF, for example, has deployed substantial sums both in Vision Fund and directly into ventures such as AI virtual reality unicorn Magic Leap ($400 million) and "ghost kitchen" restaurant delivery startup Cloud Kitchens ($400 million), as well as Uber.

Around the time of its record-breaking Uber investment, PIF also made a direct investment in Tesla, the electric-car manufacturer. Even for the shrouded world of Mohammed bin Salman (MBS), Saudi Arabia's effective ruler and the force behind the transformative investments of PIF, and the unpredictable cosmos of Elon Musk, the billionaire founder of Tesla and future Mars colonizer, the story of PIF's investment in Tesla is an outlier.

First there were the reports in early August 2018 that PIF had built a stake of between 3–5% of Tesla, already publicly traded, with a worth at the time between $1.7 billion and $2.9 billion and still making losses. The purchase reportedly took place after MBS completed his rockstar tour of the US and after he had approached Musk about purchasing shares in a new issuance. Musk, struggling to avoid further dilution of Tesla equity, declined. Fifteen years after its founding, Tesla was then one of the most heavily shorted companies in the US market.

Much more surprising was the next development. As Tesla shares continued to suffer in 2018, despite the PIF buying program that year, Musk tweeted on August 7 that he would take the company private at $420 per share, a substantial premium to the market price, and that he had secured the financing to do so. Under pressure to substantiate his claim, Musk, in a blog post, hinted that PIF was the financing source. However, Reuters then reported that unnamed PIF sources had denied any such commitment. The tweeted buyout did not proceed, and Musk and Tesla subsequently settled SEC charges about the misleading tweet; Musk stepped down as Chair of Tesla as a condition of the SEC settlement.

PIF, for its part, the month following the tweet – in what was seen by some as a rebuke of Musk – invested $1 billion in Lucid, another US electric vehicle startup competing in the same market as Tesla. To top it off, PIF in January 2019 fully hedged its Tesla position, effectively freezing its economic interest in Tesla. One year later, Tesla shares had climbed to an all-time high, more than tripling from its 52-week low, mostly due to its joint venture and banking financing agreement with the Chinese government in late 2019. PIF reportedly exited Tesla completely in 2019, missing out on the big runup in the value of the shares, which quadrupled to over $968 in early 2020 from their 2019 lows ((before stumbling early in the pandemic and then climbing yet again, this time to a new all-time high of $1228, making it the largest auto maker by market value).

But what has fundamentally changed the venture investment landscape is the $100 billion **Vision Fund** that PIF jointly established with Mubadala and Japanese telecommunications giant SoftBank Group in 2017 (see **Figure 3.5**). To put things in perspective, in 2018 the entire venture capital fund industry was reported to have raised a total of $53.9 billion, slightly

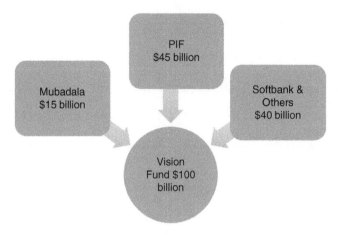

Figure 3.5    **$100 Billion Vision Fund**

over half of Vision Fund's war chest. It's also an innovative structure where the SIFs take a significant anchor position as LPs and leverage that position for a deeper role in portfolio construction, as well as value creation after the acquisition. While SoftBank as the general partner still serves as the overall lead, the SIFs effectively participate as equal partners.

SoftBank's charismatic leader, Masayoshi Son, wasted little time in putting the SIF's money to work feeding the growing herds of unicorns. In the US alone, apart from WeWork, chronicled elsewhere, sizeable amounts were handed out in short order across a variety of tech sectors (see **Table 3.4**). The scale and speed of these and its multitude of other investments across the globe fundamentally altered the VC ecosystem. Vision Fund would back two competitors in the same market, encouraging each to spend fund capital to compete for market share without regard to profits.

Vision Fund pursued this Darwinian policy across continents. For example, it poured money into both Didi Chuxing and Uber, who compete directly in Asia and Latin America. Also in Latin America, it funded Colombian food delivery unicorn Rappi which is vying for business in the region against another portfolio company Uber Eats, as is Vision Fund-backed DoorDash in the US. Fueled by sovereign investor cash, Vision

Table 3.4    Representative Vision Fund US Investments.

- **Mobility**
    **Uber,** with a troubled IPO and governance challenges, received a $9.3 billion
    investment.
    **GM Cruise,** the electric vehicle venture of GM, got $2.25 billion for a 20% holding.
- **Fintech**
    **Lemonade,** AI powered insurance fintech, where Vision Fund led a $300 million
    Series D funding round.
    **Kabbage,** an online lending platform, received funding of $250 million in one
    round, and, in another round, additional funding of an undisclosed amount.
- **Enterprise**
    **Slack,** where Vision Fund had invested in a $250 million round at a valuation of
    $5.1 billion, performed well at its direct listing, nearly doubling in value, but
    has since fallen below its debut price.
    **Cohesity,** a cloud storage secondary vendor, in which Vision Fund led a $250
    million Series D round.
- **Services**
    **DoorDash,** a food-delivery company, where Vision Fund teamed up with GIC,
    among others, in a $535 million financing round.
    **Wag,** a dog-walking service (known as "Uber for dogs") benefited from a $300
    million commitment, although this stake was recently sold back to Wag,
    reportedly at a loss.
- **Realty**
    **Compass,** digital home realty broker, where Vision Fund in 2017 led a $400
    million round and then invested $450 million more; and in 2018 QIA and
    Vision Fund co-led a $400 million round.
    **Opendoor,** home sales platform, in which Vision Fund invested $400 million.

Fund created an alternate universe in which growth counted for everything and the bottom line counted for nothing.

Derision and awe greeted the pageant of deals in the VC community as $100 billion was swiftly committed and Son began to talk of raising a second fund of similar size with a planned close in 2019. There was also schadenfreude among the VC crowd as massive failed investments began to appear. Ultimately, Softbank was cornered by activist investor Elliott Management into a forced selldown of its original bonanza investment in Alibaba. PIF and Mubadala were not lining up to invest in the second fund. Yet Silicon Valley, the cradle of disrupters, had been massively disrupted itself.

Compared to its fellow Middle Easterner, PIF, and especially the vehicle it co-funded with PIF, Vision Fund, **Mubadala**

**of UAE** has taken a less visibly disruptive route into the Silicon Valley VC ecosystem (see **Box: Learning to Play the Game**). Mubadala Ventures was formed in 2017 and it formally opened its Silicon Valley office in 2019. Leveraging relationships formed through its Vision Fund investment and with deep experience as a direct investor, Mubadala has gained traction as a tech investor in North America, notching up direct deals in close succession with its new California office, including:

- 2018: **Cologix,** $500 million investment in the network-neutral, interconnection and hyperscale edge data center company.
- 2019: **Collective Health,** $205 million round (alongside Vision Fund) in the digital health solution for employer health insurance.
- 2019: **Recursion Pharmaceuticals,** $121 million round participant in this drug discovery biotech.
- 2019: **Platform9,** SaaS-based, hybrid cloud platform, $25 million round.

## Learning to Play the Game and Leveling the Playing Field

Operating in any competitive milieu is not just about building a contacts list and attending the right conferences. In the US fund management world, government relations and lobbying play an important role. While SWFs have shied away from government relations for the most part, Temasek recognized the benefit of opening a Washington DC office.

Meanwhile, the public pension funds have benefited from a US tax law change that resulted from savvy government relations. Real estate and infrastructure have long been a favored asset class for SIFs and the US is the largest destination for foreign direct investment. However, as a part of the reaction against Japanese investments in iconic US trophy properties – such as Rockefeller Center in the 1980s – US tax laws were revised to increase the tax burden of non-US investors under the Foreign Investment in Real Property Tax Act (**FIRPTA**). As a result, SIFs were at a bidding disadvantage vis-a-vis US institutional investors, particularly when up against US pension funds that enjoy tax advantaged status.

Not to be deterred, some non-US pension funds managed to distinguish themselves from the more easily demonized SIFs and secured passage of the Qualified Foreign Pension Fund tax changes. The result, for the non-US pension funds that qualified (**QFPF**s), is the leveling of the playing field with US pensions in investments in real estate and infrastructure, eliminating the FIRPTA burden. SIFs were not similarly favored as a group, although many are examining the possibilities of fitting within the favorable treatment where pension elements can be found in their remit.

Mubadala has learned to play the game in its own way. Mimicking the corporate sponsorships common in financial management circles, Mubadala, in addition to having a Northern California office, is a sponsor of the "Mubadala Silicon Valley Classic" – an annual professional Women's Tennis Association tournament in San Jose. Tennis courts are very level playing fields.

**Third, the Canadian pensions.** Like those intergenerational wealth and economic development-driven sovereign funds, the public pension funds are pursuing tech investments for similar reasons. OMERS has been a pathfinder with its **OMERS Ventures** making direct, early stage venture investments in Canada, the US, and Europe. After long maintaining an informal base in Silicon Valley, its Ventures team established a presence in Northern California. Featured in Chapter 7, the OMERS Ventures tech investments include, for example, Rover, the e-dog-walking service, Shopify, and Crunchbase. The other large Canadian pensions have plans to join the hunt.

In April 2019, **Ontario Teachers' Pension Plan (OTPP)** announced it was launching a new investment department, Teachers' Innovation Platform (**TIP**). OTPP is Canada's largest single-profession pension plan, with approximately $200 billion in net assets. "TIP will focus on late-stage venture capital and growth equity investments in companies that use technology to disrupt incumbents and create new sectors," according to the press release. Only months after TIP was announced, the group got off the ground with its very first investment, putting an undisclosed sum into SpaceX, the Elon Musk space-launch venture in June 2019.

**Canadian Pension Plan Investment Board (CPPIB)**, Canada's largest pension plan with assets of more than $400 billion, claims to manage more than 80% of its assets in-house (see **Box: Canada's Global Footprint**). Opened in 2019, its San Francisco office's principal focus is on fund investments and co-investments, but it has also made late stage investments in a few unicorns. AI in fintech is one area, where it has made a direct investment in a subsidiary of payment processor Square, known as Square Capital, which employs AI to acquire loans made to small businesses in the US. As with PIF, there also seems to be a mobility theme in its AI portfolio, which includes an investment in California-based autonomous vehicle company Zoox, which has plans for robo-taxis.

Joining forces with **Mubadala Ventures,** in March 2020, CPPIB co-led a $2.25 billion investment in Waymo, the AI-based autonomous driving system spun out of Alphabet, Google's parent (see **Figure 3.6**). Originally known as the "Google Self-Driving Car Project" and one of Alphabet's "moonshot" units, Waymo is potentially an engine of disruption with its application of AI to mobility. In early 2020, Waymo revealed it would initiate mapping and then testing its "autonomous" long-haul trucks in Texas and parts of New Mexico. Doubtless, Mubadala's 2017 investment into another Alphabet unit, Verily Life Sciences (for which Temasek is also an investor), had posi-

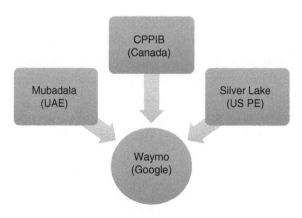

Figure 3.6    **Mobility theme across SIFs**

tioned it for the Waymo opportunity. CPPIB's San Francisco presence could not have hurt it – either with Alphabet or with Mubadala.

**Finally, the best of the rest.** The IE Foundation 2018 report names **Australia Future Fund** and **Ireland Strategic Investment Fund (ISIF)** as joining GIC, Mubadala, and Temasek as leaders in VC investors among sovereigns. Future Fund was an early beneficiary of fund investments in some of the well-known unicorns, such as Uber, Pinterest, Airbnb, and Snapchat, earning annual net returns over 20% from its venture investments. Future Fund's strategy in tech investing reflects its role as an intergenerational fund, keen to grow and protect its assets.

In addition to healthy returns from its early fund investment – as well as hoped-for returns on its most recent, eclectic bets – Future Fund's CIO in 2017 expressed a further motivation: "Venture is very important to us as it gives us access to the current innovation and disruption trends." More recently, Future Fund featured as a direct investor in no less than six US tech startups in only a 12-month period which ended January 2020: NextNav (geolocation service), Everactive (Internet of Things (IoT) data end-to-end solution), Coursera (online learning startup), Bitglass (cloud access cybersecurity), Eargo (direct to consumer healthcare startup), and Gladly (digital customer relations solution, where Future Fund led the financing round).

Playing a different hand, the ISIF has a development role and is mandated to make its investments support economic activity in Ireland, fostering the country's reputation as a tech center. Aided by the fact that Ireland is already a darling of US tech firms as a European base, it has succeeded in its dual goals of achieving a return while supporting Ireland's economy. Good examples are its investments in unicorns Kabbage, a fintech which we saw earlier in Vision Fund's roster, and InsideSales.com, a digital CRM startup, both of which committed to open offices in Ireland.

Last but not the least, **CIC** has been active on the scene as well. Because of its origin in China, a rising innovation center of the world of different strengths, CIC is busy investing in both Silicon Valley (having created an innovative platform and affiliated team, detailed discussion in **Chapter 7**) and its home market. In fact, the two nations together account for over 80% of the world's tech investing. We now move to the other side of the ocean where the sovereign investors are also participating in the hunt for unicorns.

## China: Wild Wild East

As China's mobile economy and e-commerce leaps forward, foreign financial investors have emerged as some of the biggest winners. The investment themes for these Chinese mobile e-commerce players are obvious: they are basically directional bets on the fast growth of China's consumption power as well as the irreversible trend of mobile e-commerce vanquishing traditional retail. Their high valuation not only reflects their dominance in the world's largest mobile commerce market, but also the investors' optimism in the special business models or product features that they are pioneering.

The sovereign investors, both domestic in China and overseas, have become significant shareholders of Chinese Internet and tech firms from the very beginning. For example, at its IPO, Alibaba, China's dominant e-commerce company, already counted China's sovereign wealth fund **CIC, Temasek, Khazanah,** and **CPPIB** in its ownership structure (see **Figure 3.7**). **GIC** in 2016 purchased $500 million of Alibaba shares from SoftBank in a secondary transaction and became a major shareholder as well.

Similarly, Alibaba's main competitor JD.com also had Temasek and Canada pension **OTPP** (Ontario Teachers' Pension) as key investors at its IPO (see **Figure 3.8**). For the mobile economy, the China market is poised to be a trend-setter, rather than the trend-follower, in next-generation

## Alibaba Ownership at IPO

- ■ Softbank (Japan) –34%
- ■ Yahoo (US) –23%
- ▨ Jack Ma –9%
- ■ Others (including CIC, Temasek, Khazanah, CPPIB)

Figure 3.7    **Alibaba's Ownership at IPO**

## JD.com Ownership at IPO

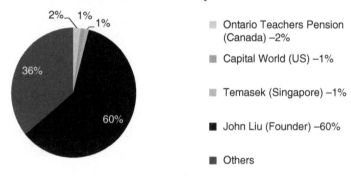

- ▨ Ontario Teachers Pension (Canada) –2%
- ▨ Capital World (US) –1%
- ▨ Temasek (Singapore) –1%
- ■ John Liu (Founder) –60%
- ■ Others

Figure 3.8    **JD.com's Ownership at IPO**

mobile devices and services. Going forward, as the tech world leaps into "intelligence first" from "mobile first," the China market is setting itself as a leading player. During China's digital boom, these investors are richly rewarded with billions of capital gains.

As the market shifts from mobile e-commerce to tech innovation, **Temasek** has made the transition. Its investments include Chinese unicorns Rokid and SenseTime. Hangzhou-based Rokid Corporation specializes in robotics research and AI development, and Temasek led the recent funding round in 2018. Rokid's augmented reality glasses feature facial recognition, which can pull up the social-media accounts of people that it scans and recognizes. In the consumer smart device market, Rokid more or less competes with US-based Magic Leap, which is backed by Saudi's PIF.

SenseTime specializes in deep learning-enabled computer vision technologies. The company's AI-based technologies can recognize faces, characters, and images as well as provide video analysis for many industries, from finance to security, online entertainment to healthcare, and more. SenseTime has supplied automatic face scanning systems to many railway stations and airports across China, with a near perfect accuracy rate (for example, it has signed agreements with China's largest subway operator, Shanghai Shentong Metro Group, to use AI to monitor metro traffic).

What's remarkable is that the company successfully completed multiple rounds of funding during a two-year span in 2018–2019 (Temasek invested in one of the rounds with China's e-commerce giant Alibaba) and its valuation jumped from $3 billion to $7.5 billion following the recent round from investors including SoftBank Group. At $7.5 billion (according to media reports from late 2019), SenseTime Group Ltd is the world's largest AI startup, illustrative of the significant power of sovereign capital in investing in innovation and pushing up valuation at the same time.

With ample funding in hand, the company declared that it would explore several new strategic directions, including smart city data centers, autonomous driving (with Honda), AI training chip development, augmented reality, and international expansion. Indeed, the company set up an operating office in Singapore as a hub for its South-east Asia expansion. According to a company executive's interview in late 2019, the company plans to triple its staff in Singapore within three years to some 300 people, and it is collaborating with a university in Singapore as well as its education ministry for research. Such an "investment and integration" theme brings extra value to Singapore (just like Ireland, Saudi, UAE, and many more), as the country is positioning itself as a global hub for AI research and development.

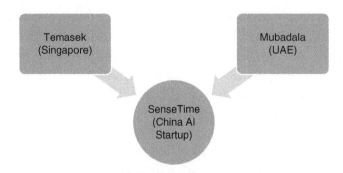

Figure 3.9    **Temasek and Mubadala into SenseTime**

Also invested in Sensetime is **Mubadala** (see **Figure 3.9**). As mentioned, it is a major LP investor in Vision Fund, which has invested in US tech companies such as Uber and WeWork. Like Temasek, it is also an active investor in Chinese unicorns. In an interesting twist, Mubadala also invested in Didi Chuxing, China's ride-hailing startup for which CIC is a long-time shareholder. After a costly price war to acquire driver and passenger users, Didi Chuxing eventually acquired Uber's separate business in China – Uber China.

Based on the Mubadala investment relationship, SenseTime in late 2019 entered into a strategic alliance with Abu Dhabi on the 35th anniversary of the Diplomatic Relations Establishment between the UAE and China. In Abu Dhabi, SenseTime is setting up an EMEA (Europe, Middle East, and Africa) Artificial Intelligence R&D center, and it will support UAE AI development in multiple industries including healthcare and education. Just like Singapore, United Arab Emirates are looking to invest in tech startups as part of a wider plan to create a technology hub in UAE and diversify its economy (the domestic mission of Mubadala will be discussed later).

Just a short drive from Mubadala's offices on the corniche, in the same capital city of Abu Dhabi, another sovereign investment fund **Abu Dhabi Investment Authority (ADIA)** has also been busy. It joined Alibaba to invest into another Chinese AI unicorn, Megvii Technology Inc (more commonly known as Face++, see **Figure 3.10**), which is a competitor to SenseTime

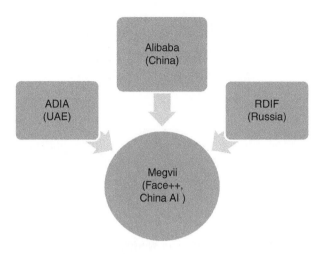

Figure 3.10    **ADIA and RDIF into Megvii**

in many fields. Megvii's face recognition technology was adopted by Alibaba's financial arm Ant Financial Services Group for the "Smile to Pay" function, which allows users to pay using a facial scan on their smartphones. This $750 million equity financing raised by Megvii, which was led by an ADIA subsidiary and other strategic investors, was the second-largest funding round among AI startups in 2019.

Another important and strategic investor of Megvii is the **Russian Direct Investment Fund** (**RDIF**), a sovereign wealth fund of the Russian Federation with $10 billion in reserve capital under management. In RDIF's 2018 annual report with the headline title "investing for the future," Megvii is listed under "selected portfolio members." The annual report further highlighted that RDIF's tech portfolio is "the largest channel for attracting foreign investment into innovative Russian companies" – Megvii's expansion into Russia probably is expected, and "RDIF's projects form the basis for the country's technological breakthrough."

The most prominent example of SIFs in China's tech unicorns is, no doubt, the fintech firm Ant Financial, a company spun off from the e-commerce giant Alibaba before that firm's 2014 listing (see **Figure 3.11**). Ant Financial is known for its flagship Alipay payments platform, which enjoys the largest market

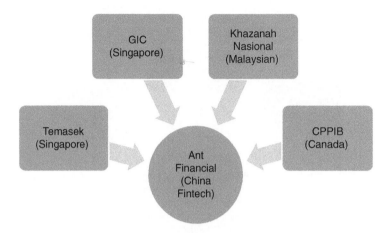

Figure 3.11    **Global Sovereign Funds into World's Largest Unicorn**

share of consumer mobile payments in China (Apple Pay, by comparison, has a much smaller market share), but its increasing focus is on business-oriented financial technology, including assisting financial institutions on big data solutions as well as providing fraud prevention services.

In 2018, Ant Financial raised around $14 billion in what market watchers called the biggest-ever single fundraising globally by a private company (according to market data firm Crunchbase, $14 billion amounted to the largest confirmed single fundraising round in history). The fundraising valued the company at over $150 billion (in Chinese RMB yuan currency over 1 trillion). Ant Financial became the highest valued unicorn in China (and the world), and the imputed valuation was greater than the market capitalization of Goldman Sachs, the famous US investment bank. Not surprisingly, the early SIF investors of Alibaba, whom we saw at the beginning of this section, again rushed in. Their eagerness seems to be justified: the press reported in August 2020, that a planned IPO valued Ant Financial at over $200 billion, the highest value ever for an IPO on a major exchange.

## London, India, and Rising Innovation Hubs

The EU is well behind China and the US in the production of unicorns. India enjoys scalability over the EU, even before

Brexit trimmed the single European market, but remains behind as well. Nonetheless, the hunt for unicorns is playing out on the continent that spawned the medieval legend, on the subcontinent of India, and elsewhere.

Europe's digital e-commerce unicorns have been rewarding for a pair of sovereign investors. In the UK, **Khazanah** operating from its now-shuttered tech hub high in London's iconic skyscraper, The Shard, profited from its unicorn investment in Skyscanner, the Scottish travel search website. Khazanah invested at a $1.6 billion valuation in January 2016 (in a GBP 128 million round) and exited with a sale to China's largest online travel company, at a $1.74 billion valuation, in under 12 months. (A perfect storm of underperformance and a new government critical of Khazanah's expansion into early stage tech investing overseas led to the en masse resignation of the entire board of the fund in 2018 and closure of its London presence. But Khazanah looks primed to stay the course in China and the US.)

The transaction epitomized a late stage pre-IPO investment of the type that initially attracted sovereign investors but became difficult to duplicate as the runway for founders grew ever longer and direct listings began to be preferred over IPOs. In Sweden, Abu Dhabi Investment Council (**ADIC,** now part of Mubadala) was in for the long (but ultimately successful) haul when it invested in Spotify in a $400 million round at a valuation of $8.4 billion in 2015. AP6, the Swedish pension fund for private market investments, also had Spotify on its playlist via a venture fund investment. Both did well (AP6 reported receiving 8.4 times its original investment with an implied IRR of 33%), when Spotify went public via a direct listing at a valuation of roughly $28 billion years later in April 2019.

While sovereigns achieved healthy returns on Skyscanner and Spotify, the consumer-focused digital platforms featured in these deals, other sectors are scoring higher in attracting sovereign investors in Europe. SIFs have favored AI, healthtech, and fintech in a trio of UK deals in recent years, three sectors that have played interesting roles in that economy's digital transformation.

In the field of **AI,** according to a 2019 McKinsey report, the UK has fostered firms at the cutting edge, citing DeepMind, founded in 2010 and acquired by Google in 2014 for $500 million, and SwiftKey, founded in 2008 and acquired by Microsoft in 2016 for $250 million. **Temasek** selected AI for its 2017 investment in a UK unicorn, Improbable, participating in a $502 million Series B round after also investing in the Series A (amount undisclosed). Improbable uses cloud-based distributed computing to enable the creation of virtual worlds for use in games and massive-scale simulations of the real world. With proceeds from the round, it is also applying the same technology to the simulation of complex real-world systems. Potential applications include simulating transport infrastructure, telecommunications networks, or the behavior of fleets of autonomous vehicles.

**Healthtech** is the next area in the UK to benefit from the government's role in the economy. With its massive National Health System (NHS), lovingly featured in the 2012 London Olympics opening ceremony, the UK has fostered healthtech as well. In 2019, PIF led Babylon Health's $550 million Series C round. The company combines AI and healthtech. The NHS provides the large data set to benefit from AI-assisted health-care and to feed the growth of startups like Babylon, now valued at over $2 billion. Its apps now enable the NHS to substitute video consultations for doctor visits and to deploy a chatbot to screen patients seeking to visit a doctor.

Finally, the **fintech** sector in the UK has benefited from the 2014 creation by its Financial Conduct Authority of a fintech "sandbox," freeing startups that are admitted to experiment in the real world financial economy without full regulatory burdens. Out of more than 1500 requests, 700 have been admitted. CPPIB opted for UK fintech when it invested GBP 765 million for a 30% stake in BGL Group in 2017. The fintech is a leading digital distributor of insurance and household financial services as well as a leader in price comparison for financial services. BGL cancelled its IPO plans upon the CPPIB investment, preferring SIF capital to the public markets for its continued growth. CPPIB claimed a board seat but management continues to run the business. And the trend continues in the pandemic with June seeing GIC participate in a Series B round of Checkout.com. At $5.5 billion, the UK startup is among the most highly valued fintech startups in Europe.

While the UK's regulatory regimes could be credited with creating an environment favorable to the development of unicorns and attracting SIF investors to them, other countries, not always considered hotbeds of digital innovation, have produced digital unicorns leading to their sectors sometimes enjoying a government regulatory tailwind, sometimes not. The SIFs have not overlooked these spots.

Even tiny **Switzerland** has spawned a fintech unicorn to go along with its banking gnomes. **Investment Corporation of Dubai (ICD),** the $70 billion sovereign fund of the emirate, whose oil reserves are, like its sovereign fund, dwarfed by those of Abu Dhabi, invested $27 million in Numbrs, a bank account managing app that has, quite sensibly, launched in the much larger German market. In the **German** market itself, WeFox, an insurance fintech in Germany, reached a valuation of $1.8 billion and received an equity investment from Canadian pension OMERS through its OMERS Ventures unit (profiled in Chapter 7) in Europe.

**Brazil** is not generally regarded as having a regulatory regime friendly to startups. That image is not up to date. According to the *Financial Times,* its central bank approved 13 new fintech firms in the last quarter of 2019 (among them, startups in direct lending, payments, peer-to-peer lending) and goes on to report that Brazilian fintechs raised $18 billion in funding in 2019. At the head of the pack is Nubank, a startup mobile virtual bank there. With more than 20 million customers, according to CB Insights, at $10 billion, it is the most valuable digital bank startup in the world. GIC noticed and, in 2019, participated in a $400 million round.

In **Australia,** another loosening of banking regulations favored new digital entrants. Quickly joining the unicorn ranks, Judo Bank broke private capital startup funding records when, in successive rounds in 2018 and 2019, it raised AU$$$540 million (approximately $350 million) from Canadian pension **OPTrust,** among others. The investment was unusual in several respects. While Australia is home to wallabies and koalas, it is not known for unicorns. And the appearance, particularly in a very large Series A round, of a pension fund from the other side of the globe demonstrates how the SIF pursuit of the unicorns knows no bounds.

Less surprising, perhaps, is the activity of SIFs in **the vibrant startup ecosystems in India and South-east Asia.** There are several reasons for this cluster of unicorns in the region. First, the region is rapidly entering the digital mobile economy. Second, India and Indonesia are the second and fourth largest nations on Earth in terms of population. (The other two comprising the top four, China and the US, as we have noted, currently receive 80% of tech investing between them.) Finally, the region is in the backyard of Singapore, home of the two SIFs most active in direct investing in the digital economy. While **GIC and Temasek** are not alone in pursuing digital opportunities in the region, they certainly set the tone with investments in fintech, mobility, and e-commerce.

For **fintech,** Temasek alone has poured money into unicorns in India, sometimes investing in multiple rounds.

- $1.6 billion **Pine Labs,** a cloud-based mobile POS start up, included Temasek in its 2018 $125 million round.
- $1.5 billion **Policy Bazaar,** a digital insurance marketplace which claims 20% of India's life insurance market, has seen participation in its 2018 $67 million round from Temasek, which reportedly acquired its initial stake in a 2015 purchase from existing investors.
- $1.8 billion **Billdesk,** a digital payments company, was the object of two investments by Temasek, in the 2015 $700 million round and in the follow-on 2018 round of $200 million.

**Mobility** is another unicorn investing theme Temasek pursues in the region. Mobility in South-east Asia has shown a tendency to shade into fintech as well, as we will see in more detail in Chapter 10's discussion of the spawning of Grab Financial by Grab Taxi and a possible banking license in Singapore for the (originally) mobility unicorn.

- Temasek's Vertex Holdings unit invested in the 2014 Series A round of ride-hailing decacorn **Grab,** of reportedly $10 million; Grab has since relocated to Singapore from Malaysia, is seeking to add a Singaporean banking license to its Grab Financial unit, and is valued at $14 billion.
- In 2018, Temasek also had reportedly taken a 5% stake in $6.3 billion Indian ride-hailing unicorn, **Ola Cabs,** paying in the range $150–200 million and acquiring shares from existing investors.
- In 2018 as well, decacorn **Go-Jek,** Indonesian motorbike ride-hailing, delivery, and payments app valued at $10 billion, saw Temasek participate in its $1.2 billion round.

In the potentially vast markets of India and Indonesia, **e-commerce** is an area of interest for the Singapore SIFs, but also those from outside the region.

- **Snapdeal,** India's $7 billion e-commerce giant, counts both Temasek (since its 2014 $115 million round) and Ontario Teachers Pension Plan (2016 $200 million round) as investors.
- **Zomato,** a $2.5 billion Indian food ordering and delivery app, received an early stage investment from Temasek, in a $60 million round in 2015.
- In 2019, GIC led a $420 million round in the **Traveloka** Indonesian travel site, the largest online travel startup in South-east Asia, valuing the company at $2 billion.
- $7 billion Indonesia's **Tokopedia,** a CtoC online marketplace, had Vision Fund participate in the 2018 $1.1 billion round; reportedly Temasek plans in 2020 to invest $500 million (out of a $1.5 billion round) upping the company's valuation to $8–9 billion.

- The ubiquitous **Softbank Vision Fund** is present with more than $8 billion invested in India alone, providing its SIF backers, PIF and Mubadala, exposure to the subcontinent.

Finally, in India, two sovereign investors from outside the region have selected an entirely different sector for which India appears to provide the ideal launchpad, education tech (**edtech**). Dubbed "the most valuable edtech company in the world" by the *Financial Times* in March 2020, India's unicorn **Byju** is valued at $8 billion. The mobile digital learning platform garnered investments from two SIFs, Canada's CPPIB at about $125 million in 2018 and QIA which led a $150 million round in 2019 (see **Box: Canada's Global Footprint**).

### Canada's Global Footprint

Canadian Pension Plan Investment Board (CPPIB) not only is the country's largest pension plan by assets under management, but also has the most extensive international presence. Its Byju investment is not so surprising, perhaps, considering it has a team on the ground in Mumbai as well as San Francisco (Sydney and Sao Paulo, to finish out those starting with the letter "S"). And London, New York, Hong Kong, and Luxembourg City. Five continents.

With Canada the destination of about 15% of its assets, nearly 85% of its investments lie beyond its borders. The US leads with approximately 30% and Asia and Europe (including the UK) follow at 20% respectively. All the more remarkable, then, that up to 2000, virtually all the portfolio was in Canada. Only with the global financial crisis did non-Canadian assets outweigh the domestic portfolio. This allocation apparently strikes enough observers as unexpected that it has prompted the fund to include in the FAQs on its website the question "Why don't you invest only in Canada?"

Of course, the answer is the relative size of the Canadian economy and the diversification imperative of prudent management. Still, the geographic dispersion is eye-catching. In fact, it has prompted a 2018 study by The Fraser Institute, a Canadian think tank, calling for fiscal reform to spur local capital formation so as to counterbalance the outflow of investment capital from Canada. They may have missed the answer to that FAQ.

## 2020 and Beyond

In summary, 2019–2020 is a new milestone for SIF investors into tech investing. **First, they are well established as active, powerful investors in venture capital.** According to the National Venture Capital Association, "nontraditional investors, such as sovereign wealth funds and family offices, are more involved in the venture industry than ever before, participating in 85% of the 252 mega-deals (deals over $100 million) recorded in 2019." Pursuing unicorns of various stripes around the globe, SIFs have shaken off tradition and converted themselves into nimble earlier and earlier stage investors in the companies of tomorrow, with a heavy helping of tech, of course.

In doing so, they are fostering innovation at the host nations, expansion of the world's digital infrastructure, and the digital transformations of their own economies. In **Chapter 4,** we will follow the sovereign investors' moves as they commit capital to the digital infrastructure that underpins the digital transformation of much of the world, including IoT, "smart cities," and "smart logistics." In **Chapter 5,** we will study the role played by the sovereign investors in the digital transformation of their own economies as they underwrite the construction of actual smart cities, smart logistics systems, and the digital future. Finally, in **Chapter 6,** we see how the sovereign investors move to the very source of innovation as they invest earlier and earlier in the standard bearers of the digital future.

**Second, the SIF are becoming sophisticated investors, shifting their focus from "fake tech" to "hard tech."** Years ago – as illustrated by many case studies in this chapter – the large size of SIF capital powered the rapid creation of "Internet" companies that had little "tech" edge. The design and manufacture of such unicorns were industrialized, with the central ingredient being online service, supported by mobile apps and marketed by social media. Growing as large as possible and as soon as possible (so-called "blitz-scaling") was the best – possibly the only – business strategy of these "fake tech" companies. The result is many capital-intensive firms without a visible path to profit. (Of course, some did become great companies, such as Alibaba and Amazon.)

Therefore, these days the SIF investors are shifting focus from user gathering to intellectual property (**IP**). They carefully select "hard tech" startups that have IP and unique technology that creates barriers to entry for rivals. The rule is simple: for a unicorn to claim itself a genuinely "tech" pioneer – and therefore profitably scalable (not scalable by burning cash for a loss) – its actual product (better yet, invention) must be technology, not merely using technology to create a new business model. For example, an e-commerce business selling everyday goods online most likely won't make the cut, even if it uses mobile video contents to advertise, thanks to high-speed 5G networks. On the other hand, a data-solution company that provides cloud-based services to corporations to help their digital operation would qualify.

**Third, they must quickly become mature investors and behave like business owners in the 2020 global downturn.** Established players with a long history in tech investing, such as GIC, have made a constant effort to avoid being pro-cyclical, having seen the boom and bust during the dot-com era. However, for many younger SIFs – especially those that only started active investments after the 2007–2009 global financial crisis – the market break-down triggered by the coronavirus pandemic could be their first direct experience of how cycles really operate, and how the portfolio companies cope with difficult times.

The downturn will depress startups' growth and severely test some of the unicorns' business models. That means after many years of capital deployment, the SIFs must focus more on their existing portfolios. The growth at all cost credo is out of the window. Path to profitability is the new catchphrase. They now think like business owners, working closely with the investee companies to rein in costs, streamline their operation plans, and review their strategic options. At the end of day, they have to behave like the real venture capitalists and do something that the long-term investors are not the most familiar and comfortable with: cut the loss on the dying unicorns.

One example from the pandemic era is the March 2020 Delaware lawsuit filed by WeWork against Vision Fund and its manager SoftBank over the decision to walk away from a previously agreed $3 billion share buyout. The special committee of the board of WeWork parent We Company contested Vision Fund's position that the conditions to the deal had not been satisfied, thereby permitting it to walk away from the commitment without penalty. The complaint alleges breach of contract and of fiduciary duty. The $3 billion was part of a larger multi-billion-dollar rescue package to stave off bankruptcy at the shared workplace startup. Without the $3 billion, the founder, Adam Neumann, drops out of the billionaire's club, having been included as recently as a year before with a net worth estimated at $14 billion. Lessons learned all around.

Meanwhile, the global downturn actually plays to the advantage of the long-term capital of sovereign funds. When both IPO and private capital markets are disrupted, these super asset owners are the capital of last resort. The SIF capital is critical to the unicorn community, both for those who are already listed and worry about the departure of "cornerstone" shareholders in the public market, and the majority that remain private and are struggling with capital scarcity.

That will deepen the relationships among the trillion-dollar club, and the sovereign investors may opportunistically find attractive deals to strike when the startups' valuation correction kicks in. Some unicorns may disappear, and some decacorns must be fed – but only at a fraction of even a unicorn's price. The SIF capital has been the oil for the unicorn making machine so far. They will be key players when it's time to clean up the pasture, too.

*Their names are not emblazoned on the skyscrapers of Manhattan, nor do they appear on the discrete signboards of the low-rise office parks of Sand Hill Road. That absence should not be read as lack of power and influence. They enjoy the huge advantage of having cash available. As we shall see in the following chapters, sovereign investors are not only chasing unicorns, they are leaders of the digital transformation.*

# CHAPTER 4

# Long-term Capital into Digital Infrastructure

*Lighting up the February night sky over the desert steppes, and live-streamed on YouTube, the massive Soyuz rocket lifted off from the Soviet era Cosmodrone in Baikonur, Kazakhstan, launch site of the first human spaceflight with Yuri Gagarin. The enormous craft shed its four boosters as it headed north into the darkness high above the Kazakh steppes. Powered by over 340 tons of lift, its path was monitored by mission control in Moscow. Soon, it was hurtling out of Earth's atmosphere at over 8 kilometers per second.*

*This time, the cargo was not a Soviet cosmonaut. Instead the payload was a bevy of 34 satellites, each about the size of a dishwasher, and the vanguard of a "constellation" ultimately numbering 648 low Earth-orbiting spacecraft. The Soviet era Cosmodrone has a new role in digital age infrastructure.*

*But the real action is not on the steppes or in the frozen reaches of space. The constellation is being put in orbit by SIF-funded OneWeb to provide the Earthbound among us Internet service at a competitive price and in regions not yet served by broadband. If the proposal flies, access to the digital economy will become available not only to those who have never flown in a rocketship, but also to millions who have never left the Earth's surface in an aircraft.*

*We turn now to the story of how direct investing in infrastructure moved to space (cyberspace) as SIFs refocused their expertise to participate in the expanding demand for digital infrastructure on Earth, as well as in the heavens.*

## Data to Information to Knowledge

The digital economy is powering ahead, riding a tsunami of digital data. Machine-readable data is generated from the digital footprints of personal, social, and business activities. Data flows (as measured by reference to Global Internet Protocol (GIP) traffic), have grown from roughly 100 gigabytes (GB) per day

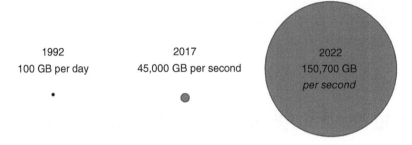

| 1992 | 2017 | 2022 |
| --- | --- | --- |
| 100 GB per day | 45,000 GB per second | 150,700 GB *per second* |

Figure 4.1    **Growth in Global Internet Protocol (GIP) Traffic**
Date Source: UNCTAD Digital Economy Report 2019.

in 1992 to over 45,000 GB *per second* in 2017 (see **Figure 4.1**). But the traffic is nowhere in sight of peaking: by 2022, it is estimated to reach 150,700 GB per second. This hypergrowth is attributable to the massive number of users coming online (or, perhaps, "on satellite" would be a better way to put it) for the first time and the ever expanding universe of the Internet of Things (**IoT**).

The IoT is the term adopted to describe a future world with pervasive connectivity. According to news reports, as of 2020, every item sold by one of the global electronics manufacturers would be enabled to connect to the Internet. For some, this might be viewed as the pinnacle of digitalization. But this is just one manufacturer. IoT is poised to be a tsunami of transformation for every industry sector. Clearly, the explosion of digital data is set to continue apace.

The impact this massive increase in Internet-capable devices will have on digital infrastructure requirements is profound. The boom in interconnected objects – when added to the continued penetration of smartphones in developing economies such as India and Africa – entails the sending, receiving, and analysis of unbelievable amounts of data. The vast quantities of digital data are fostering a data-driven world. To make it work, the end customers, the device manufacturer, and service providers need connectivity with low latency.

But that's the mere tip of the iceberg. Digital data is generated and flows through multiple systems that enhance its utility and profit from its application. Starting from raw,

Figure 4.2    **Digital Data Empowerment**

machine-readable data from devices and terminals, they can be processed to become information, often employing artificial intelligence (AI) and big data applications. When analyzed and transformed into knowledge, data becomes valuable, creating economic value-add to business sectors and customers (**Figure 4.2**).

Therefore, managing this gargantuan dataflow requires correspondingly epic investment in digital infrastructure. The telecommunications industry – which is the main funder of the Internet network, fiber expansion, and other digital infrastructure developments – cannot independently raise the financial resources needed for IoT expansion over the next decade. Fresh capital will be needed on a global basis to support network buildout and prepare for the implementation of 5G, IoT, AI, and other forms of next generation networks.

Hence come the sovereign wealth and public pension funds. With their immense capital power and long time horizons, they are already experienced in deploying patient capital into infrastructure assets, and they continue to chart a more adventurous course in technology infrastructure projects. Capitalizing on their know-how from traditional infrastructure, the sovereign investment funds (SIFs) have moved forward to underwrite the infrastructure of the digital economy, from data centers to smart logistics, smart cities to IoT. This chapter is the story of how they made that leap.

## SIFs and Global Infrastructure Gap

As mentioned in Chapter 2, one of the first alternative assets classes in which SIFs began to invest as LPs and then directly was infrastructure. That's most obvious in large-scale infrastructure with a long-term horizon, for which the SIFs can use their deep pockets to grab infrastructure assets that have best-in-class operators, strong cash flow, and which provide the ability to capitalize on megatrends such as urbanization and climate change. GIC (Singapore), OTPP (Canada), and Wren House (Kuwait), just to name a few, have all accessed traditional infrastructure assets directly, without relying on, or co-investing with, PE fund sponsors.

Even before the digital revolution, the world already had a financing gap in infrastructure. A widely quoted McKinsey (2013) report estimates that a grand total of $2.5 trillion is annually invested in infrastructure systems such as transportation, power, water, and telecommunications, and with that amount not being sufficiently mind-numbing, it adds that, each year, another $3.3 trillion will be needed over and above that. The infrastructure needs and financing gap are the most significant in the emerging markets.

However, not only are developing countries struggling to unleash finance for infrastructure, infrastructure investment as a share of GDP has declined as well across G20 members such as the United States, the EU, and Russia. The government of China and, more recently, the US have pursued multinational initiatives to address this need with each taking a very different approach. One similarity: names that defy branding convention (see **Box: What's in a Name?**).

---

### What's in a Name?

One wonders: who is in charge of branding for these initiatives? In February 2020, India's Prime Minister Modi officially expressed interest in joining the US, Australia, and Japan in the curiously named Blue Dot Network (**BDN**). Like China's much better known and funded (but similarly puzzlingly named) Belt & Road Initiative (**BRI**), its focus is global infrastructure development.

The "Blue Dot" Network reflects an approach to facilitate identification, at least, of suitable projects. At a February 2020 summit in Delhi between Prime Minister Modi and US President Donald Trump, India "expressed interest" in the US-led Blue Dot Network that responds to the desire to identify responsible infrastructure projects for international investment in the region. Suitably vetted projects would earn a "Blue Dot" for alignment with sustainability and similar goals. Backers claim that such a seal of approval would facilitate financing for such projects from public–private initiatives.

Details remain sketchy for the program, announced in November 2019 by the three founding nations in Bangkok at the Indo-Pacific Business Forum. The more recent joint India–US statement issued upon India's expression of interest did not go much further. Blue Dot is described, officially, as promoting global, multi-stakeholder "sustainable infrastructure development in the Indo-Pacific region and around the world." Apparently, this network initiative is named after astronomer Carl Sagan's observation that Earth looked like a "pale blue dot" when viewed from space.

What is clear is that BDN reflects the contest being played out between China and the US in infrastructure development in the region. The initiative appears largely to be a certification program for infrastructure projects that comply with G-20 principles for Quality Infrastructure Investment along with other international standards relating to sustainability and the management of the social and environmental risks of such projects. In return, the sponsor nations would provide a "seal of approval" (in the form of a "Blue Dot" which could be likened to the stars awarded by the Michelin Guide to top restaurants) thereby opening the door to public–private backing for such projects.

BDN is jointly headed by US International **Development Finance Corporation** (**DFC,** formerly Overseas Private Investment Corporation), Japan Bank for International Cooperation, and the Australia Department of Foreign Affairs. Despite the involvement of US and Japanese government finance vehicles, none of the founding troika has committed to any financing (see **Figure 4.3**).

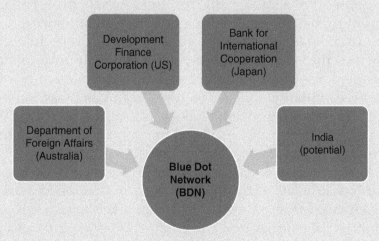

**Figure 4.3    The Inception of the Blue Dot Network**

Commentators were quick to cast it as an effort by the US to boost its regional profile in a sector that has seen China provide financing, know-how, labor, and materials for numerous and substantial infrastructure projects in countries that have signed on to the BRI. India notably elected not to join the BRI but is the exception where most others in the region have done so.

BRI was accompanied by a massive China-led multilateral funding source, the Beijing-based Asian Infrastructure Investment Bank (**AIIB**). The bank, founded in 2016, has more than 100 members with total capital commitments of nearly $100 billion, the US not among them. By early 2020, the bank notched up 64 approved projects with total commitments of $12.25 billion, several digital infrastructure projects among them: fiber optic networks in Cambodia and broadband infrastructure in Oman. On the other hand, the US government reportedly has committed $2 million for the BDN's organizing committee expenses. That sum should at least cover the tab at Tokyo's Michelin-starred sushi restaurants when the committee meets there.

The SIFs have long been touted as the ideal sources of capital to bridge the global infrastructure gap. So why isn't that much-needed flood of investment happening? Many naturally think that the SIF investors, which manage large sums of capital and have a long-term investment horizon, are the institutions best suited to finance the infrastructure gap. However, that is not always the case. Many SIF investors are interested in infrastructure because of its potential to provide lower-risk, inflation-linked revenue streams that can support their long-term payout obligations (especially true for SWFs that stabilize the countries' fiscal budget, and PPFs that have defined-benefit annuity-type liabilities).

As such, these investors tend to prefer mature or brown-field (constructed) infrastructure assets in developed markets with established cash flows. They are less likely to favor projects with material construction and completion risks, and untested demand. For infrastructure that is social in nature, they fear any investor who does achieve outsized returns could later face political pressure or adverse regulatory rulings. Furthermore, emerging market infrastructure carries higher risk, including the risk of nationalization. Overall, these investors are deterred from greenfield (new from ground zero) projects because they believe the inherent risks are not rewarded with an appropriate upside – out of their fiduciary duty considerations.

The sovereign funds of larger scale are potentially more capable of dealing with the risks of greenfield infrastructure projects in emerging markets – the ability of well-established, resourceful internal teams to assess new assets in new regions while understanding the risks. But even for those with the capability to do so, the country risks cannot be fully eliminated, especially when the investors are based on different continents from their investments. These could be mitigated by sovereign-to-sovereign relationships: diplomatic relationships at state level and co-investing relationships at sovereign fund level, of which India's new sovereign fund is a great example.

The **National Investment and Infrastructure Fund (NIIF)** was created by the Government of **India** with the specific mandate to help deepen India's infrastructure sector. The Indian government has committed seed capital to NIIF with the remaining capital flowing from long-term investors such as sovereign wealth funds, public pension funds, and other development institutions. As such, the Indian government has a 49% stake in the NIIF with the rest held by marquee foreign and domestic investors.

The collaborative mechanism set up by NIIF and international investors provides better interest alignment and risk mitigation for the foreign players than direct investing by the latter. It helps catalyze overseas capital into infrastructure and allied sectors in India (see **Box: NIIF – Indian Master of Infrastructure**). (Many SIFs today have an even broader domestic mandate to promote economic development than mere infrastructure. In **Chapter 5** their increasing focus on domestic digital infrastructure and venture capital ecosystem will be discussed in detail.)

## NIFF – Indian Master of Infrastructure Fund

The NIIF is India's first-ever sovereign wealth fund (SWF). It was established in 2016 to invest into critical infrastructure across India. It manages three funds under NIIF:

- The **Master Fund:** primarily invests in infra-related projects such as roads, ports, airports, and power (details below).
- The **Fund of Funds:** more passive, invests as anchor investors in funds, and this enables the fund managers to accumulate more funding from capital markets.
- The **Strategic Fund:** invests primarily in equity and equity-linked instruments.

The main vehicle is the Master Fund, whereby outside investors will provide founding investor capital to gain ownership stakes in the vehicle. The Master Fund will then invest in specific platform companies in different infrastructure sectors such as roads, railways, airports, and waterways to build a diversified portfolio. The NIIF Master Fund is not only attracting investor capital into the vehicle itself, but also providing co-investment side-cars into the platform companies that the vehicle invests into (see **Figure 4.4**). By 2020, NIFF had already secured many prominent SIFs and major financial institutions as investors.

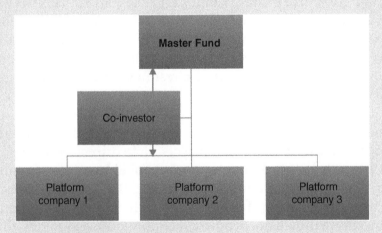

**Figure 4.4    NIIF Master Fund Structure**

The first international investor in the master fund was the **Abu Dhabi Investment Authority (ADIA)** which kicked in at $1 billion in 2017. A sizable commitment, yes, but just a fraction of 1% of its $800 billion in assets. Founded in 1976, ADIA is the marquee fund of the UAE at its sleek skyscraper in Abu Dhabi, as described in the introduction to **Chapter 1.** The ADIA portfolio is weighted half or more to public equities and debt, with smaller allocations to alternative assets, including real estate, private equity, and infrastructure. Its passive allocator approach is in contrast to its sister SIF, **Mubadala,** which is much more active in direct investing and private equity (and an LP in the Vision Fund).

In August 2019, **AustralianSuper,** Australia's largest superannuation fund ("Superannuation fund" is Aussie parlance for pension fund), and **Ontario Teachers' Pension Plan (OTPP),** Canada's largest single-profession pension plan, announced that they will invest $1 billion each in the NIIF Master Fund. The agreements each include commitments of $250 million and co-investment rights of up to $750 million in future opportunities alongside the fund. Together with **Temasek of Singapore,** these SIFs join the government of India and domestic institutions including the HDFC Group, ICICI Bank, Kotak Mahindra Life Insurance, and Axis Bank as investors in the fund, making it the largest infrastructure fund in India with assets under management of over $1.8 billion and a co-investment pool of $2.5 billion.

As such, SIF investors' appetite has mostly focused on mature Western infrastructure assets in recent years. Attracted by strong fundamentals, including strong equity returns and perceived low risks, many investors – beyond the community of SIFs themselves – including Japanese trading houses, British university pension funds, and German insurance companies have turned to prominent infrastructure assets. Consequently, SIFs face challenges to deploy capital in this highly suitable asset class, whether directly or as LPs, as increasing competition for assets and the resulting effect of rising asset prices lead to low returns from traditional infrastructure.

For example, London Heathrow Airport now has seven institutional investors, including sovereign funds from China, Qatar, and Singapore. Meanwhile its biggest competitor in London, Gatwick Airport, has five owners, including sovereign funds from Abu Dhabi and Korea, and public pension funds from Australia and Canada. The impact of this chase for yield has been a sharp increase in the prices that investors are prepared to bid for investments.

**This is where direct investment in new digital infrastructure enters the picture.** The challenges of such greenfield investing, including construction, commissioning, and inherent tech risk (innovation means the new tech itself could be disrupted by further innovation in the near future), make it a very different proposition from investing in stable, existing infrastructure. Nevertheless, digital infrastructure presents attractive investment opportunities for SIFs with an interesting return profile, sustainable development goal (SDG) element, and, most importantly, growth potential.

**First,** the inflation of prices of available infrastructure assets forces sovereign investors to look into infrastructure projects offering a better risk–reward profile, such as greenfield projects where the competition is not as strong as it is for brownfield sites. Similarly, when SIFs are presented with fewer opportunities to acquire core infrastructure assets, they expand their reach to regions outside the OECD markets where they are compensated for the incremental risk.

**Furthermore,** from an SDG perspective, innovation stemming from the digital economy and smart cities has the potential to lower both the cost and the environmental impact per infrastructure unit in urban areas. As such, a part of the projected infrastructure gap in the emerging markets could be closed through productivity increases, allowing lower expenditures per infrastructure unit (although the world cannot rely solely on productivity to fix the severe financing gap for infrastructure, SDGs, and climate resilience).

**Lastly,** investments in digital economy infrastructure can be a *proxy* to invest in technology. Cognizant of trends towards a digital economy, many sovereign investors have significantly reduced investing in sectors that are already disrupted by e-commerce, such as retail malls. Instead, they are increasingly allocating capital to data centers, digital warehouses, and smart logistics platforms to gain exposure to e-commerce, artificial intelligence applications, and other tech innovation.

For the sovereign investors, the digital economy infrastructure has become a new asset class that turns data into value.

## Network Infrastructure and Data Center

Armed with deep experience in investing in traditional infrastructure and charged with fulfilling SDG, SIFs have moved to the next growth area: digital infrastructure. The foundation of the continued growth of the digital economy is the capability to manage the increasing flow of digital data. Key elements include data centers for storing and serving up the data, networks for transmitting it, platforms for utilizing data, and larger systems, such as smart cities, that can integrate huge amounts of data for real life applications. As the building blocks, data centers are being constructed across the world at an unprecedented rate.

**Australia's Future Fund,** for example, is reportedly reducing its exposure to traditional infrastructure and increasing its investments in the digital economy, like others with an eye to the digital future (as its name seems to demand). In early 2020, it invested over A$250 million to acquire a 24% stake in data centers in Canberra (capital of Australia) in what it characterized as the largest single direct investment it had made in the infrastructure asset class (see **Figure 4.5**).

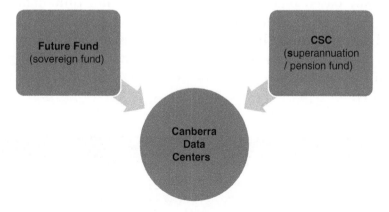

Figure 4.5    **Australian SIFs into Canberra Data Centers**

Another co-owner of the Canberra data centers is **Commonwealth Superannuation Corporation (CSC)**, a public employees pension fund. CSC was established in 2011, as part of a decision to merge the government employee and military superannuation schemes. It manages more than A$40 billion assets for Australian government employees and members of the Defense Force. It has long invested in traditional infrastructure and now digital infrastructure assets.

The Australian sovereign fund and superannuation funds are among the most experienced infrastructure investors in the world (see **Box: Super Investors in Infra**), such that their push into digital assets features infrastructure is the least surprising. Another major player, **Queensland Investment Corporation (QIC)** runs an active infrastructure direct investment program, managing funds for various state entities. Its A$85 billion (US $60) billion portfolio includes ports (Melbourne, Brisbane), utilities (Adelaide, Brisbane, Thames Water), transport (Ohio State University and Maspark parking, Brisbane and Brussels airports, Sydney toll roads), and other asset types.

QIC was created in 1991 by the Queensland government to manage long term assets for its components and has focused on alternative assets from its founding. Starting in 2016, QIC released a series of "red papers" on the impact of 11 disruptive technologies in infrastructure, including, most particularly, digitally based technologies. It highlights not only data centers and cloud computing, but also smart grids, ride hailing and autonomous vehicles, and AI. As a leading infrastructure investor, it is clearly focused on digital infrastructure disruption (interestingly, its US office is in Los Angeles – not Silicon Valley).

---

### Super Investors in Infra

Australia boasts about a million different native species with 80% of many types found nowhere else on the globe, according to the WWF. Australia's SIFs are also unique in several respects. Despite being a resource-based economy (Australia exports iron ore, gas, coal and other minerals to the world), **Future Fund,** its sovereign wealth fund is funded not from recurrent surpluses from oil and gas or mineral wealth but rather from the one-off proceeds of privatization.

Another unique feature of Australia's system is its superannuation funds (Supers). The **CSC** and **QIC** are examples of major "supers." These massive, fast-growing pools of capital are the result of high mandated pension contributions across many sectors of the economy, private as well as public. Implementation of this policy has led to investable assets that are large in relation to the scale of its capital markets and which reached almost A$3 trillion at the end of 2019 (per the Australian Superannuation Fund Association).Together with the drive for higher returns, these features have contributed to a move by its SIFs into alternative assets, particularly infrastructure.

As we will see in Chapter 8, this abundance of cash to put to work coincided with a privatization push by Australia's states. The stage was set for the Supers to lead the way into infrastructure as an alternative asset class. As discussed previously, the long time horizon of the SIFs fits well with the profile of infrastructure assets – large initial investment in regulated monopolies with inflation-adjusted returns. Australia's funds led the way into this asset class in many respects as attested by the diaspora of Australian investment professionals to the "infra" teams of Canadian, Singaporean, and other SIFs.

**Future Fund,** as our Canberra Data Centers example shows, is already deeply focused on the digital economy and, from an Australian perspective, digital infrastructure seems a natural next step. Founded in 2006, its initial funding largely derived from, appropriately enough, privatization of Telstra, the telecoms provider. Unlike many peers, Future Fund has not received subsequent additional funding and its growth is dependent entirely on its investment performance. It maintains its sole office in Melbourne, relying on a small internal team relative to its size.

Peter Costello, Australian Treasurer at the time the Future Fund was conceived, saw the fund as a way to offset future government pension liabilities. Costello is currently Chair of the fund's Board of Guardians and has witnessed a growth in its assets from an initial A$60 billion to over A$160 billion at year end 2019. History teaches that it is worth keeping an eye on Australia's unique SIF flora and fauna.

Another experienced direct investor, **GIC of Singapore,** has actively built up a portfolio of data centers across continents. In its Asia-Pacific neighborhood, GIC created a joint venture with Polymer Connected to build hyperscale data centers in Indonesia. In Europe, GIC in June 2018 invested in Equinix, a "wholesale" data center operator that builds data centers for huge global cloud technology companies like Google, Microsoft, Oracle, Amazon Web Services, and Alibaba Cloud. More recently, in April 2020, GIC announced a US $1 billion initiative with Equinix to construct new data centers in Japan.

Major cloud providers are often better credits, stable data center customers, with clear business expansion plans. Once viewed as a possible threat to data center growth, the cloud has been a significant growth driver as the demand for premium connectivity to cloud networks across the world surged. The GIC investments enable Equinix to build data centers for the "FLAP" markets (see **Figure 4.6**) – Frankfurt, London, Amsterdam, and Paris – that have emerged along with Dublin as the focal point for data center deployment in Europe, as well as in Japan for the Asia Pacific market.

Adding the western hemisphere to its globe-spanning strategy in this sector, GIC has teamed up with Denver-based investment firm Mount Elbert Capital Partners and Canadian pension **OPTrust** to create EdgeCore Internet Real Estate LLC, a vehicle that will develop, acquire, and operate data centers in North America. The EdgeCore venture will have an initial capitalization of over $800 million of equity, which is expected

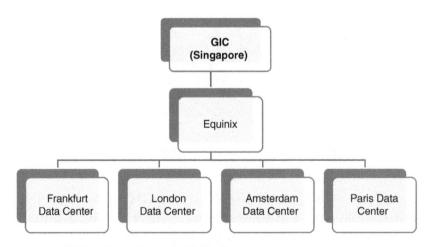

Figure 4.6    **GIC into Data Center FLAP Markets**

Table 4.1    GIC's Global Portfolio of Data Centers

| Partner for GIC | Region | Starting positions |
|---|---|---|
| Mount Elbert Capital Partners; OPTrust | North America | United States |
| Equinix | Europe, Asia-Pacific | "FLAP" markets and Japan |
| Polymer Connected | Pan-Asia | Indonesia |

to support about $2 billion in development and investment. EdgeCore will kick things off by building six hyperscale campuses across the United States and also plans to hunt for land in three complementary top-tier markets for expansion.

GIC's North American partner, OPTrust, manages the OPSEU Pension Plan, which is jointly sponsored by the government of Ontario and the Ontario Public Service Employees Union (OPSEU). The trust has net assets of approximately C$20 billion. They have a shared vision of creating a scalable North American data center platform. "As a long-term value investor, we believe the secular growth in data consumption and public cloud usage will generate attractive returns in the data center sector," commented Lee Kok Sun, Chief Investment Officer of GIC Real Estate in connection with the EdgeCore transaction. The GIC globe-spanning portfolio of data centers (see **Table 4.1**) clearly attests to such belief.

High above the Earth's data centers, smart grids, and connected homes and businesses, another kind of digital infrastructure is being launched to support the connectivity required by the IoT. As described in the introduction to this chapter, in February 2020, in a nighttime launch live-streamed from Kazakhstan on YouTube, OneWeb added 34 satellites to its low Earth-orbiting constellation intended to provide global Internet. They join the six presently in orbit after a 2018 launch. The company's goal is to place a total of roughly 650 satellites in service with beta testing of its Internet service in 2020 and commercial service in 2021.

This constellation would provide Internet service to users on the ground – leapfrogging fiber and other ground-based systems for much of the developing world. Satellites can also monitor land use, poaching, and seawater incursion, as unique elements of sustainable environmental action. Of course, this mission is capital intensive. OneWeb pocketed US $1.25 billion in March 2019 in a round led by the **Vision Fund** that saw the **Government of Rwanda** invest as well. Vision Fund, backed by PIF and Mubadala, reportedly owns nearly half of OneWeb after participating in an earlier round as well. (The company has raised a total of $3.4 billion.)

OneWeb is only one of several entrants in the highly competitive space-based Internet race. Its valuation has already taken a hit after Vision Fund wrote off an estimated $465 million of the initial investment when the March 2019 round proceeded only at a lower valuation (a "down round"). (Elon Musk's SpaceX had already deployed 240 satellites by the time of OneWeb's live-streamed launch.) And then, eyes in Riyadh, Abu Dhabi, and Kigali may have been scanning the skies when OneWeb ran out of rocket fuel and filed for bankruptcy in March 2020, leaving its future and that of dozens of satellites up in the air. A crash landing seems to have been averted, however, when in July the UK government announced its $500 million equity investment in OneWeb, keeping the project aloft for now.

## Smart Global Logistics

Many SIFs have made significant investments in e-commerce players, including Alibaba and JD.com in China as well as their peers in other digital retailer markets (see details in previous **Chapter 3**). Behind the scenes of online marketplaces, the logistics system that supports the actual physical delivery of the online-ordered goods is at the center of e-commerce operation. The pressure on the global logistics has grown exponentially as e-commerce penetrates more and more markets and regions, and the SIFs are now chasing investments into the rapid development of smart, inter-continental logistics ecosystem.

The logistics headache is the most evident on Singles' Day, the e-commerce festival in China. Every November 11, billions of Chinese, at home or abroad, passionately participate in the 24-hour online shopping extravaganza. It is also a global festival, as international buyers and sellers from more than 230 countries and regions get involved. By transaction volume, it is the world's largest online shopping day, beating Black Friday and Cyber Monday combined (see **Box: November 11 – From Singles' Celebration to Global Festival**).

The story behind the shopping extravaganza scene is that, on each year's Singles' Day, the e-commerce giants struggle with the logistic issues – the inventory, distribution, and delivery of numerous orders in a short span of time. They typically would be forced to add temporary workers for extra help. In 2019, at the speed of the Internet, $1.5 billion (10bn RMB) worth of orders was placed in the first two minutes. The total trade volume of the day ("Gross Merchandise Value" or **"GMV"**) was more than $38 billion. Of course, AI rode to the rescue on digital infrastructure, providing new solutions in the hectic scene.

### November 11 – From Singles' Celebration to Global Festival

November 11 was first known as the "Guanggun Jie" (Bare Sticks Festival or "Bachelors' Day") in the 1990s. It was celebrated by male students at Chinese universities because the numerals that form the date, 11/11, looked like four solitary stick figures. Over the years, this loosely defined holiday has become a celebration for all singles. The day has also become much more gender-inclusive by becoming the "Singles' Day" that we see today.

Gradually, as the Chinese economy continued to flourish, the event started to feature shopping as an intrinsic part of the celebration. When Chinese Internet giant Alibaba provided access to e-commerce through its website, Singles' Day became a virtual festival for everyone, single or married, local or a part of the diverse Chinese diaspora overseas.

Alibaba launched the Singles' Day shopping festival in 2009 as a promotional event to raise awareness of the value of online shopping. Initially having just 27 merchant participants, Singles' Day in just a few years has exploded into the largest shopping day in the world. Each successive year's event breaks the previous year's record. And because of the vast size of the participating population, its transaction volume has exceeded Cyber Monday sales in the US by multiple times.

Furthermore, it is increasingly a global festival. According to Alibaba, about 200,000 international brands and merchants, including Apple, Burberry, and Uniqlo, took part in recent years' sales. On the holiday eve, Alibaba hosts an annual gala celebration titled "Double-11 Night Carnival." During the four-hour Carnival TV show leading to the midnight festival start, Western brands such as Columbia, Levi's, Budweiser, and Corona compete over time slots for advertisements, because it is the single most important day for companies to target young, tech-savvy consumers.

The SIF-backed Alibaba has upgraded its supply chain management, called Ali Smart Supply Chain (ASSC), to apply AI to help online and offline merchants to forecast product demand. The model processes a range of historical and real-time data, including seasonal and regional variations as well as consumer preferences and behaviors. That is critical for same or next-day delivery services planning, and, furthermore, it enables merchants to respond quickly to shifting consumer tastes based on trends sniffed out of transactional data, allowing merchants to coordinate the flow of merchandise more efficiently – hence reducing costs and lost sales due to out-of-stock items.

For actual delivery, Alibaba's logistics affiliate, Cainiao, has used AI techniques and GIS (Geographic Information System) to determine the fastest and most cost-effective delivery routes in a variety of complex road networks, including both rural villages and crowded urban areas since 2018. New digital technologies, such as low-cost satellites accessed by handheld smart devices, could provide real-time supply chain visibility to merchants so they know when a shipment will arrive and can plan operations in advance (see **Figure 4.7**).

Cainiao also uses AI technology to predict what size box should be used to efficiently pack orders consisting of items of

Figure 4.7    **Smart Logistics behind Singles' Day**

various sizes and weights. For the November 2018 Singles Day period, Cainiao's total number of delivery orders processed exceeded 1 billion for the first time, yet it managed to accelerate its delivery, using 2.6 days for the first 100 million parcel deliveries, faster than 2.8 days the previous year.

As the new data technology is now reshaping Singles' Day, it illustrates that the global logistics system and related infrastructure needs are also going digital. The same trend is also obvious in the US market. According to the data service company Mastercard SpendingPulse under Mastercard Inc., between November 1 and Christmas Eve of 2019, total retail sales were driven more by the increase in online e-commerce (18.8% increase from same period 2018) than retail shops (1.2%). E-commerce contributed 14.6% of total retail, a record high, which also led to tremendous pressure on the express delivery system.

Going forward, in the global context, companies will likely all install digital warehouse and inventory management systems to save costs and resources on shipments. Throughout the supply chain, there is a high level of expectation from vendors that because of technology, there will be new methods to do analytics and planning, and greater visibility in terms of information and product, materials, and goods flowing across countries and continents. As such, smart logistics has become a strong growth sector for SIF investors who have long invested in the traditional logistics system of warehouses, ports, and roads.

**GIC** initially increased its exposure to infrastructure for the digital economy with its 2016 $2.4 billion acquisition (from TPG and fellow SIF **Ivanhoe Cambridge – CDPQ**'s real estate unit) of P3 Logistics Parks, a pan-European specialist owner, developer, and manager of logistics properties. Riding the e-commerce boom, P3 at the time of the acquisition owned and operated 163 warehouses in 62 locations across nine countries. The investment strategy seems to have delivered. As e-commerce continued to expand rapidly in Europe, GIC invested a further $1 billion in late 2019 to acquire another

28 locations known as the Maximus portfolio in logistics hubs principally in Central Europe.

**Malaysia's Khazanah** is also pivoting from a portfolio heavy in traditional domestic infrastructure investments, such as state utility Tenaga Nasional, Malaysia Airlines, Malaysia Airports, and Telekom Malaysia, to a digitally focused, post-carbon portfolio. Profiting from its early investment in smart logistics trailblazer Alibaba, Khazanah recently reached out to add to its board a high-profile tech star from China, Tang Xiao'ou, the founder of artificial intelligence start-up SenseTime. Tang became the first non-Malaysian appointed to the board, and under a more "digital-oriented" board, Khazanah is likely to increase allocation to smart logistics infrastructure.

While traditional infrastructure is getting smarter, numerous digital logistics startups are emerging around the world, capitalizing on the industry's high number of transactions and large amounts of data. (Conquering a particularly difficult robotic feat, Fast Retailing's Uniqlo recently announced the success of a T-shirt folding robot, developed by start-up Mujin, conquering the final frontier in automating its flagship Tokyo warehouse – now 90% automated. Mujin tech was also deployed in Shanghai for JD.com in what is called the first humanless, fully automated e-commerce warehouse.)

These young and agile newcomers are disrupting the entire logistics value chain, working to digitalize everything from freight forwarding, to brokerage and long-distance transportation, to warehousing, contract logistics, and last-mile delivery. As such, sovereign funds are also flocking to technology companies facilitating the logistics chain. For example, **Mubadala** Ventures led the $60 million series B funding of Turvo, a real-time collaborative logistics platform that provides end-to-end visibility and collaboration for the logistics and supply chain industry.

The **Vision Fund** has, again, helped create a few unicorns. In 2019, Vision Fund led a $413 million Series F round investment into the logistics company Delhivery Pvt Ltd. in India. Months later, **CPPIB** invested US$115 million for an 8% stake

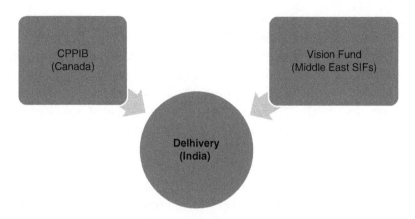

Figure 4.8    **Long-term Investments into Indian Logistics Unicorn**

in the company, bringing the logistics company into the unicorn club with a valuation of $1.5 billion. For CPPIB and Vision Fund, the burgeoning Indian e-commerce sector has generated significant high-growth opportunities in India's express logistics space for long-term investors (see **Figure 4.8**).

Delhivery, one of India's leading third-party logistics providers, operates in more than 2000 cities (more than 17,500 pincodes) offering a full range of supply chain services, including express parcel transportation, freight, business-to-business, and business-to-consumer (B2B and B2C) warehousing and technology services. With the 2019 financing from the major SIFs, the company planned to expand capacity and technology investments to help customers meet their needs for dependable, time-definite delivery service, with enhanced visibility and flexibility.

Also in 2019, Vision Fund led a $1 billion round in the software-focused shipping and logistics company Flexport, which describes itself as a "modern freight forwarder." Freight forwarding – businesses transporting their goods to their point of sale – is the circulatory system for global trade, but it is "as ancient as mankind" according to the Silicon Valley-based founder. It still largely run on paper. From Flexport's view, it is the only player that connects all the parties in global trade – importers, exporters, trucking companies, ocean carriers, airlines, customs agencies, port terminals – through a single, secure cloud-based platform.

Equipped with digital technology, Flexport moves freight across the globe by air, ocean, rail, and truck, handling the packages as well as all the customs information required. Its service makes the freight system more efficient too because it can cover small customers well. Flexport sees a whole universe of small-scale merchants, and its service includes support for smaller LCL (less than full container) shipments that bigger players often treat as low priority. Best summarized by the investment team of the Vision Fund, Flexport's business model is unique in "going after what is essentially a pretty boring space and doing it in an incredibly innovative way."

Speaking of global logistics upgrade, the world's largest project is China's Belt & Road Initiative (BRI) mentioned earlier in this chapter. To overcome the logistical choke points of sea routes through the straits of Malacca and the Suez Canal, the BRI, started in 2013, envisions a new Silk Road, reminiscent of the trade routes that connected the Tang Dynasty with the Roman and Byzantine Empire. The "Belt" refers to the Silk Road Economic Belt, an overland push that runs through Central Asia to Europe; and the "Road" is the 21st century Maritime Silk Road, a maritime route that runs through South-east Asia, Africa, and Europe. More recently, a new digital dimension has been added to BRI as the Digital Silk Road (see **Figure 4.9,** more details in the next section relating to smart cities).

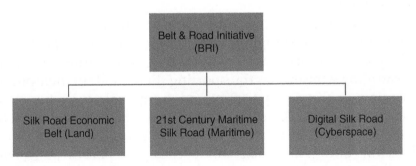

Figure 4.9   **Three Prongs of BRI**

The BRI project casts **Kazakhstan** in a central role, given its position astride the ancient routes (right next to China, it is the very first node and largest country on the transcontinental route of the Silk Road Economic Belt). The logistical aspects of this modern trade route dovetail with the programs targeted by Kazakhstan's sovereign wealth fund, **Samruk-Kazyna (SK)**. The fund's assets under management are primarily in large domestic companies covering almost all key sectors of the Kazakhstan economy. For most of its portfolio companies, SK is the sole or major shareholder. SK has broad mandates from Kazakhstan government: improve the long-term value of its holdings and modernize the country's economy for sustainable development.

With more than $70 billion in assets, SK has announced plans to privatize its industrial assets (national airline, uranium mines, etc.) and pivot to investments in the digital economy, as part of a national plan, **Digital Kazakhstan,** adopted in 2017 by the government. Digital Kazakhstan aims to do nothing less than improve quality of life and economic competitiveness through the development and application of digital technologies. SK sees its role as an "engine" of the transformation by solving business problems with digital solutions.

As part of Digital Kazakhstan, SK's rail company is implementing a smart logistics project to automate multimodal transport, as well as a transportation management system to search and select the best logistics routes with the help of big data. The digitization projects of SK and its units are playing out in the world's largest "dry port" lying 1600 miles from the nearest ocean and very nearly the farthest point on Earth from any ocean. Khorgos, embedded in the new Silk Road, furnishes an enormous proving ground for digital solutions in the logistics sector. The massive dry land free port straddles the China–Kazakh border.

The two countries use different gauge railways, meaning that every railcar must be handled at the dry port. Giant cranes lift the railcar-sized shipping container off one carriage and lower it onto another of a different gauge. Still, its contents will arrive in Europe twice as fast as seaborne shipments. The expected annual volume is 30 million tons, providing ample opportunity for stress testing new digital logistics systems. The boost to the global logistics supply chain will be significant: currently more than 70% of land transit between China and EU passes through Kazakhstan, according to SK CEO Akhmetzhan Yessimov in a 2019 interview.

Lying not far from the massive "dry port" at Khorgos, the Cosmodrone hosted the OneWeb constellation launch described in the introduction to this chapter. Meanwhile, satellites already play a role in the logistics and transport sectors, as witnessed by the potential use by Alibaba's logistics affiliate, Caianiao, of handheld devices connecting with Earth-orbiting satellites. Before Asian goods reach the European e-commerce users, they may take a brief stop at one of the digitalized warehouses in Hungary, Poland, or Slovakia of Logicor company, the largest owner of logistics and distribution properties in Europe, which was acquired by **CIC** in 2017 for $13.8 billion, in one of CIC's largest direct investment transactions.

## Smart Cities – Urban SDG

Zoom out from smart logistics to the bigger picture and you will have a view of the next level of smart infrastructure: smart cities. The mounting infrastructure finance gap is especially profound in cities. Urban areas are already home to 50% of the world's population, generate around 80% of global economic output, and account for 70% of greenhouse gases. With the lack of enough finance for investment in infrastructure – especially in the "smart" dimension at a time of the fourth industrial revolution – urban populations are prevented from reaching their full potential of productivity, which impedes economic progress and increases the overall costs of municipalities.

The term "smart cities" conjures visions of a future where digital technology monitors and connects everything from buildings to streetlights to self-driving cars. It empowers governments to provide better city services more efficiently, creating a more accessible, safer, and cleaner environment in the process – with, on the other side, the city's citizens utilizing all the city has to offer from the convenience of their smart devices. However, if smart city projects are long-term investments, the investor may worry about the risk that the underlying technology could be superseded before the investment pays off (in other words, technology in the near future may render the investment obsolete). Given the nature of smart city projects, a traditional infrastructure financing model may not work well.

The Smart City Infrastructure Fund – the first of its kind globally – was established by the **Dutch pension fund APG** with Australian PE fund Whitehelm Capital in November 2018. First off, some background on APG, the largest pension fund manager in the Netherlands. The comprehensiveness of the Dutch pension system stands out among developed countries. Approximately 90% of the labor force is enrolled in a pension plan, and pension benefits aim to be about 70% of average lifetime earnings. Dutch workers save on average 16% of their disposable income (Eurostat, 2015), which is second only to Germany in the Eurozone.

Headquartered in Amsterdam, APG, the largest pension fund manager in the Netherlands, was established in 2008 as a spin-off of Stichting Pensioenfonds **ABP,** the Dutch pension fund for government and education-sector employees. This followed a law passed in 2007, which required pension funds to turn their asset management functions over to independent firms (before this, ABP conducted asset management in-house). Now, in 2020, APG manages more than $600 billion assets for the pension funds in numerous sectors (education, government, construction, housing associations, energy and utility companies, and medical specialists, to name just a few), providing the pension for one in five families in the Netherlands (about 4.5 million participants).

The Smart City Infrastructure Fund by APG and its partner will start out with an initial investment of $300 million, with subsequent tranches expected to be more than $1 billion. The fund was established to meet the growing demand for financing the scale up of digital infrastructure in cities and communities worldwide, such as smart lighting, parking, waste collection, and pollution control, which currently do not have access to long-term institutional financing and capability. According to APG and its partner, this initiative will complement existing financing channels to enable a sustainable transition from small-scale pilot projects to mainstream applications (in other words, to bring the traditional infrastructure investment model to "new business models and use cases").

The first "smart city" that the Smart City Infrastructure Fund invested in was the City of Fullerton, California. In 2019, the fund partnered with SiFi Networks America Ltd ("SiFi") to invest over $75 million in the deployment of "smart city ready" digital infrastructure in Fullerton. It will be home to the country's biggest privately funded open access network from international fiber optic network developer SiFi Networks. The roll-out of fiber network in Fullerton will not only provide a significant upgrade to Internet speeds and accommodate a growing demand for data in households and businesses, but it will also facilitate the proliferation of smart city solutions in key urban services, such as traffic control, street lighting, and emergency services (see **Figure 4.10**).

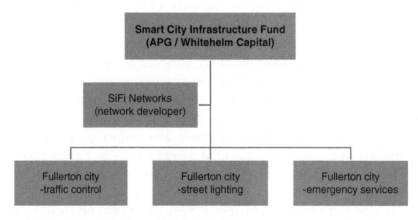

Figure 4.10    **City of Fullerton – first Fiber City**

Fullerton has a population of approximately 135,000, with some 50,000 homes and 5000 businesses. It is expected that between 33% to 50% of broadband customers (residential and commercial) will migrate to the new network over time. The network will also be used by the municipality to deliver city-wide services, such as wi-fi, public sensors, traffic control, CCTV operations, and streetlighting control systems. Additionally, the fiber network will provide a platform for the future expansion of 5G mobile and IoT networks into the area when next generation smart devices are adopted by individuals and businesses. With the view to unlock societal benefits and facilitate a rapid transition towards low carbon, resource efficient, and competitive economies, the Smart City Infrastructure Fund has a clear SDG element in its investment theme.

Another smart city example is the city of Hangzhou, hometown of SIF-backed Alibaba in China. Hangzhou City uses an artificial intelligence transportation management system developed by Alibaba, called the "City Brain," to gather traffic information through videos and GPS data. It then uses artificial intelligence to analyze the data and coordinate more than 1000 key traffic lights and road signals to guide real-time traffic flow. Hangzhou, a megacity of 10 million people, once ranked fifth among China's most congested cities, became 57th on the list as of 2019.

On the other side of the globe from Fullerton, Smart City solutions are gaining traction in Manama. **Bahrain's Mumtalakat** has earmarked a $100 million fund investment in the Al Waha fund of funds, including smart cities technology. The move is consistent with the government's rollout of a 3D digital image of Manama, Bahrain's capital, mapping everything above and below ground. The project will integrate information in machine readable format showing structures, power grids, water, and sewers to enable building information management (BIM).

Other Gulf countries are not simply digitally retrofitting existing cities. Kuwait and Saudi Arabia have much more ambitious plans to raise entirely new shoreline cities in the desert, Silk City and Neom City. Both are slated to receive SIF funding in the region, and China's sovereign capital also plays a role through the Chinese government's Digital Silk Road initiative (see **Box: Silk Road in the Cyberspace**), the digital prong of the BRI (UAE and Saudi Arabia are signatory countries already).

---

### Silk Road in the Cyberspace

China's Belt & Road Initiative (BRI) had two major prongs when President Xi Jinping unveiled Belt & Road, or *"yi dai yi lu"*, in September 2013: one is the Silk Road Economic Belt, an overland push that runs through Central Asia to Europe; and the other, the 21st century Maritime Silk Road, a maritime route that runs through South-east Asia, Africa, and Europe.

The initiative aims to build a trade and infrastructure network, thereby opening up new space for the world's economic growth and realizing "high-standard, livelihood-improving and sustainable development." Whereas skeptics warn about the scheme's risk of raising developing countries' debt burden, its potential climate impacts, and the geopolitical ambitions of a rising great power (all of which are legitimate concerns deserving their own analysis, and see the earlier box on the **US Blue Dot** initiative for a reference), supporters see it as a timely injection of fresh capital and a catalyst to global development long held back by the West-dominated institutions.

The BRI has become a globally recognized initiative as written into a UN resolution in November 2016. The global recognition of BRI was illustrated by China's successful hosting of the BRI summit in 2017, which was attended by almost 30 world leaders and representatives from nearly 110 countries. And its influence keeps spreading as 5000 representatives from over 150 countries and 90 international organizations attended the Second Belt and Road Forum for International Cooperation held in April 2019 in Beijing.

By jointly investing into critical infrastructure, the BRI is poised to be the 21st century's most extensive and transformative economic integration project. Such efforts are now being accelerated by the new digital prong of the BRI, promoted by President Xi mostly recently at the 2017 BRI summit. "We should pursue innovation-driven development and intensify cooperation in frontier areas such as digital economy, artificial intelligence, nanotechnology and quantum computing, and advance the development of big data, cloud computing and smart cities so as to turn them into a digital silk road of the 21st century."

The Digital Silk Road initiative is powered by the fact that China is the largest homogenous digital market in the world. The Digital Silk Road is expected to supplement the Belt and Road's physical infrastructure with advanced IT infrastructure, such as broadband networks, e-commerce hubs, and smart cities, for better global connectivity. With that, the digital dimension of the BRI is poised to develop the pathways on which the global digital economy will run.

In the desert of **Kuwait,** a \$10 billion Kuwait–China Silk Road Fund is reportedly being formed jointly by Kuwait and China, reaching, with leverage, \$30 billion. The goal is to invest in the futuristic Silk City planned to rise in a barren stretch of Kuwait at a cost exceeding \$100 billion over a 25-year period. So far, there is a bridge to nowhere: the newly opened 36-kilometer, \$3.6 billion Sheikh Jaber Al Ahmed Al Sabah Causeway has connected Kuwait's capital directly to its undeveloped northern territories, reducing a previously three-hour drive to 30 minutes.

On the causeway's now barren terminus, a 250-square-kilometer city is to rise, including a kilometer-tall tower, an international airport, an Olympic stadium, and duty-free trade area with housing, workspace, retail, and entertainment for three-quarters of a million residents. The development, known as Madinat al-Harir in Arabic, will include several ports, each, like Silk City, employing digital technology to speed logistics and eliminate paperwork.

By far the most ambitious smart city plan, hands down, is **Saudi Arabia**'s Neom City. The nation's sovereign fund, PIF, has pledged \$500 billion to start this futuristic megalopolis – at more than 10,000 square miles, 33 times the size of New York City. Sprawling across parts of Jordan and Egypt as well as Saudi Arabia, it will feature flying taxis, an artificial moon, robotic maids, holographic teachers, not to mention a theme park featuring robotic dinosaurs. The smart city technology will include crime monitoring AI, facial recognition, and public services including sanitation and robotic caregivers. The plans foresee digital technology mediating health and safety as well as traffic, not to mention the fleet of drones seeding clouds for rain and, in the evening, simulating a rising and setting moon.

The project is part of Vision 2030, the Kingdom's transformative plan to ensure a prosperous post-carbon future for the nation by reducing the country's dependence on oil and increasing employment in the private sector. The hope is that the semi-autonomous zone will attract foreign direct investment, particularly in the tech sector, and facilitate tourism in the otherwise alcohol-free Kingdom.

### IoT: Financing the Hyper-connected World

The global development of digital infrastructure eventually leads to a world of IoT – the Internet of Things (or Internet of Everything). Hence the SIFs are also actively investing in new digital infrastructure emerging from all sectors – new businesses as well as traditional industries. The digital payment system and digital health systems are briefly mentioned below; even more such examples are evolving in numerous other sectors that are being transformed by the digital revolution. For a start, network connectivity, smart logistics, and smart cities host people and facilitate trade, but another cornerstone of the digital infrastructure is needed to cement all the elements of e-commerce: the **digital financial infrastructure.**

The world of payments is becoming cashless and a digital infrastructure is fast evolving. As the pandemic raged in the second quarter of 2020, Mubadala ($1.2 billion), ADIA ($500 million) PIF ($1.5 billion) piled into India's Jio Systems, following Facebook's $5.7 billion investment in Jio hoping to use the platform to convert WhatsApp into the Alipay of India. Even Visa, the world's largest digital payments platform, felt compelled to shell out $5.3 billion in early 2020 to acquire Plaid, a startup that facilitates integration of financial accounts for its users. As we become a cashless world, digital technology takes center stage. Accenture reports that by 2023, annual in-store and remote transactions authenticated via mobile biometrics are predicted to reach $2 trillion. Not surprisingly, SIFs have invested in unicorns that bring innovation to mobile payments and instant credit digital infrastructure that underpins the digital economy now shaping the world of commerce:

- India's booming e-commerce sector attracted **Temasek,** alongside Paypal, to invest in a 2018 $125 million round in Pine Labs, a New Delhi-based POS (point of sale) and instant credit startup providing both the technical framework and financing infrastructure for e-commerce transactions.
- In China, Ant Financial, the payments and online asset management giant born out of Alibaba, landed financing from **CIC** in 2016 and then investments from multiple SIFs in early 2019, at $150 billion valuation that far exceeded the market cap of Goldman Sachs.
- In Europe, **GIC** invested at the earliest stage in Checkout .com, a London-based payments platform, which raised $230 million in 2019 in what it called the largest ever Series A round by a fintech in Europe, according to a press release. The company's technology processes global payments across multiple payment methods, including credit and debit cards, online banking, Apple Pay, PayPal, and other digital wallets.
- And even before that, in 2014, **GIC** led a $150 million series E round in Square, whose mobile credit card payment devices have powered its rise to a NYSE listing with a market cap over $25 billion.

**Digital health** is another key digital infrastructure sector that has benefited from SIF direct investment. Digitizing aspects of healthcare, such as facilities management, diagnoses, health monitoring, patient records, therapies and much more, digital health is a fast-evolving sector. The American Medical Association identifies the application of big data as one of the key trends in digital healthcare in 2020. Venture capital has taken heed and digital health is now seen as an important venture field, attracting over $7 billion in each of the past two years. SIF-backed deals include:

- **Kuwait** as far back as 2014 invested $350 million (two rounds total) in Nanthealth, a cloud-based clinical decision support platform used by hospitals.
- More recently, in 2019, **CPPIB** invested alongside EQT VIII Fund to acquire control of another cloud-based provider to the healthcare sector, Waystar, at a valuation of $2.7 billion. The company's cloud-based revenue cycle technology is used by over 45,000 healthcare providers.
- Also in 2019, **PIF** invested $550 million in the Series C round of UK-based Babylon, which uses an AI-powered chatbot to book virtual doctor's visits and order prescriptions. The PIF round is intended to finance expansion outside Babylon's home market to China, North America, and the Middle East.
- Both Montreal-based Canadian pension **PSP** and **Mubadala** joined the **Vision Fund**-led $205 million 2019 Series E round of Collective Health, a US employer healthcare solution platform that uses predictive analytics to manage and navigate healthcare plans.
- **Temasek** led a $64 million 2019 Series C round for Pear Therapeutics, a Boston-based startup that develops digital therapeutics to treat substance abuse (the first software app to receive FDA clinical approval), schizophrenia, opioid abuse disorder, and multiple sclerosis.

In summary, technology has fundamentally changed the way sovereign investors invest in all aspects of infrastructure. Around the world, all markets face an acute need for new or modernized infrastructure. The estimated shortfall in global infrastructure investment is at trillions per year, and that number may multiply – when considering the latest infrastructure needs from the digital revolution. The SIFs are the critical source of capital for this need, even though greenfield projects present a different risk–reward profile from mature infrastructure.

Here is the constructive thinking: the digital revolution may lend itself to better perspectives on due diligence and projects review for greenfield digital infrastructure. The more smart cities are set up, the more data centers and network are connected, the more infrastructure gets smarter, the more construction parameters, public–private partnership (PPP) contracts, procurement practices, and more will be standardized. And above all, with digital infrastructure systems capturing data of everything, there will soon be exponentially more performance data to make digital infrastructure investments easier to monitor and analyze (and the same for more new investments).

However, as is true for anything so powerful, the IoT has the potential to be misused and can create serious national cybersecurity and individual data privacy issues if not controlled appropriately. The trend is increasingly obvious in recent years. The rising concern over the vulnerability of digital infrastructure and the data flowing through it, particularly personal digital data, has led to SIF investments being subjected to increased scrutiny under foreign direct investment reviews.

As we will see in more detail in **Chapters 8 and 9,** several of the sectors described in this chapter have been called out for special national security review under new CFIUS rules in the US and similar rules in other countries, among them "critical infrastructure" such as data centers and digital platforms managing sensitive personal data. In that respect, SIFs have a playbook to fall back on, as their investments in traditional infrastructure were one of the areas to first set off alarms and trigger increased national security concerns around SIFs in the US.

Overall, the sovereign funds' digital infrastructure investments have a tremendous positive impact on the global economy. That's especially true for the emerging markets, which are facing unprecedented levels of urbanization development and corresponding infrastructure bottleneck. The key – you guessed it – is to leverage an existing sovereign fund or set up a new one to be the catalyst. As SIFs have traversed the globe during the tech boom, they have gained experience and developed a keen sense for attendant risk and opportunity. All this makes them prime candidates to play a role in the domestic innovation ecosystem, which we turn to in the following chapter.

*What goes up, must come down. Scan the night sky and you will not yet see the OneWeb satellite constellation featured in the introduction to this chapter. Nor may you ever. The company's March 2019 down round is mentioned earlier in this chapter. That was only the beginning of the return to Earth for the rocketship unicorn.*

*One year later, in March 2020, OneWeb filed for bankruptcy protection, citing its inability to secure the additional financing needed to complete its low Earth-orbiting satellite constellation, which had been slated to begin offering satellite-based broadband as early as the end of 2020. The company blamed the disruption in capital markets caused by the coronavirus pandemic. But, judging by the hit its valuation already took in the 2019 equity round, the competition in the digital satellite sector likely played a role. Even unicorns are subject to the laws of gravity, it seems.*

CHAPTER 5

# Spurring Domestic Digital Transformation

*$1.5 trillion is a big number. Bigger than the January 2020 combined market value of Germany's DAX, the stock market index composed of the country's 30 leading enterprises.*

*As 2020 dawned, it was also the approximate market cap of a single tech company, Apple, the iPhone maker. The icons of vaunted German technical prowess, Daimler-Benz, BMW, Siemens, Bayer, and the rest of the DAX were each the scale of garden gnomes in comparison. Looked at this way, the captains of German industry feared that their country was being left in the dust by the digital revolution born of data and software, not based on their skills of metal bashing and high-finish assembly.*

*This dawning realization gave rise to harsh criticism of the staid investment management of Germany's well-endowed pension plans. In the US, German executives complained, big pension funds have long invested in technology startups via venture capital; in contrast, German pension funds were ultra-conservative, placing the bulk of their investments in low-yielding sovereign debt, while the digital revolution bypassed German industry. (In their angst, the critics apparently had not yet realized from this book's earlier chapters that an even more striking comparison was available: Canadian pension funds and emerging economy sovereign wealth funds had been making even more aggressive strides into future tech investing than their US counterparts.) The industry leaders demanded that the pensions correct the absurd investment allocation: go and invest more in venture capital in Germany – you will bear less risk than holding Italian government bonds.*

Across the globe, not every sovereign investment fund has a single objective. Some of the SIFs have domestic and strategic objectives, and some combine two or more of the functions, mixing fiscal stabilization, intergenerational savings, and economic development. Besides overseas investments, they also see strong opportunities to accelerate their domestic development agendas. For example, having contributed to the rescue of the Irish banks since the global financial crisis, the **Ireland Strategic Investment Fund (ISIF)** is now focusing on domestic economy development.

These funds see tech investments as a way to support economic activity and job creation at home, while simultaneously achieving commercial returns from new businesses. In the earlier chapters of this book, global sovereign funds were seen to rush to Silicon Valley, China, and other innovation hubs of the world to join the unicorn hunt. This chapter will look into sovereign funds nurturing the technology sector in their own backyards. For example, one of the goals of **Turkey**'s sovereign fund is to develop the domestic entrepreneurial economy and become the "investment gate of Turkey."

While these funds of hybrid missions arise the world over and include Khazanah in South-east Asia, CDPQ in Canada, Mumtalakat Bahrain in the Middle East, the Trinidad and Tobago Heritage and Stabilization Fund in Latin America, and the State Oil Fund of Azerbaijan in Central Asia, they are emerging particularly from the frontier economies in Africa. For example, **Botswana's Pula Fund** is a SIF in sub-Saharan Africa whose mission is a combination of savings, stabilization, and development. Similarly, **Fundo Soberano de Angola** allocates capital separately to an international investment portfolio and a local portfolio for Angola and sub-Saharan Africa to support "socioeconomic development."

Amid the global tech revolution, these state funds of emerging countries have thrown themselves into the technology race. They are investing overseas, domestically, or both, to support and facilitate the digital transformation of their home countries. The cases in this chapter will illustrate two main ways for SIFs to achieve strategic tech investment objectives: (a) facilitate cross-border technology transfer; and (b) build a domestic innovation ecosystem and infrastructure.

The latter can provide a longer and more powerful catalyst for the emerging markets, and hence is the focus of this chapter.

**Cross-border technology transfer**. This involves investing in innovative companies abroad to encourage them to set up shop in their home market. For example, a SIF acquires a direct stake or total control of a tech company. The invested company owns proprietary technology, controls a unique process, or has access to rare materials. Via their board seat and oversight of corporate operation, the SIF develops ongoing dialogue with the company management. The company is convinced to open a factory, set up an operation, create a subsidiary or joint venture or form a research facility in the home country of the fund. In connection with the strategic knowledge transfer, employment opportunities are also created in the SIF's home country.

Such a transfer could be a win–win for both sides. For the SIFs, they could get access to the latest digital development, for example in Silicon Valley, then contribute to their own countries' digital transformation. For the technology companies with ambitions to expand their business to overseas markets, SIFs can be ideal local partners in helping startups to develop a better knowledge of the potential markets – the sovereign funds can open doors in their home countries. Furthermore, the SIFs may find prospective synergies that exist between the overseas tech companies and the domestic firms they invest in. Third, the SIFs may provide startups with better understanding of public policy and regulations – such as data privacy and cybersecurity issues – in new product experiments and avoid potential reputational crises.

For example, **Oman's State General Reserve Funds (SGRF)** in 2016 bought a 32% stake in Mecanizados Escribano, a family-owned Spanish precision mechanical components maker for the aerospace, defense, and other industrial sectors. Following the investment, the Spanish firm set up a local manufacturing entity in Oman, as the SGRF hoped to leverage the transaction to expand the company's machining capabilities and technologies in Oman and the Gulf (see **Figure 5.1**). Another example is Khazanah of Malaysia, a large shareholder of Telecom Malaysia

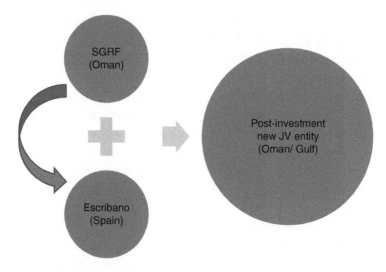

Figure 5.1 **Oman/Spain Cross-border Technology Transfer**

and with telecom and media assets constituting 25% of its port-folio. For its portfolio companies in Silicon Valley, Khazanah is clearly the best partner for their expansion into Malaysia and South-east Asia.

**Domestic innovation ecosystem and infrastructure.** In recent years, more SIFs are now choosing – or being encour-aged – to invest in their domestic markets and cultivate an innovation ecosystem at home. Such an ecosystem requires the integration of three key ingredients: digital infrastructure, venture capital, and entrepreneurial talents. The following sections will show that as the SIFs effectively help their gov-ernments to shape national policies on digital transformation, they potentially find unicorns of their own breed.

## Quest for Additionality: from NPRF to ISIF

The **Ireland Strategic Investment Fund (ISIF)**, managed and controlled by the National Treasury Management Agency (NTMA), is a good example of a sovereign development fund that focuses on domestic economic development. The fund's performance is evaluated using two criteria: financial and economic returns. This Irish saga has gone on about two decades, and the fund and its mandate has evolved over time.

The fund was set up at the turn of the century, in 2001, and was known as the **National Pensions Reserve Fund (NPRF)**. It was a classic sovereign wealth fund for national "savings," which was investing globally and was aiming to build a pool of assets to support public sector and social welfare pensions in Ireland between the year 2025 and 2055 (in other words, an "intergenerational fund"). Similar to NZ Super and Australia's Future Fund, the NPRF's role was to generate financial returns from an international portfolio to help reduce the country's future pensions bill.

By the time the financial crisis hit Ireland in 2009–2010, the mandate for NPRF had changed. The fund had grown to €23–24 billion (approximately $35 billion), which was about 10% of Ireland's GDP. Ireland then entered into a €85 billion program of financial support with the IMF, the European Commission (EC), and the European Central Bank (ECB). Under direction from the Ministry of Finance, 80% or more of the assets of the fund were used to bail out two main banks in Ireland which were in major distress in 2009–2011 (capital markets were closed and no capital was flowing whatsoever).

In 2014, following the global financial crisis, the NPRF changed its mission and investment scope, as the new government decided to convert it into a strategic investment fund. In 2014, the National Treasury Management Agency Act kick-started the legislative process that changed the NPRF into the ISIF (see **Figure 5.2**). From global investor and then bailing out the banks, the Irish fund entered into its third phase acting as a strategic investment fund with a mixed mandate to "invest on a commercial basis to support economic activity and employment in Ireland."

The ISIF has been in full operation under the new mandate from 2014 onward. On the one hand, the concept of investing on a commercial basis is familiar to the sovereign fund community, who are encouraged to invest "to maximize risk-adjusted financial returns." On the other hand, supporting

Figure 5.2    **The Evolution of ISIF**

economic activity and employment represents a new role for the investment team. For this mixed mandate, the ISIF fund has a "double bottom line" requirement for its portfolio, necessitating that all of the fund's investments generate both investment returns and positive economic impacts in Ireland.

In more recent years, the Irish economy has recovered dramatically, and the Minister for Finance has slightly revised the ISIF mandate, reflecting the strong growth in the Irish economy and abundant capital flows to the country of late. In July 2018, the Minister for Finance and Public Expenditure and Reform announced a refocusing of the ISIF within its overall policy mandate centered on five key economic priorities: (i) indigenous industry; (ii) regional development; (iii) sectors adversely affected by Brexit; (iv) projects to address climate change; and (v) housing supply. The fund still has the same broad double bottom line mandate for commercial investment and economic impact; however, it was asked to focus on five particular priority themes that are relevant to the Irish economy at the moment.

But what exactly is the economic impact? The most important concept that the ISIF applies is "additionality," which is around additional incremental economic activity in Ireland that will arise from its investments. As a long-term investor, the ISIF seeks to achieve sustainable additionality, as this will have "a more prolonged effect on economic activity and will result in a greater impact than one-off, short-term gains." The "additionality" that ISIF is looking for can be found in

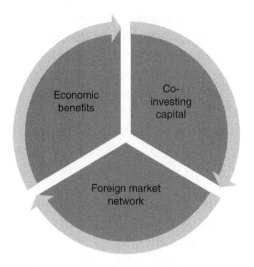

Figure 5.3    **"Additionality" Economic Concept by ISIF**

three main aspects: economic benefits, co-investing capital, and the foreign market network (see **Figure 5.3**).

**Economic benefits.** This refers to the economic benefits additional to gross value added/gross domestic product that are likely to result from the investment in question, over and above what would have occurred anyway. This would classically be in an infrastructure or in a real estate type of transaction that would enable future economic activity that would not otherwise be enabled. More recently, tech investments are taking the front seat, as will be illustrated in the deal examples later.

**Co-investing capital.** The ISIF has invested widely across the Irish economy in infrastructure and energy, commercial real estate and housing, food and agri-technology, as well as the healthcare sector and into SMEs. That has helped the fund build acceptance and visibility as an attractive "investor of choice" for companies and other investors. As such, the ISIF is a huge comfort blanket for prospective co-investors, both domestic and international, and it gets more bang for the Irish buck. According to a recent report, for every euro that the ISIF has invested in Irish projects, it has attracted more than 1.5 euros, thus more than doubling the impact of its investments.

**Foreign market network.** Following the concept of co-investing, the idea of networks and collaboration in foreign markets is a major underlying principle in ISIF, as illustrated by the Irish life sciences company case below. Furthermore, peer sovereign funds are a main part of this network, not only because, like ISIF itself, they are capital for a long investment time horizon, but they also bring connections and networks in their respective domestic markets. The joint venture project the ISIF launched with **CIC,** China's sovereign fund, is another case study below.

In 2018, with Chinese biotechnology giant WuXi NextCODE, ISIF co-led a $400 million investment in Irish life sciences company Genomics Medicine Ireland (GMI). The investment aimed to help make Ireland an important hub for genomics research and the development of new disease treatments and cures. WuXi biotechnology also saw strategic interest in establishing a presence in Ireland as a gateway into the broader European market. ISIF as the lead investor put $70 million in the project, and it managed to attract fellow SIF Temasek and major Silicon Valley investors including ARCH Venture Partners and Sequoia Capital as co-investors (see **Figure 5.4**).

With CIC, the ISIF fund has launched a co-investment joint venture to link the Ireland and China markets specifically on fast-growing technology companies. In 2018, ISIF and the CIC announced a €150 million China–Ireland Fund, which was a successor to the fully-invested China Ireland Technology Growth Fund, started in 2014 by NPRF (ISIF's predecessor before the new mandate) and CIC. The new fund would continue targeting companies in core technology sectors such as Internet, software, semiconductors, and clean technology and other areas of technology such as agriculture and financial services.

As in the previous fund, the China–Ireland Fund aims to invest in both high-growth Irish technology firms with an ambition to access the Chinese market, and Chinese firms seeking to use Ireland as a base for European operations. The earlier $100

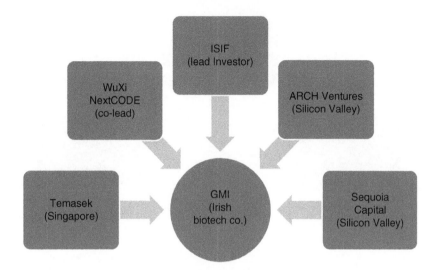

Figure 5.4    **ISIF Biotechnology Investment Attracted Co-investors**

million China–Ireland Technology Growth Fund supported six Irish technology firms expanding into China and helped the firms develop relationships with Chinese customers. For example, Irish-founded Movidius has become a global leader in machine vision technology, with the ISIF–CIC JV assisting in facilitating relationships with new Chinese customers. (Movidius was subsequently acquired by Intel in 2016.)

What's unique about the JV structure is that, at the LP level, ISIF and CIC invested 50% each, and at the GP level, there is also a joint venture on a 50/50 basis, with both the Irish and the Chinese GPs having people on the ground (see **Figure 5.5**). The Irish general partner is Dublin-based Atlantic Bridge, whereas the China side general partner is Beijing-based West Summit Capital, a new team that CIC seeded shortly before the 2014 fund (see **Chapter 7** for details). The JV GPs offer cross-border expertise and local networks in China and Ireland to support investees' international expansions.

For Irish businesses to expand in China, and for prospective Chinese businesses to navigate the Irish system, the collaboration of the two sovereign funds has made a huge difference. The ISIF uses the phrase: "Thinking in decades,

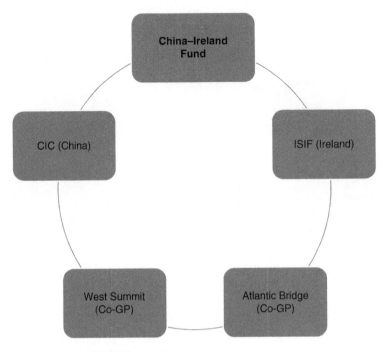

Figure 5.5    **China–Ireland Fund – JV at LP and GP**

making a difference." That is really its long-term time horizons and the quest for additionality. And the high-tech sectors are the best place to apply that.

## Tech Hub in the Desert

States like Abu Dhabi and Dubai in the United Arab Emirates (UAE), as well as other countries in the Middle East, are increasingly pumping cash into local tech ecosystems. On the one hand, the Gulf states have some of the most plugged-in populations in the world, with the rate of Internet penetration in Bahrain, Saudi Arabia, Kuwait, and Qatar all exceeding 70% – far outpacing the global average of 50%. On the other hand, tech helps reduce their reliance on oil-dependent industries. Shifting away from simply acting as global technology investors, the Gulf states have focused on investing domestically with the goal of becoming emerging hubs for digital innovation.

However, despite its tech savvy population, the Middle East could not boast its own unicorn until 2016, when ride-hailing service, Careem, breached the $1 billion line to join the club. It competed so successfully with world-beating Uber that in March 2019 it became the region's largest tech buyout with Uber paying $3.1 billion to acquire it. Among its investors, only one SIF appears: KIA participated in the 2015 $60 million Series C round.

Fintech is another sector on the rise in the Middle East, with its large unbanked population of expatriate laborers. The region generated outbound remittances of $120 billion in 2017 according to the World Bank. Now Money, in Dubai, has brought to market a smartphone app to facilitate that flow. Entrenched incumbents, high regulatory hurdles, and partner banks concerned about anti-money-laundering rules meant that it took four years from startup to product launch for the app.

While local startups were largely overlooked by the sovereign investors, **Mubadala** was looking far outside the Gulf states for ways to kick-start the local tech scene – sometimes very far. As early as 2009, Aabar Investments (now consolidated into Mubadala) made a $280 million investment to acquire a 31.8% stake in Richard Branson's Virgin Galactic, a space tourism startup. With a $110 million follow on investment in 2011, the stake was boosted to 37.8%. At the time of the initial investment, $100 million was also committed to building a spaceport in Abu Dhabi which could serve as a launch site for the Virgin Galactic spacecraft.

The initiative to develop a local space tech sector continues to aim higher. In 2019, Hazzaa Al Mansoori became the first UAE astronaut, making a weeklong visit to the International Space Station. Mars is next. The Emirates Mars mission completed its July 2020 launch to study the Martian atmosphere and learn about climate change. While the Martian visit is the mission, the goal is more down to earth. Omran Sharaf, project manager for the mission, told Euronews, "The UAE government wanted to see a big shift in the ecosystem that we have when it comes to building a creative, competitive and innovative knowledge-based economy. And it looked at space as a means to do that and Emirates Mars mission is the catalyst for that big shift and change."

While Saudi Arabia's **PIF** fund and the Vision Fund it backed frequently hit headlines, and its Neom City under planning is set to be the model smart city of the world (see **Box: Neom City**), Mubadala has been equally strategic. (In fact, Mubadala is a cornerstone investor in the Vision Fund as well and both SIFs have backed Virgin Galactic.) This government-owned investment company from Abu Dhabi, which recently merged with the International Petroleum Investment Company to form Mubadala Investment Company, is a pioneering global investor. Mubadala's multi-hundred-billion-dollar portfolio has one main theme: economic diversification towards new industry sectors. Its focus has finally turned to fostering local entrepreneurs.

---

### Neom City

Neom is at the forefront of the digital transformation of the Saudi economy. It is the brainchild of Mohammed bin Salman, the next generation Saudi crown prince who is set upon transforming the Kingdom. The Prince has set in motion huge changes in Saudi society, permitting women to drive, relaxing rules on dress in public, opening movie theaters for the first time in decades, hosting the world heavyweight boxing championship. But Neom surpasses all in its potential for transformation of the Saudi economy and society.

Saudi Arabia's oil-based economy fostered a young, growing, and well-educated population. Over a third of its citizens are under the age of 30. What is missing is career opportunities, an issue that only becomes more acute as the workforce enlarges to include Saudi women for the first time. At the same time, the government is seeking to secure its future in the post-carbon world. A perfect storm.

Neom presents the digital future as the solution to the social issues of the present and the looming post-carbon economy. It would start from scratch, on a patch of barren desert, stretching more than 450 kilometers along the Red Sea coast. Relying on abundant solar power, it would attract digital entrepreneurs from around the world with its appealing lifestyle (more robots than people) its own legal code (read: alcohol permitted), and tax (read: low) system.

The goal for this megacity is nothing less than the transformation of the economy and society by introducing a raft of liberalizing reforms and embracing digital technologies and services. While an initial target is the development of tourism, the coastal lifestyle is intended to be a magnet for new economy founders seeking to operate in a low-tax, high quality of life environment. The government is also reportedly luring large tech companies which already supply services to the Kingdom.

According to its website, Neom's industry will focus on 16 economic sectors, namely: future of energy, future of water, future of mobility, future of biotech, future of food, future of manufacturing, future of media, future of entertainment, culture, and fashion, future of technology and digital, future of tourism, future of sport, future of design and construction, future of services, future of health and well-being, future of education, and future of livability as the foundation of all the sectors.

In this context, Mubadala launched Hub71 in early 2019 as part of a broader effort by the UAE government. It is a flagship initiative of the AED 50 billion (approximately $15 billion) economic accelerator program, Ghadan 21, which means "tomorrow" in Arabic. The tech hub is located in Abu Dhabi's financial district, which will also house local offices for Amazon and Softbank. For startups operating within it, Hub71 provides fully subsidized housing, office spaces, and health insurance packages. Microsoft will provide its technology and cloud services.

To address the funding needs of startups within the hub, Mubadala launched two MENA tech investment vehicles – both a $150 million fund of funds and a $100 million direct fund targeted at early-stage companies. The US$150 million "fund of funds" program invests in funds that are committed to supporting the Abu Dhabi-based Hub71 ecosystem through investing in companies that leverage Hub71 for regional expansion and growth.

The first investment, from the direct fund, is Bayzat, a Dubai-based startup that is focused on delivering an exceptional employee experience that is accessible to every small and medium sized enterprise through a free cloud-based platform. Bayzat has raised US$16 million (AED58 million) in Series B funding from, besides Mubadala, global investors including Point72 Ventures. As Mubadala's Deputy Group CEO Waleed AI Muhairi indicated in a statement, "Hub71 will bring together three key factors essential for the success of Abu Dhabi's tech ecosystem – capital providers, business enablers and strategic partners – all under one roof."

## Innovative SWF Structures in Africa

In comparison with their peers, African sovereign funds have experienced notably rapid growth of late. Many African countries created their sovereign wealth funds following the recent commodity super-cycle of the 2000s, which led to a boom in resource revenues, and more countries on the continent have announced their intention to create SWFs. Like their Middle East peers in Saudi Arabia and UAE, African SWFs are largely funded from oil export revenues, such as **Nigeria's Sovereign Investment Authority (NSIA), Algeria's Fonds des Regulations des Recettes (FRR), and the Libyan Investment Authority (LIA).**

Locking away capital for future generations is important for these resource-rich countries, whereas their high levels of poverty and pressing infrastructure-development needs also demand investments to stimulate economic developments. To balance development and saving, African countries have successfully used sovereign funds as flexible tools, articulating various policy goals. They created innovative SWF structures that often integrate multiple sub-portfolios respectively designated to a range of purposes.

The **NSIA of Nigeria,** the largest economy in Africa, is one of the best examples. Despite its resource wealth, Nigeria is still in the bottom third of countries by GDP per capita (PPP).

Meanwhile, Nigeria – like many other developing countries – is challenged by a substantial infrastructure funding gap counted in billions. Furthermore, its population is exploding at a time when digital automation and artificial intelligence threaten to make job creation more difficult. In short, amid the ongoing global fourth industrial revolution, educational, healthcare, and infrastructure investments are much needed to transform Nigeria's economy into one that is competitive and innovative.

NSIA has effectively implemented a home market technology and innovation investment strategy in Nigeria, as will be illustrated by the case studies of its investments below. Equally important, NSIA has developed excellent governance and transparency to top the African Sovereign Wealth Fund Ranking. It is one of the best public institutions in Africa in terms of its leadership, operations, performance, and engagement with its stakeholders. For both reasons, NSIA is able to attract quality co-investors globally, which is extremely significant for Nigeria, given that NSIA does not have the same scale of capital as the earlier examples in this chapter – ISIF of Europe and Mubadala of the Middle East.

The NSIA was set up in 2013 with $1.5 billion seed capital from the federal government. In line with government mandates, the NSIA established and manages three funds for different objectives, namely: (a) the Fiscal Stabilization Fund, to provide relief to the economy in times of financial stress (e.g., a sharp drop of oil price as the market witnessed in March 2020); (b) the Future Generations Fund, which undertakes growth investments to provide for future generations of Nigerians at such time that the crude oil has been depleted; and (c) the Nigeria Infrastructure Fund (NIF), which undertakes investment in domestic infrastructure projects (hence the focus of this chapter).

The establishment of different sub-funds to reflect different investment objectives is used by a few resource-rich countries. **Chile** is another example that has adopted a two-fund structure – one that combines its short-term stabilization fund, the Economic and Social Stabilization (ESSF), and a long-term savings/income fund, the Pension Reserve Fund (PRF). To highlight domestic infrastructure needs, Nigeria has a third sub-fund to focus on domestic infrastructure and economic development. Similarly, **Ghana** also has set up three sovereign wealth funds that are strongly ring-fenced and have clearly delineated purposes (in parallel to NSIA's three funds): the Ghana Stabilization Fund (for fiscal contingency), the Ghana Heritage Fund (for intergenerational endowment), and the Ghana Infrastructure Investment Fund (for developmental objectives).

These three separate, ring-fenced funds account for 20, 40, and 40% of the NSIA portfolio (see **Figure 5.6**). Accordingly, they invest into different securities and assets of different liquidity, time horizon, and risk–reward profiles:

- Stabilization Fund: in liquid assets, to help to smooth out fiscal bumps due to short-term fluctuations in commodity prices (1–2-year horizon).
- Future Generation Fund: in global assets and securities to appreciate over a long time for future generations.
- Infrastructure Fund: in new enterprises and development projects that drive social and economic impact.

Lately, NSIA, through the infrastructure fund, has invested heavily in healthcare technology. NSIA is interested in strategic "high-impact, high-value" opportunities across the entire

■ Fiscal Stabilization Fund  (20%)

■ Future Generations Fund  (40%)

▦ Nigeria Infrastructure Fund  (40%)

Figure 5.6    **NSIA Divided into Three Ring-fenced Sub-Funds**

healthcare value chain that will facilitate the delivery of high-quality, affordable, and accessible healthcare services to Nigerians. Even though building and operating top-quality medical facilities in Nigeria is challenging, requiring specialist personnel and knowledge – as well as meeting the robust sectoral and regulatory requirements – NSIA is determined to expand investment in this sector, in the belief that improving medical care in Nigeria is critical to the country's future.

Consequently, NSIA has entered into strategic partnership agreements with the Federal Ministry of Health and leading global healthcare sector participants to identify and invest in healthcare infrastructure projects. In 2018–2019, NSIA committed $20 million in three landmark projects in the health sector. The main project is the NSIA-LUTH Cancer Centre (NLCC) at the Lagos University Teaching Hospital (LUTH), Idi-Araba, Lagos, the first investment to develop tertiary healthcare services in Nigeria (inaugurated by President Muhammadu Buhari in early 2019).

The NLCC, an $11 million in partnership with LUTH, will rebuild and equip the hospital's cancer center to provide cutting-edge radiotherapy and chemotherapy treatment services. To equip the cancer center, NSIA has also built strategic partnerships with leading oncology equipment manufacturers, including Varian Medical Systems and GE Healthcare. The two other projects are medical diagnostic centers located at the Aminu Kano Teaching Hospital (AKTH), Kano State, and the Federal Medical Centre (FMCU) in Umuahia, Abia State.

These healthcare investments have served an obvious social need for new medical technology and have been "very profitable" for NSIA, according to senior executives. They see healthcare remaining a focus area going forward with the implementation of the next phase of diagnostic and treatment centers. The NSIA investment team has an active pipeline and a plan to aggressively increase investments in the coming years. The long-term vision for Nigeria? Over time, NSIA expect the country to be a net-beneficiary of global medical tourism.

Just like the Irish ISIF, alliances and partnerships formed by NSIA in its investments, as shown in the healthcare tech transaction above, are a strategic priority to achieve Nigeria's growth objectives. Currently the total assets under management are around $2.5 to $3 billion (which includes additional government monies managed by NSIA, in addition to the three funds described above). Additional capitalization from the government will help NSIA to broaden its investments, but a lot would depend on the oil price movement (in 2020 the oil price was especially challenged, and the global ESG movements are steadily building pressure on fossil fuel's long-term price).

Therefore, the fund's current focus remains on achieving growth through joint investments. As a professionally managed institution highly rated internationally for governance and transparency, the NSIA is uniquely positioned to attract sovereign funds from Africa, the Middle East, and beyond for co-investments in Nigeria. For example, NSIA is co-investing with **Morocco**'s sovereign fund, **Ithmar Capital,** in an offshore/onshore Trans-African gas pipeline which will provide energy to West African states as well as Europe (see **Figure 5.7**). In the agriculture sectors, it has a $200 million partnership

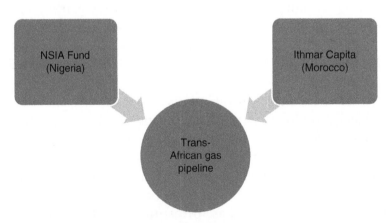

Figure 5.7 **Nigeria/Morocco–African SIF Partnership**

(50/50) with **Old Mutual of South Africa,** and it also has a joint venture with **OCP Morocco** (a government office of Morocco, later transformed into a limited company) to invest in an ammonia plant.

Beyond co-investing capital, NSIA has used financial innovation to reduce the "risk premium" perceived by foreign investors, which may be a game changer to solve the infrastructure bottleneck in Nigeria as well as Africa in general. There's a high perception of risk held by international capital about investing in Africa, and many would place a premium on expected return from projects – sometimes as much as 20 to 30% higher in Africa than in the developed markets, solely because of risk perception.

As such, NSIA as a successful sovereign fund has developed InfraCredit, a specialized financial guarantor, to bring down this risk premium (see **Figure 5.8**). InfraCredit was capitalized with $100 million by NSIA in partnership with the Private Infrastructure Development (PID) Group and GuarantCo, as well as KfW Development Bank and Africa Finance

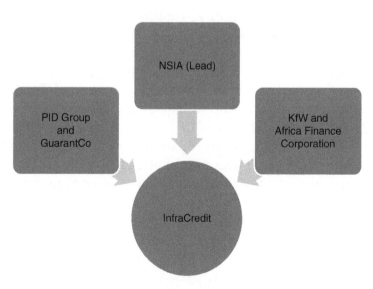

Figure 5.8     **SWF Innovation to Lower "Africa Risk"**

Corporation (AFC). InfraCredit provides local currency guarantees for debt instruments issued for finance-qualifying infrastructure projects in Nigeria, making it possible for infrastructure projects to raise capital efficiently from broader capital sources.

The InfraCredit innovation is the best example of NSIA serving as a catalyst to drive investments into the country. By enhancing the credit quality of local currency infrastructure debt instruments, NSIA and InfraCredit become a multiplier of capital for Nigeria infrastructure needs. Now the qualifying projects can tap long-term capital from international sovereign funds and pension funds at lower cost and longer tenure of such credit than before. In summary, NSIA is pioneering frameworks for financing social impact projects through tech-related investments, and the corresponding economic impact will lead Nigeria into the league of fastest growing economies in the world.

### Digital Africa – the Bigger Story

As illustrated by NSIA's infrastructure and healthcare investments, sovereign funds in Africa are making impactful investments to promote the economic developments of the country. The majority of African sovereign funds are funded from exports of natural resources, for example Botswana's Pula Fund was originated from diamond exports, and **Kenya** and **South Africa** announced a plan in 2019 to set up a sovereign wealth fund based on mining royalties (among other sources), similar to **Namibia**'s **Minerals Development Fund,** while many more were capitalized by hydrocarbon revenues (see **Figure 5.9**).

Because natural resources are depletable and unsustainable, most African SWFs have development and diversification mandates that include investing in the innovation and technology sectors of their economies, as well as supporting Small and Medium Scale Enterprises (SMEs). Looking forward, the digital transformation is the biggest story for African next-generation development. With its 1.2 billion inhabitants

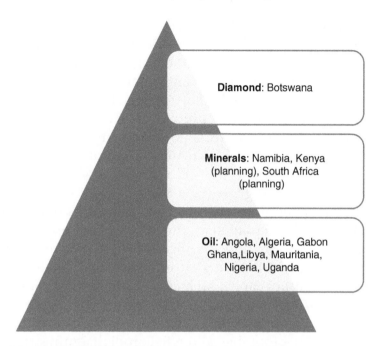

Figure 5.9    African SWFs Largely Funded by Commodity Exports

and rapid deployment of digital technologies, Africa could potentially leapfrog its current development challenges and deploy its youthful population for tech-driven sustainable economic growth, for which the African SIFs may become important tools.

In 2015, the African Union Heads of State and Government adopted Agenda 2063: The Africa We Want ("**Agenda 2063**"). The Agenda 2063 articulates Africa's most pressing development aspirations, including its digital transformation, and seeks to transform the continent into a global economic powerhouse "underpinned by science, technology and innovation" by 2063. Accordingly, it affirms Africa's commitment to developing its digital economy as well as providing information communication technology (ICT) infrastructure that will facilitate manufacturing, skills development, technology, research and development, intra-African trade, and investments in the continent.

In furtherance of the digital aspirations laid down in Agenda 2063, the African Ministers of Communication and Technology adopted the 2019 Sharm El Sheik Declaration, which focuses on the Digital Transformation Strategy for Africa (**DTS Africa**). It plans to develop Africa's digital infrastructure as an enabler for efficient delivery of goods and services across all sectors, including government services, manufacturing, job creation, financial services, agriculture, healthcare, education, and trade. Specifically, the DTS Africa is geared towards creating an Africa "Digital Single Market" by 2030.

Although many different financing sources abound for realizing Africa's digital potentials, the SIFs are well placed to catalyze digital transformation in Africa through long-term investments to bridge: (a) the digital infrastructure financing gap and (b) the venture capital financing gap across the continent.

**Digital infrastructure.** The DTS Africa highlighted that the digital transformation in Africa is being hampered by lack of reliable, affordable, and efficient digital infrastructure, such as "broadband and high speed networks, terrestrial optic fiber networks, fiber over power lines, submarine cables, satellite communication, mobile communication, IXPs, postal infrastructure, digital terrestrial broadcasting, data centers." Currently, antiquated infrastructure, inadequate broadband penetration, and poor Internet and telecommunication services are the major bottlenecks stifling the growth of Africa's digital economy.

There is huge room for African SIFs to lead the way in developing the continent's infrastructure, especially the new telecommunication and digital infrastructure. In addition to direct investing into projects, the African sovereign funds can bring in equity co-investors and guarantee the debt of infrastructure projects to bring in more international long-term capital. As illustrated in the NSIA and InfraCredit case, credit enhancement by local African SIFs can catalyze debt financing from pensions, insurance companies, and other institutional investors to facilitate infrastructure investments.

**Venture capital financing.** Compared to digital infrastructure investing, the African SIFs can become even more profound catalysts by making venture investments and boosting the entrepreneurial ecosystems. Venture capital (VC) financing, typically provides interest free, collateral free, long-term equity finance to startups, allowing for funding that is much more "entrepreneur-friendly" than short-term collateral requiring interest-bearing bank lending. The sovereign funds are well positioned to fill the VC void and enable African entrepreneurs.

Since the last decade, Africa has experienced a startup boom led by the rapid penetration of Internet access, uptake of smartphones by users, and the spread of digital social networks. Just like the large population of mobile Internet users in China, in Africa, especially in rural areas, the Internet users are "mobile only" and "mobile first" – their first and only Internet experience is often mobile instead of PC-based – the moment they start using a smartphone. Although Africa's digital ecosystem is still considered small by Silicon Valley standards, it is considered one of the fastest growing technology markets globally, based on the volume of activities and year on year expansion of tech hubs, venture capital (VC) activities, and startup formation across the continent.

Currently, Africa has more than 400 active tech hubs, accelerators, and incubators, and Nigeria, Kenya, and South Africa are some of the leading countries, and host well-known clubs like CcHub of Nigeria and iHub of Kenya. Young digital entrepreneurs are emerging in Africa that attract global players' attention. Take Andela in Nigeria, for example. This is a software company that trains Africa's software developers for contract work with Fortune 500 companies remotely. They received a $24 million investment from Facebook founder Mark Zuckerberg's foundation in 2016, followed by $100 million investment round led by former US Vice President Al Gore's investment firm.

---

**BongoHive Buzzes with Tech Startups**

The Digital Economy Report 2019 from UNCTAD profiles one tech hub that started informally and rose to run a World Bank-funded project "Zambia AgriBusiness BootCamp." BongoHive, in Lusaka, **Zambia,** has evolved from its beginnings in 2011 as an informal meeting place for software developers into a support system for entrepreneurs to stress test ideas, start businesses, accelerate growth, and secure investment.

The hub began simply as a way for enthusiasts to gather to exchange ideas that would help them bridge the divide between their academic studies and the real world of software and tech solutions. That led to hackathons, workshops, "fireside chats" with established entrepreneurs, and other events to foster knowledge-sharing and networking.

From 2016, BongoHive added programs aimed at supporting startups. Several have succeeded, including ZPOS, an android mobile app which allows SMEs to track sales, manage inventory, and run P&Ls through their point-of-sales systems. Another, Musanga, has pivoted from food delivery to logistics. Plans call for adding an incubator program "Thrive" intended to facilitate shared business support systems for startups, including HR and accounting.

Digital technologies have spawned a variety of startups. As noted, in 2018, the World Bank program was launched for agribusiness. But that is only one of the sectors – delivery, edtech events management, fashion, fintech, professional services, to mention a few – that keep things buzzing at BongoHive.

---

Some of the existing hubs already have funding and operation partnerships with development finance institutions like the World Bank, which can be supported or expanded by African SIFs (see **Box: BongoHive Buzzes with Tech Startups**). Since 2019, NSIA has teamed with two development finance institutions – Bank of Industry and Afreximbank – to develop special economic zones (SEZs) in Nigeria. The focus of SEZs is on export-oriented manufacturing, with new technology and processes a main theme. It would be only natural to expect that NSIA will soon become a leading sponsor for innovation hubs in coming years.

In fact, the NSIA in its short lifetime has already made the largest number of fund investments in venture capital and private equity funds of any domestic institutional investor in

Nigeria. It's poised to become a leading player in Nigeria's innovation ecosystem – similar to the case of Mubadala and its Hub71 in UAE – cultivating and sustaining more unicorns like Jumia (see **Box: Short-lived First Unicorn**).

## Short-lived First Unicorn: The Amazon of Africa

The rise of the e-commerce marketplace, Jumia Technologies AG, testifies to the boom of mobile Internet economy in Nigeria. According to a 2019 media interview by Nigeria's Vice President, at about 200 million GSM phone users, Nigeria is in the top ten of telephone users in the world, and like China it is also a "mobile only" Internet economy, i.e., it has a high percentage (more than 95%) of people who use Internet on their mobile phones. As a result, the country ranks high on the mobile Internet banking scale of the world. Following from that is the ever-growing number of tech startups.

In 2012, Jumia was founded in Lagos, Nigeria, which led the early years of African online shopping developments, before expanding its presence across more than ten African countries. Jumia's marketplace supports electronics, fashion, and other retail sales with a simultaneous payment service, which facilitates the transactions between sellers and consumers. Like Amazon in the US, Jumia also provides logistics services, which enable the shipment and delivery of packages.

After seven years of rapid growth, Jumia had its public listing on the New York Stock Exchange with a US $200 million IPO in April 2019. That was a huge milestone for Africa's venture industry: for one, Jumia was the first VC-backed startup operating in Africa to get listed on a major global exchange; for another, for the first time ever, a Nigerian company was valued at over $1 billion, which sent Jumia into the global unicorn universe of billion-dollar companies.

For a moment, Jumia was set to be the Amazon of Africa. To that end, the company's website even copied the font, color schemes, and product arrangements directly from Amazon.com. But its crown as the first African unicorn didn't stay in place long due to its operational issues. From a peak price of $49.99, Jumia stock fell off a cliff and shortly the share price fell below its IPO price of $14.50. By March 2020, the stock was trading at around $2 a share.

It remains uncertain whether Jumia can build up a solid e-commerce business across Africa and, hopefully, a fintech business as well like Alibaba in China. The bottom line is that merely making it to an IPO on the New York Stock Exchange is in itself a great achievement for the African startup. To enable more African entrepreneurs to develop their startups into unicorns – and stay there – the sovereign funds in Africa have a lot to contribute.

Like NSIA in Nigeria, many African countries have modified the mandate of their SWFs to include fostering innovation and developing the local digital economy. For example, **Angola's Fundo Soberano de Angola (FSDA)** has established the "Mezzanine Investment Fund," which will focus on emerging sectors including startups and provide venture financing, with a view to meeting the financing needs of entrepreneur-driven sectors of the Angolan economy. Furthermore, FSDA allocates 7.5% of its capital to the Social Charter, which is dedicated to investing in viable projects that will generate sustainable wealth through entrepreneurial development. Recently the subject of an attempted diversion of funds and looting, fortunately for the entrepreneurs of Angola, FSDA has regained its assets to fund this and other programs (see **Box: When Good Governance Fails**).

---

### When Good Governance Fails, Employ other Methods

With her assets frozen, Isabel dos Santos, daughter of Angola's former President (who left after nearly 40 years in office) has been featured in the press in recent years and touted as "the richest woman in Africa" and been the subject of allegations of corruption and theft of state assets. The storyline has eclipsed that of her brother, Jose Filomena dos Santos, former head of Angola's sovereign wealth fund. A pity. His is a colorful story.

Involving a cast of characters out of "Ocean's Eleven," as the *Wall Street Journal* put it, the tale of the looting of the fund in the days before the elder Mr. dos Santos left office does have a Hollywood tone to it.

Reportedly, in a scheme hatched at the Portuguese beach city of Cascais and involving shell companies, Jose Filomena dos Santos allegedly arranged to have $500 million of Angola's funds wired to the London account of Perfectbit Ltd, a company registered to the North London address of an accountant. An alert teller at a suburban HSBC branch contacted her superiors after being requested to transfer to Tokyo $2 million from the newly opened account which suddenly had a $500 million balance. Ultimately, after HSBC froze Perfectbit's account, the $500 million found its way back to Angola. Arrests followed for the accountant and others allegedly involved in the UK. Jose Filomena dos Santos was detained and charged in Angola after being removed as head of the fund.

But that was just the tip of the iceberg. In December 2019, the country announced it had recovered an additional $3 billion stolen from its sovereign wealth fund, saying a business partner of the younger dos Santos returned the huge sum, without further explanation. The funds had reportedly been in banks in Britain and Mauritius.

Around the same time, Jose Filomena dos Santos was released from custody, although not cleared in the $500 million fraud case. Good governance was evidently lacking at the fund. But the government also evidently had access to other means – not necessarily found in the "best practices" handbooks – to compensate for its absence. In any event, it got its Hollywood ending.

Some other African SIFs have also embarked on creating venture capital funds to meet the funding needs of local startups. The **Strategic Investment fund of Gabon** backed the venture fund Okoume Capital to finance entrepreneurship in the country. In Rwanda, the **Rwanda Innovation Fund (RIF)** provides venture financing to local entrepreneurs, and the RIF is building a $420 million Digital Innovation Precinct within the Kigali Innovation City. With increased assets under management, experience in venture investing, and learning from the global venture capital community through VC fund investments, the market will see African SIFs getting increasingly comfortable with venture investments into tech startups.

In summary, more and more African sovereign investment funds are finetuning their strategies to increase their focus on technology and innovation investing. They will play a critical role in financing the digital infrastructure gap and venture capital gap in the continent. However, the African funds are quite small and young (mostly established in the last two decades, with a few billion dollars of capital under management) compared to more established sovereign funds. Co-investing with peer SIFs, therefore, should be a top priority for the African funds when they join the hunt for unicorns in the innovation economy.

### The Rise of Strategic Collaboration Rising

Years ago, "sovereign wealth funds" referred to those primarily established to manage a global investment portfolio and provide intergenerational savings, whereas "sovereign development funds" were domestically oriented funds with a pure local agenda. In the age of digital revolution, more sovereign funds are making tech investments both overseas and domestically, hence the line between "sovereign wealth funds" and "sovereign development funds" becoming increasingly blurred. And more funds on the same track are being established and planned. (In this book, sovereign investment fund – SIF – is used to cover both.)

The case studies on the ISIF of Ireland, Mubadala of UAE, and the NSIA of Nigeria have shown how these sovereign funds can serve multiple functions. They promote their own countries' digital economy development, attract foreign capital, and achieve financial returns at the same time. Furthermore, these double bottom-line investment considerations are not a topic specific to sovereign wealth funds, particularly given the rising importance of environmental, social, and governance (ESG) and "impact" considerations among the international pension fund community. Public pensions may invest into emerging markets' innovation ecosystem for UN sustainable development (SDG) considerations.

On the receiving end of the emerging markets, their SIFs are part of the solution as well, because they are the necessary local counterpart to foreign co-investments. In less developed countries, their SIFs signal credibility and maturity of the local economy to foreign investors. As such, a collaborative investment model is emerging, where the SIFs develop joint platforms among themselves to invest in long-term projects together, and the global economy will see SIFs collectively making an increasingly bigger impact in the less-developed markets. For example, the **Indonesian** government as mentioned is establishing a sovereign wealth fund modeled on Temasek and has formed a partnership with Mubadala.

Another neighborhood pairing of SIFs has arisen on the Malay peninsula, where high-income **Singapore** abuts middle-income **Malaysia.** As mentioned in the introduction to this chapter, **Khazanah** has a dual mandate including domestic development. A high-profile investment has been the development of Iskandar special economic zone, sometimes called "Malaysia's Shenzhen," as it sits across a short strait from Singapore. (The city of Shenzhen is a major tech hub of China, across the river from Hong Kong.)

The massive development, which has reportedly attracted $25 billion in foreign investment into Malaysia, contemplates the development of four artificial islands, each with its own theme. The first is a digital smart city targeted at high tech with the hope of luring tech companies to relocate from Singapore to lower cost Iskandar in Malaysia. Another of the islands, Medini, is the site of the project's central business district and tourism sector. A 50:50 joint venture between **Temasek** and Khazanah was formed to develop two wellness-themed resorts there.

In the Middle East, **Egypt** and **Saudi Arabia** announced the launch of a $16 billion joint development fund in 2016, funded by Saudi Arabia for development in Egypt. Egypt certainly could use the money. Its own sovereign fund, the Sovereign Fund of Egypt, set up in 2018, is looking for foreign investors to participate in the privatization of army-owned assets, including infrastructure. Its authorized capital is $13 billion, small by SIF standards, and not even yet fully funded – with only $63 million paid in as of early 2020. The balance will arrive in the form of state-owned assets which it hopes to privatize through a 2020 deal with private equity fund sponsor Actis.

In **Canada, CDPQ** presents an example of a public pension in an advanced economy that has embraced its dual role of long-term management of pension assets with a mission to develop the local Quebec economy. Pairing with government, CDPQ has directly invested in Quebec infrastructure for local economic development. Speaking in 2017 of CPDQ's investment in REM, a high-speed rail system to serve Montreal,

Michael Sabia, then CEO of CDPQ, made the link of dual objectives, "We want to put this expertise [of infrastructure management], acquired in Europe, the United States and Australia, to work here in Québec."

As mentioned at the beginning of this chapter, the European countries fear that they are behind the tech revolution curve. In fact, the US and China have the world's top 20 largest tech companies, and they are also the home base of the world's super-majority of unicorn startups. To cover this tech gap, the EU is currently contemplating a pan-European sovereign investment fund to promote "tech champions of Europe" (see related discussions in **Chapter 1**). At the individual country level, some have already set up their own SIFs with the mission to attract foreign capital and invest into new tech sectors. The ISIF of Ireland is a great example, and countries like Italy and France are also marching forward aggressively.

**Italy**'s economy is characterized by small enterprises and a low technological level of production (despite its reputation for excellence), which is challenged by the tech revolution and globalization trends. Even though Italy is the eighth largest economy in the world and fourth largest European economy in terms of GDP, its tech ecosystem is still underdeveloped. The lack of tech development is a heavy burden for corporations. Not only are the companies not fully covered by broadband connectivity, but also there is a delay in the corporate adoption of technology for management of supply chain and business activities.

Italy's sovereign fund Fondo Strategico Italiano (**FSI, Italian Strategic Fund**) was established in 2011 under the state-controlled lender Cassa Depositi e Prestiti Group SpA (CDP). In its early years, its main mission was to acquire and manage direct holdings in companies of "significant national interest" and help them to compete globally. Such transactions included investments in manufacturing, bio-pharmaceutical, aerospace, as well as high-speed Internet connectivity (for example, the 2012 investment into fibre-optic company Metroweb Italy spa). Notably, its 2014 transaction

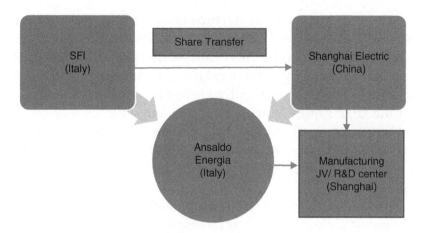

Figure 5.10    FSI/SEC – China/Italy Tech Transfer Transaction

with Shanghai Electric of China (SEC) well played out the "cross-border expansion" investment theme (see **Figure 5.10**).

In 2014, SFI sold 40% of power engineering company Ansaldo Energia (AEN) to SEC for €400 million. Headquartered in Shanghai, the SEC is a leading diversified heavy industrial equipment manufacturing group in China. Following the investment, two joint ventures between AEN and SEC were formed in China – one for manufacturing gas turbines for Asian markets and, for another, the creation of an R&D center in Shanghai. The deal enabled AEN to boost sales by entering the Asian Chinese market and gave the Chinese access to the Italian company's gas turbine technology for its clean energy equipment businesses.

On 31 March 2016, Fondo Strategico Italiano was renamed **CDP Equity** and it remains wholly owned by the CDP Group. In recent years, it has focused more on its parallel mission to "support the innovation and competitiveness of the Italian industrial system." To that end, CDP Equity has signed co-investment agreements with top SIFs like Samruk-Kazyna (Kazakhstan), Kuwait Investment Authority (KIA), Qatar Investment Authority (QIA), Korea Investment Corporation (KIC), Russian Direct Investment Fund (RDIF), and China Investment Corporation (CIC).

At a time when Italian startups are creating a new generation of entrepreneurs, CDP Equity's effort to bring more global capital and network into the country is invaluable. In 2018, CIC proposed establishing a bilateral fund, namely the China–Italy Industrial Cooperation Fund, to invest into Italian enterprises, and the CDP Equity is involved in the ongoing discussions. In mid-2019, a new €1 billion fund Fondo Italiano Innovazione (**FII, Italian Innovation Fund**) was set up (under CDP again) to specifically invest in tech startups and attract more capital from overseas.

**France** has similarly explored setting up collaborative investment platforms to attract foreign investment to the country. The **Caisse des Dépôts' (CDC)** objective is "to make a major contribution to attracting foreign capital to multiple asset classes in order to provide long-term finance for the French economy and improve its competitiveness." The Russian RDIF, Russia's Bank for Foreign Economic Affairs, and the CDC signed a 2013 Memorandum of Understanding to develop cooperation in direct investment between the two countries.

Similarly, CDC in 2016 entered into a memorandum of understanding with **CIC of China** for the development of a joint investment fund for infrastructure projects in the greater Paris metro area. This is a notable turnaround from the 2008 creation of the **Fonds Strategique d'Investissement** (51% owned by CDC and 49% by the French government) when then President Sarkozy made it clear that the new fund had a defensive aspect, in light of the rising alarm at SIF investment in the French economy. Times change.

The **Russian Direct Investment Fund (RDIF)** is especially active in developing co-investing relationships with peers to attract capital to Russia. It has developed numerous collaborative platforms with various countries, including deep ties with China. In 2012, CIC and RDIF established the Russia–China Investment Fund (RCIF) together to enhance

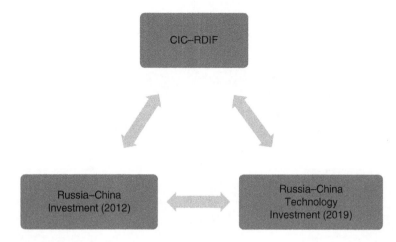

Figure 5.11    **RDIF–CIC's New Focus on Tech**

economic cooperation and investments between Russia and China (see **Figure 5.11**). The RCIF fund received $2 billion commitments from RDIF and CIC on an equal basis. In 2019, and focusing on tech innovation, RDIF partnered with CIC again to establish a $1 billion Russia–China Technology Investment Fund; in the same year, RDIF teamed up with China's Internet giant Alibaba Group, among others, to create a social commerce platform.

Overall, the SIF co-investment platform mechanism probably is the most important for sovereign funds in frontier markets like Africa. Most African sovereign funds are below $5 billion in size (Algeria and Libya are the rare exceptions with more $50 billion each under management), hence the co-investing peer SIFs can significantly scale up capital injection into investment projects. For example, **Ithmar Capital of Morocco** established Wessal Capital (see **Figure 5.12**), a co-investment vehicle for Morocco infrastructure investments, through which it raised $2.5 billion from major SIFs from the Middle East, including PIF (Saudi Arabia), KIA (Kuwait), QIA (Qatar), and Mubadala (UAE).

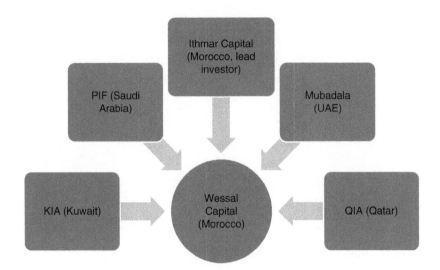

Figure 5.12    **Morocco Leveraging Middle East Capital**

Another obvious benefit is that investing alongside mature and established institutional investors helps to increase the acceptability of African SIFs in the global financial community, thereby enhancing their reputation and legitimacy in pursuit of their mandates. Subsequently, the African SIFs could signal the credibility and maturity of the local economy to foreign investors, thus making their home countries more attractive to overseas capital.

The more profound benefit of co-investing for African SIFs is to improve fund governance and transparency. To increase their chances of effectively stimulating digital transformation in Africa, African SIFs must overcome extant challenges including their poor governance and disclosure scorecard, which reduces their international credibility. While some African funds like the NSIA have been scored high on governance and transparency, there is still little or no insight into how most African SIFs operate. For example, the SIFs of **Mauritania, Libya, Equatorial Guinea, and Algeria** were the lowest ranked in this regard, with almost no financial disclosures.

## Who Are You Calling a "Political Animal"?

"Every sovereign wealth fund is a political animal," Zafer Sonmez, CEO of the $33 billion **Turkey Wealth Fund,** was quoted by the *Financial Times* as saying on February 18, 2020. Responding to attacks that President Erdogan was using Turkey's sovereign wealth fund to political ends, Mr. Sonmez, former head of the Turkey office of Khazanah, went on to say "Can someone say to me, for example, that GIC of Singapore, chaired by the prime minister of Singapore, has no political relationship . . . [or that] the Public Investment Fund in Saudi Arabia, chaired by [Saudi crown prince] Mohammed bin Salman . . . is not politically related?"

Well, it did not take long before he heard from someone. The next day, on February 19, the *Financial Times* published a letter from no less than Singapore's Ministry of Finance in the person of Lim Zhi Jian, the Ministry's Director (Reserves & Investment). He put it succinctly, in five short paragraphs, concluding: "Governance models for SWFs will vary, and there is no one right approach. Singapore's SWF model combines state ownership with autonomous operations insulated from political pressures. It has worked for us." (If PIF also wrote a letter, it was not run by the *FT.*)

The rare public exchange highlights the sensitivity of the issue of political influence to SIFs. The issue often has resonance within the host country, as politicians and the public look for apparent conflicts or inequities. We will see in Chapter 7 the furor raised by Texas legislators over seemingly posh new offices for that state's public pension fund for teachers. And in Chapters 8 and 9, the specter of political or policy motives behind investments by SIFs is raised in support of stricter and stricter national security reviews for government-linked investors.

As Mr. Sonmez's fund is largely domestically focused, the latter concern may not be paramount. For GIC, which by its mandate only invests outside Singapore, and for Temasek, which has expanded from a domestic investor to a regional and global player, being seen as commercially motivated is key to executing their strategies.

Hence, their co-investing with well-established sovereign funds will bring valuable learning such as peer reviews, capacity-building, and sharing of institutional knowledge and best practices. Meanwhile, the involvement of global sovereign funds could also help the African SIFs properly deal with political interference, as domestic investments often lead to excessive involvement by politicians in operations (see **Box: Who Are You Calling a "Political Animal"?**).

Worse, political intervention may also lead to a higher risk of political rent-seeking (see **Box: When Good Governance Fails**), especially for countries with fewer experienced professionals, weaker regulations and accountability, and poorer investment opportunities. The loose definitions of "economic development" may be employed by government officials, and sovereign capital could be forced into inefficient or politically driven domestic investments. The presence of an experienced foreign SIF (even better if institutional investors, pensions, and development banks appear as well) in a transaction could act as a counterweight, helping to prevent potential deviations from economic and sustainable development.

In summary, the previous chapters focused on sovereign investors' global hunt for tech unicorns, mostly in leading innovation hubs like the US and China; meanwhile, this chapter examines an emerging global trend to use sovereign investment funds for developing tech industry sectors and diversifying their domestic economies. Therefore, a striking number of SIFs are both development finance institutions in their own countries and major players of development throughout the world. As they move ever closer to the source of digital innovation, they are already acting as powerful agents of development. The result is exciting progress in tackling imbalanced economies in the world.

*There's little evidence that the German pension plans took heed of the advice, recounted in this chapter's introduction, to seed venture capital in Germany rather than invest in Italian government bonds. There is a German listed company, Rocket Internet, that has successfully invested in startups. Maybe it should have followed the advice about investing in German startups.*

*A sort of Vision Fund with family office money, Rocket has made and successfully exited numerous venture investments in startups in Europe. However, on April 2, 2020, it announced that it had exited its 11% holding in the ill-starred "Amazon of Africa," Jumia, after having seen the e-commerce company's US listed shares plummet from a high of $49.99 to $2 in a year, as described in this chapter.*

*Rocket is still sitting on more than $2.3 billion in cash after the exit and so no tears are being shed for it. Its diversified venture investments have produced the requisite home runs to more than balance out Jumias.*

*Something tells us, nonetheless, that we are not going to see the German pension funds transform themselves any time soon into early and nimble venture investors in Germany, let alone elsewhere in the world, as our next chapter shows that leading SIFs have done.*

C H A P T E R

# Go Early, Go Nimble

*Looking less like the unicorn tapestries and more like the Brothers Grimm, the story of WeWork and its pulled IPO is a fairy tale without a happy ending for its investors, although the SIFs have largely managed to escape the reputational hit taken by Vision Fund. In the tale of Snow White, the seven dwarves return from their shared workspace one day to find their beloved Snow White asleep under a spell broken only by the kiss of a handsome prince. Unfortunately for the investors, the CEO did not turn out to be the handsome prince and the company never cast off the evil spell after filing for its IPO.*

*Fueled by the magic of endless capital, WeWork transformed the workplace in cities around the world, becoming the largest single tenant in New York City in the process. Its principal backer, Vision Fund, injected billions of sovereign investment funds' (SIF) cash into a transformative phenomenon. Although not truly a "tech" company, WeWork and its founder, Adam Neumann, benefited from the fairy tale rise of the tech unicorns.*

*Then everyone woke up when the IPO was filed in August 2019 and the fairy tale was over: it turned out that Adam Neumann was no handsome prince. According to the* Wall Street Journal, *during the IPO process, Neuman and friends chartered a private jet to Israel, smoking marijuana en route, and leaving a cereal box crammed with the substance on board for the return flight. Reports of tequila shots at company meetings and the purchase by the loss-making company of a $60 million corporate jet also contributed to the questioning of his management style and judgment.*

*In October 2019, Neumann was ousted as CEO (with a "happily ever after" payout of over $1.7 billion). Masayoshi Son and the Vision Fund took over the company at a valuation of $8 billion to avert financial disaster and the IPO was "postponed indefinitely." By the end of November 2019, over 2400 WeWork employees had been laid off, never to return to their shared workspace.*

The WeWork story is not just about a first-time massive venture fund (equipped with an unheard-of $100 billion in venture capital) invested into an eccentric startup founder. In the decades before the current tech boom, one recurrent theme has been the hazard of the increased availability of open checkbooks of passive investors seeking outsize returns without the scrutiny and attendant discipline of public markets. That tendency was exacerbated by the rise of the sovereign funds, their entry into the hunt for the unicorns, and overstretched startup valuations from mega venture capital (VC) fundraising. Even before the impact of the pandemic, cracks were showing in the WeWork façade.

## The Year WeWork Failed to Work

January 2019 was an auspicious start for WeWork. At a valuation of $47 billion, the iconoclastic unicorn was transforming the office workplace. It was the largest commercial office tenant in New York City, and it provided furnished, shared office space to startups and some of the world's largest companies. Traditional real estate developers and landlords emulated its millennial-friendly workplaces as WeWork itself expanded into residential and other ventures outside its core office space business.

From its founding in 2009, WeWork raised substantial amounts in the private markets with ever increasing valuations. Benchmark started the action with a $17.5 million Series A investment. DAG Ventures bought in at a later round at a $440 million valuation. JPMorgan, at $1.5 billion. T. Rowe Price came in at a $5 billion valuation in late 2014. Six months later, Fidelity Investments followed at a $10 billion valuation round.

Then things really got rolling when sovereign investor-backed Vision Fund and its manager SoftBank, headed by Masayoshi Son, came along in 2016, investing $4.4 billion into the startup. By the beginning of 2019, with Son putting in over

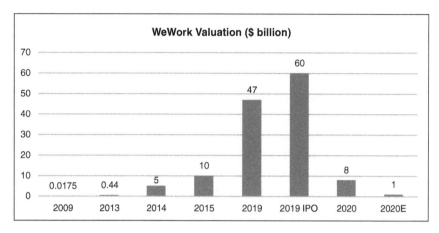

Figure 6.1    The Rise and Fall of WeWork

$10 billion cumulatively, WeWork was valued at $47 billion, all without a public market check. For its IPO, investment bankers were engaged to offer the public the opportunity to top even this lofty figure and invest at a valuation of $60 billion or more (see **Figure 6.1**).

As a leading sharing economy unicorn, it checked all the boxes of the "growth at any cost" model, championed by Softbank's Masayoshi Son and underwritten by the SIF investors who were the LPs. But it was attracting attention for other reasons as well. Its business model predicated committing its balance sheet to long-term leases and deriving its revenues from short-term occupancies. The skeptics were many. *The Financial Times* characterized earlier valuations of WeWork as built "on thin air." When Wall Street began looking at the books of the company with the mission statement: "to elevate the world's consciousness" for IPO preparation, the scrutiny – and skepticism – intensified.

In the summer of 2019, things began to come apart – and down to earth. Disclosures of the mounting losses, the lack of a path to profitability, the presence of nepotism, and comparable market multiples all contributed to reducing the valuation to less than half of the January figure. Within a month, the valuation was slashed from $47 billion to under $10 billion. By the end of October, the IPO had been canceled, the CEO replaced, and Vision Fund had acquired 80% of the equity as the valuation was slashed to $8 billion. By April 2020, Softbank decided to walk away from the planned buyout, which resulted in a litigation between the two (hence, for Figure **6.1**, $1 billion is used for the 2020 estimated valuation as a pure guess).

WeWork is not a unique case. The marketplace for "innovation" – the commercialization of new research and technology – is complex, opaque, and, by its very nature, risky and inefficient for institutional investors (on a deal-by-deal basis). Technology risk, market risk, business model validation, and execution risk all await the early stage technology players. Uber, the San Francisco-based car-sharing app unicorn, is another example.

As its first high-profile foray, **PIF,** before the formation of Vision Fund, in 2016 injected $3.5 billion into Uber, giving the startup a $62 billion valuation. Softbank then made a $1.2 billion direct investment in the company at the end of 2017, but by 2020, Uber's value had dropped below $45 billion. (Just like WeWork, Uber had significant losses from its operation.) This represents a massive loss for Vision Fund and even worse for the investing public: Uber IPO-ed in 2018 at a valuation of over $82 billion. As mentioned, the PIF also had a direct stake in Tesla, the electric-car manufacturer, which apparently also led to a significant loss for the investor.

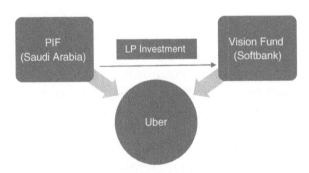

Figure 6.2    **Compounded Investments into Uber by PIF and Vision Fund**

## Temasek: Bumpy Road even for Established Players

The challenge of tech investment is not limited to a first time $100-billion venture fund and unconventional startup founders. Even an experienced SIF investor like **Temasek** has encountered failures along the way.

The most prominent among these probably is NIO – a five-year-old electric vehicle startup making its name as a premium brand – which has cultivated a devoted fan base and managed to meet its delivery goals for last year, all without even having its own factory. Created in 2014, NIO positions itself as a Chinese rival to Tesla, and it was pitched heavily to institutional investors before its IPO in 2018. According to media reports, Softbank looked into NIO's stock during the company's IPO roadshow, but eventually Masayoshi Son (wisely) decided to pass on the investment.

In June 2016, NIO announced its C round of financing led by Temasek. That round of financing raised several hundreds of millions of dollars. Investors included leading PE funds like TPG, HOPU, and Lenovo Group. These sophisticated PE funds were following Temasek, validating its position as an established investor in the VC arena.

Over NIO's short, five-year lifespan, total losses exceeded $5 billion (it took Tesla 15 years to cross that threshold). At the end of 2019, the company disclosed another big loss (again) for

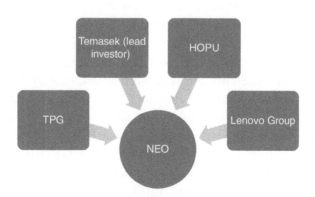

Figure 6.3    Temasek Led the June 2016 Financing Round of NIO

the quarter and reported an early warning on "going-concern" risk. Its tale of woes does not end there. NIO recalled 5000 vehicles in 2019 and ran a negative gross margin on its sales. The company postponed its earnings calls for two successive quarters and its CFO resigned. There was likely little champagne popped even though it held its annual shareholders meeting in 2019 on New Year's Eve.

At its lowest level in early 2020, NIO's stock fell more than 70% from its IPO valuation. After NIO was listed, Temasek's SEC filing in February 2019 showed that it owned 5.4% of the company. One year later, according to an updated SEC filing, by early 2020 Temasek's ownership in NIO had dropped to 1.8%.

In another foray into the Chinese market, Temasek had its own share of investing in the "sharing economy," such as Uber's Chinese counterpart Didi Chuxing, whose schedule for IPO is still unknown. (Temasek is an investor in Uber rival Grab in South-east Asia as well.) What's interesting is that China's sharing economy has veered away from the term's original meaning: as a peer-to-peer exchange of underutilized goods and services. Unlike Airbnb and Uber, which provide a platform that connects users to underutilized, existing resources like spare rooms and private cars, the sharing economy in China has evolved into something like an Internet-enabled rental business, where the sharing companies own assets of all kinds that they hope to rent out to users.

Of course, not all new ideas will work out. Most of the sharing services need to put in substantial upfront capital investments to acquire the goods before "sharing" (or "renting"), whether large, like cars and bikes or small, like umbrellas and portable batteries, but the fee per use is set very low in order to attract the largest possible pool of users. As a result, young companies are constantly in the capital markets to raise funding, whereas their paths to profitability are far from clear. For some, there is a fundamental question on whether users have a real need to share those products, or whether the underlying goods are suitable for sharing (see **Box: The Worst Idea Ever Heard**).

### The Worst Idea Ever Heard

The umbrella sharing startup E Umbrella was much laughed at for its questionable business model. For a start, compared to a car or even a bike, an umbrella is a lot cheaper, which raises the question of whether it is something people prefer to own or even like to share.

E Umbrella launched with an investment of 10 million RMB yuan (approximately $1.47 million), charging users 20 RMB (nearly US$3 dollars) for the first time use, plus 19 yuan per umbrella as a deposit, and an additional yuan ($ 0.07) for one hour's use. Immediately China's netizens questioned the business logic. "The company demands a 20-yuan deposit fee," some commented, "I have a better idea than that – Go buy a new umbrella with that 20 RMB."

Furthermore, E Umbrella seemed to overlook the fact that, unlike bikes, umbrellas have to be kept at fixed locations. Bikes can be "docking free" and parked anywhere, but an umbrella needs to be hung on railings or a fence. In practice, E Umbrella's stands were set across the cities near train and bus stations, which limited its convenience value for the broad population.

For the same reason, it was also challenging for the company to ensure that users would return the umbrellas to the stands when done with them. Most users just ended up keeping their rentals – or did what they did with their own umbrellas, forgetting where they left it after the last use. According to news reports, just under three months after launch, E Umbrella had lost almost all of its 300,000 umbrellas across 11 Chinese cities.

Actually, the shared umbrella idea was not from China alone; the same venture idea also appeared in the US market. One startup named BrellaBox pitched a similar concept on Shark Tank, and the venture pitch was called "the worst idea ever heard" on the show by one of the panelists. To be fair, one could easily fill many episodes of Shark Tank with sharing economy ideas competing for the "worst idea ever heard" title.

For example, folding stools were put on the streets of Beijing near bus stops and train stations to be shared. Similar to bikes and umbrellas, the stools also have a QR code on their seats to be scanned before being used. However, they are fundamentally different from bikes and umbrellas in that the goods to be shared are not even "mobile": people don't have to move the stools when using them. Hence, many people reacted with ridicule on social networks: "If I just sat on the stool without scanning, would the company know?"

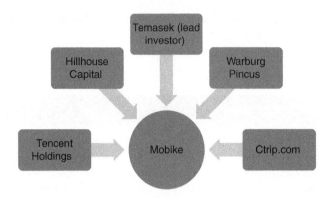

Figure 6.4    **Temasek Led the February 2017 Financing Round of Mobike**

During the bike sharing boom, Temasek jumped on Mobike, one of leading players in this crowded market. The business involved no intellectual property and the startup companies copied each other, competing on price and availability. Since 2016, the sidewalks in China's major cities were filled with a rainbow assortment of colorful "sharable" bicycles, in orange (Mobike), or yellow (Ofo, Mobike's main rival, whose investors included the ride-hailing startup Didi Chuxing), or blue (Bluegogo), or other color combinations.

In February 2017, Temasek Holdings and PE fund Hillhouse Capital led one major funding round of Mobike, with other investors including Internet giant Tencent Holdings, asset manager Warburg Pincus, and Chinese travel firm Ctrip .com International (see **Figure 6.4**). However, even these deep-pocket investors were not sufficient for the cash burn of Mobike, as the race for market share among essentially identical startups soon intensified. In the fall of 2017, there were up to 70 bike-sharing brands with 16 million cycles on the streets for a customer base of about 130 million, according to China's Ministry of Transport.

Mobike successfully expanded into 170 cities worldwide, owning 7 million bikes and claiming more than 100 million customers. But, at the same time, its losses were also mounting due to:

- **Large capital expenditure:** Typically, sharing economy platforms don't necessarily own the operating assets: Airbnb doesn't own hotels nor does Uber own cars. But the bike sharing companies have to expend capital to buy and own all the bikes.
- **High operating costs:** The companies need to maintain bicycles and replace the damaged ones. They need to repair, repaint, and reinstall locks on old bikes, and turn them back into inventory ready for use.
- **Low revenue:** All the bike-sharing companies are providing essentially the same commodity service, which leads to an oversupply. Price per ride is very low to start with, and, to compete for more market share and active users, companies have to provide various discounts and incentives for riders.

Since 2018, many of the bike sharing startups have declared bankruptcy. Their former fleets of various color were dumped at "bike graveyards" scattered across major cities and their outskirts, forming a decaying monument to an investment craze. Mobike survived (sort of): it was acquired in April 2018 for nearly $3 billion by Meituan-Dianping, the largest mobile life services platform. Starting in group discounts and restaurant reviews (hence it is often described as China's version of Groupon and Yelp combined), Meituan-Dianping sought to build a "super app" offering consumers everything from online retail and food delivery to hotel bookings and taxi rides – and bike rides was added in.

Mobike is now rebranded as "Meituan Bikes." For a mobile platform business like Meituan-Dianping, a bike-sharing company with a big database of users may potentially supply some value. However, it has continued to make losses. According to China's securities firms' research report, Mobike will continue to be loss-making through to 2021 and be a drag on overall company (Meituan) profitability. Of course, Mobike's investors had already done much better than those of bankrupted competitors:

Mobike's acquirer, Meituan-Dianping, achieved a public listing (IPO) in September 2018.

WeWork, whose global meltdown was detailed earlier in this chapter, also had a Chinese episode and Temasek played a role. WeWork China, presently 59% owned by WeWork, added outside investors as well. In 2018, only a year after WeWork China launched, Temasek, along with Softbank, Turnbridge Partners, and others, invested in the second of two $500 million rounds, valuing the unit at roughly $5 billion. Given that the Softbank/Vision Fund rescue in late 2019 valued all of WeWork at only $8 billion, by then the valuation of WeWork China was likely also well below the $5 billion mark at which Temasek invested.

Early in 2020, press reports indicated that Temasek was in talks to increase its stake, together with fellow investor Trust-bridge Partners, to take majority control of WeWork China. The valuation at which the deal was being discussed was about $1 billion – 20% of the valuation at which the two invested back in 2018. This sally into the Chinese workspace sharing economy so far has left Temasek and Turnbridge sharing only losses.

In summary, the "growth at any cost" unicorn business model has created an opportunity for sovereign investors to put large amounts of capital directly in a sector previously inaccessible to them outside VC funds. As a result, the investment environment is conducive to the evolution of unicorns, but also to the risk of investors (not least of which is that the IPO market is not providing the exit path anticipated by those who invested at high valuations). The newer entrants begin to rethink their strategy – not questioning the startup business models but, rather, asking themselves: have we invested too late in the funding cycle of startups?

### New Strategy, New Setup

The cases in this chapter illustrate that implementing an ambitious tech investment program is a daunting challenge for sovereign investors in practice. The fundamental reason is that direct venture investments into the tech sector involve the asset class "furthest away" from the traditional activities of sovereign funds.

For the major sovereign funds, their sweet spot equity check's size is over $100 million for each transaction (for a comparison, most VC funds are between $50 to $500 million in total fund size), as their institutional setup typically is a small staff diversifying a large pool of assets into global public equity and fixed income markets. Even if the funds have the expertise and resources to handle such investments in-house (which is generally not the case, as demonstrated in the following **Chapter 7** covering staffing and recruiting issues in more detail), they often find it difficult or impractical to invest into startups because the deal size they are seeking is too large for the young companies.

That's why the sovereign funds, whether from Middle East or China, Canada or Singapore, have been active in unicorns' late stage financing rounds, often referred to as "growth capital" or "expansion capital." Timing wise, this is the area between venture rounds (Series A, Series B) and IPO (initial public offering), where investments have gone beyond the initial tech risk but still require capital before they might go public (see **Figure 6.5**). Meanwhile, many private market investors like VC funds and private equity (PE) funds (and even peer sovereign funds) have already invested in the startups, which provides a useful reference for late stage sovereign investors.

Dollar size wise, these deals are rather too large and late stage for the venture capital funds, but don't really suit buy-out or listing. Many of these new economy businesses are quite capital-intensive (for example, the "sharing economy" of Uber

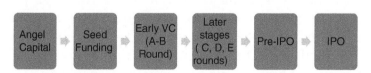

Figure 6.5    **The Life (Financing) Cycle of a Unicorn**

and Mobike), which is attractive for long-horizon investors who have the ability to provide that liquidity. When the startup's valuation reaches a billion dollars, the investment size becomes sufficiently large for the sovereign funds. (Consider that this is actually a challenge for people managing a half-a-trillion-dollar portfolio.) For the startups in their early days, the deal sizes are much smaller, ranging only up to $50 million, and it is difficult for large institutional investors to invest at scale on a direct basis.

However, opportunities in the private equity market often arise by investing early in small firms with high growth potential. Access, capabilities, and timing are fundamental drivers of success in this space. Because many sovereign funds consider themselves long-term investors, their strategies naturally lead to targeting fewer, larger investments than VC funds, hence they like to join the late stage financing rounds of unicorns – frequently the so-called "pre-IPO" round, which by definition means the last round of private market financing before the unicorn gets listed in the public market.

Such late stage investments provide sovereign investors the opportunity to write a large equity check, usually in hundreds of millions of dollars, into an established unicorn that has many years of operating history. Before their investments, there are already branded investors in the company, which may include famous VC funds, blue chip mutual funds, major asset management firms, and other sovereign funds who are active in the field. But all these don't necessarily mean the late stage investments involve less risk. The reality may be the opposite.

**First, startup companies, even quite mature ones, often have far less robust internal controls and governance procedures than most public companies.** Just because a company can raise money from major investors at a very high price, it does not guarantee everything is going well at the company, as the Vision Fund/WeWork case clearly shows. It wasn't until WeWork filed its IPO prospectus that the rest of the venture market saw just how greatly corporate governance was lacking. For example, the company seemed extremely comfortable with transactions involving the CEO/Founder and his affiliates, such as CEO Neumann owning stakes in some of the office buildings that WeWork leases; his wife joining the process of choosing a successor if he is incapacitated; and his family members working for the company's Creator Awards, which its biggest outside shareholder committed $180 million to fund.

**Second, the last round valuation is not the permanent price for startup shares.** During the last tech bubble of 1999–2000, record valuations of "dot-com" startups co-existed with record IPOs, from which shareholders receive transparent pricing and cash liquidity. In recent years, the scenario is the exact opposite, as record private unicorn valuations come hand-in-hand with increasingly fewer and fewer IPOs. Most investors look successful on paper by marking up their holdings' value based on the valuations from private financing rounds of unicorns, but in terms of real public trading and cash-on-cash returns, there are far fewer successful outcomes.

In practice, one shocking reality is that, often, the financial information on the unicorns is quite limited. And when it is presented, it may be presented in a way that is inconsistent with GAAP (Generally Accepted Accounting Principles) standards (see **Figure 6.6**). Because many of them are still far away from operating profitability, their financial reports tend not to proactively address measurements like earnings and profits, nor focus on net revenue or gross margin under GAAP. Instead, they would highlight large number of "active users," high level "gross merchandise value" and "run rate," or even "forward bookings." These favored parameters aim to show the rapid growth of the business, not too different from the

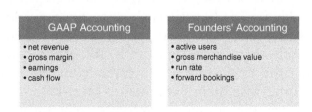

Figure 6.6    **GAAP Accounting vs. Founders' Accounting**

"eyeballs" and "website visits" used by the "dot-com" founders two decades ago.

Even if an audit is included, it might have massive "qualifications," where the auditor lists all the reasons that this particular audit may not comply with GAAP standards and highlights that things could change materially if they dig in deeper. Even for the unicorns in the "pre-IPO" rounds, there is often a relative absence of pertinent financial information with nothing approaching the formal disclosure in an IPO prospectus. (In fact, some unicorns delayed their IPO listing plans after their "pre-IPO" rounds and went on to seek additional financing in the private market.)

**Third**, **famous investors from early rounds are not a proxy for due diligence.** When there are branded investors already in the startups, such as famous VC funds, blue chip mutual funds, major asset management firms, and peer sovereign funds that are active in tech investments, many sovereign funds take comfort and join in the late stage investments. That's a dangerous shortcut, because the early investors, especially the VC funds, PE funds, and mutual funds, are more aligned with the startup founders than the late stage investors (see **Figure 6.7**). Just like the founders, they are likely sitting on significant paper-based gains that have already been recorded as a success. More importantly, they may have presented such "success" to their own investors – their LPs.

If a startup is currently struggling, these anxious private funds investors might have multiple incentives to prevent a down round (financing by selling company shares to new shareholders at a valuation below the last round), because a valuation write-down means that their "booked" early success would quickly shrink. In turn, such write-downs could impede their ability to raise their next fund from the potential LPs, which include many sovereign funds. It's in their interest to ensure that the new sovereign investors come in at a higher valuation, otherwise their investment is "at risk."

**Finally,** even though sovereign funds are being approached as the lender of last resort, they may not get the best terms.

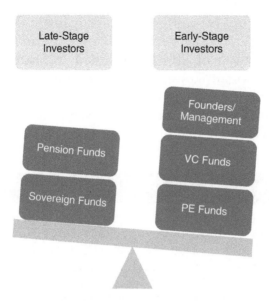

Figure 6.7    **Early Investors more aligned with the Startup Founders than Late Stage Investors**

Despite their large capital injections, late stage sovereign investors in the unicorn deals often have to accept unequal terms vis-a-vis investors from the earlier rounds, due to the pressure to own parts of high-flying companies. For example, the earlier investors tend to enjoy in their term sheets better downside risk protection provisions (such as "ratchets" provisions to receive more shares if the shares are priced at IPO below what they paid, and superior preferences in liquidation), which means these sovereign investment funds are accepting more risk. Furthermore, their shareholder rights may also be limited, having little say on material corporate matters, such as compensation, indebtedness, major capital purchases, and material business agreements. And, unlike the early round investor, they are less likely to get board seats and the opportunity to view management up close.

**In summary,** sovereign investment funds must rethink their bias in recent years on growth capital, not early stage, for direct investments into tech startups. (Small ticket investments into the early stage opportunities were mostly made through external fund managers.) To recall, Chapters 2 and 3 chronicled the transformation of SIFs from passive allocators of capital to direct investors in key emerging technology unicorns. This move has driven changes in the SIFs themselves, how they make decisions, how they are staffed, and the responsibilities the staff assume as a consequence of making those decisions.

---

### Working on the Railroad

As a SIF with the dual mission of furthering the economy of Quebec while delivering a bottom line for the pensioners and other beneficiaries of its funds, CDPQ could be expected to encounter special difficulties in transforming itself. The pending sale of the train division of Bombardier tells the tale of a successful transformation process. CDPQ, regarded pre-transformation as an arm of the Quebec government, was seen by critics as succumbing to political pressure to bail out failing local businesses or block takeovers by outsiders.

CDPQ was again called upon in 2016, as its transformation took hold, to inject cash into Bombardier, one of Quebec's largest employers. Bombardier was desperately in need of the cash to finance plane and train orders delayed by production issues. CDPQ was one of the few institutions willing to back the company. CDPQ's team negotiated strong terms as a condition of investing $1.5 billion in the company's train unit. This will result in CDPQ cashing $2.5 billion on its $1.5 billion 2106 outlay, a return of over 70%, when Alstom completes its acquisition of the Bombardier train division.

The 2016 terms included a guaranteed 15% annual compounded return to CDPQ if, as is happening, the train unit were sold. Michael Sabia, the CDPQ CEO called upon to transform the fund after it had sustained a massive $40 billion loss in the global financial crisis (and who had retired from that post just as the deal was announced), had succeeded beyond expectations. He has moved on to head the Munk School of Global Affairs and Public Policy at the University of Toronto. Wondering what he did before joining CDPQ? Good question. He ran a railroad.

---

For example, CDPQ found it necessary to transform itself at the depths of the global financial crisis. The timing probably contributed to its acceptance as well as its success (see **Box: Working on the Railroad**). CDPQ currently manages up to 90%

of its assets using internal teams, allocating very little to outside mangers. In areas in which it has the expertise, its internal team can be massive: its Ivanhoe–Cambridge unit, which invests in, builds, and operates shopping centers and office towers, alone has a headcount of more than 1000.

Michael Sabia, until recently President and CEO of CDPQ, puts it this way: "The 'what' of the transformation was a new investment strategy, based on what we call a 'business-owner mind-set.'" To effect the transformation, CDPQ had to change its culture by (a) rethinking its recruitment and personnel, (b) restructuring its decision-making processes to introduce more rigor and collaboration – including replacing IT platforms to break down silos, and (c) revamping the compensation structure. Now for sovereign funds to become better tech investors, they must further transform their institutional setup, in the same way they moved to "go direct" years ago, as illustrated by the CDPQ example.

## Becoming VC: Early, Nimble, and Portfolio Approach

To find less overheated areas in technology investments, sovereign investment funds must behave like venture capital funds themselves to venture into early stage investments in tech startups. Such a move will have profound implications for the business model those sovereign funds operate on. In addition to "going direct," the gigantic sovereign funds must further transform their institutional setup, such as governance, benchmark, compensation, and much more, to meet the unique dynamics of innovation investing.

**First, the accountability issue.** Accountability is a fundamental aspect of the functioning of sovereign investors. Such a concentration of the country's wealth in one entity has inevitably drawn intense interest, not just from every fund manager in capital markets, but also from state bureaucracy, financial media, and the general public. Investment performance is often made publicly available, and rewards (or punishment) and performance must be perceived to be proportionate. Each stakeholder has its own ideas on how the money can best be spent, and they especially have a lot to say when some deals lose money – the perception of accountability.

As the sovereign fund management targets more assets directly, its accountability grows commensurately. No longer can underperformance be parked at the door of the (subsequently fired) outside money manager, hence the fund staff become even more accountable – to the government ministry in the reporting chain, legislators, and the public. The widespread criticism that CIC, China's sovereign wealth fund, received from the public for its investment into Blackrock, the prominent US asset manager, is a telling example (see **Box: CIC Hit by Blackstone**).

---

### CIC Hit by Blackstone

When CIC, China's sovereign wealth fund, announced it was buying a $3 billion stake in Blackstone back in 2007, the watershed deal marked the country's first move to diversify the investment of its vast foreign exchange reserves into direct, concentrated equity investments in a company; reserves which until then had mainly been stored in US Treasury bills and fixed income securities.

In connection with Blackstone's June 2007 initial public offering, CIC bought approximately 10% of the company for $3 billion. In just a few months, the value of its investment began to sink as the financial turmoil started in the US credit markets. Soon, the financial crisis became global, Blackstone shares slumped, and by 2008 the CIC holding had lost more than two-thirds of its value. The shares were valued at $31 apiece at the IPO; at the nadir of the crisis, the Blackstone stock was trading below $5 a share.

The sharp loss – on paper only, as CIC marked its holding to the market value of the shares – of the investment immediately prompted widespread criticism. The fact that CIC jumped at the chance to get in on Blackstone's IPO even before it was formally set up (which did not occur until October of that year) exacerbated that pressure. CIC was questioned for its duty of care, as it may have lacked the staff needed to do thorough due diligence on its investments in one of the largest US financial institutions. The public even asked why China's national fund used foreign reserves to bail out the Wall Street (for a loss) rather than support China's development.

It's especially complicated for tech venture investments, which by nature involve failures – quick and many. As portrayed in the media, the tech startup story is always so easy: an entrepreneur with an amazing technology and timely venture capital funding becomes a billionaire in his 20s. But that has a lot to do with the industry culture: venture capitalists bury their dead very quietly; they emphasize the successes, but they don't talk about the failures at all.

In practice, the nature of venture investment is that the majority of the startups will fail. The definition of failure has a wide range, from closing the business and liquidating all assets, with investors losing all their money (big loss), to an undesirable exit, such as an asset sale or an acquisition for less than the total funding raised by the company (moderate loss), to not meeting the projected return on investment (small loss). Even the most well-funded startup companies can ultimately fail. When sovereign funds focus their investments into a few concentrated positions, they have no portfolio diversification.

By contrast, venture capitalists play a game of "large numbers." They make lots of high-risk investments, each in a small amount, anticipating many of them to fail and a few to become home runs. Can sovereign funds do the same? If early stage venture investments are evaluated deal-by-deal, the sovereign fund staff would worry too many "failed deals" will be pinned on them. The truth is that if venture investors don't have a lot of failures, then they're just not doing it right, because that means that they're not investing in risky ventures. In short, to behave like a VC fund, the sovereign investment funds need to take a portfolio view (instead of deal-by-deal) and have a high level of tolerance for "failure" and "accountability."

**Second, performance benchmark.** Sovereign investment funds tend to look at each deal valuation in isolation, but instead they should treat direct venture investments holistically, just as the accountability issue should be viewed in a portfolio context. Because the sovereign investors have a sizable portfolio of tech-related investments, they should recognize that the broader portfolio gains are more significant

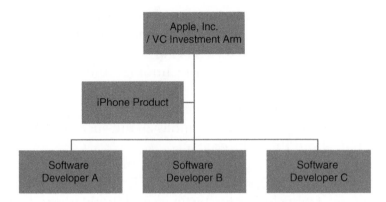

Figure 6.8   **Apple's iPhone Product and related VC Investments**

than pure financial returns from individual stakes in startups. For that, corporate venture capital funds can be a useful reference, whose investments target businesses which have some strategic connection with the corporation.

For example, when Apple Inc. first launched the iPhone, its VC investment arm invested extensively in software developers, usually through taking minority stakes, which helped to build an ecosystem around the smartphone platform (see **Figure 6.8**). Earlier than Apple, when Intel launched the 86-series microprocessor during the age of the PC, its VC fund used the same mechanism to support firms that would write software for Intel chips, which shortened the natural time-lag between the availability and usage of new computer technology. At the end of the day, the success of the iPhone ecosystem is far more valuable than the gains from individual smartphone apps. (The same is true for Intel chip monopoly and the financial returns from the individual software developer in its VC portfolio.)

In other words, sovereign funds should also consider how different investments may interact with each other in an ecosystem and benefit each other. An active digital economy investment portfolio can provide them with advanced insights into emerging trends that benefit their wider portfolio. For one thing, a window into industry-changing technologies may allow sovereign funds to take advantage of such disruption in different asset classes, such as listed equities, infrastructure, real estate, and more. For another, the tech investing portfolio can help them make judgment calls on more traditional investment sectors; for instance, new energy storage tech and power sector investments.

**Third, investing in emerging digital and technology businesses requires fundamental adjustments to a fund's due diligence practice.** Early stage investing is historically a difficult area for sovereign funds because a small capital investment requires a huge staff commitment. Compared to late stage investments (more like private equity transactions in traditional industries), early stage investing techniques relate to different key performance indicators, revenue standards, business models, growth estimates, and more. The digital revolution is accelerating. As a result, investors have to develop an internal mechanism able to review brand new technology – like Blockchain applications and non-traditional issues such as data privacy – quickly while fulfilling their fiduciary duty of care.

For all that, a very special team, a diverse range of investment professionals with different skills and backgrounds, is much needed to deal with the endemic challenges of small scale and big complexity. Can such expertise be developed organically in-house? Or maybe some infusion of VC veterans is necessary to augment the process? The recent move toward more fundamental research investments calls for deeper talents in "hard tech" and intellectual property than mere understanding of Internet-based business models. (Much as was the case with Michael Sabia and the CDPQ, where Sabia's chief financial officer experience at CN, Canada's largest railway, was called upon for the restructuring of the train division of Bombardier.)

## From Alpha to Omega

In fact, "going early" for tech investment is essentially in line with former CEO Michael Sabia's observation when the CDPQ moved into direct investments: be like an owner. For the most part, early investors in unicorns eventually end in the same position as founders and employees. This is because by the time these startups become unicorns, they have raised so much capital that the early investor is no longer a substantial portion of the equity ownership, voting rights, or the liquidation preference stack. As a result, most of their interests are aligned with the common stockholders, and key decisions about return and liquidity are the same as for the founder.

In the years before 2017, sovereign funds' direct investments focused on growth stage, whereas early stage investments, for the most part, were almost entirely conducted through external VC fund managers. In recent years, several SIFs have already made big steps into early stage investing. With competition rising in the buyout and mid-market spaces, experienced SIFs are developing the skills to allocate capital for direct investment in companies at earlier stages. It's not for the faint of heart, but for those with sufficient resources and long-term time horizons to weather startup cycles, the commensurate outsized opportunity will follow.

For example, Singapore's **Temasek** recently set up a new Strategic Initiatives unit, seeking greater agility for opportunistic deals requiring fast turnaround and senior-level assessment. To be nimble, the unit can pull in resources from other parts of the company. It created so-called "experimental pods" to explore opportunities in artificial intelligence (AI) and blockchain technologies, which Temasek sees as long-term trends impacting multiple industries and geographies.

Similarly, **OPTrust** of Canada established an "incubation portfolio" of about C$300 million, accounting for 1.5% of assets under management (approximately C$20 billion). The new portfolio aims to make small investments of around C$20 million to C$40 million for emerging growth. Companies at that stage may have just got off the ground, have a sample product, and their first few consumers.

Of course, not all pension forays into the startup sector have borne fruit. **Sweden**'s state pension fund dedicated to private assets has publicly retreated from the strategy. The fund **AP6,** which was set up to invest solely in early stage Swedish firms, made a formal plea in 2009 to its government overseers to relax its investment rules, as it was finding it difficult to make money. In response, Swedish Finance Minister Mats Odell stated that the fund's first objective should be returns – and so the rules were relaxed to allow AP6 to invest more in companies that have already proven their worth. As described earlier, it got back in the game, however, a few years later via an investment in VC fund Creandum IV, run out of Stockholm and Silicon Valley, which was an early backer of Spotify. With this move, AP6 resumed its exposure to venture investing, but unlike its more progressive peers, solely as an LP.

Overall, the trend is accelerating. In 2018, sovereign wealth funds continued to invest more in growth-capital financing for startups in disruptive industries. According to data from IFSWF, in 2018, SWFs completed 29 transactions at growth-capital stage (series C, D), up from 19 the previous year, and doubled their commitments at early stage (A, B, B+) with 20 deals versus nine in 2017 (see **Figure 6.9**).

Furthermore, new models have also emerged from the pension fund and endowment communities: PGGM, ATP, and the University of California Board of Regents have all made widely publicized developments in this sector. Some are taking

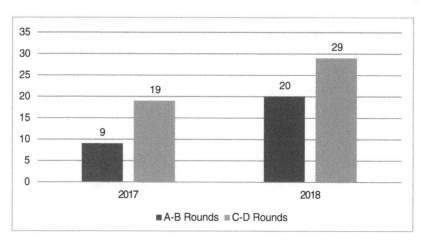

Figure 6.9    SIFs Increase Early Stage Investments

extra steps to establish a dedicated subsidiary – independent of the "mother" sovereign fund – to pursue high-risk venture investments more independently from the convention of sovereign funds. At times, a SIF has even founded or seeded its own VC entity, either through partnership with an external firm, as exemplified by the new PIF/Softbank initiative, or – in the style of OMERS Ventures – as a wholly owned subsidiary.

**OMERS** in 2011, not long after the global financial crisis, surveyed the Canadian venture scene and concluded that it could deploy capital directly in startups, a tactic shunned by its fellow pension plans in Canada due to the scale and labor intensive nature of venture investing. A venture-focused team could not hope to invest anywhere near as much in startups as a similarly sized team could invest in infrastructure, real estate, or other private assets over a similar timespan. As such, venture did not fit the traditional pension plan investment model.

Today, OMERS Ventures has over C$1 billion in assets under management and operations in Silicon Valley as well as Europe, where it has established an incubator in collaboration with Dutch pension funds and is launching a European venture fund. Operating as a separate entity within OMERS, OMERS Venture has forged its own path.

It invests at all stages of a startup's existence. An early success was its investment in Shopify, an e-commerce company started in Ottawa in 2004. OMERS Ventures led a C$200 million Series C round in 2011. Shopify's successful IPO in 2015 saw it go public at $17 per share; the NYSE-listed company recently traded at nearly $600 and has a market cap in excess of $60 billion. OMERS Ventures had vindicated its business model.

By 2015, OMERS Ventures, having deployed its initial C$210 million funding from the OMERS pension fund, launched its C$260 million Fund II and brought on board corporate venture capitalist CISCO Investments and BMO Capital as LPs. At the time, OMERS speculated that this fund was the first in which a pension fund had acted as GP for third-party money (see **Figure 6.10**), a huge step forward for the

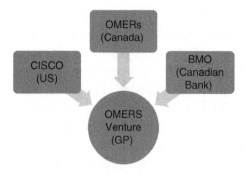

Figure 6.10    **OMERS Venture as GP**

asset owner community. In 2017 came fund III (C$300 million) with additional outside investors including Kuwait's sovereign investor via Wafra. Having landed investors, it expanded its global footprint.

In 2019, it opened an office in Silicon Valley to participate more intimately in the startup ecosystem. The same year, it announced the launch of a €300m venture capital fund in Europe with former Uber executive Jambu Palaniappan as Managing Director (more details in Chapter 7). In Europe, it has invested €76m into companies including content management infrastructure provider Contentful, insurance tech startup Wefox, and digital veterinarian FirstVet. The Global Head of Private Equity at parent OMERS, Mark Redman, says the fund is proud of what he calls "cuddly capital" – the reputation of Canadian pension funds as being "the nice guys" in capital markets.

The OMERS Ventures story is being replicated by other SIFs, including **Mubadala.** In fact, the two crossed paths in the Wefox Series B round, with Mubadala Ventures leading the March 2019 $125 million round and OMERS Ventures leading the December 2019 Series B extension for an additional $110 million (total $235 million). Like OMERS Ventures, Mubadala's venture investing is done through venture funds it operates. The Wefox deal was the first from its $400 million European directs fund.

In addition to the newly launched European directs fund, Mubadala Ventures launched a US-focused $400 million fund in 2017. It made early stage investments in startups Recursion Pharmaceuticals (biotech), Color Genomics, and Turvo (smart logistics). More recently, Mubadala Ventures co-led (with Silver Lake and CPPIB) in the $2.25 billion round to provide outside funding to Alphabet unit Waymo. While not an "early stage" investment in the traditional sense (although no valuation was disclosed for this round, Waymo was previously valued at over $100 billion by Wall Street analysts, well above a Series A-B level), the deal represented the very first outside fundraising for the unit, making it more like a SIF-sized Series B round.

Finally, Mubadala recently announced two new venture capital funds. One – in what appears to be an effort to develop a venture ecosystem around Abu Dhabi's government-backed Hub71 tech hub – where Mubadala announced a $150 million fund of funds to support that initiative (detailed discussion in Chapter 5). But the more telling new fund is a $100 million directs fund with another geographic focus, this time, MENA. Learning from its experience in tech investing around the globe, Mubadala has turned its attention to early stage investing in disruptive technology in its own backyard. The fund's first investment, as mentioned, was in the $16 million Series B round of Bayzat, a cloud-based HR solution based in Dubai.

The most interesting example is that some forward-thinking SIFs have gone into the very beginning of research and innovation – the universities and research institutions, even before a business model exists. At the same time, they are also innovative enough – maybe bold enough – to set up an evergreen vehicle. Their task is to identify game-changing technology, not evaluate business plans. One noteworthy example is Oxford Sciences Innovation plc (OSI), whose stakeholders include **Temasek** and the **Oman Investment Fund (OIF)**. (In June 2020, Oman's government announced the creation of Oman Investment Institution which will consolidate OIF with Oman's other SIF, State's General Reserve Fund.)

In the past, institutions have tried innovative VC structures to incentivize research commercialization on a specific campus or university basis. From a SIF perspective, however, often these efforts are too small scale to warrant attention. OSI represents instead a phenomenally interesting new model at scale. Operating in partnership with Oxford University, this manager provides investment assessment and lifetime financing to research originating from the university in return for a certain percentage of free equity, even where OSI has chosen not to invest.

OSI has tackled very early stage investing with an innovative approach, raising £600 million in its initial fundraise, bringing together SWFs with value-added tech investors Google Ventures and Sequoia (see **Figure 6.11**). Structured as a *corporation*, in which the university has an equity interest, it is an evergreen fund, which frees it from many of the time constraints of a traditional VC.

Like a traditional VC, OSI brings more than cash to a startup, seeking to combine deep experience of building successful businesses with OSI's network of investors, entrepreneurs, industrialists, and experts from Silicon Valley to Shanghai to offer advice, experience, relationships, and hands-on support. OSI promises to furnish Oxford's researchers with help in writing business plans, creating pitches, recruiting the board, and setting up the company.

Here the investors are not LPs but hold equity directly in the venture and receive returns in the form of stakeholder dividends and perhaps eventually capital appreciation. While quite new, founded in 2015, this model of innovation investing at

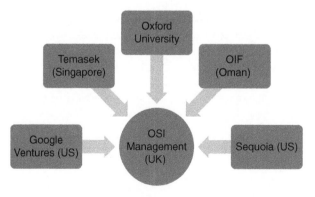

Figure 6.11    **OSI Structured as Evergreen Corporation (Shareholders)**

scale is getting serious consideration by many. These innovation investment experiments are worth following closely (see **Box: Muscat to Oxford and Back**).

## Muscat to Oxford and Back

Oman Investment Fund has done more than follow the OSI case closely. Oman's sovereign fund has signed on to OSI's approach, giving it a very early look at innovative technology. It is an interesting move for the Sultanate of Oman's SIF. OIF was founded in 2006 but traces its origins to the State General Reserve Fund created in 1980 to invest the state's oil surplus abroad (Oman is the largest Arab oil-producer outside OPEC), which then combined with it in 2014 when oil prices collapsed. (Subsequently, the UAE similarly combined its International Petroleum Investment Company, Mubadala Development Company, and Abu Dhabi Investment Council in a series of mergers to create Mubadala Investment Company.)

OIF is much smaller ($34 billion AUM per data of the SWF Institute) than Mubadala and for much of its existence has focused on joint ventures with other countries: India, Vietnam, and Qatar formed joint funds with it. Egypt's sovereign fund has reportedly discussed the concept. The approach is consistent with Oman's relationship with the rest of the Gulf states; outside OPEC, not siding with the UAE and Saudi Arabia on the Qatar boycott, opening its key port to China's Belt and Road Initiative.

But as a small nation with a growing population and little local industry to provide employment, as evidenced by the OSI relationship, OIF has recently turned to venture capital and innovative technologies. While learning at Oxford, it is doing its homework back in Muscat. Positioning itself to become an early stage investor, in 2016, OIF partnered with three VCs (Atlantic Bridge Capital, from Ireland, 500 Startups, from Silicon Valley, and Techstars Ventures from Boulder, Colorado) to form the $200 million Oman Technology Fund.

The Oman Technology Fund is majority owned by OIF with a mandate to invest and nurture startups that will benefit the broader Omani economy and deliver sustainable economic dividends. OIF is in a position to benefit from working with its VC partners and increase its exposure to direct investing in potential high-growth tech ventures in Oman and the region as it aims to do through OSI. The fund has certainly grasped the fundamental concept of early stage investing: spread your bets.

In summary, going early is the new trend for sovereign tech investors. Success is equated with investing early stage directly – in an idea right at the center of an ecosystem – and then watching everything develop around it. This way, the investor hopes to avoid missing that game-changing, breakout success. But this requires more than being nimble. The funds need top notch talents in-house and a proprietary network of industry so as to nurture early relationships with businesses before their need for funding arises, as will be discussed in the following chapter.

*WeWork, as described in the introduction to this chapter, spectacularly plummeted in value even prior to the advent of the coronavirus pandemic and the impact on the shared workplace model. The carnage did not stop there. Mighty Vision Fund suffered not only a blow to its reputation, but was the target of a lawsuit by the board of the (likely, former) unicorn for walking away from its $3 billion buyout proposal. The courts will sort that out over time. The markets have reached judgment more quickly. SoftBank is now trading at a fraction of the value of its investments, even after they have been battered; and for Vision Fund, it has announced a $17 billion write-down. No shots of tequila at the next meeting it is safe to guess. Still, Masayoshi Son is unfazed: "Tactically, I've made regrets. But strategically I'm unchanged. Vision-wise? Unchanged."*

CHAPTER 7

# The Hunt for the Hunting Party

*Branded as Europe's tallest office tower, The Shard – as its name flaunts – slices the London skyline and is visible from over 40 miles. At 310 meters its glinting glass is nearly three times the height of St. Paul's Cathedral, the historic landmark of London's financial district, and nearly twice that of The London Eye. Not surprisingly, Qatar Investment Authority is a major investor in the iconic tower. And, stepping off the high-speed elevators on the 22nd floor, shortly after the tower opened, the visitor had a choice of launch tenants: one direction houses the headquarters of global digital marketing agency Jellyfish; the other, Khazanah Nasional Berhad, a Malaysian sovereign fund.*

*Khazanah's offices are no less alluring than one might imagine those of Jellyfish to be – the striking vistas include an overhead view of toy-like Tower Bridge. In addition to housing its professional staff of ten, the open, shared workspace is enjoyed by the occupants of its incubator. James Wales, a pioneer of Wikipedia, was once hosted for a subsequent startup venture. London's first Muslim Mayor, Sadiq Khan, attended the festive opening reception, along with hundreds of others.*

*Like other SIFs before and after it, Khazanah sought its place in the digital transformation with a presence, if not on the ground, then multiple floors above it. A successful investor in Alibaba and in Scotland's digital travel service, Skyscanner, Khazanah had good reason to commit to a ten-year lease that put it closer to its unicorn prey, while Qatar took the more traditional role of landlord. This is the next chapter in the transformation wrought by, and wrought upon, SIFs pursuing unicorns. The story involves the challenges of the pursuit, in multiple hunting grounds, often far from the hunter's home base, of the talent to build a hunting party.*

## Nantucket Sleigh Ride

**Khazanah**'s London office is not its only international foray; the US, Mumbai, and Istanbul figured in its hunt. In fact, Sovereign

Investment Funds (SIF) have their hunting parties out in force in London, New York, and Silicon Valley in pursuit of unicorns. (See Table 3.1 for New York and Silicon Valley offices, and Table 7.1 below for London offices.)

One view of this evolution can compare it to the rise in the New England whaling industry of the 19th century. Whales were the goal, not unicorns. The reasoning goes, large sums of money were raised to outfit expeditions, most of which failed to return with a profitable catch, or simply failed to

Table 7.1    The London Offices of Sovereign Investment Funds

| Sovereign Funds | Full Name | Country |
|---|---|---|
| AIMCo | Alberta Investment Management Corp. | Canada |
| BIA | Brunei Investment Agency | Brunei |
| BCI | British Columbia Investment Management Corp | Canada |
| CDPQ | Caisse de Depot et Placement du Quebec | Canada |
| CPPIB | Canada Pension Plan Investment Board | Canada |
| GIC | GIC Private Limited | Singapore |
| KIA | Kuwait Investment Authority | Kuwait |
| Khazanah | Khazanah Nasional Berhad | Malaysia |
| KIC | Korean Investment Corporation | South Korea |
| Mubadala | Mubadala Investment Company | UAE |
| NBIM | Norges Bank Investment Management | Norway |
| NPS | National Pension Service | South Korea |
| OMERS | Ontario Municipal Employees Retirement System | Canada |
| OTPP | Ontario Teachers' Pension Plan | Canada |
| PIF | Public Investment Fund | Saudi Arabia |
| PSP | Public Sector Pension Investment | Canada |
| QIA | Qatar Investment Authority | Qatar |
| SAFE | State Administration of Foreign Exchange | China |
| SOFAZ | The State Oil Fund of the Republic of Azerbaijan | Azerbaijan |
| Temasek | Temasek Holdings | Singapore |

As noted in this chapter, Khazanah has closed its office in London.

return. However, as the elegant whaling captains' mansions on Nantucket attest, those that succeeded more than covered the losses of the majority, just as one unicorn can make up for a string of losses in a portfolio.

Persuading investors to wager their capital was one thing; recruiting the captain with the ability to find and land whales was another. Not to mention outfitting the ship and, in a key move, locating and incentivizing sailors who would crew the long voyage to remote locations under challenging circumstances. In the 21st century, as the competition for frontier technologies intensifies, the sovereign funds seeking unicorns encounter challenges of a different nature but sufficiently daunting in their own way.

The reality is that, until recently, sovereign funds had been passive investors at their quiet headquarters making them a special class of institutional investor that managed most of their portfolios in remote jurisdictions. For many sovereign investment funds, their headquarters were far away from the global financial centers (let alone tech innovation hubs), without even a representative office where most financial activities happened. Historically, there was a geographical mismatch between the source and the use of funds of these investors (correspondingly, an unprecedented flow of capital from emerging economies to developed markets). In fact, the first ever overseas office of a sovereign investor was just a little more than half a century ago (see **Box: Kuwait the First SWF Overseas Office**).

## Kuwait the First SWF Overseas Office

The Kuwait Investment Authority (KIA) is known not only for being the first Sovereign Wealth Fund (its origins date back to 1953 – before the emirate had gained independence from Great Britain), but also for having opened the first ever overseas office of a Sovereign Investor, with the 1953 establishment of the Kuwait Investment Board (predecessor to today's Kuwait Investment Office (KIO)) in London. Kuwait actually did it in reverse: first, a London presence with a four-person board, including two Bank of England directors, was established to oversee investment of the oil revenue account at the Bank of England.

Only later, in 1965, after independence, was the Kuwait Investment Board reorganized into the KIO and became part of the newly formed KIA. Not until opening in Kuwait City in 1985 did the KIA have a physical presence other than London. The KIO continues to operate quasi-independently, although it is now officially an office of the KIA.

In 1976, KIO's mandate was formalized with a decree entrusting management of the new Future Generations Fund (**FGF**). The law dedicated a minimum of 10% of the State of Kuwait's revenues to the FGF, creating a constant flow of funds to invest. KIO also manages other state monies. The secretive fund's assets under management are estimated at nearly $600 billion as of December 2019.

The value of having such a fund with a well-staffed and functioning London office – over 100 professionals – was underscored by the outbreak of the Gulf War in 1990. Saddam Hussein invaded and occupied Kuwait – and was notoriously reported to have stripped occupied infant incubators from the Kuwait hospital maternity ward. During the occupation, the KIO functioned as the finance ministry, providing remittances to refugee Kuwaitis. The Iraqi forces were driven out in a fierce rout, leaving oil fields ablaze and the country devastated. Recovery and rebuilding cost more than $85 billion (nearly twice that amount in today's dollars); the cost was funded by the FGF.

In 2013, KIO established a subsidiary. Named after the London building it occupies next to St. Paul's, Wren House Infrastructure is staffed with 21 investment professionals. Its portfolio includes investments in airports, ports, water, energy generation (conventional and renewables), distribution, and transmission, and spans 12 countries and over 10,000 employees in the UK, Europe, Australia, and Central and South America. Wren House is also active in midstream, digital infrastructure – including towers, fiber and cloud computing, healthcare, and education infrastructure.

As the first of its kind, Kuwait's sovereign fund in many ways created a template. The British government granted a special tax exemption which today has formed the fiscal model for the host of SIFs operating in London. Its penchant for secrecy seems to have set the tone for many sovereign investors as well. One report is that a Citibank trader dared to mention KIO to the press, resulting in the fund pulling all its business from the bank.

That might be fine when their portfolios were essentially comprised of investments into external managers. However, when they do more direct investing, especially amid the fierce competition for successful unicorns, they are challenged to build up in-house capabilities from their headquarters. The overseas arena is critical for the unicorn hunt: for one thing, this complex game requires a deeper knowledge of the local markets, so they need to create a presence on the ground to get closer to their quarry. For another, the in-house team needs to attract international talent to build up diverse capabilities.

Deal (investment target) wise, the sovereign funds need to position themselves in the tech hubs they are focusing on. Overall, there are many great startups in the Silicon Valley and similar innovation hubs such as London, UK and Beijing, China. But at the same time there is already so much capital – thanks to the booming domestic venture capital (VC) funds and local Internet giants (for example, Google and Intel in the Silicon Valley, as well as Alibaba and Tencent in China, are also busy investors into startups themselves) – that it was a really crowded marketplace even before the sovereign funds and their capital moved in.

Meanwhile, as the sovereign investors bring assets management in-house (putting less capital into external managers' hands), they are, in effect, giving up many of the agglomeration economies enjoyed by asset managers and private VC funds. What troubles these enormous financial firms is that no matter how successful they are in their home markets, they are not necessarily networked into the startup community of Silicon Valley and other innovation hubs automatically. For example, startups may not view large financial institutions as preferred business partners, because the perception is that they tend to require more paperwork. Relating to sovereign capital, the stereotype may also involve slow decision-making and additional regulatory hassles (detailed discussions in the following chapters).

The investment team side of thinking is similar. Generally speaking, as employers with prestigious name brands, the sovereign investors can attract ambitious young talent, domestic and internationally. For dealmakers, having a ready source

of capital is a huge advantage: they can focus on closing transactions, without the hassle of being constantly on the road to
visit potential limited partners (LPs) for repeated fundraising.
Furthermore, the access to scale of capital is also compelling,
which means the investment team can pursue the largest
game – not only unicorns, but also decacorns.

However, the typical location of their headquarters makes
it more challenging for sovereign investors to attract talent.
Kuala Lumpur, Oslo, and Doha are not necessarily first choices
for top MBA graduates or investment professionals. Although
sometimes touted, work–life balance does not seem to be a
driver for the cool guys in the digital economy (see Box: **Chill
Out at Work**). Of course, it's possible for the sovereign funds
to make their headquarters more appealing and to develop a
somewhat metropolitan living environment nearby. Still, the
long-distance travel between the distant headquarters and
the markets they are investing in is a difficulty that cannot be
changed.

Historically, those with no overseas offices who had investments outside the country had to fly people in and out. "It's
very simple: logistics," commented the CEO Leo de Bever of
**AIMCo** (out of Alberta Province, Canada), when his firm set up
its London office in 2014. "We had people making 40 flights
a year between London and Edmonton." These frequent
long trips create substantial wear and tear on the investment
teams. (By way of reference, for a **CIC** Managing Director to
attend a board meeting at a Uruguayan company, the one-way
flight from Beijing to Montevideo includes making two flight
transfers at Paris and Buenos Aires and sitting on different
airplanes for more than 24 hours. And the same for the return,
plus 12-hour jet lag.)

---

### Chill Out at Work

The **Alaska Permanent Fund Corporation** (**APFC**) may face special challenges in
recruiting staff, even to its HQ in Juneau. It rains there, on average, 230 days

annually; snow falls October through April; Juneau is accessible only by boat or air, like only one other US state capital: Honolulu.

Nonetheless, the "careers" section of the fund's website touts: "Juneau residents rank quality of life as the number one reason they live here. From the moment you step off the plane it is easy to see that Juneau is one of the best kept secrets in the country. Beautiful forested mountains, glaciers, flowing rivers, and ocean channels are around every turn. With minimal traffic, no pollution, and some of the cleanest water you will ever have, Juneau is just secluded enough to balance small town charm with a strong political and economic presence.

What is it like to live and work here? For many it is the chance of a lifetime to escape the hassles/stresses of city life, live more simply, and enjoy the adventure of a lifetime. Traffic in Juneau is negligible relative to the average large city; the average commute is just 7–12 minutes. This can save you up to 130 hours (almost 17 work days) a year spent commuting. What an incredible opportunity to work with a dynamic progressive organization while maintaining exceptional work life balance."

The **Alberta Investment Management Corporation (AIMCo)** of Canada, located in Edmonton, Alberta, ignores the climate in its pitch, probably wisely. For reference, the University of Alberta website for international students helpfully points out winter days at –35 Celsius are the coldest students will encounter and goes on to furnish information on frostbite and hypothermia. For its active infrastructure investments in the UK and Europe, AIMCo set up its London office in 2014.

In summary, the tech investment teams and their locations are not just about the SIF investors themselves, but about where the unicorns and hunt captains are. Faced with the challenge of attracting international talent to their headquarters, the sovereign funds may find the best solution is opening international offices and hiring bespoke foreign professionals and experts on the ground. Then, what's the best way to set things up? Two case studies in the PE and infrastructure/real estate world, which relate to the sovereign funds' going for direct investments in earlier years, may provide some reference for the digital era.

## AlpInvest "Captive" Asset Manager: A Sexier Employer?

AlpInvest is one of the largest private equity fund-of-funds investment managers in the world and is fully owned by The

Carlyle Group ("Carlyle"). Managing more than $40 billion, AlpInvest has offices in New York, Amsterdam, Hong Kong, Indianapolis, and San Francisco, with professionals also located in Carlyle's London and Tokyo offices. Impressive surely, and also with origins that are not what the outside observer would expect, given its role today within one of the largest PE fund managers. Hiding in plain sight in the promotional language above, the Amsterdam office provides a clue.

AlpInvest was the stepchild of two of the world's largest pension funds, both Dutch. (See Figure 7.1 below.) **APG** had assets under management in 2019 of €529 million while **PGGM,** the Netherlands' second-largest pension fund, which manages the savings of health and welfare workers, managed €252 million. As the 21st century dawned, both sought to increase their exposure to alternative assets, principally private equity – both buy-out as well as venture capital. As pension asset managers, their DNA was adapted to public equities and debt. And, as pension managers, they were not likely to attract the talent necessary to penetrate the private equity (PE) and VC markets quickly and to win the large co-investment opportunities they sought in Europe and in the US.

The move had an additional motivation for the two pension funds. It was hoped that dabbling in private equity would also make APG a "sexier employer" in an increasingly tight Dutch labor market. Portfolio managers and analysts who would normally take a pass on a job offer from a staid pension fund, preferring instead to join a high-flying investment bank,

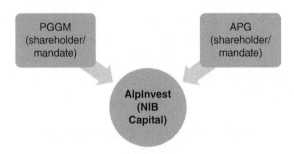

Figure 7.1　**Unique Strategy – AlpInvest/PGGM/APG Structure**

were more inclined to give APG a second look, APG officials said – according to the *Wall Street Journal* coverage at the time.

Things worked out better than planned, perhaps too well. Within the decade, AlpInvest was Europe's largest PE manager and, apparently, sexy enough to attract high-earning talent. PGGM and APG decided to sell AlpInvest after public criticism in the Netherlands over the high pay packages received by some of its top executives. AlpInvest paid €32.6m in salaries and wages in 2009 to its 118 staff, of which 71 are investment professionals, after making €60m of revenues from management fees and carried interest (a share of investment profits).

Despite the apparent success of the "captive" arrangement, the pension managers determined it was best to assuage their critics rather than defend the high-ticket management team. The two funds managing the pension savings of much more modestly compensated Dutch workers then initiated an auction process and completed a sale to a joint venture of AlpInvest management and Carlyle at an undisclosed price, estimated in the range of several hundred million dollars (see **Figure 7.2**). For Carlyle, the deal cemented its position as the world's biggest private equity group by assets under management (eventually Carlyle fully acquired 100% of AlpInvest).

On the positive side for the two funds, the foray into a captive management unit probably accelerated the desired increase in their allocation to private equity assets. And did

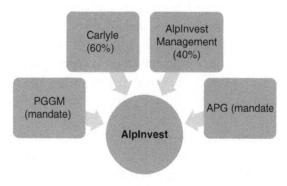

Figure 7.2    **AlpInvest/Carlyle Take-Private Structure**

so at a cost that was certainly no greater than the fees that they would have paid to an outside fund manager, while the two benefited from the accretion in value to the management company when they exited. On the other hand, considering that the "unique structure" appeared to function well, the reputational hit and public pressure sustained from the disclosed high compensation of their captive must have been substantial.

Overall, it seemed a net positive for the two Dutch pensions, with the downside to reputation balanced by exiting on profitable terms. What is the lesson to be drawn? Perhaps it is the Rubik's Cube nature of the challenge – is it possible to combine: (1) the staid and prudent demeanor of a pension fund manager with (2) the social media profile of the sexy employer necessary to attract the alternative asset management talent that (3) the outsized returns essential to meet the pensioners' expectations? In this instance, the arrangement seems not to have been sustainable.

### OMERs and Oxford Properties

As with the Dutch pensions, the Canadian pension fund OMERS sought more exposure to an alternative asset class to boost returns and cover its defined benefit obligations – in this case the target asset was real estate. OMERS also bought – rather than built – to facilitate this transition, and its addition of Oxford Properties Group Inc. ("Oxford"), a publicly listed company from Western Canada, is another case study in how SIFs engineer transformations and compete for talent. OMERS found the path lay through a take-private, like the Dutch. Unlike the Dutch, there has not been a subsequent exit forced by Canadian public reaction to compensation packages.

In August 1998, OMERS acquired shares of Oxford Properties to reach approximately 12% ownership of the real estate investment, management, and development company, which made OMERS one of the largest shareholders. The transaction was described by OMERS as a move into real estate

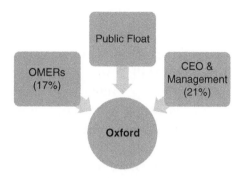

Figure 7.3    Oxford Properties Structure before Taken-private

investments through public equities (besides direct property and debt instruments). By 2001, OMERS had grown its stake to a commanding 17% (see **Figure 7.3**).

Shortly after that, Oxford Properties and OMERS jointly announced in August 2001 that an agreement had been reached whereby BPC Properties Ltd., a related company of OMERS, would make a cash bid to acquire 100% of Oxford's common shares at $23.75 per share for a total equity value of $1.5 billion. With the absorption of the Oxford team, OMERS was ready to grow its alternative assets portfolio in the real estate sector. And the Oxford team, relieved of the need to constantly raise capital, dipped into the OMERS cash pile and got to work.

APG and PGGM captured the benefits of a dedicated, experienced team that could transform the funds' portfolios, increasing access and exposure to high returns in PE and VC deals in funds and co-investments. OMERS got the talent it needed to transform itself into an important player in real estate. Both resorted to take-private transactions in which the target's deal makers were richly rewarded. This strategy not only enabled them to jumpstart their transformations but positioned them to attract talent in markets more competitive than Amsterdam and Toronto.

Not every sovereign investor, however, can take this path to build an international talent pool. As noted, Oxford was the only target then available in Canada to fill this void when

OMERS acquired it. And, in the end, AlpInvest's days as a captive alternative asset manager were numbered under public pressure. In practice, many sovereign funds, including Canadian pensions like OTPP and CPPIB as well as OMERs' private equity team, build up their direct private investment team internally and organically (and more slowly).

Similarly, for digital and tech investments, different approaches are adopted by different funds. As illustrated by the case studies below, the players with a longer operational history, for example Singapore's GIC and Temasek, have evolved their direct tech investment strategies more organically. On the other hand, the in-house capability needs of the younger sovereign funds, such as CIC of China and PIF of Saudi Arabia, is immediate in light of their increasing focus on venture capital and new geographies. As a result, they try to leapfrog that organic process a bit and get a kick-start by "seeding" external teams for "semi-captive" managers.

## Stepping Out: Singaporean Funds and Canada Pensions

For SIFs that have already been in direct private investments for a long time, there's the build-it-yourself approach to developing a tech investment team. Tech deals, which may have taken months or years to mature, move frighteningly quickly once in play, hence a local office is much needed soon after sovereign funds allocate significant capital and time to a tech hub. Typically, they start the new initiative at the headquarters before sending expatriates to overseas offices. As needed, they recruit investment professionals from the local markets to complement the overseas team.

The tension between different cultures is usually highlighted by the working team's composition. On the one hand, headquarters may feel uncomfortable incorporating a completely new local team to manage their overseas assets (the speed at which tech deals move on the ground, combined with the time zone differences, means that a fair amount of autonomy is required for the team to operate); on the other hand, it can take years for foreign sovereign funds to build a management team and related network of local stakeholders from ground zero. As a result, the overseas office staff usually are a mix from the SIF's home country and local or third-country hires.

To make the mix work, the overseas office must be organically integrated into the headquarters, because a few trips a year by headquarters executives alone are not sufficient for local integration. No doubt the HR function is always run out of the headquarters, and the overseas market's unicorn hunting must fit in the sovereign fund's total portfolio construction. Therefore, a successful integration requires a global team from the very top, including domestic members acutely clear about the headquarters' culture and strategy, while hiring and incentivizing local talents to deeply localize day-to-day operations (see **Figure 7.4**).

**Temasek of Singapore** has implemented its global expansion successfully (**GIC**, another major SIF of Singapore, shares the same development story). In 2002, the fund decided to "step out" in accordance with Singaporean government policy and transform itself from a domestically-oriented investor to a regional direct investor in Asia. Probably relating to the boom of emerging markets – recall the time of BRIC (Brazil, Russia, India, and China) – Temasek stepped out into Asia in 2002, investing beyond Singapore into markets such as China and India (Beijing and Mumbai were the first moves abroad

Figure 7.4   **Overseas Office Integration**

Table 7.2    Temasek's Worldwide Offices before 2010

| Country | City of Office(s) |
|---------|-------------------|
| India | Mumbai |
| P. R. China | Beijing, Shanghai |
| Vietnam | Hanoi |
| Brazil | Sao Paulo |
| Mexico | Mexico City |

in 2004). Soon, it also expanded into Latin American opportunities in Brazil and Mexico, establishing offices in São Paulo and Mexico City subsequently (see **Table 7.2**).

In connection with the recent tech boom, Temasek opened offices in London and New York in the same year, 2014. Soon it further set up office in San Francisco, getting even closer to the Silicon Valley. Interestingly, Washington, DC was added to mix most recently in 2018 (see **Table 7.3**). (As the following chapters will discuss, with sovereign funds building out local offices and teams to enable direct investing in tech startups, national security regulators of the host countries are on alert.)

Today, Temasek has 11 offices worldwide and is successfully attracting staff to fill them globally. The offices outside Singapore are, in the aggregate, as large as those in Singapore. There are 400 investment professionals, roughly 200 sit in Singapore and the remaining 200 are spread over ten overseas offices. To bolster its teams, Temasek has also been known to bring on specialized external advisers. Jamie Vachon, former global head of technology at various funds, in 2019 became a senior external consultant for the data solutions field.

Table 7.3    Temasek's New Offices During the Tech Boom

| City/ Country | Year of Opening |
|---------------|-----------------|
| London (UK) | 2014 |
| New York (US) | 2014 |
| San Francisco (US) | 2017 |
| Washington, DC (US) | 2018 |

The internal organization of this global fleet reflects Temasek's pursuit of digital opportunities in the developing digital economies of the world. Temasek operates in teams divided by market (e.g., Americas) and industry (e.g., TMT). To proceed, deals must be championed by both industry and market heads and then be approved by the single firmwide investment committee (IC). Temasek's IC is composed of members from around the globe, most of whom attend the sessions, held in Singapore, in person.

As a balance to its industry/market team divide, Temasek has also created a Strategic Initiatives unit that can pull in resources from different parts of Temasek, seeking greater agility for opportunistic deals requiring fast turnaround and senior-level assessment. The effort is delivering: Rohit Sipahi-malani, who leads Temasek's startup focus as a joint head of the investment group, commented in media that Temasek possesses dense information networks in the US, China, India, and elsewhere that enable it to discover promising companies before others do and revise its portfolio quickly, which trans-lates into broad unicorn investments in China, South-east Asia, and the US, among other regions (see **Table 7.4**).

The Canadian pensions, which have a long history of "go-ing direct" like their Singaporean peers, take a similar organic growth path and may be a bit more aggressive in external hir-ing. Headquartered in Toronto, **CPPIB** had eight offices for direct private investments (see details in Chapter 3) before it opened its San Francisco office in September 2019. Among

Table 7.4    Temasek Representative Tech Investments in Major Markets

| China | SE Asia | US |
|-------|---------|-----|
| Ant Financial | Go-Jek | Airbnb |
| Didi Chuxing | Grab | Amazon |
| Meituan Dianping | Pine Labs | Doordash |
| NIO | Snapdeal | Impossible Foods |
| SenseTime | Zilango | Verily Life Sciences |

the first team members were several important internal transfers from the Direct Private Equity, Thematic Investing, Private Equity Funds, and other departments.

The leadership for venture investments is a mix: Ryan Selwood, Head of the Direct Private Equity Department, was the interim lead of the new San Francisco office, and Monica Adractas was hired from a Facebook unit to become the Head of Venture Capital Funds, responsible for the development and implementation of the Venture Capital (VC) funds program. Adractas had spent time at Facebook, Box, Starbucks, and McKinsey; immediately prior to joining CPPIB, she was Global Director at Workplace, an area of Facebook she helped launch in 2016.

Another Canadian pension fund, **OMERS,** has pursued even more external recruitment for its venture arm. Even before going into the venture world, OMERS was already among the most active Canadian pensions to make direct private investments, and it was the first Canadian fund to open an office in London in 2009. As covered in Chapter 6, OMER Ventures is set up as part of the private equity family at OMERS, but OMER Ventures has created a GP management company itself and raises venture capital funds to include funding from other institutional investors.

As such, the OMER Ventures' funds operate at arms-length with OMERS Private Equity, similar to the operation of Oxford. Initially it was seeded with $200 million from its parent OMERS in 2001, had the management team staffed by Canadian professionals, and operated from the same office building. After a few years of successful development, in January 2019 OMER Ventures opened its Silicon Valley office and hired a US venture capital veteran to lead it, as part of its North American OMERS Ventures team.

Soon, in March 2019, OMERS Ventures took a bigger step: it expanded to Europe with a sole-sourced €300 million fund at the new office in London, with the recruited team in Europe running its own fund (see **Figure 7.5**). Given the difference in the markets between Europe and North America, plus the time

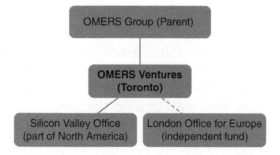

Figure 7.5    OMER Ventures: Mix of Development and Seeding

difference involved, the autonomous decision power given to the London office probably is sensible. This latest move is similar to young SIFs make bold, direct "platform seeding" far away from the headquarters, at the overseas markets of their focus, which will be covered in detail later in this chapter.

## JIC: Don't Try this at Home

The markets in which the sovereign funds seek to source and execute deals are naturally among the most competitive, not only for bagging deals, but also for landing staff. The overseas offices need to make competitive offers in the red-hot talent markets of Silicon Valley and other tech hubs to attract and retain key staff. However, the different compensation schemes are not always easily explained back at headquarters. Some countries, such as Singapore, have a policy of compensating public employees on par with the private sector. As a result, the Singaporean sovereign funds seem to enjoy a recruiting advantage not only at home but abroad as well. Just like Temasek in the previous section, GIC has also steadily expanded into overseas markets, building up a sizable team out of its headquarters.

It's worth noting that the Singaporean funds and others may have leveraged their sovereign status to provide a bit of a perk for the staff in the US offices, where the tax code provides some potentially interesting catnip. For those SIFs (including some pension savings plans) that satisfy the arcane criteria of Section 893 of the US Internal Revenue Code, their non-US employees may enjoy exemption from US income taxation. That's a significant benefit not, of course, replicable by PE or VC fund managers for their US staff, hence it may provide a tool to narrow the yawning compensation gap often evident between Wall Street and government fund employees. It is not clear how widely SIFs have availed themselves of this recruitment tool, given that it is not without its own complications: because US nationals are not eligible for the tax break, the disparity may have to be addressed to maintain peace in the workspace between foreign staff and local hires.

Pension funds, as the earlier Dutch example (public pushback experienced by APG and PGGM over AlpInvest payouts) and the **Teacher Retirement System of Texas (TRS)** tale below demonstrate, are often more challenged in offering compensation packages on par with their private sector competitors. The Canadian pension funds appear to have come close to breaking the code. For the pension assets in Canada, the investment community has successfully developed a model of managing public assets with market rate-compensated professionals. (The onboarding of alternative assets team, Oxford Properties, through a take-private in Canada provided a case study earlier in this chapter.)

Today, many of the Canadian pensions have nurtured world-class deal teams that comb the globe for opportunities. They also enjoy physical proximity to US venture capital centers on the West and East Coasts, enabling them to be competitive employers in Toronto or Montreal, for example, while augmenting teams with fly-ins as needed, even on short notice. Still, they are building up teams in New York and San Francisco offices to better access investment opportunities and deepen relationships within the global technology ecosystem.

On the other hand, US and European pension funds have different governance structures with trustees who are not yet ready to sanction the cost of retaining top talent with million-dollar salaries (it's worth noting that the Canadian media has kept a close eye on CPPIB's $3-billion-a-year operation budget lately, and it's not unlikely that the "Canada

model" will be pushed back by stakeholders as in other jurisdictions). Especially in the US, public employee pension funds
are actually not able to blur the line between modestly paid
public servants and outperforming alternative asset managers.
For some, even the headquarters office rent is a tough topic,
let alone overseas offices and expatriate staff (see **Box: The
Texas Office of Wrath**).

## The Texas Office of Wrath

Austin, Texas enjoys a reputation as a tech magnet due to its quality of life and
active tech scene. Nonetheless, to build up its direct investment team, the $160
billion **Teacher Retirement System of Texas (TRS)** recognized that the competition
for talent was intense and workplace amenities could improve its standing. Thus,
the biggest public pension fund in Texas planned to move into what is billed as
Austin's tallest office tower – natural enough? Absolutely not.

Going into direct investments should lead to net substantial savings, as
TRS reckoned that it could save $1.4 billion in management fees and carried
interest by building out its internal private assets team (vis-a-vis investing into
PE funds). To carry it out, its CIO, Jane Auby told its board that the fund would
be competing for talent against other large pension funds as well as the private
sector and seeking to lure talent from New York, San Francisco, and Chicago.
The expansion space was not available in its existing building and new space
offered the amenities that would help it to attract the talent it sought.

As planned, the new office would be in a gleaming downtown tower, with
amenities including a fitness center, outdoor terraces, and restaurants and
stores in Austin's biggest downtown office complex. For a $3.9 million-a-year
lease to occupy three floors, the $160 billion pension fund unexpectedly took
heat from all sides, including comments from pensioners like: "It is shameful
that our money is spent for the luxury of those who are entrusted with our future
while retired teachers must go without what they deserve. Needless to say, we
are all furious. Do something about it."

Soon a firestorm was generated, and all stakeholders rushed to weigh in:

- 3506 comments on Facebook;
- 12 direct communications from legislators, in addition to several tweets
  by others;
- both the Texas Senate and the Texas House scheduled hearings; and
- 21 news stories from the state and national media.

> It will come as no surprise that the board backed down and canceled the move in light of the uproar. TRS will find expansion space in the building next to the freeway it has occupied for the last 11 years. And attempt to recruit talent in the tech hub that is in its backyard. Austin is not seen as a frozen outpost, like Edmonton or Juneau. Still, recruiting for a public pension even in a growing tech hub can be a minefield.

The tension on market-competitive compensation and operations budgets could seriously hamper sovereign investors' endeavor for tech deals and direct investments in general. When an institution does not enjoy a significant operations budget, it will likely allocate less to private assets because it cannot attract enough external talent to manage the activity. Meanwhile, internal teams also require scale; therefore, for funds that don't have large enough private equity allocations, such a team building exercise may not be worthwhile. As the high-profile case of **Japan Investment Corporation (JIC)** below illustrates, the compensation issue can completely derail a major sovereign fund, initially aiming to pursue innovation investments globally, even before it takes off.

By 2018, Japan had come to the conclusion that it had fallen behind in the competition to transform its economy into the digital future and foster its own unicorns. In a telling analysis produced by Japan's Ministry of Economy, Trade, and Industry in 2017, the size of Japan's VC funding (seed and growth stage) was unfavorably compared to other advanced nations. Based on the ratio of VC funding to GDP in 2015, Japan (at roughly 0.025%) stood well below the US (over 0.3%), was dwarfed by Israel (approaching 0.4%) and lagged behind Canada, the UK, France, and Germany.

The solution proposed by the METI? A sovereign fund to foster innovation and explicitly generate Japanese unicorns. In September 2018, the Japanese government created the new JIC under the supervision of METI and the Ministry of Finance (MOF). "Our mission is to enhance competitiveness of industrial sectors and create future industries, and deliver long term maximum return from investments, acting on principles of fiduciary duty," according to the official presentation; and an articulated goal of the new entity was to create "unicorn ventures." To this end, the government sought to recruit "world-class talent" to run the $18 billion fund focused principally on investing in startups and bringing new technologies to Japan.

Soon, Maasaki Tanaka, the former Deputy President of Mitsubishi UFJ Financial Group, Japan's largest financial firm with more than $2.8 trillion in assets, was hired as President and CEO. By October, JIC's first fund – "JIC-US" – was announced as launching in Silicon Valley. The California-based JIC-US would invest $2 billion in global startups that possess cutting-edge technology in the biotech and drug discovery fields. The fund essentially is JIC's US platform for broad mandates in direct investments and LP investments in both VC and public equity funds (see **Figure 7.6**). The fund would foster cooperation between the startups and Japanese businesses in the sector, so the team also needed cross-border expertise to link Silicon Valley investments with Japan's domestic pharmaceutical industry.

That's quite a team for a one-month-old fund to quickly put together. Just like earlier SIF examples, JIC planned to form JIC-US leadership with a mix of in-house executives (Yasunori Kaneko, Deputy President of JIC and a former Managing

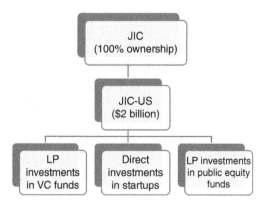

Figure 7.6     **Ambitious Mission of First JIC Fund**

Director at Skyline Ventures, a Silicon Valley healthcare fund) and external recruitment (a serial entrepreneur in the biopharmaceutical field was targeted, without disclosing the name). In his October 2018 public presentation on JIC-US, CEO Tanaka emphasized that JIC would "attract and develop best-in-class investment professionals."

But within a few short weeks, the wheels started to come off. In December 2018, all the private sector board members (leaving only the two from METI and MOF) had resigned in protest over the decision of the Ministry to backtrack on promised compensation arrangements. The executives complained that the ministry had betrayed their trust by lowering initially agreed terms: fixed annual pay of ¥15.5 million ($137,000), up to ¥40 million in short-term performance-based pay, and further incentives that collectively could boost the annual compensation above ¥100 million (approximately $900,000).

Apparently, the terms were agreed upon in October, but in November, the METI had a change of heart and requested that the management team lower their demands. The government said it withdrew the promised incentive compensation plan because it concluded such a package would never win public approval. The head of the ministry, Hiroshige Seko, apologized for what he said was a mix-up and said he would forgo one month's salary to take responsibility. At the same time, the ministry urged Tanaka to resign voluntarily as the head of JIC.

"We need to promise a certain level of compensation to secure world-class personnel," Mr. Seko said at a news conference in early December 2018. "But this is Japan. Compensation at an institution that manages public money needs to be in line with what the people find acceptable." The CEO Tanaka and eight other board members resigned. JIC-US was never mentioned again. More than one year later in early 2020, JIC finally had its new board and management team in place, but no investment had yet been started.

## Seeding: West Summit and Vision Fund

In-source development takes time and has its own challenges, and if the road to bringing in a "captive" team through a take-private deal is not possible, then what's a digitally hungry SIF to do in the wars for talent? For a young sovereign fund that wants to leapfrog the organic development and avoid internal debates, the fast way to build up a team is to "seed" a new team: one sovereign fund or a group of like-minded investors may set up a structure to sponsor a *de-novo* asset manager staffed by a seasoned investment team.

For instance, **CIC** was set up in Beijing late 2007, and right after the financial crisis it recognized in 2009 that tech investing was going to be an important investment theme for the decades to come. But there were few tech-background staff at CIC (and the North America office of CIC was not established until late 2011). How to jump-start in the Silicon Valley?

What CIC did was to sponsor a team of experienced entrepreneurs with both China and US backgrounds to form West Summit Capital. The four founding partners were native Chinese; they graduated within three years of each other from China's prestigious Tsinghua University and after that they all studied and worked in the US. They all had experience as entrepreneurs themselves (and investors), which provided perspectives different from CIC investment professionals. For West Summit's first fund, CIC provided all of the original $300 million as the sole backer, thus forming a strategic cooperation with West Summit.

Since 2009, West Summit has occupied a unique position as one of the only captive funds backed entirely by CIC, thanks mostly to the specifics of investing in the technology industry. At that time unicorns were, as the term itself suggests, rare; therefore, not too many technology startups could absorb equity checks in the hundreds of million dollars that CIC were writing in its early years of capital deployment. Instead, CIC made a large commitment to West Summit Capital, which could then invest in growth-stage technology companies for an average 10–20 million dollars per transaction.

The West Summit fund provided a high return for CIC, and the strategic value of West Summit for CIC was demonstrated in deals where, after West Summit's early stage investments, startups eventually became unicorns that suited CIC's larger size investment. One good example is Unity Technologies, a San Francisco-based software company that makes development tools for video game creators. It became a major player in the game engine space since it fully embraced mobile in 2008 and became one of the first platforms to support the iPhone during the earliest days of the App Store.

West Summit Capital first invested in the company's Series B round of funding (just $25.5 million). Soon, at the $181 million Series C round of funding in 2016, West Summit brought the deal to China Investment Corporation, and both West Summit and CIC invested in that round (see **Figure 7.7**). Less than a year later, when Unity Technologies raised $400 million from the private equity firm Silver Lake, the company's valuation reportedly reached $2.6 billion.

For particularly specialized sectors, even long-term tech investors like **Temasek** seek partnership with industry players to seed investment platforms together. For example, the logistics business is a traditional industry with a long history, little touched by venture capital. However, driven by the explosive technology developments, companies across global value chains are increasingly re-evaluating business models and investing in technology to optimize capture of demand as

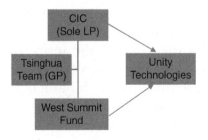

Figure 7.7    **CIC Co-invested with its Seeded-Platform West Summit in Unity**

well as improve operational efficiencies. Amazon and Alibaba, for instance, are investing in startups to innovate in last-mile delivery; mobility providers like BMW and Mercedes are working with startups to advance their work in cargo transport platforms as well as autonomous driving solutions.

Temasek sees a whole realm of startups developing products and capabilities to disrupt the supply chain and logistics space. They will bring in industry-changing new methods to carry out analytics and planning, and seek greater visibility in terms of information, materials, and goods flowing throughout the supply chain. For example, many are using AI, deep mind tech, digital logistics, and the Internet of Things (IOT) to solve problems such as analyzing supply chain data, tracking logistics flow, and making forecasts to manage the system risk.

Meanwhile Temasek recognizes the synergy from working with logistics incumbents to invest in the digital disruptors together. For Temasek, an established supply chain player would bring industry know-how and experienced operators not to be easily found in its existing investment portfolio. For the startups, they could form valuable partnership with incumbents since the latter are looking to gain access to new technologies to make their existing businesses more competitive.

As such, Temasek formed a partnership with Kuehne + Nagel, a transport and logistics giant headquartered in Switzerland, for this venture. In late 2019, Temasek teamed with global logistics company Kuehne + Nagel to launch Reefknot Investments, a $50 million joint venture fund for logistics and supply chain startups (see **Figure 7.8**). For high-growth technology businesses, they could gain business insights from Temasek, as well as the supply chain and logistics industry expertise of Kuehne + Nagel. This joint venture model bridges the gap between traditional business, the technology space, and the startups.

Compared to the modest size of West Summit Capital (China) and Reefknot Investments (Singapore), the setup of the **Vision Fund** team by Japan's SoftBank, plus the two major sovereign funds, PIF and Mubadala, took a more radical

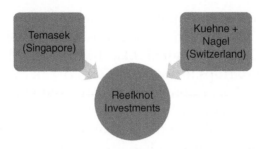

Figure 7.8    **Temasek forms JV Platform for Supply Chain and Logistics Industry**

approach. Japan, home of the Walkman and master of 1980s tech, had long been overtaken in the quest for the digital economy, as the story behind Japan Investment Corporation (JIC) reveals (case study earlier in this chapter). But there was one exception, SoftBank and its rockstar CEO, Masayoshi Son.

With SoftBank's early $20 million investments in Chinese e-commerce platform Alibaba turning into $130 billion recently, Son acquired a deserved reputation as a visionary. He parlayed that into raising, at $100 billion, the world's largest venture fund and enticed PIF and Mubadala to invest the lion's share (the Vision Fund's $100 billion fund size was roughly what all US venture capital firms *combined* had raised in the two boom years of 2018–2019). To cover the fast-moving world of venture capital that spans the globe and its time zones, Vision Fund operated out of SoftBank's Tokyo headquarters with offices in London, Silicon Valley, and Singapore. Meanwhile, Masayoshi Son recruited and formed an unconventional world-class team to lead the brainchild of Japan's SoftBank.

In general, top private equity and venture capital firms have a group of four to five managing partners that lead their respective firms, and in most or all of these cases, these partners have worked together for a long time (i.e., fight together through multiple investment cycles). Vision Fund, however, had a 12-person managing partner group. Among them, a former Google executive was recruited from Silicon Valley, and at least five were former Deutsche Bank traders, who came from a very different world far away from VC fund investments. This large team started to work together for the first time, changed the landscape of venture investing, and landed more unicorns than anyone else. However, as investment case studies in earlier chapter have shown, not all has worked out as planned.

The tension within the leadership team started almost immediately after the fund got off the ground. The *Wall Street Journal,* starting in 2017, recounted rival Vision Fund executives' payments to offshore accounts of private investigators, "honey traps" involving prostitutes to lure colleagues, "burner phones," and an Italian operative. All efforts allegedly aimed by one Vision Fund executive against another, commencing not long after the top talent was lured there. After the valuations of unicorns like WeWork started to shatter in 2019, the situation worsened. By early 2020, a few senior partners departed, followed by senior investment staff that were unhappy about what they saw as a toxic culture with "competing teams, inexperienced investment executives, and poor communication" (see **Box: Stalking the Unicorn Hunters**).

---

### Stalking the Unicorn Hunters

The SoftBank Vision Fund's team is an interesting mix. To start with, the common image of SoftBank is of a cutting-edge Japanese technology firm. But in fact, SoftBank's roots were in traditional, industrial Japan. A large number of Soft-Bank's executives came from the railway industry through its 2004 purchase of Japan Telecom which emerged from the privatization of Japan Railways. Besides railway and telecom industries, the company's executive team also included bankers and private equity specialists picked up in SoftBank's 2017 acquisition of Fortress Investment Group.

To manage the largest VC fund in the world, Vision Fund set up offices in London, Silicon Valley, and Singapore outside of its Tokyo headquarters, and Masayoshi Son needed to have an experienced team in place quickly on the ground in key locations (see **Figure 7.9**). One key managing partner was Rajeev Misra, a former fixed income trading executive at Deutsche Bank; another, Nikesh Arora, was snatched from a top position at Google. Misra worked from London, Arora from Silicon Valley. Son, the founder, was based in Tokyo.

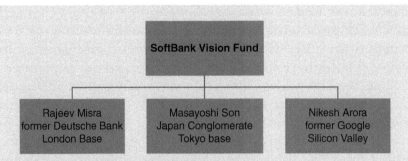

**Figure 7.9    Vision Fund Team in Global Locations**

But things went south quickly. Misra is cited by press reports as having operated a "dark art campaign" to discredit other executives at the fund and SoftBank. Notable among them was Arora, then SoftBank President. Misra allegedly arranged to lay a "honey trap" to lure Arora to a Tokyo hotel room, outfitted with hidden cameras, where he would have been filmed in compromising positions with women waiting there. Luckily for Arora, he never went. Internal investigations have not resulted in any reported actions.

Things got even more tense when failed bets on WeWork and other unicorns made PIF and Mubadala, Vision Fund's lead investors, leery. Son approached them and others about funding a second Vision Fund. As the WeWork debacle unspooled in the summer of 2019, investors shied away from Son. He then turned to Vision Fund and SoftBank staff to bridge the gap. The *Financial Times* reported that senior executives were being pressured to borrow up to ten times their annual salary to invest in Vision Fund 2. The commitment amount allocated to staff in Fund 2 was trebled over their goal in the first, to $15 billion. While the Vision Fund spokesperson stated that the intent was to align the interests of staff with those of the investors, some staff have spoken instead with their feet.

Senior executives have been departing or rumored to be weighing departure. Among them, in February 2020, one of the top five executives in the US, Michael Ronen, ex-Goldman Sachs and one-time Israeli Air Force Intelligence Analyst, exited; Michelle Horn, Senior HR Executive in the US, also departed in February 2020, after less than a year on the job; two other partners, David Thevenon and Praveen Akkiraju, made for the door even earlier, in October 2019. More investment staff left on their own, unhappy about what they saw as a toxic culture with competing teams, inexperienced investment executives, and poor communication, as well as a risky incentive structure.

By early 2020, senior staff had begun to exit: US-based Managing Partner Michael Ronen said he was leaving, following partners David Thevenon, Praveen Akkiraju, and around ten midlevel investing and operating staff who had shortly preceded them out the door. In a move that may or not be related, Jack Ma, Alibaba CEO left Softbank's board in June, 2020. While Son has long argued that his company is in the best position to capitalize on the coming artificial intelligence revolution for the long term, his team has far greater near-term problems.

The case of SoftBank Vision Fund is an important case study on seeding a new platform and building up a new team. It's hard to imagine that this alleged unseemly state of affairs could come to pass at the fund, where top dealmakers were supposedly stalking unicorns rather than one another. From the summer of 2019 (less than three years since the original fund was announced), SoftBank and Masayoshi Son started talking to potential investors about a comparably sized $100 billion for the Vision Fund 2, but the major sovereign investors were hesitant, according to media reports, and the future of this young platform looked challenging. In May, 2020, Son remarked that, in light of the performance of Vision Fund to date, he would not be seeking outside investors for Vision Fund 2 "for a while."

## Diversify and Participate: Building up an Ecosystem

Many challenges of "platform seeding" were illustrated by the Vison Fund saga. The charismatic Son built the team but found it difficult to maintain under the pressures of performance and geography. The world-class team assembled across continents appeared to crumble when the going got tough. (The opposite risk also exists: in the case of West Summit, the initial team of four departed in different directions after the *success* of their first fund together.) Meanwhile, asset managers in the tech sector are expensive, with uneven track records. Given the relatively long time horizons, past track records may not be the best indicators of future performance. And access to those managers with the best historical records is limited. All these are important factors for sovereign funds to consider before making a big bet on a new team.

The obvious risk mitigation, of course, is diversification. Instead of writing one single check of several tens of billions of dollars to a new team, a SIF may choose to commit a much smaller amount to a few different platforms. Furthermore, SIFs could even sponsor one new platform, which takes the job of seeding multiple new management teams. One example of this trend is Capital Constellation, a $700 million joint venture established in 2018 by the Alaska Permanent Fund Corporation (**APFC**), Railways Pension Scheme in the UK (**RPMI Railpen**), Public Institution for Social Security of Kuwait (**PIFSS**), and **Wafra,** a unit of the PIFSS (see **Figure 7.10**).

Among the founding members, the APFC was created by the Alaska Legislature in 1980 to invest and manage the assets of the Alaska Permanent Fund that had approximately $64 billion of assets under management. RPMI Railpen is one of the UK's largest pension funds with approximately £28 billion of assets under management. The PIFSS runs the social security system for all Kuwaiti nationals, spanning public and private sector professionals working at home and abroad, and its assets under management are approximately $60 billion. As a unit of PIFSS, Wafra is headquartered in New York with an additional office in Kuwait, managing approximately $20 billion private equity and alternative investments.

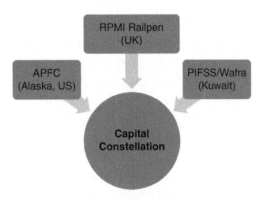

Figure 7.10    **Capital Constellation – JV to Fund Emerging Managers**

The four founding partners of Capital Constellation in 2018 initially committed $700 million to the venture and were expected to deploy over $1.5 billion over the following five years. The objective of Capital Constellation is to provide a long-term capital base and operational support for the next generation of promising PE and VC managers around the world. It pledges an anchor investment in a debut fund by new firms launched by experienced dealmakers, enabling talented investment teams to break through the challenges of initial fundraising; furthermore, it provides operational support such as back office setup, which is also valuable to investment teams launching their inaugural funds.

By providing institutional stability for new fund managers, Capital Constellation in return also receives a minority stake in the GP firm, which translates into an annuity-like cash flow from its share of management fees and carry. When the new funds develop successfully and move into follow-on funds, the SIF backers of Capital Constellation are incentivized, as partial owners of the GP management team, to continue investing. This structure plays to their strength as providers of long-term capital while facilitating exposure to deals that would be challenging to source and manage entirely in-house.

So far, the model is getting traction in mid-market private equity, as managers respond favorably to the prospect of a long-term LP relationship potentially over the lives of multiple funds. Four alternative asset managers have received commitments of at least $100 million each. The four all concentrate on mid-market deals with each specialized in a different sector. Among the four, two are digitally focused: Astra Capital Management, in communications and technology services, and Motive Partners, in fintech.

From the in-house capability building perspective, Capital Constellation is especially interesting in two ways. For one, by taking on LP and GP roles simultaneously, Capital Constellation is in a position to increase know-how for its own staff and those of its founders through GP involvement, something seldom on offer to LPs in large funds of established managers.

For another, by investing into a portfolio of new funds, Capital Constellation could gain broad market intelligence and diversify the risk of untested teams.

Actually, this long-term, portfolio approach should be applied in a broader context as many sovereign funds are embarking on venture investing for the first time. The best way to gain experience of this highly esoteric sector is for each SIF to build up a portfolio of diverse tech investments – LP investments in VC funds, co-investing, direct investing, all the way to GP stakes in new or established managers – and actively participate in them, so as to develop an ecosystem of fund managers, knowledgeable SIF peers, startup founders, university researchers, and tech company CEOs around itself (see **Figure 7.11**).

The sovereign funds can develop an investment approach that maximizes the learning, such as:

> **Investing in every vintage year.** Even though vintage year is critical to investment outcome, it's difficult to pick and choose the best moments. By investing through all vintage years, sovereign funds can gain a deeper understanding of how cycles really operate, and how the fund managers and portfolio companies cope with difficult times.
>
> **Making very long-term commitments to managers.** SIFs' long-term commitment, as well as their willingness to enter at less popular points during the cycle, will gain them access to the managers they want to work with. For new teams launching their inaugural funds, SIFs

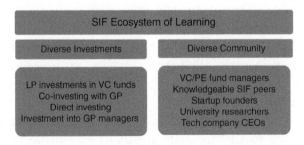

Figure 7.11   **SIF Ecosystem of Learning: Diversify and Participate**

need to look beyond the funds the managers are raising right now and consider the potential for the funds they'll raise in future.

**Co-investing with peer SIFs.** Learning from more sophisticated SIFs that have a longer history in tech investments can be very constructive, because it's a friendlier peers' relationship, drastically different from the LP–GP relationship within VC and PE funds. Considering many SIFs are cutting PE and VC funds investments, they need to actively network with its peer group to replace some of the ecosystem formerly provided by those funds in New York and London.

**Actively squeezing knowledge out of VC managers.** Venture capital managers do not tend to devote much time or resource to educating their LP investors, and engagements are generally limited to standard LP meetings. To derive more insight, SIF teams should arrive highly prepared at these sessions and keen to dig into the details. To step further, SIF may consider acquiring a stake in selective funds to get in the driver's seat with the GPs.

**Adding value to startups at VC funds' portfolio and own direct investment portfolio.** For tech companies that aim to grow globally, the SIFs have a lot to offer, such as domestic market knowledge, political and policy influence, and the value chain downstream/upstream network from the broad portfolio that the sovereign funds invest in. For example, CIC is an investor in both Alibaba and its unlisted fintech subsidiary Ant Financial (valued at more than $100 billion, the highest valued unicorn globally). Meanwhile, CIC's fully owned subsidiary, Central Huijin, is the government shareholder in ICBC bank, the largest commercial bank of China. In 2019, Ant Financial and ICBC formed a strategic partnership in mobile payment, online asset management, and other fields, creating a win–win for all stakeholders involved (see **Figure 7.12**).

Figure 7.12    **CIC Expands its Ecosystem in Fintech**

In summary, technology investment requires a diverse range of people with different skills and backgrounds, and for many sovereign funds building out a high performing team in global tech hubs remains a challenging exercise. However, it's critical and completely feasible for SIFs to leverage their capital, portfolio, and influence to better position themselves in the tech world and develop their in-house capabilities.

Besides their financial capital power, thinking like an operation partner not only helps SIFs establish direct relationships with startup management to gain tech industry knowledge, but also develops valuable due diligence and operations skill for future direct investments. With a long-term investment perspective, a strategy consciously developing over time, and institutional learning, the sovereign funds will get their investment strategy sharpened and world-class investment teams fully established.

## After the Shard

> *Approaching a decade after the Renzo Piano tower was topped out, Jellyfish still occupies half the 22nd floor of London's The Shard. The Qatari government is still the principal owner. But someone else is looking down on London Tower Bridge from the former Khazanah offices. Admittedly, there's Brexit, although this was not said to be the rationale; and with a change in government and government policy, Malaysia's sovereign fund has refocused its strategy on domestic priorities and vacated its ldeuxe Petronas Towers HQ for less iconic quarters at home.*

*But securing a team in a competitive tech hub like London was never going to be easy. That fact has not dissuaded SIFs from trying in places like Silicon Valley, where their numbers continue to grow. Khazanah left the Shard, but its offices in the US and China "remain relevant" because it has "a very big interest in technology." We hear that the views of the Golden Gate and Great Wall are compelling.*

CHAPTER

# Overseas Expansion and National Security Collide

*You enter, maybe a little groggy from jetlag and an early conference call. Or maybe bright-eyed after a morning jog through the thronging streets. Either way, you are ready for the breakfast buffet at your business class hotel. There's the full English: cooked tomatoes, baked beans, bacon, and eggs. Or the continental selection of croissants, jams, and coffee.*

*But that's only the beginning of the choices. Dim sum, one-hundred-year-old eggs, congee, smoked salmon, pots of steaming soups, spicy meats, avocado toast, black tea, green tea, flat blacks, lattes, pastries, 15 types of bread, fruits familiar and otherwise, marmite, cornflakes, smoothies, vegan options ... Lots to choose from.*

*Just like the sovereign investor, feasting on an investment buffet of assets from around the globe, traditional to trendy. But there comes a moment when you are asked for your identity and room number to verify that you are entitled to fill your plate(s) in NYC, KL, BJ, or elsewhere on the global investor circuit. Even for the well-heeled, there is no such thing as a free meal. SIFs must similarly follow the local rules when they serve themselves helpings of assets from around the globe.*

**W**e have reviewed the rise of the sovereign investment funds (SIFs); their transformation from passive allocators of capital to fully-staffed tech investors with enormous appetites for assets around the world. As the SIFs raised their forks or chopsticks and hunted their next unicorn meal, the host countries began to take note as well. And a collision course was set.

The startups seeking capital, then their corporate competitors, the host country capital markets, and, eventually, the governments and politicians gradually awakened to the actual or perceived impact of sovereign investors, sometimes in the role of "white knights" – as in the 2007 global financial crisis, when SWFs in particular were eyed as saviors of the developed world's financial institutions and, as the crisis unspooled, of the world's advanced economies.

## White Knights, Damsels in Distress, not so Happily Ever after

With their transformation from passive to active investors, their government links, and their massive cash piles, sovereign investors have, not surprisingly, garnered special attention. They have become big players and, as such, have attracted the attention of the press and the policy makers. Given that SIFs generally maintain a low public profile (and many are largely opaque), commentators in the host country often set the terms of discourse. The creation of a term for the category was symptomatic of the increased awareness. The term "sovereign wealth funds" is first noted in print in 2005, although the concept had existed for decades before.

A catalyzing event was the global financial crisis of 2007–2009. Financial institutions from the developed economies faced a liquidity crisis and were desperate to shore up their balance sheets, over and above cash injections from their own central banks. Bankers flew off to China, the Gulf, Singapore, and other SIFs, seeking large cash infusions and offering attractive terms. Deals ensued. (See **Table 8.1.**)

In December 2007, the newly established **CIC** purchased $5.6 billion mandatory convertible securities in Morgan Stanley's common stock, representing approximately 9.86% equity ownership. Its stake was diluted to approximately 7.86% after Mitsubishi UFJ Financial Group Inc bought into the bank in October 2008, and CIC in June 2009 invested an additional $1.2 billion to buy 44.7 million shares of common stock in Morgan Stanley to stay at approximately 9.9% ownership.

Table 8.1    SIF White Knights for Wall Street

| SIF Funds | Troubled Wall Street Firms | Fund invested |
|---|---|---|
| CIC (China) | Morgan Stanley | $5.6 billion + additional $1.2 billion |
| ADIA (Abu Dhabi) | Citibank | $7.5 billion |
| KIA (Kuwait) | Citbank | $3 billion |
| GIC (Singapore) | UBS | $11 billion |
| GIC (Singapore) | Citibank | $6.88 billion |
| Temasek (Singapore) | Merrill Lynch | $5.9 billion |

**ADIA** was also on the front line, committing in November 2007 to the $7.5 billion purchase of convertible interest-bearing securities of Citibank, representing 4.9% of the total equity when converted. The investment bore interest at 11% until a mandatory conversion at a price that turned out, however, to be ten times the trading price at conversion, locking in a multibillion-dollar loss. In a rare move for a SIF, ADIA commenced (and later lost) an arbitration with Citibank. Another SIF from the Gulf, **KIA,** invested $3 billion in Citibank in 2008, after the bank's shares had already lost most of their value. KIA's timing was better: it exited in 2009 realizing a profit of $1.1 billion, a return of 36.7% in the year it held the Citibank stake.

**Singapore** made similar investments. GIC pumped $11 billion into UBS in 2009, after the bank announced a $10 billion loss. GIC also converted $6.88 billion in Citibank preferred shares into an over 9% stake in the bank as the financial crisis proceeded. GIC subsequently profited on its Citibank exit but took a loss on UBS. Its sister SIF, Temasek, jumped into Merrill Lynch in the early days of the global financial crisis, and took a loss of $4.8 billion upon its exit shortly after Bank of America acquired Merrill in a US government bailout.

During the financial crisis, SIFs were in the headlines, sometimes seen as "white knights," sometimes as foolhardy. Nevertheless, foreign direct investment (FDI) was generally

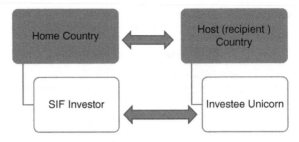

Figure 8.1　**Mixed Investment and International Relations**

regarded as having substantial benefits to both sides, including the recipient or host country that benefited from the capital. It was considered key to developing and sustaining national economies, including both China and the US.

Since the 2007 global financial crisis, the sovereign funds have been recognized as important participants in the international monetary and financial system. Today, it is hard to avoid the headlines their activities attract. As earlier chapters illustrated, they are especially in the spotlight as a recognized investor class in the tech boom. The SIF investments into unicorns not only form cross-border business relationships, but also play a part in the international relations between home country and host (recipient) country (see **Figure 8.1**).

That moment of glory and good feeling soon came to an end when the rise of SIFs as direct investors collided head on with another strong force: the growing political and popular perception of FDI as a threat. Not unlike the populist backlash recently witnessed against immigration in Europe, the United States, and elsewhere, foreign direct investment has lately been tagged as a potential threat and subjected to increased scrutiny at the border.

The current global tensions around the artificial intelligence (AI) race and tech competition have exacerbated such misperceptions, and this collision has played out in the arena of "national security" reviews of FDI. If there was gratitude to these "white knights" for their service in the global financial crisis, it was short lived. Regulatory regimes of host countries began to be recalibrated to take account of the identification of the new players and their more active roles. The modus operandi was the ever-expanding scope of national security reviews. In their global hunt for unicorns, the SIF investors are now subject to unique governance, legal, and regulatory constraints.

## Not all National Security is the Same

Host countries have pursued different strategies in border checking FDI. Some remain generally open to FDI while tracking it. Others have upped scrutiny, mandated notifications, or required prior approvals. The US, volume leader in inbound investment, bases its analysis solely on the (elastic) concept of "national security." Meanwhile, Canada screens on the basis of "net benefit" and Australia pays extra attention to the "critical infrastructure" (see detailed case studies later this chapter). Yet, both also include a "national security" element in screening FDI.

The concept of "national security" is a slippery one, subject to changing with the vagaries of public reaction. In the beginning, "national security" was generally seen as synonymous with military security, involving military suppliers, technology, and facilities. It has since ballooned to encompass much more. The US is a bellwether in this expansion of "national security" into surprising corners of the economy.

In the US, the **Committee on Foreign Investment in the United States (CFIUS)**, which will be discussed in detail below, reviews and decides on most investments. Occasionally, presidential actions may also be involved at the recommendation of CFIUS. Since the creation of CFIUS, presidential action has blocked seven transactions based on CFIUS recommendations, with the tempo noticeably increasing from Obama onwards in the most recent decade; coincidentally, all seven of them involved Chinese buyers (or the China factor, in the Broadcom/Qualcomm case).

In order to best understand the evolution of "national security" reviews, we examine the creation and evolution of the "national security" review of FDI in the US (the short list of

Table 8.2    Seven Transactions Blocked by US Presidential Actions

| Year | US President | Investor | Target |
|------|--------------|----------|--------|
| 1990 | Bush | China National Aero-Technology Import and Export Corporation (CATIC) | MAMCO Manufacturing |
| 2012 | Obama | Ralls Corporation (a China-controlled company) | Oregon wind farm project |
| 2016 | Obama | Fujian Grand Chip Investment Fund | Aixtron, a German-based semiconductor firm with US assets |
| 2017 | Trump | Canyon Bridge Capital Partners, a Chinese investment firm | Lattice Semiconductor Corp. of Portland, OR |
| 2018 | Trump | Singapore-based Broadcom | Qualcomm, a US semiconductor chip maker |
| 2020 | Trump | Beijing Shiji Information Technology Co., Ltd | StayNTouch, a US software supplier to the hospitality industry |
| 2020 | Trump | ByteDance Ltd | TikTok, US social media app |

presidential actions provides a glimpse into that evolution; see **Table 8.2**) and parallel developments in Australia and Canada. The frequency of reviews and the rationale behind them grew in fits and starts, often in reaction to specific deals, some of which form the basis of our case studies.

We will witness the transformation of such reviews from an approach intended to facilitate foreign direct investment, to a tool to further industrial policy in the digital economy – all leading to an inevitable collision with these former "white knights" when the motives of foreign government-controlled entities came under suspicion. As a result, there are high uncertainties in the regulatory environment for foreign sovereign funds in major investment recipient countries.

## CFIUS Origin: Japan before China

The Committee on Foreign Investment in the United States (CFIUS) dated back to a 1975 executive order from President Gerald Ford. Ironically, CFIUS was established to "dissuade

Congress from enacting new restrictions" on foreign direct investment. Ford's predecessor in office, Richard Nixon, under the pressure of OPEC-induced concerns over the weakness of the US dollar, had been forced to suspend the convertibility of dollars into gold. And the increasing investment by the oil-rich Gulf States in particular was seen as politically – not commercially – motivated.

The creation of CFIUS appeared to have appeased these concerns by instituting a review mechanism consisting (today, after expansion) of nine cabinet members and other officials in the executive branch of the US federal government (see **Figure 8.2**).

CFIUS takes the form of an interagency committee headed by the Secretary of the Treasury and includes the Secretaries of Commerce, Defense, Energy, Homeland Security, and State, as well as the Attorney General, the US Trade Representative, and the Director of the Office of Science and Technology Policy. In addition, the Secretary of Labor and the Director of National Intelligence are non-voting members and five White House offices hold observer status. Treasury staff handle the administration and all communications with parties to a CFIUS

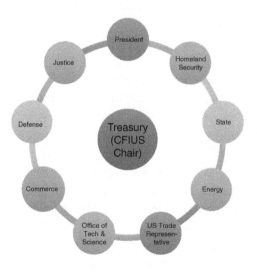

Figure 8.2   **CFIUS Member Agencies**

Table 8.3    Legislative History of CFIUS

| | |
|---|---|
| 1975 Executive Order | Created by the Ford administration to keep foreign investments from being politicized, at a time when Congress was worried about oil-rich nations' investment in US companies |
| 1988 "Exon-Florio" amendment to Defense Production Act | Codified the process used by CFIUS to review foreign investment transactions and formalized Presidential authority to block deals on national security grounds. |
| 1992 "Byrd Amendment" to Defense Production Act | Required reviews in cases where foreign acquirer is controlled by or acting on behalf of a foreign government. |
| 2007 Foreign Investment and National Security Act | Replaced Executive Order and codified CFIUS. |
| 2018 Foreign Investment Risk Review Modernization Act | Provided a comprehensive reform of the CFIUS process. |

review are conducted through them. Decisions are reached by consensus. Reviews were conducted without public disclosure and, for decades, CFIUS operated in relative obscurity.

CFIUS has evolved in recent decades (see **Table 8.3**), and the concept of "national security" has evolved accordingly. Most recently under the Trump administration since 2017, CFIUS appears to have "stepped up" restrictions on foreign, and particularly Chinese, investments for "national security" reasons. As America's technological hegemony is under threat from China, a rising innovation superpower, the remit of CFIUS is being significantly expanded to cover all transactions in the new digital economy.

In the early years, Japanese capital was at the frontline, and such foreign direct investment was seen as a threat to national cultural identity, if not national security. In 1988, during the Reagan administration, the US Congress enacted the Exon-Florio Amendment to clarify the legislative basis for presidential authority to block foreign acquisitions and to provide a more robust framework to replace President Ford's ad hoc executive order that originally establishing CFIUS.

The initial focus was on military technology and ensuring US capability to manufacture key military components on US soil and under US ownership. The textbook example was the 1987 Fujitsu bid for control of Fairchild Semiconductor, which was a main catalyst for the Exon-Florio Amendment (see **Box: Japan Inc. and the US Reaction**). Fear that a key military supplier would be bought and relocated to Japan (as was perceived to be the case with the electronics and auto industries) was enough to stir concerns in Washington, then in the throes of a trade war with Japan. No dealmaker thought that CFIUS would bother with any deal not involving military security.

### Japan Inc. and the US Reaction

Difficult as it may be to imagine today, the Reagan era currency realignment (known as "The Plaza Accord" after the New York City hotel where it was announced), led to a tsunami of Japanese direct investment in United States assets. Although sovereign investors were not the perpetrators – corporate Japan was – Americans viewed mounting Japanese investment as the workings of a foreign power.

Iconic US assets were scooped up: Rockefeller Center, Pebble Beach Golf Course, Columbia Pictures. The alarm was general: Paul Harvey, a leading syndicated newspaper columnist put it bluntly, "We are fat and soft and they are eating us alive." The flood of cash coincided with the dominance of Japanese automakers (Chrysler underwent its first US government bailout in this era) and the ubiquity of Japanese consumer electronics. (2019's 40th anniversary edition of the SONY Walkman was a non-event, but the device was the iPhone of the 1980s). Parallels were drawn to Pearl Harbor. New York City's then mayor, Ed Koch, publicly called upon New Yorkers not to panic over the sale of Rockefeller Center.

Amid this cultural ferment, in 1987 Fujitsu, a Japanese electronics firm, sought to buy 80% of Fairchild Semiconductor, a US semiconductor producer, from Schlumberger, a Franco-American NYSE-listed company that had previously acquired its parent. Fairchild was a military supplier to the US armed forces and senior members of the Reagan administration put intense pressure on Schlumberger not to sell to Fujitsu.

The Secretaries of Defense and Commerce as well as the CIA called upon the White House to block the sale. The deal was called off by the parties before the power of the President could be put to the test. Although national security was the stated basis for scuttling the deal, an important factor was an ongoing trade war with Japan.

Dealmakers learned to scrutinize potential foreign ownership of US military technology and would peruse the US government's export control list to judge the sensitivity of the target from a "national security" standpoint. It came as little surprise, then, that in 1990, President Bush directed the China National Aero-Technology Import and Export Corporation (CATIC) to divest its acquisition of MAMCO Manufacturing. MAMCO was a small aeronautics parts supplier to the US military with some of its products potentially subject to export controls as sensitive military exports. MAMCO had initiated a voluntary CFIUS review but proceeded to close the sale to CATIC before the initial, then applicable, 30-day review period had run (see later in this chapter **Box: The Many Steps of a CFIUS Foreign Investment Review**).

The surprising part was that this deal constituted the first exercise of Presidential authority to block or undo deals on the basis of "national security." The action confirmed, with a clear message, that military suppliers were dangerous prey. Congress acted further in 1992, requiring an extended CFIUS review whenever there was foreign government involvement in the deal.

Two decades had passed when, in 2012, then President Obama ordered the undoing of a second deal. In 2012, Ralls Corporation, a Chinese-controlled company, was ordered to divest itself of a wind farm project in Oregon. The decision sounds surprising as well but it fits firmly into the "military" framework. The wind farm, it turns out, was in close proximity to a US Air Force base and the wind turbine towers potentially provided prime sites for monitoring the facility. It was at the midpoint in time between these two divestment orders that the concept of "national security" had profoundly changed with the terrorist attack of September 11, 2001.

## Energy Security, National Security

By 2005, it had become abundantly clear that "national security" was not limited to military suppliers or facilities. That year, China National Offshore Oil Company (**CNOOC**), the Chinese state-owned oil giant, made a $18.5 billion bid for Unocal, a California-based oil and gas producer with production in Asia as well as the US. The bid came after Chevron had agreed on a deal to acquire Unocal at a lower price, aligning it against a US oil major with considerable clout in Washington.

Heightening concern was the Chinese government ownership in CNOOC. In the course of one of the largest takeover battles up to that time, foreign government control of US energy assets became a rallying cry for the opposition. Although the deal died before CFIUS handed down its decision, its mere announcement had led to calls by US congressmen to block it on "national security" grounds. Natural resources were now seen as part of "national security."

CNOOC walked away from the deal (Unocal eventually was acquired by Chevron), but it had not given up on North America. Resource-rich **Canada** next grappled with the issues raised by natural resources, again forced by a CNOOC bid (see **Figure 8.3**).

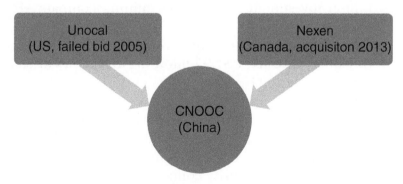

Figure 8.3    **Two CNOOC Bids, Different Outcomes**

In 2012, China's national oil company CNOOC and the government of Canada faced off in what was, in a way, a second chance for both. CNOOC made a $15.1 billion bid to acquire NEXEN, a Canadian oil producer with operations in Canada's oil sands as well as the North Sea and the Gulf of Mexico. While the US and the UK looked at the Gulf of Mexico and North Sea, Canada's concern was with its massive oil sands reserves, third in the world behind only Saudi Arabia and Venezuela.

The bid attracted considerable public attention in light of the perception that China's companies were scooping up Canada's natural resources at a heady pace after having been stymied in their quest in the US. Before the CNOOC offer for NEXEN, Chinese investment in the oil sands as well as in other natural resource industries in Canada had been on the rise, putting the spotlight on CNOOC's large public bid:

- CNOOC in 2011 made a major move into the oil sands by purchasing 100 % of troubled OPTI Canada for C$2.1 billion.
- Sinopec (another top three national oil company of China) acquired Daylight Energy in 2011 and made a C$4.65 billion investment in Syncrude in April 2010.
- China Investment Corporation (**CIC**), China's sovereign fund with an office in Toronto, made an investment of C$817 million in a new oil sands joint venture with Penn West Energy Trust in 2010; it also made a C$1.5 billion investment in Canadian mining company, Teck Resources, in 2009.
- Petro China (another top three national oil company of China) invested C$1.9 billion in Athabasca Oil Sands Corp. in late 2009.

Not to mention the burdensome backstories for both players. CNOOC came with baggage: its 2005 bid to acquire US oil and gas producer Unocal had ended in tears when US political backlash and national security concerns resulted in the deal's withdrawal. Canada, meanwhile, had raised doubts about its openness to foreign direct investment with its invocation of the Investment Canada Act (ICA) to block BHP's 2010 bid for another Canadian resources company, Potash Corporation. Both parties had a great deal weighing on the outcome.

**Investment Canada Act:** The Investment Canada Act (ICA) provides for reviews of foreign direct investment in Canada. Among the stated goals of the ICA is to attract beneficial foreign investment to Canada. The review is conducted confidentially without public disclosure. The final determination is made by the Minister of Industry, who is required only to issue written reasons for the decision, which may not be appealed. The process is consequently opaque – not too different from a CFIUS review.

There are two types of reviews: a "net benefit" review and a "national security" review.

**"Net benefit" review:** The better known of the two reviews is the "net benefit" test, addressing the question: is the proposed acquisition "likely to be of net benefit to Canada"? The considerations are primarily economic (with some cultural elements meant to protect Canadian creative industries from US domination). They include its effect on economic activity in Canada, employment and resource processing; degree of participation by Canadians in the business; the effect of the investment on productivity, product variety, industrial efficiency, technological development, innovation and competition in Canada; compatibility of the investment with Canada's industrial, economic and cultural policies; and contribution of the investment to Canada's ability to compete in world markets.

ICA reviews cover proposed direct acquisitions by a foreign acquirer of a Canadian business above the statutory dollar threshold. The threshold varies with the nature of the investor and is adjusted annually. (For example, currently the threshold for a WTO member-based state-owned enterprise (SOE) is C$428 million; different thresholds apply to non-WTO member-based acquirors, private sector acquirors, etc.)

SIFs are called out in Canada as well. A proposed acquisition by a state-owned entity (SOE) must further be assessed for: the corporate governance and reporting structure of the acquiror, the degree to which the acquiror is owned or controlled by the state, and whether the Canadian business being acquired will have the ability to operate on a commercial basis in the future.

**National security review:** A "national security" review under the ICA casts a wider net than a "net benefit" review. It can apply to any investment to establish a new business, to acquire control of a Canadian business, or to acquire, in whole or in part, or to establish an entity carrying on all or part of its operations in Canada. Decisions are final and cannot be appealed, but they can be subject to judicial review.

In the case of a "national security" review, the process is even more opaque than that for "net benefit" reviews. There is no definition for a "threat to national security," no written decision, and no appeal. Nor is there a disclosure that a national security review was conducted.

Both CNOOC and Canada's government seemed to have studied history. CNOOC was agreeable to mitigation measures to satisfy the Ministry on "net benefit" terms, despite their adding a considerable drag to its financial performance over time:

- CNOOC's NYSE and HKSE listings subjected it to corporate governance and disclosure.
- CNOOC also listed NEXEN securities on the TSE.
- CNOOC offered to establish its Americas head offices in Canada.
- CNOOC kept senior NEXEN management and agreed not to cut Canadian staff.
- CNOOC committed to increased investments in the oil sands.

Canada, for its part, did not repeat Potash and approved the massive investment. (And did so even before the US completed its – also favorable – national security review of the indirect transfer of NEXEN's Gulf of Mexico assets.) But the government added a caveat, drawing a line in the oil sands for non-Canadian SOEs. (As will be seen in **Chapter 10,** however, the SIFs have become active ESG investors in recent years, with many of them committing to avoid investments in traditional hydrocarbon energy such as oil sands. The grand political gesture of drawing a line in the sand turns out to have been meaningless in the end.)

Prime Minister Harper stated, when announcing the approval (together with that of a smaller deal by Malaysian state-controlled Petronas of another Canadian oil producer) before the deal's 2013 closing, that "Foreign state control of oil sands development has reached the point at which further such foreign state control would not be of net benefit to Canada." With this decision, a hard cap was effectively placed on SIF investment in a major sector in Canada's economy, adding oil sands to the "hands off" list.

## Critical Infrastructure, Expanded Review

It will come as no surprise that the next expansion of national security reviews was also born in the USA. With this next major shift, the collision course with SIFs was locked in. The Dubai Ports deal witnessed the crumbling of the firewall that CFIUS was meant to provide between the free flow of cross-border investment and political meddling.

In 2006, public and congressional concerns about the proposed purchase of commercial port operations of the British-owned Peninsular and Oriental Steam Navigation Company (P&O) in six US ports by **Dubai Ports World (DP World)** sparked a firestorm of criticism. It's worth highlighting that the Dubai Ports deal involved the transfer by one foreign entity to another of a lease (instead of ownership) to operate ports (see **Figure 8.4**). After a voluntary submission, CFIUS blessed the investment. The story could have ended there.

But times had changed after 9/11 and the trajectories of national security and direct investing by SIFs were doomed to cross and generate lasting fallout. Congressional and public reaction upon learning of the approval was swift and fierce,

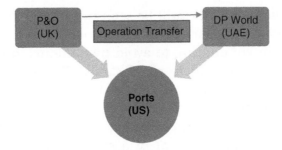

Figure 8.4    **Dubai Ports World and US Ports**

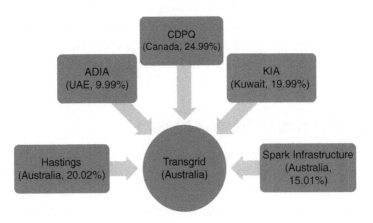

Figure 8.5    **Australia Transgrid's Winning Bidders**

focusing on the Dubai government's control of the acquirer, and the rallying cry was "national security." As a result of the unwanted attention by the public and Congress, Dubai Ports hastily sold the US port operations to a US insurer before the year was out.

The Dubai Ports affair made it evident that the September 11, 2001 terrorist attacks had dramatically changed the political landscape for CFIUS, which was clearly blindsided by the ferocity of the reaction from Congress. The public discussion centered on foreign government control of critical infrastructure. The Dubai Ports affair led directly to the adoption of new US legislation (FINSA) giving Congressional committees oversight of CFIUS reviews in real time, irrevocably politicizing the process.

Most importantly, the legislation formalized the expansion of "national security," under which FINSA subjected to CFIUS review foreign investments in "critical infrastructure." Like "national security" before it, the new term was undefined. The door was open to even greater expansion of reviews.

With the addition of "critical infrastructure," the impact fell on SIFs, which often favor infrastructure investments. Infrastructure can provide the scale and long life most attractive to the large, long-term investors. The earlier Byrd Amendment extension of the timeline for CFIUS review of SIF deals had lengthened the period of uncertainty (see **Table 8.3**), making SIFs less appealing bidders to sellers seeking certainty as well as the best terms. Subjecting this asset class to national security reviews now presented a major issue for SIFs.

History rhymes. We have seen how Canada widened the scope of its FDI review to include natural resources after the US had pioneered the category with CNOOC-Unocal. A decade after Dubai Ports led to CFIUS reviews of investments in "critical infrastructure," the "critical infrastructure" tale played out again, this time with even more drama, at the opposite end of the globe – **Australia.**

In 2016, as part of a movement to privatize assets, the government of New South Wales, Australia put half the interests in state-owned Ausgrid, an electrical distribution business, up for bid. Ausgrid supplies electricity to more than 1.5 million customers in Sydney and other parts of New South Wales. Its sale was anticipated to raise billions of dollars for the state government. The successful bidders for a 99-year lease over a 50.4% stake were Chinese government-owned State Grid Corporation and Hong Kong-based Cheung Kong Infrastructure.

As a foreign acquisition of a majority stake in an Australian business, the proposed transaction was subject to review by Australia's **Foreign Investment Review Board (FIRB)**. With a green light from the federal government, the deal proceeded to an advanced stage when suddenly the government pulled the plug on the sale.

At the last minute, the federal treasurer rejected the deal, citing national security. Seller and buyers were surprised by the decision, which enjoyed bipartisan political support at the federal level. It was particularly surprising given that the previous year New South Wales had successfully privatized Transgrid, another electricity distribution system, to a consortium with nearly 65% foreign ownership (including 40% owned by two SIFs based in the Gulf).

As is customary, the treasurer provided no basis to justify the national security grounds for the rejection of the Chinese bid for Ausgrid. The parties were left to speculate and the 50.4% stake was subsequently sold to the only all-Australian bidder, a consortium of IFM, which manages infrastructure investments for Australian superannuation funds and Australian Super, Australia's largest superannuation fund (in **Chapter 9,** the Australian IFM and China's State Grid Corporation will get involved in another critical infrastructure case together – 50Hertz, a power grid operator in eastern Germany).

No surprise then that the rejection – reportedly only ten days before the deal was scheduled to close – provoked cries of discrimination and a negative reaction from China as well as Australians favoring increased foreign investment. The story that later came out is revealing. The failure to identify and address the issue in a timely manner revealed a severe disconnect in the Australian national security review apparatus, the consequences of which would have been far reaching.

The story was that Australia had long maintained a list of critical infrastructure, but no one noticed the presence of Ausgrid on the list until, at the last minute, the Australian Signals Directorate, the Australian spy agency, spoke up. Ausgrid serves the Joint Facilities at Pine Gap, near Alice Springs. Pine Gap is the top-secret monitoring station of the Australia–US alliance. Its activities are key to US capabilities in the event of a nuclear war. A sale of Ausgrid to Hong Kong and Chinese government-controlled bidders would have been a major blunder infuriating the US. To do so unwittingly would only have been worse.

The fumble resulted from a lack of clarity as to which ministry held responsibility for the critical infrastructure element of a national security review. The solution? Another government body: **Australia's Critical Infrastructure Centre (ACIC)**. And heightened awareness in the federal government and among those advising potential non-Australian investors of the national security aspects of infrastructure, particularly the electrical grid.

In June, 2020, Australia proposed an additional level of review of foreign investment in "sensitive national security business." This potentially broad term is not defined nor, unlike the current review regime, does the proposal contain minimum investment amounts or ownership percentages to trigger the additional scrutiny. The change would grant the government broad discretion to block or undo investments. Advisers will now certainly add this proposal to the factors generating deal uncertainty for foreign investors.

## Tightening the Digital Screw

Since the creation of CFIUS, the ever-expanding rationale for "national security" reviews doubtless contributed to the increased number of submissions and reviews shown in **Table 8.4** below. Still, until the 2016 Presidential elections, the number of transactions reviewed remained limited and the number of outright rejections (not counting deals abandoned due to CFIUS scrutiny) remained a handful. The numbers, however, spiked in 2017 as the Trump administration dramatically expanded the use of CFIUS reviews. (And, although CFIUS has not yet provided figures for the subsequent years, we will see in Chapter 9 that the trend continues with more tech transactions challenged, withdrawn, or blocked.)

The stage was set for further tightening. The 2016 US elections had resulted in an executive branch that, unlike its predecessors, was as politically motivated against foreign ownership of US assets as the elements of Congress that CFIUS had been created to blunt. The force of the reaction to foreign direct

Table 8.4     Foreign Investment Transactions Reviewed by CFIUS, 2009–2017

| Year | Number of Notices | Notices Withdrawn During Review | Number of Investigations | Notices Withdrawn During Investigations | Presidential Decisions |
|------|------|------|------|------|------|
| 2009 | 65 | 5 | 25 | 2 | 0 |
| 2010 | 93 | 6 | 35 | 6 | 0 |
| 2011 | 111 | 1 | 40 | 5 | 0 |
| 2012 | 114 | 2 | 45 | 20 | 1 |
| 2013 | 97 | 3 | 48 | 5 | 0 |
| 2014 | 147 | 3 | 51 | 9 | 0 |
| 2015 | 143 | 3 | 66 | 10 | 0 |
| 2016 | 172 | 6 | 79 | 21 | 1 |
| 2017 | 237 | 36 | 561 | 145 | 3 |

Source: *Annual Report to Congress*, Committee on Foreign Investment in the United States, CY 2016 and CY 2017, as of December 2019 (due to the CFIUS reporting schedule, the figures for years after 2017 are not yet available).

investment in the US became evident when the White House and both parties, in one of the most politically divisive moments of US history, circled the wagons and fortified the role of CFIUS and its scrutiny of foreigners buying in the US.

As the numbers in **Table 8.4** show, even before Congress acted in the summer of 2018 to codify the new rules of the game, a distinct trend in US presidential actions emerged. Conceived by the White House as a bulwark against political hindrance of foreign direct investment in the US, CFIUS had already increasingly become a policy tool of the White House and more attuned to the political winds. Through the history of CFIUS, presidential action blocked seven transactions based on CFIUS recommendations, with the tempo noticeably increasing from Obama onwards, especially in the last five years – as along with the global tech revolution, more digital economy transactions were reviewed and challenged:

- In 1990, President Bush directed the China National Aero-Technology Import and Export Corporation

(CATIC) to divest its acquisition of MAMCO Manufacturing.

- In 2012, President Obama directed the Ralls Corporation to divest itself of an Oregon wind farm project.
- In 2016, President Obama blocked the Chinese firm Fujian Grand Chip Investment Fund from acquiring Aixtron, a German-based semiconductor firm with US assets.
- In 2017, President Trump blocked the acquisition of Lattice Semiconductor Corp. of Portland, OR, for $1.3 billion by Canyon Bridge Capital Partners, a Chinese investment firm.
- In 2018, President Trump blocked the acquisition of semiconductor chip maker Qualcomm by Singapore-based Broadcom for $117 billion.
- In 2020, President Trump directed Chinese acquiror Beijing Shiji Information Technology Co., Ltd to divest its 2018 purchase of StayNTouch, Inc., a US software supplier to the hospitality industry.
- In August, 2020, President Trump directed China's Bytedance to divest its 2017 acquisition of TikTok (originally musical.ly) the wildly popular social media application, as discussed in the following chapter.

The actions of the Trump administration in two 2018 cases outlined below, Qualcomm and Ant Financial, dramatically expanded the use of "national security" reviews into new areas. Neither involved any plausible military technology or facility. Absent also were natural resources and "critical infrastructure," at least in the physical sense in which it had been understood. Instead, they illustrate the simmering "America First" and "Tech Supremacy" atmosphere that boiled over into the adoption of FIRRMA that summer.

**Qualcomm/Broadcom transaction:** On March 12, 2018 President Trump blocked Singapore-based Broadcom Limited's $117 billion bid for Qualcomm Incorporated. Broadcom, a US tech company based in Singapore for tax considerations, was viewed as an aggressive cost cutter. It was feared that the acquisition would lead to severe cuts in the R&D investments at

Qualcomm and hence America's loss of the battle to dominate fifth-generation (5G) wireless technology, where China's Huawei is in the lead.

The Treasury Chair of CFIUS even sent an unprecedented letter to the parties in the CFIUS proceeding on March 5, 2018 to this effect. Complicating matters, Broadcom was in the process of redomiciling as a US entity, which would have arguably deprived CFIUS of jurisdiction. CFIUS reacted by requiring Broadcom to provide advance notice before so proceeding – presumably to allow CFIUS the power to block the deal. It all added up to a sweeping land grab by CFIUS where many viewed the transaction as not involving national security, but rather a blatant effort to favor the home team in the 5G race.

The Qualcomm fighter jet scramble made clear the Trump administration's concern about Huawei's leading role in 5G wireless technology. The no-holds-barred nature of the reaction served to lay bare that the US is strategically disadvantaged in the 5G battle by the lack of a US competitor to Huawei. If CFIUS is one of the arrows in the quiver, interestingly, the concept of sovereign funds is another. Attorney General, Bill Barr, has suggested a US national fund to acquire a controlling stake of the European firms, and Congress is separately contemplating a 5G tech-specific fund to develop alternative products to Huawei's 5G network (more detailed discussion in **Chapter 10**).

**Ant Financial and MoneyGram transaction:** The Trump administration, eager for action and not interested in waiting for Congress, employed CFIUS in yet another novel area, money transfers. Most associate the sector with Western Union outlets in immigrant neighborhoods or truck stops, not with national security. Not the Trump administration, judging by the roadblocks thrown in the way of Ant Financial, the Chinese fintech.

Ant Financial is the mobile finance and asset management arm of China's Internet giant Alibaba. As discussed in earlier chapters, both Ant Financial and its parent have major SIFs – from China's CIC to South-east Asian SWFs and Canadian pensions – as their shareholders. At the beginning

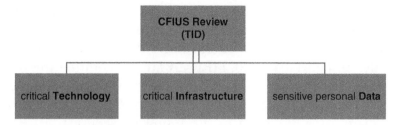

**Figure 8.6    The TID Focus of CFIUS**

of 2018, Ant Financial cancelled its bid to acquire US money transfer company MoneyGram International Inc. after CFIUS rejected the proposed action over national security concerns. At the time, it was the most high-profile Chinese deal to have been annulled under the administration of President Trump.

Dallas-based MoneyGram has approximately 350,000 remittance locations in nearly every country in the world. Ant Financial, looking to expand outside its home market, sought MoneyGram not principally for its US presence, but rather to expand in growing markets elsewhere outside China. Struggling MoneyGram saw a lifeline in an expanding Ant Financial. Once the deal died, Ant Financial and MoneyGram announced that they would explore and develop initiatives to work together in remittance and digital payments in China, India, the Philippines, and other Asian markets, as well as in the United States through some form of commercial agreement.

The scrutiny and eventual withdrawal of the deal highlighted the increased perception of "sensitive personal data" as an area of concern in both China and the US, again expanding the concept of national security to encompass yet another sector of the economy unrelated to the military. MoneyGram's financial records of US nationals were extensive. Ant Financial would have acquired the data and, the argument went, as a Chinese company potentially have exposed it to the Chinese government. The CFIUS action was a precursor to the 2018 legislation and the eventual articulation of TID (see **Figure 8.6**), casting personal data of American citizens into the national security bucket.

Playing catch up with the transformative Trump moves, Congress enacted the Foreign Investment Risk Review Modernization Act (**FIRRMA**) in 2018 and the final rules became effective in February 2020. FIRRMA largely codified the practices that had become fait accompli with the Qualcomm and MoneyGram blockages. While the entire CFIUS process was still opaque (as discussed in the following section), FIRRMA articulated for the first time CFIUS practices that, under the Trump administration, CFIUS had already been pursuing in the digital economy.

The most revelatory and impactful element of FIRRMA for SIFs wishing to participate in the global digital economy is the emergence of the new concept, the TID (critical **technology,** critical **infrastructure,** and sensitive personal **data** of US citizens, see **Figure 8.6**). In a significant departure from a nearly half century of CFIUS practice, the existence of a Foreign Government Interest (FGI) in an acquirer triggers a *mandatory* filing when the transaction involves acquisition of "substantial interest" in a "TID US business."

Prior to FIRRMA, CFIUS submissions had been voluntary. Although they were customary and frequently employed to de-risk deals involving foreign investors, the imposition of a mandatory regime was a sea change. In another significant expansion, CFIUS was granted expanded power, where TID is involved, to review and block transactions that did not involve "control." The sovereign funds, which fall squarely into the Foreign Government Interest (FGI) category, face mounting barriers for TID transactions.

## Changing Game for SIF/The CFIUS Review Process for SIFs has Changed

Post FIRRMA, SIFs investing in the US digital economy can expect greater scrutiny and longer reviews. The process, as updated by FIRRMA, imposes considerable uncertainty for those subject to it. A few of the more surprising aspects include:

- CFIUS is secretive; its proceedings are exempt from compulsory disclosure to demands lodged under the US's Freedom of Information Act.
- There is no mechanism for appeal of its determinations either in administrative tribunals or courts.
- In fact, no rationale is provided when a determination is reached, typically only in the form of a one-page notification letter.
- Despite its "national security" mission the "lead" agency is Treasury, not Defense or Homeland Security, although these and other agencies with seemingly more relevant expertise play "behind-the-scenes" roles.
- As a result, all communications are through Treasury staff and not with the other agencies that are often the real parties in interest, adding further opacity.

Navigating CFIUS requires understanding its unusual structure and process. **First,** no longer are CFIUS reviews even nominally voluntary for SIFs, as they had been for all from the start. FIRRMA introduced a mandatory "declaration" applicable to SIFs (and others with a "substantial interest" by a government) in transactions involving TIDs. The foreign investor and the target company typically prepare a submission – called a "notice" – jointly. The preparation of the notice is often burdensome and time-consuming. Detailed information about the foreign investor and the target must be gathered and set forth. The process proceeds, ideally, on the timeline in **Box: Many Steps of CFIUS**).

## The Many Steps of a CFIUS Foreign Investment Review

With the expansion of the concept of national security to include many of the areas of potential digital growth, the investment teams at the sovereign investors now look at the process for review by the US Committee on Foreign Investment in the United States (CFIUS) as a gating issue which determines whether it is even worth considering submitting a bid for an asset with a US component or connection.

On paper, the process appears straightforward with specific time periods set out for each step. Instead, the process will be prolonged by a pre-filing period during which the CFIUS staff declines to "accept" a filing until the staff is ready – after having received a full briefing from the applicants. And, once the formal process begins, it is not uncommon that the time periods are effectively extended when the applicants are encouraged (by CFIUS staff offering as an alternative the prospect of a quick "no") to restart the clock by withdrawing and resubmitting. The increasing practice of negotiating detailed mitigation agreements can consume even more time. Experienced deal lawyers recommend planning on five to six months from deal signing to exiting the CFIUS process.

Not so fast. **Figure 8.7** shows a sample schedule of the steps for a SIF deal involving a TID business. But expect delays.

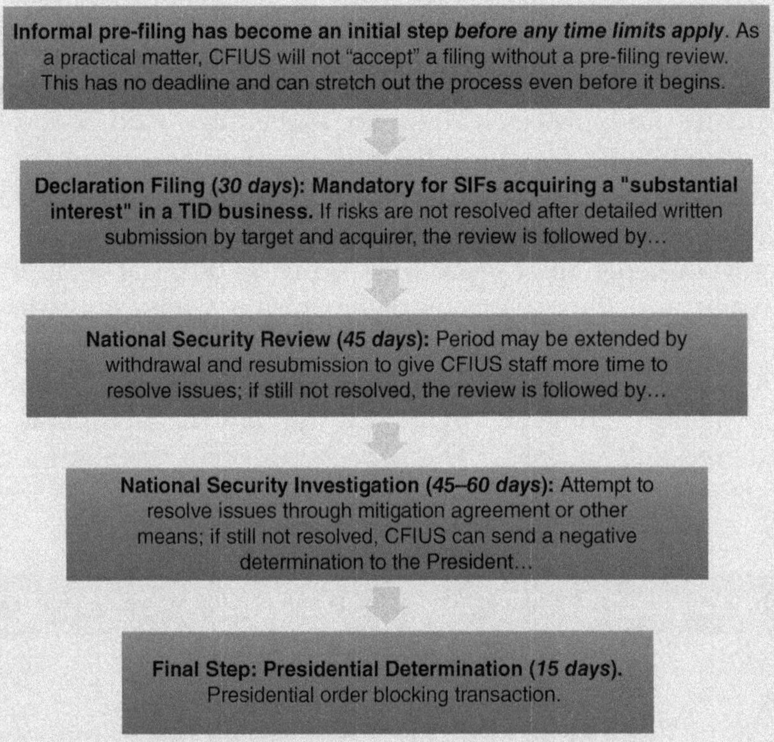

**Informal pre-filing has become an initial step** *before any time limits apply*. As a practical matter, CFIUS will not "accept" a filing without a pre-filing review. This has no deadline and can stretch out the process even before it begins.

**Declaration Filing (*30 days*): Mandatory for SIFs acquiring a "substantial interest" in a TID business.** If risks are not resolved after detailed written submission by target and acquirer, the review is followed by...

**National Security Review (*45 days*):** Period may be extended by withdrawal and resubmission to give CFIUS staff more time to resolve issues; if still not resolved, the review is followed by...

**National Security Investigation (*45–60 days*):** Attempt to resolve issues through mitigation agreement or other means; if still not resolved, CFIUS can send a negative determination to the President...

**Final Step: Presidential Determination (*15 days*).** Presidential order blocking transaction.

Figure 8.7 **The Many Steps of CFIUS**

Not only the opacity but even more so the unpredictability of its timing means that the CFIUS review process itself often precludes SIFs from deals, even if the outcome is highly likely to be favorable.

**Second,** for the purpose of jurisdiction, "US business" means US businesses and, well, a bit more. Existing law before FIRRMA defines a "US business" as any entity "engaged in interstate commerce in the United States, *but only to the extent of its activities in interstate commerce*" (emphasis added). The final investment regulations, however, intentionally omit the underlined phrase, which appears to expand the scope of CFIUS's jurisdiction in cases involving investments in global business with a US presence. Despite receiving numerous comments on this point, CFIUS noted the definition "tracks the language of FIRRMA and is not intended to suggest that the extent of a business's activities in interstate commerce in the United States is irrelevant to the Committee's analysis of national security risk."

**Third,** for the scope of investments to be reviewed, "Covered Investments" expands the CFIUS review well beyond controlling stakes. In the past, non-controlling investments were outside CFIUS's jurisdiction. Now "Control" is not a predicate to a CFIUS review of TID investments; it is sufficient simply that there be access to certain information in the possession of the TID business, certain rights in the TID business, or involvement in certain decision-making at the TID business.

**Finally,** the process is now prolonged and potentially never ending. National security concerns that arise from the filing, review, or investigation may be addressed by mitigation. For example, the access of foreign nationals to sensitive information can be restricted, the ability of the foreign acquirer to influence management can be limited, a division or subsidiary can be "ring-fenced" or restrictions imposed on the disposition of the target. These restrictions can be reflected in various instruments, including agreements with provision for ongoing monitoring after closing.

The result has altered a process that was designed to end with a clear "yes or no" decision and protect the buyer and seller from later reversal of their deal. It has now become a means for continued government involvement in the operation of the business, including screening foreign nationals from information to periodic US government compliance visits. Due to the increasing imposition of "mitigation" measures, the transaction may continue under CFIUS oversight even after the deal is "cleared" and closed.

FIRRMA did not stop there in altering the process to disadvantage SIFs from most nations. Specified nations were granted a free pass and PE/VC fund managers were favored. **Certain specified nations** were excepted from review of non-controlling covered investments (the exception does not apply to control transactions which remain subject to CFIUS). The status is subject to review after two years but reveals the schism developing between the US and its allies and China and the rest of the world. Enjoying this special status – for initially two years – are three English-speaking nations (see **Figure 8.8**); Japan, despite being a close ally of the US, did not make the cut (see **Box: The Yellow Peril**).

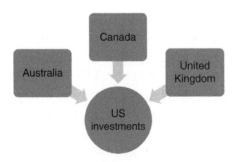

Figure 8.8    **CFIUS Excepted Foreign States**

**The Yellow Peril**

As the history of restrictions on foreign direct investment in the US demonstrates, it has been investment by Japan, Dubai, and now China that has caused Congress to rally to action. It is remarkable that, in a period of intense partisan division in US politics, there was solid bipartisan support for FIRRMA. Today's reaction against Chinese investment in the US is reminiscent of the US reaction to the Japanese investment growth in the 1980s.

Despite all the headlines of China capital buying up Silicon Valley and the US, cumulative Chinese investment is low compared to many European countries. The more than $500 billion cumulative total for UK and Canadian direct in investment in the US (2018 figures) dwarfs that of China, which falls below Sweden in the rankings. Some commentators believe that the underlying cause of the strong, bipartisan response to Chinese investment may be motivated by racism. Paul Musgrave, writing in *Foreign Policy,* read the truth in a slip of the tongue.

He reported public remarks in April 2019 by the State Department's Director of Policy Planning, Kiron Skinner, who noted that US competition with China would be especially bitter, she argued, because "it's the first time that we will have a great-power competitor that is not Caucasian."

Whether or not Musgrave has put his finger on the cause, the heightened reaction to Chinese investment bears striking resemblance to the near panic that greeted the wave of investment in the US in the 1980s by America's staunch ally Japan, lending credence to the view that American policy is not grounded in simply national security or industrial policy. Not to mention the CFIUS "white list" featuring Australia, Canada, and the UK but not Japan.

**Investment funds** were given favorable treatment to accommodate offshore structures of US PE funds and their rosters of SIF LPs. Of relevance to how SIFs can access US investments post-FIRRMA, the legislative and rulemaking processes also provided an opening for the private equity managers to strengthen their positions as intermediaries for SIFs seeking exposure to private assets in the US.

If the following are satisfied, a SIF will not satisfy the "substantial interest" for TID investments (and thereby avoid triggering a mandatory filing and extended review) by a PE or VC investment fund in which the SIF is merely an LP, with no interest in the fund's GP:

- Fund GP manager is US (not a foreign person).
- LP advisory board has no investment power nor portfolio company governance.
- No non-US LP investors has access to material non-public technical information.
- Non-US LP investors have no access rights or involvement in the businesses.

This last carve-out provides a major incentive for SIFs to partake in US investments in sensitive sectors via US fund managers. Given the lobbying savvy of the US PE and VC industries, this is not surprising. With this provision, SIFs may reconsider their path to direct investment in the TID sector and return to passive LP roles with US PE and VC managers, or decide to invest in other, more receptive markets. Time alone will reveal the impact of this bone thrown to the PE/VC industry.

## Widening the Net

The national security threat posed by ham was not immediately apparent to the casual observer when CFIUS in 2013 accepted for review a submission of the proposed purchase for $4.7 billion of Smithfield Foods, America's largest ham producer, by Shuanghui International, a Chinese meat processor. At the time, the transaction was the largest purchase of a US company by a Chinese firm. Although US lobbyists raised specters of threats to food security in a letter to CFIUS, and the Senate Agriculture Committee held hearings on foreign takeovers in the US food sector, even CFIUS could not uncover a national security issue in pork.

But the trend toward wider application of the powers of CFIUS was now baked in. More serious efforts to expand the scope of CFIUS ensued. A pair of CFIUS actions shortly before the passage of FIRRMA swiftly brought home the more aggressive stance of the Trump administration. The first case in point: Cofense, a US cybersecurity firm that simulates and detects attacks transmitted via email as a defense against security threats faced by US companies and others.

BlackRock acquired Cofense in February 2018 (six months before FIRRMA was signed into law) together with a group of investors, including Pamplona. Pamplona is a PE firm with Russian investors founded by Alexander Knaster, a former CEO of Russia's ALFA Bank. Pamplona obtained a board seat as part of the deal but was otherwise apparently a passive minority investor, with Black-Rock running the show. Nonetheless, CFIUS intervened in the following months. Pamplona ultimately relinquished the board seat and agreed to sell its stake. (After a failed auction, BlackRock took Pamplona's stake in a deal which kept the economics with Pamplona, win or lose, and off BlackRock's balance sheet.)

The scenario seems to fall clearly within the CFIUS wheelhouse, particularly in light of FIRRMA's curtailment of foreign access to material non-public technical information in the TID context. However, the passive nature of Pamplona's upstream investors was probably what gave the parties – Cofense and BlackRock as well as Pamplona – comfort in proceeding without seeking CFIUS clearance. (Seeking such approval was still voluntary pre-FIRRMA but CFIUS risk would likely have been taken into account by the target and BlackRock as lead investor.) Lesson learned: CFIUS is looking deeper into access to information resulting from investment.

At the same time, CFIUS was casting a wider net, entangling more nations and sectors, including some that most observers would have considered – like pork – outside any rational discussion of "national security." In late 2018, CFIUS blocked a transaction whereby a Japanese building supplies maker would have sold its loss-making Italian subsidiary to a Chinese construction group. The players were Lixil Group of Japan, Grandland Holdings of China, and the target, Italian Permasteelisa (see **Figure 8.9**). The national security concerns arose over the US unit of the target, a company which produces exterior building products, such as materials for New York's Museum of Modern Art and Apple's headquarters in Silicon Valley.

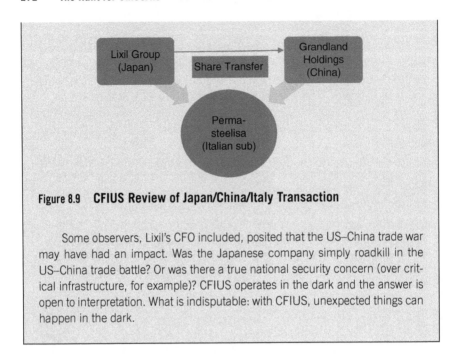

Figure 8.9   **CFIUS Review of Japan/China/Italy Transaction**

Some observers, Lixil's CFO included, posited that the US–China trade war may have had an impact. Was the Japanese company simply roadkill in the US–China trade battle? Or was there a true national security concern (over critical infrastructure, for example)? CFIUS operates in the dark and the answer is open to interpretation. What is indisputable: with CFIUS, unexpected things can happen in the dark.

In summary, the United States has led the way in tightening the rules on national security review of FDI again with FIR-RMA, just as it did with Exon-Florio in a time of trade tensions, then with Japan, now with China. Australia and Canada most notably, among others, have also increased scrutiny on inward investment and now enjoy special friends' status under the US CFIUS review process. The scope of investment subject to reviews has exploded in recent years (see **Box: Widening the Net**). The focus on government investors, including SIFs, has become intense.

We will assess the continuing and accelerating impact of this expansion in the following chapter. The world is dividing into camps and yet SIFs continue to have a mandate to invest and achieve returns that are increasingly to be found in high growth digital startups. The table is set for the next course.

> *Breakfasting at the hotel buffet, you may notice those who sample from multiple cuisines. Others stick to their morning routine and do not touch the choicest items from the breakfast fare of other nations. Not feasting on foreign delicacies may simply be habit at the first meal of the day. The motivation may be different for SIFs as national security tests increasingly restrict their diets, morning, noon, and night.*

CHAPTER

# Tech Transactions Snared by Geotech Tension

*The Grindr Multiple Choice Quiz*

*Now for something different. We start with a quiz. It's about Grindr, the gay dating app. First, the background: over 3.6 million daily active users rely on this gay-dating app to see profiles of other users in their immediate vicinity. Using geolocation tech, the most popular all-male mobile social networking site loads your screen with a "cascade" of men looking to hook up, ranked by proximity to you.*

*You can tap to view the profiles, which display "tribe" (Bear, Clean-cut, Geek, Jock, Otter, Poz, Twink, etc.), height, weight, as well as HIV status (and date last tested). The chat function can be used to send photos. (Profile photos cannot include nudity or underwear shots, limitations that do not apply to chats.)*

*The app – frequently referred to as a "hookup" app – has been downloaded over 27 million times and has won industry awards, including the TechCrunch 2011 award for best location application. Criticized for contributing to the demise of traditional gay social hubs such as gay bars, it has also been praised as a low-risk way for gay men located in remote or intolerant locations to find social connections.*

*Did you catch it? The vital national security issue? The one that aroused the wrath of CFIUS and resulted in a forced divestiture? Millions of its users did not, evidently. Nor did the dealmakers who had arranged the 2016 sale of the West Hollywood company to new Chinese owners.*

*If you are a quick study, you might have caught it. As the contours of the value – as well as the potential for weaponization – of personal data become clearer, a plausibly correct answer emerges. CFIUS isn't saying, of course, and so we list multiple choice answers:*

A. *Geolocation allows access to activities of millions of users, some of whom may be military or sensitive government employees or contractors.*

B. *Sensitive personal data, such as HIV status, can be used to compromise users.*

C. *Explicit photos, sexual practices, and other personal data can be used for blackmail.*

D. *Where gay sex is prohibited, disclosing use of the app may result in legal action.*

E. *All of the above.*

*We are giving you full credit if you answered "E." (To learn more and for extra credit, study **From Hard Tech to Invisible Data** in this chapter.)*

Years ago, the sovereign funds' direct investments in the tech industry were focused on "2C" services, such as consumer technology, e-commerce, and the sharing economy (such as Grindr). Such investments have slowed down lately, partly because those sectors have largely consolidated, leaving a few dominant players that enjoy either regional or even global monopoly (for e-commerce, Amazon in the US and Europe and Alibaba in China; for ride-sharing, Uber in the US and Didi in China, and so on). Consequently, many funds view themselves sufficiently exposed to these sectors.

The more powerful force behind this shift is that the global *consumer-focused* Internet is transforming into a more *enterprise-oriented* Internet. Consumers have long embraced digital technology to improve their lives, whereas industry is just starting to figure out how digital tools – including AI (artificial intelligence), the latest – can improve their productivity. The connection between Internet businesses and manufacturing sectors is deepening, and the upgrade of traditional industries (financial services, retail, healthcare, and so on) is accelerating.

If the years 2014–2015 marked the start of global mobile Internet economy, the years of 2017–2018 are an even more important inflection point for the world's digital transformation. Now the frontline of the digital economy is moving into an enterprise-led transformation characterized by more advanced technologies such as the Internet of Things (IoT),

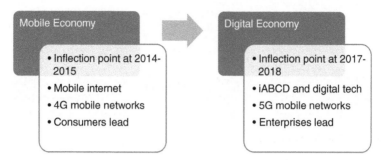

Figure 9.1    **From Mobile Economy to Digital Economy Investments**

artificial AI, blockchain, cloud computing, and data analytics (iABCD), 5G mobile networks, and more digitalized industries (see **Figure 9.1** below).

As a result, the sovereign funds are now thinking more systematically and focusing more on disruptive innovation. Rather than investing in a mobile Internet platform that attracts large user traffic for everyday services or entertainment content, they are looking to invest in a disruptive idea or technology that will transform industries. Such companies are often more reliant on their intellectual property for success (more barriers to competition vis-a-vis e-commerce), while requiring relatively large capital investment to support deep tech research and subsequent global expansion – a good fit for the long-term investor.

However, in a climate of resurgent nationalism and trade wars, host governments are becoming more cautious about foreign direct investment, particularly in those sectors that they perceive to have greater national security issues. As discussed in the previous chapter, the new FIRRMA legislation in the US mandates that CFIUS view national security through a wider lens: in addition to the more traditional indicia such as protection of defense facilities and infrastructure, government contracts, etc., the innovation capability to develop emerging "TID" technologies is the new focus (see **Figure 9.2**):

- Critical technology: including the sorts of military- and defense-related items with which CFIUS has traditionally been associated, as well as certain "emerging and

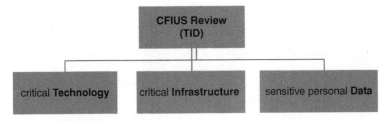

Figure 9.2    **The TID Focus of CFIUS**

foundational technologies" used in industries, such as computer storage, semiconductors, and telecommunications equipment.
- Critical infrastructure: identified by reference to a list of 28 subsectors, including, among others, telecommunications networks, electric power generation, transmission, distribution and storage facilities, certain oil and gas systems, financial market utilities and exchanges, and airports and ports.
- Sensitive personal data: including any business that maintains or collects genetic information or other "identifiable data" such as financial, health-related, biometric, or insurance data for more than one million individuals.

This chapter focuses on the tensions arising from sovereign investors' active role in the digital economy, especially those "TID" fields. The sovereign investors are keen to make direct investments into the cutting-edge technology sectors. Meanwhile, their activities have also contributed to geopolitical tensions and tightened cross-border regulations. Especially for Chinese sovereign capital, corporate sanctions and deal blocking are on the rise under the US CFIUS and other regimes including the EU, Israel, and Australia. And the Western capital is not cage-free either: domestic regulations are also on the rise for US institutions seeking to invest into tech companies in foreign jurisdictions like China.

## Tech and Semiconductor Chips

Leading-edge technology has always been a major focus of the US CFIUS for "national security" analysis. Back in 1987, Japanese electronics firm Fujitsu sought to buy 80% of Fairchild Semiconductor, a US semiconductor producer, from Schlumberger, a Franco-American NYSE-listed company. Fairchild to Intel and many other US semiconductor companies was like the more recent Netscape to today's Google and Facebook, and a *Los Angeles Times* news story then described it as "a pioneer of America's high-technology industries" and the "mother company of Silicon Valley."

The deal was viewed by many in the Reagan administration and industry officials as a test case in Japanese efforts to invest in the United States, particularly in strategically important high technology. Fairchild was a military supplier to the US armed forces, and then Defense Secretary Caspar W. Weinberger, Commerce Secretary Malcolm Baldrige, and the Central Intelligence Agency (CIA) collectively asked the White House to block the Japanese electronics company's bid (see **Box: Japan Inc. and the US Reaction** in the prior **Chapter 8**). The *Los Angeles Times* suggested that the potential transaction with "foreign rival Fujitsu of Japan" is like "selling Mount Vernon to the redcoats." Under intense pressure, the parties called off the deal.

History rhymes. In 2016, capital from China made a $2.49 billion acquisition offer to the same Fairchild Semiconductor company (see **Figure 9.3**). The buyer consortium consisted of China Resources Microelectronics Ltd., a state-owned company, and Hua Capital Management Co., a China-based investment fund (whose LPs probably also included a China state investor). The Chinese well understood the deal might be tied up in a lengthy national security review; hence the consortium promised to pay the company $108 million if the deal failed to clear the bar with CFIUS. Nevertheless,

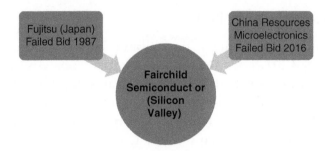

Figure 9.3    **Japan and China's Bids for Fairchild**

the Fairchild board decided the proposed deal wasn't worth the regulatory headaches (again), and it rejected the offer, citing concerns over the uncertainty of obtaining CFIUS approval.

The same year, 2016, also saw the launch of a deal that later fell foul of CFIUS. President Trump blocked Chinese government-backed PE firm Canyon Bridge from buying US chipmaker Lattice Semiconductor Corporation for $1.3 billion. As discussed in detail in Chapter 1, Oregon-based Lattice is a publicly traded semiconductor company that manufactures programmable logic devices which can be used by customers for specific uses such as vehicles, computers, and mobile phones.

One of the main issues arising in the Lattice/Canyon Bridge Deal was the strong connection with the Chinese government. Lattice started seeking potential acquirers in February 2016, and on April 8, 2016 China Reform Fund Management Co ("**CRFM**") approached Lattice for a potential takeover bid. CRFM owns businesses with military applications and also invested in other sensitive industries in line with the Chinese government's military and economic agendas. As such, CRFM's bid would naturally be subject to US CFIUS review.

Probably realizing this problematic tie to sovereign capital, CRFM designed a complex transaction structure by establishing a US-based private equity fund, Canyon Bridge Capital Partners, Inc. (see **Figure 9.4**). China Venture Capital Fund

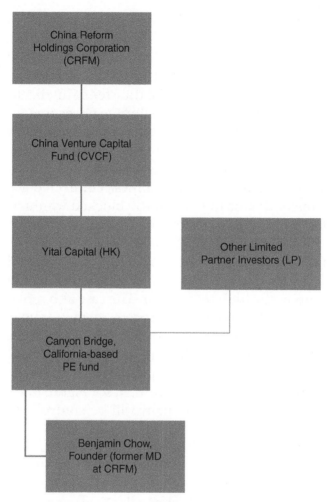

Figure 9.4    The Chain of Ownership and Control of Canyon Bridge

("**CVCF**"), a subsidiary of CRFM, was the sole limited partner
of Canyon Bridge, and two US nationals (with CRFM affilia-
tion) were appointed as the general partner (GP) to manage
the fund. This structure aimed to show that the potential purchaser, Canyon Bridge, was a US-based entity and was operated
by US-based general partner and CRFM, as the limited partner,
was only acting as a passive investor with limited operational
rights.

Still, US President Trump in September 2017 issued an executive order blocking Canyon Bridge (CRFM) from buying the chipmaker Lattice Semiconductor. According to his order, "the national security risk posed by the transaction relates to, among other things, the potential transfer of intellectual property to the foreign acquirer, the Chinese government's role in supporting this transaction, the importance of semiconductor supply chain integrity to the U.S. government, and the use of Lattice products by the U.S. government."

This constituted the second Chinese connected acquisition in the semiconductor industry to be blocked within a year (in December 2016, President Obama blocked a Chinese acquisition of the US business of German semiconductor company Aixtron SE – see the detailed case study later in this chapter), sending a signal that the US will specially oppose China-related investments in the high-tech sector. The case also reflected how the US now employs the review process: no matter how the purchaser designs the deal structure, CFIUS will eventually trace back to the ultimate controller and its affiliates (in this case, the CVCF capital even passed through a HK-based vehicle before reaching the US-based Canyon Bridge, see **Figure 9.4**) to determine whether the target company will be controlled by a foreign buyer after completion.

Similarly, CFIUS in February 2018, in effect, blocked the $580 million acquisition of semiconductor testing company Xcerra by Hubei Xinyan, a Chinese state-backed semiconductor investment fund. (Technically, Xcerra withdrew in the face of signals that CFIUS would never approve the deal.) Xcerra does not manufacture chips itself. Instead, it provides testing equipment used in the production of semiconductors. The deal was terminated due to CFIUS's concern that Xcerra equipment was used by chip manufacturers that were part of the supply chain to the US government.

### From Hard Tech to Invisible Data

Now in the age of AI and iABCD, with the new Foreign Investment Risk Review Modernization Act ("**FIRRMA**") enacted in

2018 and fully in effect as of February 13, 2020, the concept of "critical technology" has been substantially expanded (along with significant reforms to CFIUS, as discussed in the previous chapter). CFIUS traditionally associated "critical technology" with military- and defense-related items, whereas the new regulations also highlighted "emerging and foundational technologies" that would be discovered and applied in industries – as wide-ranging as computer storage, semiconductors, and telecommunications equipment.

In that context, data (the "D" of the "TID" categories mentioned at the chapter beginning) – whether personal or industrial – has emerged as a mainstream concern of CFIUS. The background: AI must be "trained" or "taught" for its cognitive abilities. From facial recognition to autonomous cars to machine translation, most AI applications must digest vast amounts of data and find hidden patterns between inputs and outcomes (so called "machine learning") before a machine algorithm can "learn" how to master human skills.

Therefore, to a significant degree, the AI innovation race is a competition for data; in addition, data collection and analytics also raise serious personal privacy issues. Lately, data technology related startups have become the new focus of CFIUS. This section will analyze related high-profile cases, including three Chinese companies being subjected to the previously rare remedy of retroactive divestment of technology startups – Grindr, PatientsLikeMe, and StayNTouch in 2019 and 2020 – allegedly due to concerns regarding access to sensitive personal data.

**First,** in March 2019, CFIUS directed Chinese gaming company Beijing Kunlun Tech to sell its stakes in the popular gay dating app Grindr. Kunlun took over Grindr through two separate transactions between 2016 (61.53%) and 2018 (100% buyout). In March 2019, spurred by data privacy concerns, CFIUS intervened. (Kunlun completed the earlier deals without submitting the acquisition for CFIUS review because the filing requirement was voluntary – and probably in light of the fact that a gay dating app was not thought by the venture capital world to be a national security risk.)

In March 2020, Kunlun announced the sale of Grindr to San Vicente Acquisition for roughly $608.5 million, ahead of the June 2020 divestment deadline. (Its final closing, however, will still be dependent on the final CFIUS review.) The sale reflected a substantial increase over the $151 million valuation at which Kunlun had acquired its majority stake in 2016, but likely reflects a discount from its true value due to the forced sale.

Previously, in 2017, Ant Financial, Alibaba's financial arm, announced a $1.2 billion acquisition of money transfer company MoneyGram. Ant Financial had a strategic view that MoneyGram could provide a platform for Chinese Alipay customers to access goods and services when traveling abroad. However, Ant Financial was not able to mitigate CFIUS concerns over the safety of data that could be used to identify US citizens, and the deal collapsed in January 2018.

In the Grindr case, CFIUS has not disclosed its specific concerns, but "data privacy" apparently is the main concern. Grindr, as described in the introduction to this chapter, gathers sensitive personal data. According to some analyses, the Grindr users (including US military and government contractors) could be blackmailed by their social data.

The iCarbonX/PatientsLikeMe case follows the same pattern. The US healthtech startup company PatientsLikeMe is an online service that links individuals by providing a social network on which patients can connect to people with similar health conditions. In 2017, iCarbonX, the Shenzhen, China-based digital healthcare unicorn, invested more than $100 million into PatientsLikeMe, becoming the majority stakeholder.

**Second,** more than a year after the investment, CFIUS ordered the China tech company iCarbonX to sell its majority stake in PatientsLikeMe. The reason apparently related to the collection and archiving of US patient data by PatientsLikeMe. In mid-2019, iCarbonX fully divested when the startup was acquired by the US company UnitedHealth Group Inc.

**Most recently,** StayNTouch/Beijing Shiji Group became the third Chinese purchase involving personal data retroactively undone by US government order (this time by Presidential order, making it one of only six transactions blocked by presidential action based on CFIUS recommendations). Beijing Shiji Group, a Chinese software supplier to hotels, restaurants, and retail, in 2018 acquired a StayNTouch, a US-based company providing cloud-based software to the hospitality sector, including MGM Resorts International, Yotel, and Miami Beach's Fontainebleau, famously featured in Goldfinger – an early James Bond film. The software enables hotel guests to check in and check out using their smartphones.

In March 2020, years after the deal closed, Beijing Shiji Group was directed to divest StayNTouch and its US assets within 120 days of the order. As with Grindr, the StayNTouch divestment order does not specify what element raised national security concerns. The order provides a clue, however. Despite the 120-day window to divest, the Chinese company and its Hong Kong subsidiary are ordered to immediately refrain from accessing guest data. This element supports the thesis that Chinese access to personally identifiable information (**PII**) of US users, no matter the industry, is now a national security risk in the view of the Trump administration (see **Figure 9.5**).

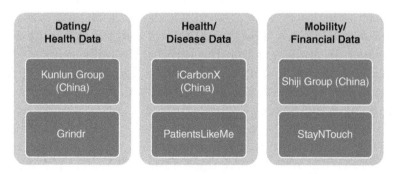

Figure 9.5    **PII Transactions Undone by National Security Review**

Now, TikTok has become the highest profile PII-based divestment order. In 2017, Chinese tech powerhouse ByteDance paid $1 billion for the startup musical.ly – the origin of the now viral social video app TikTok (its domestic counterpart app's name is Douyin, which literally translates as "shaking voice" or "vibrant voice"). CFIUS approval was not sought at the time, leaving the deal vulnerable to a subsequent divestment order from the agency.

ByteDance saw the deal as a way to expand outside its home market. Musical.ly was popular globally and ByteDance sought to leverage its strength in China with the target's international reach. The plan succeeded spectacularly. After just two years, TikTok had been downloaded over 1.5 billion times – over 40 million times in the US in 2019 alone. Apart from Apple, it is the only tech company with more than 100 million users in both China and the US. Its stunning success, particularly among younger users, was great enough to attract criticism from Facebook founder Mark Zuckerberg and US Senate Minority Leader, Chuck Schumer, who raised the specter of Chinese government censorship of TikTok content. US lawmakers called upon the government to start a national security review based on the company's gathering of personal data of Americans, particularly teenagers.

Although musical.ly has Chinese founders and its headquarters is in Shanghai, CFIUS asserts jurisdiction over its US operation and, particularly, the data of its US users – 60% of whom are between the ages of 16 and 24. Its users upload personal data and post videos. The app also automatically stores location information, an aspect that has led the US military to reverse its stance and now ban its use by soldiers. Members of Congress have called for the deletion of TikTok on all devices used by US government employees.

Bytedance had a plan to satisfy the concerns without divesting. In reaction to the informal CFIUS probe, Bytedance has reportedly ring-fenced data from US users, keeping it on servers in the US and Singapore, but not in China (see **Figure 9.6**). In another countermove, TikTok has hired its first "Chief Information Security Officer." Roland Cloutier, who

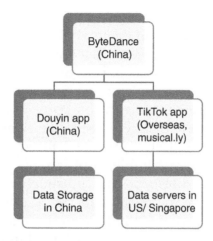

Figure 9.6    **Bytedance Ring-fenced Data for CFIUS**

began his career with the US Air Force as a combat security specialist and served in senior security capacities at US public companies, burnishes the app's US security credentials; in 2016, he literally wrote the book on his new role: "Becoming a Global Chief Security Executive Officer." Most notably, in May, Bytedance hired Kevin Mayer, former Chairman of Disney's direct-to-consumer and international operations, not only as CEO of TikTok but also, in a surprising move, as COO of the parent company. TikTok hoped in vain the measures taken to separate its China and US operations and safeguard personal data of US users would save the lip-synching video app from a CFIUS divestment order, years after the deal closed. Instead, it was hit with two divestment orders in August, 2020, the first, under emergency powers, banned Bytedance from operating in the US and set off a frantic search for a US buyer. President Trump, in a move reminiscent of his bestselling book, The Art of the Deal, asserted that Bytedance would have to pay the US Treasury a very substantial portion of the sale price, as a fee, presumably. Then, a little over a week later, the CFIUS divestment order was handed down. US tech giants Microsoft and Oracle appear as leading contenders to acquire TikTok's US assets. By the end of August 2020, Kevin Mayer had resigned. A short video indeed.

These data-driven CFIUS cases have shaped the definition of **sensitive personal data** in the final FIRRMA rules. They combine two major elements: first, the content of the information itself and second, the characteristics of the individuals, including the likelihood of their link to US national security. With respect to the former element, the regulations set forth ten categories of sensitive data. For the latter element, the definition considers one million individuals a threshold, which would capture any meaningful mobile application.

In addition, a business that outsources collection and storage of sensitive personal data to a third-party service provider, and retains the ability to access the collected data on the third party's servers, is a TID US business because it "indirectly" collects or maintains such data (for TikTok, that means extra ring-fencing for its overseas business and data).

The Grindr, PatientsLikeMe, and StayNTouch divestment orders (as well as the Alibaba/MoneyGram case and the TikTok investigation) illustrate that CFIUS considers a US target company's storage of PII as a potential national security concern. Furthermore, as these transactions closed years ago, CFIUS's treatment highlights that a foreign investment transaction is susceptible to disturbance by CFIUS at any time into the indefinite future if CFIUS has not cleared it (for those deals not subject to "mandatory review," including those that no dealmaker would have thought at the time even merited a voluntary submission). As illustrated by the following sections, the same trend is emerging in other developed markets across the globe.

## Europe: Germany, UK, France

Several advanced EU economies comparable to the United States have recently made regulatory changes, similarly increasing their focus on the high-tech and digital economy sectors. Particularly relevant countries include Germany, the United Kingdom, and France.

The German economy is a pioneer in Industry 4.0, the Internet of Things, and advanced digitization of production engineering, and in the World Economic Forum's 2018 Global Competitiveness Report, Germany came top as the world's most innovative economy. (The US came second.) Meanwhile, following a series of Chinese deals on Western technology and expertise, Germany has become the first EU country to tighten its rules on foreign corporate takeovers, providing the best case study on the other side of the Atlantic.

The 2016 takeover of Kuka, a Bavarian robotics firm, by a Chinese SOE has been described by some German officials as a "wake-up call" that underlined the need to shield strategic parts of the economy. In the same year, a louder "wake-up call" came from the US, as President Obama stopped the proposed $710 million acquisition of Aixtron SE, a German-based technology company, by the German subsidiary of a Chinese corporate buyer.

The bid for Aixtron – which makes chip equipment that produces the crystalline layers based on gallium nitride that are used as semiconductors in weapons systems – was made by Grand Chip Investment GmbH (**GCI**), a German subsidiary of Fujian Grand Chip Investment Fund LP of China (see **Figure 9.7**). In fact, in the earlier phase, the German government had already given its approval for the Chinese takeover. (Under then applicable German law, the government could block takeovers only if they jeopardized energy security, defense, or financial stability, and the review threshold was 25%.)

In October 2016, the German government canceled the clearance certificate for the transaction. The decision to

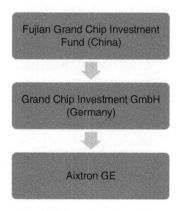

Figure 9.7    **The Bid for Aixtron**

withdraw its approval, according to Germany's Deputy Economy Minister Matthias Machnig's comment in the media, was based on "previously unknown security-related information." The confusion was more or less explained months later, when US President Barack Obama issued an order prohibiting the Aixtron transaction after an assessment by US CFIUS.

While Aixtron and GCI are German entities, CFIUS claims jurisdiction over any transaction "by or with any foreign person which could result in foreign control of any person engaged in interstate commerce in the United States." The US assessment identified the US business of Aixtron not only to include its corporate presence – i.e., its research, technology, and sales facility in California – but also the company's US patents, granted and pending.

The US thinking likely brought multiple new perspectives to the German regulatory agencies. **First,** as the Aixtron and Lattice (earlier chapter discussion, see **Figure 9.4**) decisions demonstrated, the CFIUS review is "substance over form," meaning neither a "limited partner" nor a US private equity buyout fund managed by US citizens could fall within a safe harbor. (The same is true when "US" is replaced by "Germany" in the case of Aixtron.) No matter how the deal is structured, Chinese state-backed investors cannot circumvent, and will be subject to, heightened scrutiny by CFIUS.

**Second,** the semiconductor industry remains a high priority of CFIUS and its member agencies because of its civil and military dual-use nature. The US decision specifically identified the perceived national security risk as "among other things … the military applications of the overall technical body of knowledge and experience of Aixtron."

**Finally,** the US took the far-reaching position that the existence of US intellectual property may be considered an independent ground for CFIUS jurisdiction, which is critical for future transactions in the high-tech and digital economy.

Not surprisingly, after the Aixtron episode, Germany tightened its foreign investment review process. In 2018, the German government blocked the State Grid Corporation of China from purchasing 20% of 50Hertz, a power grid operator in eastern Germany that provides electricity to over 18 million German customers. In the deal, Germany exercised its powers under its newly revised foreign investment review law, expanding its purview outside of the defense area to include critical infrastructure.

The seller was IFM, an Australian firm owned by and managing infrastructure investments for its country's superannuation funds. Before the German government intervened, IFM was looking to unload its 40% interest in 50Hertz. Elia, a Belgian transmission system company and then the owner of 60% of 50Hertz, exercised its right of first refusal for 20% of 50Hertz, leaving State Grid in talks to acquire the 20% still owned by IFM. (Before the transaction, Elia and IFM acquired 50Hertz in 2010, after it was put up for sale by Swedish company Vattenfall, see **Figure 9.8;** interestingly, when the Australian firm acquired that stake, it apparently did not experience the difficulties that the Chinese attempt later encountered.)

The German government voiced concerns, invoking the "critical infrastructure" status of the company that provides electricity for Berlin, among other places. The interesting twist was that, in this case, Germany was able to freeze out State Grid without explicitly vetoing the deal. This was because Elia, the 50Hertz majority shareholder, had the right of first refusal. At the direction of the German economics ministry, Elia exercised

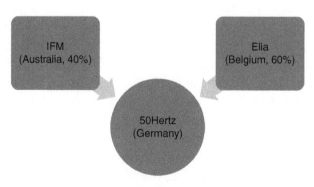

Figure 9.8    **Ownership of 50Hertz before IFM Stake Sale**

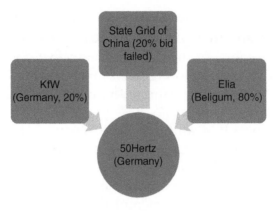

Figure 9.9   **Ownership of 50Hertz after IFM Stake Sale**

the option (IFM no longer being a shareholder), after which it immediately sold the stake to KfW, the government-owned development bank of Germany (see **Figure 9.9**).

In November 2019, Germany announced its plan to tighten scrutiny for foreign investments by formally amending foreign investment rules for critical sectors. The plan would expand "critical industries" to sectors including artificial intelligence, robotics, semiconductors, biotechnology, and quantum technology, and requiring disclosure for any purchases over 10% of companies in those areas. Meanwhile, for other sectors that had previously been identified and regulated as "critical infrastructure," including energy, telecommunications, defense, and water, the percentage threshold that triggers government review was lowered from 25% to 10%.

Although not explicitly stated, this move was widely seen as targeting Chinese state-backed investors. The pandemic may have altered that view. On June 15, 2020, the same KfW moved to preempt a US deal by acquiring a 23% stake in Cure-Vac, a German company with a promising coronavirus vaccine after the Trump administration had been rumored to be interested in acquiring the vaccine maker.

Furthermore, the German move comes at a time when the EU in general is reconsidering the bloc's industrial strategy and relations to China, in the face of increased investment in tech sectors by Chinese state capital. The same week that the KfW move on Cure-Vac came to light, the European Commission released proposals intended to leverage its state-aid rules to prevent non-EU investors enjoying government subsidies from outbidding competitors for European assets. In lieu of national security screening of foreign investment, the proposals focus on unfair advantages due to non-EU government subsidies. Like the Australian proposals described in Chapter 8, the proposals would layer yet another review on top of those already in place.

(Of course, not all SIFs are being put in the penalty box. The CFIUS "white list" appeared as part of FIRRMA, see details in **Chapter 8** and corresponding **Box: The Yellow Peril,** upon which the US and the three English-speaking nations of Australia, Canada, and United Kingdom seem to have a "mutually open" arrangement for now.)

In the Brexiting **United Kingdom,** for example, new regulations that took effect in June 2018 lowered merger control thresholds at which the government would be able to intervene, affecting advanced technologies including computer hardware and quantum technologies, the military, and dual-use sectors. The wide-ranging changes to the national security landscape, which were originally expected to have been published in 2019, have not yet been published. It is anticipated that changes will not be implemented until sometime in 2020.

Within the EU, **France** also took similar regulatory measures in November 2018. The list of sensitive activities was further expanded, and the government review now covers activities relating to "the interception/detection of correspondence/conversations, capture of computer data, information systems security, space operations and electronic systems use in public security missions." The scope of review is further widened to cover research and development (R&D) activities in "cybersecurity, artificial intelligence, robotics, additive manufacturing, semiconductors, certain dual-use goods and technologies, and sensitive data storage."

## Israel, Japan: Hard to Balance the Technology Triangle

Interestingly, the growing US–China technology tensions also led to unexpected opportunities for economic growth for third-party countries – but probably not for too long. Take **Israel**'s flourishing semiconductor industry, for example. As a workaround to US–China trade tariffs, a US semiconductor giant increased direct sales from its Israeli plant to Chinese buyers, thus boosting semiconductor trade between Israel and China by 80% in 2018. In parallel, China increased investments in Israeli semiconductor companies, driving up demand for Israeli-designed chips.

What Israel strove to form is a technology triangle with China and the US, enabled by maintaining well-thought-out controls on dual-use technology transfers (see **Figure 9.10**). However, the importance of chips for technological advancement and military use mean Israel's position in this technology triangle is bound to attract Washington's attention. This type of balance will become increasingly difficult, and soon Israel may lose its promised land allure for Chinese capital (see **Box: Playing Both Sides of the Great and Wailing Walls**).

Pressured by a Trump administration that worries about Israel's dalliance with China, Israel is moving to create an interagency government body – similar to the US CFIUS – to review foreign investments in sensitive areas of its economy.

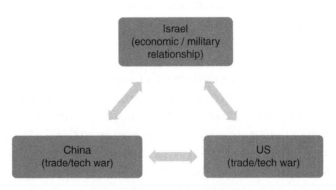

Figure 9.10    **Israel Balancing US–China Relationships**

Once set up, the regulator reportedly would focus on dual-use products that have military and commercial applications, such as semiconductors, drones, and artificial intelligence. As the next section illustrates, more and more countries would find, just like Israel, that a hard balancing act was bound to become even harder as the political and security tensions continue to escalate.

### Playing Both Sides of the Great and Wailing Walls

Israel is a tech powerhouse, particularly in cybersecurity and weapons technology. Among foreign companies listed on NASDAQ, Israeli companies trail only Chinese companies. When Silicon Valley started closing its doors to Chinese money, Israel, whose innovative tech sector inspired the nickname "Startup Nation," became an alluring destination: China gets a valuable pipeline of technology, and Israel teams up with a deep-pocketed backer.

But US–Israeli cultural ties are also close. New York City contains the largest Jewish population of any city other than Tel Aviv. The New York City mayor traditionally makes one of his international pilgrimages to Jerusalem. Trump has been a vocal supporter of Israel and its current prime minister.

Nonetheless – or perhaps because of the political support it enjoys in the US – since the 1980s, Israel has carefully walked the US–China technology tensions tightrope, trying to balance its commercial and security interests with the two great powers (see **Figure 9.10**). For example, relating to 5G networks, the Israeli government pushed back against the United States' position on completely banning Huawei due to commercial interests, while it also avoids using Huawei's equipment in its critical infrastructure for security concerns.

The growing dual-use nature (meaning they have both military and commercial applications, such as drones and artificial intelligence) of technology threatens to overthrow Israel's careful efforts to expand trade with Beijing, while avoiding the sales of security technologies that would increase Chinese military capabilities and anger Washington. Israeli entrepreneurs are also fearful that receiving Chinese investments could negatively affect business in the United States.

With mounting political pressure from its American allies and promising Chinese trade prospects, Israel is caught between its two largest and technology-hungry trade partners. If tensions escalate further, Israel could risk finding its American and Chinese trade partners less forgiving of its delicate balance.

To an even greater extent than in these European countries and Israel, the United States likely had a significant influence in nudging **Japan** to strengthening foreign investment screenings. As background, the United States is Japan's biggest and most powerful security and economic ally. In return, Japan is an indispensable key regional ally of the United States which has traditionally provided a nuclear umbrella against North Korea. China is nearby and a major trade partner with Japan; yet in cross-border investments, the United States is the biggest foreign investor in Japan.

In 2019, Japan's government expanded the scope of the industries for which inward direct investments require advance notice filings and government review. AI is a major focus of the revised rules. Industries pertaining to hardware (e.g., integrated circuits) and embedded software, which are essential for the application of AI technologies, have been added to the review list. Such a move seems to suggest that Japan intends generally to require all industries pertaining to AI developments to be subject to the prior notification requirement.

Overall, it is hardly surprising that Japan's new rules mirror FIRRMA in many aspects, both in contents and consequences. For example, the 15 industries newly designated to be put under tighter scrutiny as a result of the 2019 revision are apparently modeled after the 14 areas of "emerging technologies" that the United States Commerce Department's Bureau of Industry and Security listed in its FIRRMA rule. Furthermore, Japan's rules have provisions similar to US FIRRMA that trigger mandatory pre-filing obligations for sovereign wealth funds (SWFs) and state-owned enterprises (SOEs).

A recent episode that illustrates Japan's cautious attitude towards Chinese investors in the high-tech sector is the fallout between Japan Display Inc. (**JDI**) and Suwa, a Chinese–Taiwanese consortium led by Chinese Harvest Tech Investment Management Company. Japan Display Inc. is a key supplier of display panels for Apple Inc.'s smartphone and tablet production. Its establishment, actually, was a product of a

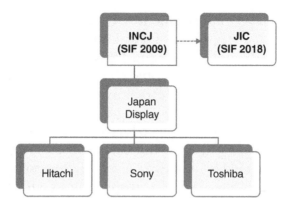

Figure 9.11    The Formation of Japan Display

Japanese SIF called INCJ Limited, which concentrated the most advanced display technology by combining the liquid-crystal display (LCD) businesses of Japan's industry-leading firms: Hitachi, Sony, and Toshiba (see **Figure 9.11**).

The **Innovation Network Corporation of Japan (INCJ)** was set up in 2009 by the Japanese government to "create next-generation businesses" in "promising new technologies." INCJ's capital was mostly from the state, with the rest from a group of major Japanese corporations. Unlike typical SIFs which consider themselves long-term investors, INCJ set its lifespan for 15 years, which means by 2024 it would cease to exist. (It should be noted that after Japan's new sovereign fund **Japan Investment Corporation (JIC)** was established in late 2018, INCJ became a 100% subsidiary of JIC; the new JIC, however, is having its own difficulty in carrying out its innovation-promotion focused mission, see details in **Chapter 7.**)

INCJ aims to promote "open innovation," by which it means to accelerate the flow of technologies and expertise beyond the boundaries of existing organizational structures, thereby boosting the competitiveness of Japanese firms. The JDI investment is a major position in INCJ's portfolio. INCJ not only has become the major shareholder of JDI but has also continued providing guarantees for the company's debt financing. The JDI investment seems to fit INCJ's mission to leverage Japanese technological and industrial prowess to create sustainable next-generation businesses.

Once envisioned as a national champion, JDI has struggled financially and incurred severe losses in recent years which the company attributed to slowing sales of display panels for Apple products. Apple and its peers are reducing the usage of LCD displays. According to industry analyses, Apple is likely to drop LCD displays altogether after 2020 in favor of organic light-emitting diode (OLED) displays that allow for more flexible handset design.

From 2018, the fifth straight year of net losses for the company, JDI teetered from crisis to crisis each quarter (as a listed company it posts quarterly earnings) requiring repeated cash injections from INCJ. It reached out to external investors for the lifeline the firm needed to pay down its debt burden and continue investing in new panel technologies. JDI still has great technology and engineers but needs funds to construct a large-scale OLED fabrication facility and shift to OLED displays production.

By early 2019, JDI had initially agreed on a capital injection of about $742 million from the Suwa consortium, consisting of Chinese Harvest Tech Investment Management Company, touch-panel maker O-Film Tech Co in China, and Taiwan's TPK Holding Co (see **Figure 9.12**). The deal negotiation led to "tech transfer" and "national champion" talk in Japan. Even though JDI failed to launch OLED products quickly, it still has leading

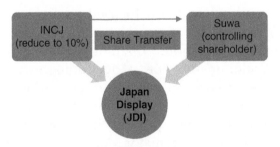

Figure 9.12    **JDI Bailout Plan with China–Taiwan Consortium**

OLED technology and excellent engineering. In addition, JDI has know-how in stably producing low-temperature polysilicon sheets, a component that makes displays more energy-efficient and faster in refreshing and which is used in Apple's top-line iPhones.

In the planned deal, JDI would issue new shares to Suwa, and Suwa would acquire additional shares from INCJ. Once the deal closed, Suwa would become the controlling shareholder and INCJ's ownership would be significantly reduced (a partial exit in light of INCJ's operation deadline of 2024). However, the deal faced too many headwinds and fell apart in a few months. According to JDI's official news release, the company sent Suwa a notice terminating the investment deal in January 2020.

Instead, Japanese asset management firm Ichigo stepped in and planned to inject about $800 million to rescue JDI. As we saw in Germany, the Chinese direct investor was squeezed out without a formal FDI review when a home team player was found to take its place. This may be the favored tactic going forward in Europe to fend off unwanted Chinese investment.

In April 2020, EU competition chief, Margrethe Vestager, publicly called upon EU member states to accelerate the adoption of regulations to fend off Chinese SOEs from buying European companies whose share prices have fallen due to the pandemic. Not only that, but she encouraged governments to take stakes in companies if needed to prevent them falling into the clutches of a Chinese SOE. Italy is not waiting on anybody, having already adopted increased measures to prevent foreign takeovers. Germany and Spain similarly announced anti-takeover initiatives, partly in reaction to recent investments by PIF and the concern over Chinese SOEs.

## China–US: Severed Cross-Border Ties

Of course, the US CFIUS review and the new rules from other countries have broad implications for the sovereign investment funds in general. However, the sovereign capital from China may take most of the hit, because CFIUS is taking on extra measures to protect sensitive technology from China acquisition as the two economic superpowers vie for tech supremacy. In fact, FIRRMA was introduced with the explicit intent to "[maintain] the U.S. technological advantage over countries that pose threats, such as China."

From the perspective of tech competition, China in Asia and the US in the West are forming two leading innovation centers of different strengths. Given that Chinese companies are dealing with the same tech issues in growing their businesses as many US companies, their cooperation may lead to a promising cross-pollination of tech innovation. However, a model for national collaboration has yet to be worked out, and the mutual distrust of the two spheres of innovation power could lead to fragmented tech worlds.

As we have seen, 5G is an arena in which the US is forcing third countries to pick sides and dividing telecoms between Huawei 5G and the as-yet-unidentified US champion. In the case of AI, algorithms are already widely shared by researchers and tech companies, but the data used to train machine-learning models are often locally managed and carefully guarded. China's ambitions and progress to date have led to talk of an artificial-intelligence arms race with the US.

That helps explain why countries like Israel and Japan are urged to modify their investment review rules to look more like US FIRRMA: if other countries leave screening for foreign investments in tech weaker than that of the United States, this regulatory loophole becomes the "weak link" within the otherwise securely guarded chain of advanced technology, of which America's competitors could take advantage.

Emblematic of this "decoupling," nothing so far has been as literal and dramatic as a severed data cable that potentially links the two sides of the Pacific. In August 2018, US media reported that the US Department of Justice was close to putting the brakes on a Google and Facebook funded Pacific subsea cable over national security concerns – because of a co-investor from China. The project remained pending through 2019 because it was not considered finally approved until the US government agencies completed the national security review, which had no specific timetable. At the beginning of 2020, the US Internet giants Google and Facebook accepted reality and dropped the controversial Hong Kong and Chinese sections from the submission to the FCC.

The Pacific Light Cable Network (PLCN), a high capacity fiber-optic cable project, is a joint venture among Google, Facebook, and a Chinese telecommunications company called Dr. Peng Telecom & Media Group, which is the fourth-largest telecom company in China (see **Figure 9.13**). The cable would run about 8000 miles (13,000 kilometers) and is intended for a high-speed trans-Pacific data route between the US and Hong Kong/China. The cable was planned to connect the builders' data centers and transport wholesale data, and it could also give US companies greater access to growing markets in Asia besides China, such as Indonesia, Malaysia, and the Philippines.

However, a US multi-agency panel led by the Department of Justice (DOJ), known as Team Telecom (see **Figure 9.14**), is reportedly objecting to the cable project. Team Telecom is a shadowy US national security unit tasked with protecting US telecommunication systems. The team comprises representatives from the Department of Defense (DOD), Department of

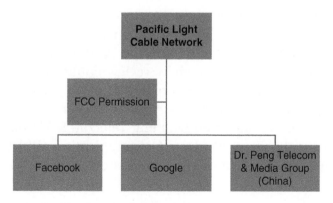

Figure 9.13    **The Pacific Light Cable Network**

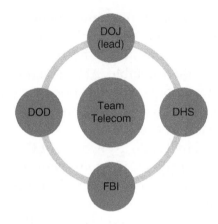

Figure 9.14   **The Team Telecom**

Homeland Security (DHS), and the Federal Bureau of Investigation (FBI, affiliated with DOJ).

While Team Telecom has no regulatory authority, the required national security agreement (NSA) has binding contractual force and can provide for substantial rights, such as site visits, oversight, and audit and can limit the acquired company's ability to locate and conduct operations. The NSA will grant the right to enforcement by injunction; in effect, regulating the acquiror's conduct through the courts. No doubt, the NSA element coming up in Team Telecom highlights the US government's focus on the digital economy.

According to the media, the Department of Justice and the Defense Department asked the FCC (Federal Communications Commission, where the companies in 2017 applied for permission to land the cable in the US) to defer action on the project until a national security review could be completed, which review continues with no specific date for conclusion. The DOJ signaled opposition because of concerns over the Chinese investor, Beijing-based Dr. Peng Telecom & Media Group, operating as Pacific Light Data Communication (PLDC). The Dr. Peng Group provides communications services in China, and its partners listed on its website include the Chinese telecom giant Huawei Technologies.

The background on global data transmission is that in the past decade companies like Google and Facebook have made significant investments into similar cables to handle ever-growing network traffic between the US and Asia. With South-east Asian countries, as with China, similarly experiencing fast growth in the data economy, ever more trans-Pacific connectivity is needed to meet the growing bandwidth requirements between East and West. Globally, thousands of miles of cable have already been placed on the seabed floor, and past projects have received approval, even when directly linking mainland China with the US.

However, given escalating US–China trade tensions and the increasing rivalry between the world's two largest digital economies, connectivity is being replaced by distrust. The national security considerations are changing the way that Internet connectivity across the Pacific is structured. In January 2020, as noted, the two US companies (with PLDC out of the picture) proposed a new approach to the FCC. They requested permission to operate just the two PLCN fiber pairs owned by the American companies: Google's link to Taiwan, and Facebook's to the Philippines.

Finally, on April 8, 2020, the FCC approved Google's request to operate the US–Taiwan link. Facebook remains on hold for the Philippines piece. The FCC deferred the Hong Kong connection entirely, saying that other US government agencies had concluded that the Hong Kong link as presented posed serious national security and law enforcement risks to the US. On June 17, 2020, Team Telecom formally advised the FCC to deny the Hong Kong link. And, with telecoms at the center of US industrial policy for the Trump administration, a Presidential order revealed in April 2020 that Team Telecom is getting an upgrade (see **Box: Team Telecom 2.0**).

## Team Telecom 2.0

Phones started ringing off the hook in Washington, DC after the President signed an executive order on April 3, 2020 that created a telecoms equivalent of CFIUS. (With the cumbersome name "Committee for the Assessment of Foreign Participation in the United States Telecommunications Services Sector," one observer has dubbed it "Team Telecom 2.0.")

The order directs the three members (the Attorney General, as Chair, and the Secretaries of Defense and Homeland Security) to agree a memorandum on operations within 90 days. It is not clear whether, unlike Team Telecom 1.0, the memorandum will be published. The order – helpfully for the likes of Google and Facebook – includes a timeline for review (120 days) but is otherwise sparse on process for the review of licenses involving "foreign participation."

Like Team Telecom and CFIUS, it is an interagency committee. Other agencies may be added and there is a long list of other agencies that will act as "advisors." That the Chair will be Attorney General Barr who has been outspoken on the key role the US government should play in 5G (and suggested no less than a new US sovereign fund for that), has created some apprehension about how the new committee will exercise its wide ranging and ill-defined authority.

The new committee is empowered to review the granting or transfer of licenses by the Federal Communications Commission for "risks to national security or law enforcement interests." What really set the phones ringing to outside counsel and lobbyists, however, was the new committee's power to "review existing licenses to identify any additional or new risks to national security or law enforcement interests of the U.S." In an echo of the power exercised in the Grindr, PatientsLikeMe, and StayNTouch cases, the committee appears to be empowered to investigate and undo licenses already granted.

Also, like CFIUS, no definition is provided for "national security." The term "foreign participation" is used, also without definition. (There has been speculation that this could cover the use of Huawei equipment, for example, in addition to foreign ownership or control of service providers.) Those phones are likely to continue ringing as everyone figures out whether Telecom 2.0 is simply an upgrade or, rather, a new operating system.

This trend is also likely to be reinforced by geopolitics, such as exogenous developments including the US–China Phase One Trade Deal agreed in January 2020, which explicitly requires China to avoid pressuring US companies to share technology with local joint venture partners or license their technology at below-market prices in return for access to China's market. Meanwhile, the decline in foreign direct investment is evident: Chinese FDI in US industries fell in 2019 to an estimated $3.1 billion – a fraction of the $46.5 billion in 2016, and a decline of 42% from the $5.4 billion in 2018, according to Rhodium Group.

## Rethinking Going Direct on Tech Investments

In summary, 2019-2020 may be remembered as an important inflection point in the global digital economy, from collaborative co-existence to head-on tension, as illustrated by the tech war between US and China, the world's two digital superpowers. While the US takes hardline national security measures, China is also stepping up efforts and bolstering defensive policies in a similar national security context, including plans to create an "unreliable entities list" of its own (reciprocating the "entity list" which the US applies to Huawei), restrictions on cross-border flow of data, and a modified foreign investment screening framework for cross-border capital investments.

In 2020 and beyond, the tensions around sovereign investors and cross-border tech investments are bound to escalate in a world where technology is global, but nations are becoming more nationalist and protectionist. **On the one hand,** all nations are experiencing "AI anxiety" and "tech anxiety":

- Data is considered the "new oil" of the "new economy," hence viewed by each nation as a national treasure.
- AI-enabled industry revolution leads to value chain transformation.
- 5G will lead to the IoT, and concern on data security will only increase.

**On the other hand,** in today's investment climate, sovereign wealth funds with high-quality technology investment programs are aiming to:

- Move toward attractive tech sectors that may have significant public policy, foreign policy, public safety, national defence, and security implications.
- Invest into digital economy infrastructure as the next generation infrastructure for the world economy.
- Seek a more active investor role given current concerns over valuations, governance, and IPOs. The latter implies more access to company data, board or observer seats, and use of voting rights.

These two ways of thinking are unlikely to match smoothly (see **Figure 9.15**). All the elements increase the likelihood of drawing greater negative attention from policymakers, perhaps creating increased impetus for regulatory intervention in cross-border activity. For SIF dealmakers, that means more deal uncertainties: more transactions may be blocked, and as the German HERE deal shows (like JDI, Pacific Light, and similar cases in this chapter), the regulators can easily send deals into limbo instead of blocking them outright.

In December 2016, Singaporean sovereign wealth fund GIC joined with Chinese technology giant Tencent Holdings and Chinese mapping company NavInfo to jointly bid for a 10% stake of the Netherlands-based HERE Global BV, a provider of high-definition maps for vehicles (see **Figure 9.16**).

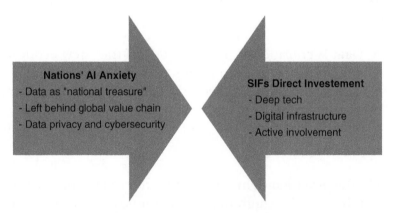

Figure 9.15  **SIFs/Host Countries Clash on Tech Investments**

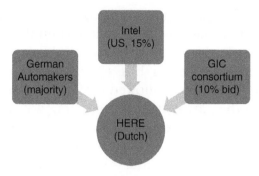

Figure 9.16    **GIC Money Not Wanted HERE**

The company was majority owned by German carmakers including Audi, BMW, Daimler, and VW and 15% owned by US chipmaker Intel. GIC provided close to half of capital for the €243 million (US$285 million) offer, but the strategic business angle – and potential value creation – would come from the mapping tech application in the Chinese market.

HERE, which is a strong competitor to Google Maps, provides world-leading location intelligence technologies. Tencent planned to use HERE's maps, location platform, and tools in its Chinese and global services, at a time when it was competing with its Chinese Internet peers Alibaba and Baidu in China's logistics and transportation industries, particularly in autonomous driving vehicles. Self-driving cars need maps to find their way around, and so HERE's cloud-based HD Live Map, with its "look around the corner" capability, becomes a valuable resource to enhance Tencent's location services and autonomous driving research. (The third player in the GIC consortium, Beijing-based mapping company Navinfo, already had a joint venture with HERE in China.)

Even though HERE is a European company headquartered in the Netherlands, approval was required from the US because it has assets in Chicago. (In a case discussed earlier in this chapter, the US similarly exercised long-arm jurisdiction over the proposed sale of the German semiconductor company Aixtron, based on the existence of US intellectual property.) The consortium spent months after the proposed deal was announced in December 2016 seeking CFIUS approval, but in September 2017 it had to ditch its plan when the US regulator continued for over nine months to withhold approval.

In a separate statement, HERE said that the decision to drop the proposed investment followed a regulatory review process "during which the parties determined there was no practicable path to receiving the necessary approval for the transaction to proceed." For dealmakers, deal uncertainty – in limbo without any clear indication of timeline – is even worse than outright deal blocking. The worst, of course, is to be forced to unwind a transaction long after it closed (as in the case of gay-dating app Grindr and TikTok). Yet an "overhang" on the deal process could occur much more frequently. In the future, many sovereign funds may find themselves in situations similar to GIC/HERE when they look into high-tech startups in foreign markets for cross-border investments.

Besides China's capital flow into the US, the other direction of capital flow is also being challenged – US capital into China, as hawkish US policymakers indicated the intention to block US pension funds' investments into China, especially China's tech sector. All these developments collectively will profoundly impact venture capital and the startup ecosystem in the US, China, and elsewhere because sovereign capital, whether foreign SIF funds or US pension funds, has been a major capital source for the latest tech boom.

How will these circumstances affect SIF investment behavior in technology companies in 2020 and beyond? Over the past few years, SIFs have become a major source of strategic capital for businesses in the new economy and an important partner for those seeking to expand into growth markets. There is no question that CFIUS and other regulators are tightening the screws, but these large investors across the world may continue to find ways to do business together across the borders.

Going forward, most sovereign funds would likely rethink their strategy and make adjustments in various ways, such as:

- **Using a balanced investment approach:** for tech investments, employing a combination of fund LP investments (private equity or venture capital funds) and direct equity holdings, which is also a combination of co-investments with funds, club deals with peers, and standalone direct investment stakes.
- **More club deals for direct investments:** in the recent cases of Chinese state-backed entities, the outcome might have been different, for example, if Canyon Bridge had been able to bring forth a more **diversified group** of investors as its limited partners to dilute the role and funding ratio of CRFM as the sovereign LP (see **Figure 9.4**) – partners coming from "exempted" jurisdictions may be even more helpful.
- **Pay more attention to portfolio companies' operation:** the negative implications of growing US–China technology tensions are reverberating around the world with disrupted supply chains and protectionist trade policies. While looking into new investment opportunities, the SIFs must well understand the operation risks to their existing portfolio companies.
- **Expand government relations and communication efforts:** use the Santiago Principles as a platform for transparency and engage not only with the FDI review agency but with the broader community, state and provincial governments, NGOs, and other stakeholders. (As an example, Temasek opened a Washington, DC office as it increased direct investment in the US.)

Overall, co-investing with domestic partners may become the mainstream for high-tech transactions, given that all business sectors are undergoing digital transformation and may involve "national security." CFIUS (like regulators in most jurisdictions) largely focuses on whether there is "control by a foreign person," especially control by a foreign government, after the transaction. Therefore, **a local partner** may not only provide local industry knowledge but also help pass the bar of host countries' transaction reviews.

**First,** for partnering, look to local financial institutions. The **CIC/** Goldman Sachs fund is a good example. The Chinese sovereign wealth fund CIC set up a joint venture fund with the US investment bank Goldman Sachs in 2017. The fund was called China–US Industrial Cooperation Partnership, and the $5 billion fund agreement was signed on the sidelines of US President Donald Trump's visit to Beijing. The fund is controlled by Goldman Sachs, and CIC is a passive investor. Without insisting on the control rights in the fund (which are CFIUS' principal concern), CIC in 2019 was able to participate indirectly in the acquisition of Boyd Corp., a California manufacturing company which is a supplier to the space and electronics industries.

**Second,** invest under the umbrella of well-connected US tech giants. We earlier discussed the investment by **Temasek** in Verily, an Alphabet unit focused on digital health whose international ambitions Temasek plans to foster. This may be part of an emerging pattern: in a deal involving not only AI but location information, **Mubadala** recently co-led a $2.25 billion investment in Waymo, another Alphabet unit, this one focused on autonomous vehicles. **CPPIB** hitchhiked along in the same deal.

**Finally,** maybe the best local partner, the local SIFs. As discussed in **Chapter 5,** many sovereign funds have the mandate to attract foreign capital and promote their domestic economy. These funds pursue joint ventures with overseas investors in order to channel foreign direct investment into their markets. They are happy to partner with foreign SIFs to make joint investments in the national strategic enterprises. At the same time, as in the example of **Italian** and **French** sovereign funds, they also have a defensive aspect. By joining the deals, the host country's own SIF could protect national firms from possible hostile acquisitions, thus avoiding the loss of productivity and technology.

Therefore, in the coming years, the market may see the headline deals – huge size, standalone direct investment by major sovereign funds – decrease significantly as the political tensions rise and startups' general valuation levels drop.

However, the sovereign investment funds will remain powerful players in the field, and as more startups stay private in the face of a volatile public market, the market may see more unicorn deals involving the SIFs at late-stage, large-size financing rounds, albeit more likely in club deals. On top of that, as the final **Chapter 10** will explain, the sovereign investment funds are developing increasing power in the worlds of tech, finance, economy, and diplomacy. They are the "super asset owners" of the 21st century.

> *Not to worry if you missed Grindr's national security threat. You were not alone. Lots of us missed the cyber moment when dating apps joined missile technology as national security threats. But here's a tip that will help next time, and, for good measure, in Chapter 10 as well. The tip? "All of the above" is not only a smart answer to "national security" questions in Chapter 9, but, you will find in Chapter 10, is a pretty good description of sovereign investors as well.*

# CHAPTER 10

# Super Asset Owners

*Known as a country that has more space than people, Australia never before experienced a summer bushfire like 2019–2020. The deadly wildfire razed an area the size of England, fueled by the nation's hottest and driest weather on record. Lives have been lost, vast swaths of property destroyed, and cities exposed to ultra-hazardous smoke clouds for months. The shocked Australians saw climate change up close and personal, and they made a connection between the massive bushfire, extreme weather, and the country's $2 trillion superannuation (pension) industry – the world's fourth-largest pool of retirement assets.*

*In 2020, the pressure on Australian SIF funds to ditch coal and fossil is mounting, from bushfire survivors, environment groups like Friends of the Earth, and most directly, young members of the superannuations, who may not access their super money until more than three decades later. They see a continent growing only hotter, drier, and more flammable as global temperature rise, and they are demanding that the custodians of their retirement assets take more direct steps to combat global warming – to protect their savings from the financial devastation that will flow from climate change.*

*While Indonesia's largest city sinks beneath the sea and Australia is consumed by wildfires, the role SIFs play in the world's sustainable future is put in the spotlight. As government-linked entities that are mandated to future-proof their nations, they are imbued with a larger mission than simply growing their, often very large, asset hoards. The sovereign investors have learned to come to terms with their visibility as large assets owners and long-horizon investors, and their reallocation of capital over the forthcoming decade will shape the global agenda on climate change, digital economy governance, and other, similarly urgent, priorities.*

## Powerful ESG Guardians

A March 15, 2019 shooting massacre in two mosques at Christchurch, New Zealand, left 51 dead, and worse, it was live-streamed on Facebook and disseminated on Twitter and YouTube. In a swift and focused response, **New Zealand Superannuation Fund (NZ Super)** took the lead in organizing a campaign, Christchurch Call, which sets out voluntary commitments for governments, companies, and wider society to work together to eliminate terrorist and violent extremist content online – the world of Facebook, Google (YouTube), and Twitter.

The linkage between the SIFs and the church shooting, forest fire, and similar seemingly non-investment topics is that, as the world's sustainability challenges become more severe and urgent, SIF investors as "super asset owners" are sending a clear message to the industries they invest in: ESG (environmental, social, and governance) and sustainability (SDG, sustainable development goals) must become the new normal. The $40 billion NZ Super has taken the lead in promoting this powerful trend, and Christchurch Call is the first global coalition to campaign about social media issues.

NZ Super is the Auckland-based sovereign wealth fund of New Zealand. All citizens and permanent residents of New Zealand aged 65 and over are eligible to receive flat-rate superannuation (pension) payments from the government. These payments are funded by present-day taxpayers. Created in 2001, the NZ Super is a pool of assets on the government's balance sheet that is used to pre-fund the future cost of New Zealand's superannuation system. The fund is managed by a Crown entity known as the Guardians of New Zealand Superannuation (the **Guardians**). The Guardians' investment objective has been to maximize the fund's return over the long term, without undue risk, in order to reduce New Zealanders' future tax burden.

The Guardians (management team) are keenly aware of a directive "to manage the fund in a manner that avoids prejudice to New Zealand's reputation as a responsible member of the world community." Some SIF investment teams would have been happy to implement a conventional approach to asset allocation and investing. The Guardians, however, have taken a more courageous approach, embracing the concept and launching its responsible investment framework. They decided to integrate responsible investing as a core principle of the fund, in the belief that responsible investing could increase returns and lower risk over the long term.

After launching Christchurch Call, NZ Super quickly rallied the major New Zealand institutional investors; within a week most had signed up to support the cause. By the end of 2019, 102 asset managers from around the globe, controlling more than $13 trillion in assets, had signed up. On March 20, 2020, the first anniversary of the mass shooting, NZ Super and its cohort of peers issued an open letter addressed to the boards and management of Alphabet (YouTube), Facebook, and Twitter, putting them on notice of the power of sovereign investors. The letter, which listed by name all 102 large institutional investors that are signatories, pulled no punches in making clear demands:

"Our request includes:

- clear lines of governance and accountability for senior executives and Board members to ensure your platforms cannot be used to promote objectionable content like the livestreaming and dissemination of the Christchurch shootings; and
- sufficient resources being dedicated to combating the livestreaming and spread of objectionable material across your platforms."

Nor did it mince words in evaluating the companies' response:

"To date, we have been dissatisfied with the response from your senior executives and Boards to us. The failure to respond to these actions creates a significant business risk, beyond the harm caused to the global community. You have a duty to address that. We remain open to continued engagement. Our expectation is that you will take responsibility for and fully address this issue."

The speed and specificity with which the movement took off under the leadership of NZ Super is a harbinger of what the world can expect from these giants. Naming names and making specific demands for changes in behavior rather than broader calls for improvement may be what's in store for the public company targets of such campaigns. The three major social media platforms have duly promised to address their complaints. However, images of the Christchurch massacre continue to circulate online. As such, NZ Super and its allies emphasized in the letter that the initiative will "continue to accept new signatories until these companies take meaningful action."

Similar responsible investing actions are being taken by the Norwegian fund **NBIM,** whose $1 trillion portfolio holds, on average, 1.5% of every listed company on Earth. NBIM's latest report on responsible investing, released in March 2020 – covering its 2019 voting, engagement with management, and follow up – runs to over 100 pages. Of the more than 9000 companies in which it holds voting shares, NBIM cast votes in more than 97%. It was not shy about voting against management even in its top holdings. In the last year, it voted "no" eight times at Google and four times at each of Amazon and Facebook, among others.

Their actions reveal a major shift: ESG-conscious SIFs are starting to campaign for a sustainable cyberspace, using tactics developed from "green investments" in sectors relating to fossil fuels and climate change. Until recently, the New Zealand and Norway funds were best known for their decarbonization efforts. Both have integrated climate risks into their investment processes thoroughly and systematically. NZ Super has developed low-carbon portfolio strategy for its whole portfolio, and NBIM divested thermal coal positions from its holdings.

Today, many funds have not only implemented climate-related investment strategies, but have also directly participated in physical, green projects. **Indonesia**'s new fund is a key element to building a new, more resilient capital. (Jakarta will soon sink under rising seas.) **PIF** is funding NEOM City, a green enclave in one of the world's largest producers of hydrocarbons. On a lesser scale, **CDPQ** is financing a massive expansion of greener public transit in Montreal, its home base. Even the most well-known passive investor, Japan's enormous **GPIF,** has taken on an active role in remaking fund management and bending it to ESG goals (see **Box: Passive Investors, Active ESG**). Indeed, SIFs acting on climate change send strong signals to other investors both at home and abroad.

---

### Passive Investors, Active ESG

GPIF Japan. The January 2020 open letter to CEOs from Larry Fink, head of Blackrock, the world's largest asset manager with $7 trillion under management, grabbed wide news coverage. It focused on climate change. And it was likely to carry weight in America's boardrooms. As the *Wall Street Journal* headlined in its coverage: "Blackrock CEO's push toward ESG investing highlights the power he wields over the direction of corporate America."

The story actually began far from those boardrooms, in an office building in Tokyo. Japan's **Government Pension Investment Fund (GPIF)** is the world's largest pension system with assets of $1.5 trillion. Its immense equity and debt portfolio is invested broadly across Japan and the world and consists of more than 5000 different stocks and bonds from more than 3400 issuers, divided 50/50 between equities and debt, with the equities split equally between Japanese and foreign stocks, while debt is more weighted to domestic issuers. It characterizes itself as a "super long-term investor" with an investment horizon of 100 years.

Since the 2015 arrival of Chief Investment Officer Hiromichi Mizuno, now recently retired, the fund has pivoted heavily to responsible investing. It is a leader in the trend in Japan, where, between 2016 and 2018, assets under management classified as ESG investments increased 4.6 times, making the country the fastest growing in ESG investment. Besides increasing asset allocation to the ESG category, the key initiative is to evaluate external managers on ESG criteria. In 2018, GPIF revised its ESG criteria and began evaluating its external managers on the new criteria.

Which brings us back to that Larry Fink letter. The Blackrock ESG funds were found lacking and GPIF reportedly withdrew billions of dollars from the manager in 2019. Seen in this context, the letter maybe was not surprising at all. Money talks and even those managing vast sums listen, and act – sometimes belatedly. Sovereign investors, working alone or together, are moving the needle on investment management towards ESG. As long-term passive investors, they stand to benefit most from the movement and as huge players they can make it happen.

Now they are focusing on the major tech companies, which reflects the increasing sophistication of the SIF investors, because tech companies are often deemed to be greater ESG pioneers than many other sectors. That's most obvious for the **E** (environmental) aspect. For example, Google and Apple have built green headquarters. The tech industry in general has earned (relatively) high ESG scores because innovations tend to do social environmental good. A December 2019 report commissioned by the telecom industry estimated that the use of mobile technology enabled people to reduce greenhouse gas emissions by 2135 million tons in the previous year, the size of Russia's annual emissions.

The SIFs are looking now at the social (**S**) and, more fundamentally, the governance (**G**) issues of the digital economy. The rapid pace of technological advancement, especially artificial intelligence (AI) and machine learning, is creating disruption and anxiety in the society; at the same time, the institutions that have traditionally had the responsibility of shaping the societal impacts of new technology are struggling to keep up with its rapid change and exponential impact. Through their influence on tech companies, the SIFs can join efforts with government and society stakeholders to usher in a sustainable digital transformation.

As tech giants such as GAFA (Google Amazon, Facebook, and Apple), as well as numerous AI-driven startups (some of which may quickly emerge as dominant global players), gather ever more data about their users, they are increasingly shaping people's lives and politics. For new investments, the SIFs' ESG policies have led to greater scrutiny of the tech companies and the impact of their innovation, especially their dealings with data privacy, information security, and their role in enabling government and corporate surveillance, at a time when data is viewed by many as the "new oil" of the "new economy," as well as playing a key role in controlling pandemics. For existing portfolio companies, they take on more active governance roles to mitigate and even pre-empt advanced tech's negative externalities on society.

## Super Fintech Institutions

The SIFs as globe-spanning asset managers not only have their fingers on the pulse of the digital economy, they are close to the beating heart of it. Along with external tech investing, they are transforming *themselves* into tech-driven "smart organizations." More and more SIFs have stepped up their operational capabilities to leverage technology to improve efficiency, use AI and machine learning to harness data, and ring-fence their large portfolios against cybersecurity risk. For **GIC,** its transformation involves multi-faceted efforts under an "ODE to technology" framework **(see Figure 10.1).**

As detailed in the previous chapters, GIC invests broadly in the tech industry, both directly and through external fund managers in startups, growth companies, and pre- and post-listed

Figure 10.1    **GIC's ODE Framework.**

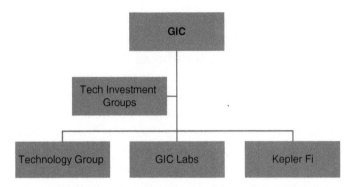

Figure 10.2    **Multiple GIC Units Focusing on Business Transformation**

companies. With a local presence in innovation hubs such as Silicon Valley and Beijing, complemented by its global presence through eight other offices, GIC could spot leads and lags across regions to capture unique opportunities. In addition to its tech investment teams, it has also set up three different units that specifically work on GIC's internal tech capabilities and business innovation (see Figure **10.2**):

**GIC Technology Group** leads innovation and transformation within the organization, and develops holistic digital solutions specific to GIC's needs.

**GIC Labs,** an in-house innovation lab, accelerates use of innovative technologies and undertakes research on tech trends that can be implemented enterprise-wide.

**Kepler Fi,** a wholly owned subsidiary, incubates and scales up innovations with the potential to disrupt the institutional asset management industry.

The unique setup of Kepler Fi demonstrates the forward-looking thinking at GIC. It is an autonomous, wholly owned subsidiary that operates out of offices in Manhattan, focusing on radical innovation ("moonshots") for the world of investment management. Among its activities: joint ventures, startup investments, as well as the development of its own proprietary products. And it attacks a range of technologies – machine learning, big data, and blockchain – and applies them to the many asset classes in which GIC is active, real, as well as digital.

If GIC is poised to become a leading smart, tech-driven asset-management institution, then the Dutch pension **APG** has set its course to transform the pension industry completely. The much bigger project that APG's innovation department (called GroeiFabriek) set out to tackle is to create a shared Dutch pension infrastructure to make pensions easier and cheaper. As the project put it: how do we create a pension product that is easy to explain to laymen, has asset management costs below 1%, and can be administered for something less than 10 euros a year? After initial assessment over the last few years, they have identified blockchain or distributed ledger technology (DLT) as the enabling technology.

To use blockchain or DLT in a traditionally centralized pension system is revolutionary. According to the project team, the main restraint is that centralizing data and processes would also mean loss of authority for most actors in the ecosystem; they would not be the master over their own data, processes, and organization anymore. As such, an ecosystem level governance model is recommended (see **Figure 10.3**). Although the assessment outcome is that most of the current Blockchain-as-a-Service (BaaS) solutions do not meet demands yet, the DLT-enabled new framework, when realized in the future, will be disruptive, since today's average pension administration costs are nearly 20 times higher than the 10 euros the APG is aiming for.

Of course, not all SIFs have the desire or available talent pool to seed a subsidiary or create an in-house disruptor. Many sovereign funds carry out their own digital transformation from external purchase and investments. Aite Group's analysis of SWF's spending costs on technology and data shows that in 2018, the total spend by the top 15 SWFs is estimated at $682 million, and this is expected to rise to US$850 million by 2021. The gradual shift toward internal investment management

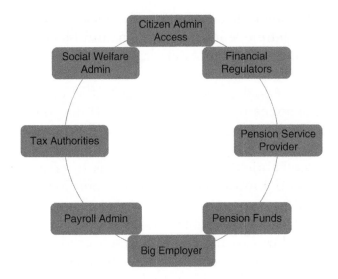

**Figure 10.3    Blockchain-based Level Governance Model**
Source: APG Pension Infrastructure Technology Assessment 2019.

within SIFs is fueling demand for more sophisticated in-house technological innovation, such as look-through capability that allows fund managers to identify exposures at any level of ownership. Their spending power is yet another reason to count SIFs as major players and masters of fintech.

Meanwhile, SIFs are active in the fintech sector, both as a suitable investment opportunity (which includes blockchain, tokens, and digital currencies) and a channel to cutting-edge technology. Deals such as Ant Financial, the financial affiliate of Chinese e-commerce giant Alibaba, Indonesian e-commerce marketplace Bukalapak, and Berlin-based mobile banking company N26, all received significant investment from SIFs. The trend continues in the pandemic: in June, 2020, Saudi Aramco Entrepreneurship Ventures, the corporate VC of the national oil company, participated in a $25 million round in New York-based, Wahed Invest LLC, a fintech offering Islamic investments. In this vein, a bevy of fintech startups have arisen to digitize investment management. **British Columbia Investment Management Corporation (BCI)**'s February 2020 investment into the UK-based ClearMacro Ltd, an independent investment analytics provider, is a good example.

With more than $100 billion of managed assets, BCI is one of Canada's largest asset managers and a leading provider of investment management services to British Columbia's public sector. BCI has taken a minority position in ClearMacro for an undisclosed investment and will hold a board seat. Because BCI has in recent years firmly established in-house investing capabilities across asset classes, this strategic investment relationship is aimed to drive forward its abilities to import best-in-class data strategies and tools to support investment decision-making and risk-management processes.

In another part of the world, Mubadala and PIF are backing, for $1.2 billion and $1.5 billion respectively, a potential Gulf-Indian regional fintech player. After Facebook splashed out $5.7 billion for a minority interest in Jio Platforms, India's fast growing digital services business, Facebook's WhatsApp launched a payments system on the platform. The move was seen as step to developing a universal digital platform along the lines of China's WeChat. The Gulf SIFs are positioned not only to fund its growth but also to foster its adoption across the vast payments corridor spanning the India Ocean.

Going forward, after many SIFs build up their own digital capabilities, they will have the opportunity to integrate the fintech resources of their subsidiaries and investments into a powerful ecosystem and form a "super fintech institution." Take **Temasek** for example. **For one,** similar to GIC, it has created Root Access, a digital tech unit to generate digital solutions to asset management problems faced by its multiple teams in multiple locations. The unit uses open source technology in AI, machine learning, and big data to capitalize on internal and external data to automate time-consuming processes and to help investment teams make better and faster decisions.

One project focused on developing an AI-powered system to quickly generate industry classifications for potential investee companies, permitting quicker benchmarking and

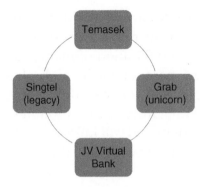

Figure 10.4    **Temasek Present at Innovation on Both Sides**

thereby accelerating the investment analysis process and reducing costs. The Root Access team contemplates disseminating its solutions to Temasek's portfolio businesses and beyond. The innovative products from within Temasek may even someday disrupt the disruptors in the market.

**For another,** by both anticipating disruption's effect on incumbents and seeking to pick the winning disruptors, Temasek has become an active participant and enabler for its portfolio companies' transformation. An instructive example is the potential entry into virtual banking in Singapore by a consortium of two Temasek portfolio companies (see **Figure 10.4**). Temasek holds a majority stake in Singtel, Singapore's telecoms incumbent, a legacy of the SIF's origin as a state holding company. It is also an investor, along with **CIC** and **Vision Fund,** in Grab, a South-east Asian ride hailing and payments unicorn. The tech disruptor was reportedly valued at $14 billion in its most recent investment round.

Grab and Singtel have now paired up to file an application for one of the two virtual banking licenses being offered by the Monetary Authority of Singapore, the city state's central bank. (Grab Financial, launched in 2016, is already active in payments, lending, and insurance.) The venture, owned 60/40 by Grab and Singtel will be able to take retail deposits and make loans. According to Grab, the digital bank will aim to cater to the needs of digital-first consumers, who have come to expect greater convenience and personalization, and SMEs that cite lack of access to credit as a key pain point.

Temasek as an equity holder in both parties to the venture stands to benefit in several ways from this combination, if successful. We recounted a parallel story in **Chapter 7,** involving the venture between two **CIC** portfolio companies, Ant Financial, the world's highest valued unicorn, and ICBC, the world's largest bank (measured by assets). Like CIC, Temasek is an equity holder in both the bank and the unicorn, and it would stand to gain by value accretion to both through a successful joint venture.

As another upside – protection against the downside of digital disruption – Temasek will also benefit by preserving its larger holding in Singtel from digital disruption by another startup entrant in which Temasek might not hold a stake. In the CIC situation, the stake in Ant Financial can be similarly viewed as a hedge for its holdings of SOE banks.

Finally, its position as a majority shareholder in Singtel and a key investor in Grab will afford it unique visibility into fintech developments, which should provide actionable information for its investment management of overall financial industry exposure, which includes over 10% of DBS Bank and stakes in other global financial institutions. Viewed as an ecosystem, Temasek, together with CIC, GIC, and peer SIFs, without question is a super fintech institution.

## Fractured Tech Future

The year 2019 may be remembered as an important inflection point for the global digital economy, from collaborative co-existence to head-on tension, as illustrated by the tech war between US and China, the two digital superpowers of the world. In the aftermath, the disrupted overseas investments, extended tech export blacklist, plus the ongoing trade and tech wars with the US, may have provided China with fresh impetus to catch up on its relative weakness in microchips. China is now putting more focus on developing semiconductor-focused sovereign funds – in China's domestic currency RMB (yuan) – to help developing R&D in the research labs and venture firms in China.

In October 2019, **China** set up a new national semiconductor fund (its second in less than five years) with 204 billion yuan ($28.9 billion) – its predecessor was capitalized with $20 billion in 2014. The fund's registered capital comes mainly from state organizations, according to company registration information, which included China's Ministry of Finance (22.5 billion yuan) and the policy bank China Development Bank (22 billion yuan), as well as state-owned enterprises such as China Tobacco Co.

The new fund plays to the tune of domestic tech development to reduce dependence on strategic imports and accelerate the digital transformation of the economy. But in semiconductors, China still faces a long path to global leadership. The 2014 fund poured billions of dollars into dozens of projects, but their electronic products still lag behind industry leaders. Taiwan and South Korea both possess advanced chip production capacity, although expertise in the manufacture of capital goods for the fabrication of chips resides in Western Europe, Japan, and North America.

For the new fund, its goal may become even broader – to cultivate China's complete semiconductor supply chain, from chip design to manufacturing, from processors to storage chips. Naturally, it has attracted fresh concern from US officials, who complained that the new fund – just like its 2014 fund predecessor – amounted to a form of state capitalism that gave its companies an unfair advantage against its US competitors. Also, the US government has an interest in the security of the supply chain in this sector because many semiconductors are ultimately used by the US government and military.

The **US**'s response? Its own sovereign fund on 5G network technology developments, an area where the US and its Western allies rely on China-sourced products – especially from Huawei. Huawei is paradigmatic of the challenge China

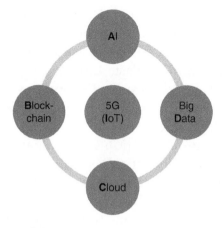

Figure 10.5    **5G-powered iABCD**

poses to the United States. It is a technological leader in "5G" telecommunications, the next-generation mobile technology that will enable new industries like the Internet of Things (IoT), AI, blockchain, cloud, and big data (see **Figure 10.5**). The desperation in the US was underscored by the highly unorthodox Trump maneuver to deploy CFIUS (described earlier in Chapter 8) to preserve Qualcomm's R&D budget, the likely best route to developing a US champion in 5G. Meanwhile, Huawei has been expanding the contest beyond 5G to the Internet itself.

In March 2020, the press reported that Huawei was putting an ambitious proposal before the ITU, the UN agency that sanctions international telecommunications protocols, including for the Internet. Huawei, together with Chinese telecoms operators and the Chinese government, advocates replacing the current TC/ICP infrastructure of the Internet with "New IP," an advanced system that would be up to the task of autonomous vehicles, IoT, holographic communications, and much more.

The current infrastructure, known as TC/ICP, was developed more than 50 years ago and the Huawei group maintains that it is insufficient for the new needs of the IoT, satellite communications, and other emerging technologies. Reportedly,

Russia supports the adoption of the new technology and Saudi Arabia is favorably inclined. Some observers indicate that New IP would accelerate the division of the Internet into two, with China, Russia, the Middle East, and Africa going the Huawei route while the US and Western Europe stay the course with TC/ICP. In any event, Huawei's emergence as a technology leader is presenting hard choices.

The Trump administration's diplomatic campaign to persuade the Western countries (as well as US domestic carrier operators) to shun Huawei has had only mixed success, due to the need to develop viable alternatives to Chinese products. While Australia has signed on, the UK government tried to pursue a middle course, permitting the use of certain elements of Huawei equipment in its wireless networks, but not without pushback from its own party in parliament. In July, 2020, the UK capitulated, banning the purchase of new Huawei 5G equipment from 2021 and mandating removal of all such equipment by 2027.

The difficulty to gain traction in the push to avoid Huawei products is hardly surprising given the actual market conditions. Competitors such as Europe's Ericsson and Nokia often do not offer the type of fully integrated solutions that Huawei does, and they come at a higher upfront cost. Countries, particularly poorer emerging markets, are reluctant to slow down 5G deployment because they see rapid deployment of 5G as important to their own economic growth. In a world of limited and high-cost alternatives, governments will be tempted to turn to Huawei despite security risks.

As with the Blue Dot program described in Chapter 4 (in combatting China's BRI), the US has championed alternatives to the Chinese initiatives (see **Figure 10.6**). This time,

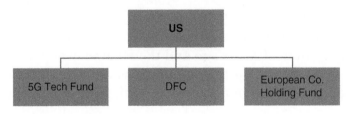

Figure 10.6    **New SIFs of US for 5G**

one took the form of a program at the newly created US **International Development Finance Corporation (DFC)**. The DFC (the successor to **OPIC,** the Overseas Private Investment Corporation), with $60 billion in funding, announced in December 2019 a program to provide finance to emerging markets in the development of mobile networks, *provided that* they do not employ Huawei equipment. Although it is not clear what alternative equipment suppliers will be tapped, Bloomberg reported at the time that shares of both Nokia and Ericsson rose with the announcement. Like a SIF and unlike its predecessor, the DFC's mandate permits it to take minority equity stakes. Where might it invest?

In January 2020, the concept of another US sovereign fund to counter China's moves was floated. During the very same week that China and US signed their phase I trade war "truce," a bipartisan group of US senators introduced legislation that would provide over $1 billion to fund the development of Western alternatives to Huawei. The bill proposes that the Federal Communications Commission (**FCC**) direct at least $750 million or up to 5% of annual auction proceeds from newly auctioned spectrum licenses to create an open-architecture model (O-RAN) research and development fund. Grants from the fund would be overseen by the National Telecommunications and Information Administration (**NTIA**) with input from other agencies. The potential recipients are not limited to US companies.

The bill would also spur the US to further its engagement in International Standard Setting Bodies – such as the ITU mentioned above – to participate in setting guidelines on telecommunications and work to make Huawei alternatives more affordable through various policies. "Every month that the U.S. does nothing, Huawei stands poised to become the cheapest, fastest, most ubiquitous global provider of 5G, while U.S. and Western companies and workers lose out on market share and jobs," according to a statement by the senators.

Finally, speaking in February 2020, Attorney General, Bill Barr, offered up a third US fund in an even more blatantly interventionist approach. Despite the efforts to launch Qualcomm on the path to 5G dominance, most observers would conclude that the US doesn't have a homegrown competitor to Huawei. The only viable rivals are two European telecoms firms. Barr is quoted as saying: "Some propose that these concerns could be met by the United States aligning itself with Nokia and/or Ericsson through American ownership of a controlling stake, either directly or through a consortium of private American and allied companies." Maybe this is where the Senators would invest the $750 million fund proposed the preceding month, or the $60 billion DFC war chest, or capital from other US government sources.

Clearly, the cross-border data governance debate – rules for who controls data, and therefore harnesses its value and increases the nation's powers of innovation – is not merely about technical problems; instead, it is at the core of geopolitical competition that will shape the 21st century. Adding an additional layer of complexity are the deep divides on the topic that are hard to bridge, not only between China and the US, but also among governments across the European Union, Japan, India, and the emerging markets that have philosophical differences on how they approach issues arising from the move into the data economy.

For example, as detailed in **Chapter 1,** the European Union has floated proposals to boost its digital economy and avoid its over-reliance on non-European companies. The EU in February 2020 unveiled a plan to restore what officials called "technological sovereignty." This echoed media reports in late 2019 that a proposal for a so-called **European Future Fund** appeared in a radical draft of plans that European Commission officials offered as an agenda of the EU's new President Ursula von der Leyen. This 173-page plan is centered on building a more defensive Europe that can take hard-hitting trade measures against Washington and Beijing, while putting more public money into homegrown business counterweights to the Chinese and US digital giants that currently dominate the European digital landscape.

Also joining in the 5G sparring match between China and the US, **Japan** in 2020 is reportedly stepping into the ring by appropriating 220 billion yen (approximately US$2.03 billion) for corporate research and development of "6G" technology (the next generation telecommunication tech after 5G). Japan's new fund will be included as part of an economic stimulus package, and the state-run New Energy and Industrial Technology Development Organization (**NEDO**) will house it. In February 2020, the Japanese government announced that it was working on a detailed blueprint focusing on 6G wireless communications network with a dedicated panel moving discussions on technological developments, potential utilization methods, and policies going forward for operations in 2030.

Having lagged behind China, Korea, and the US in the introduction of 5G, Japan is funding its efforts aggressively in order to get back in the race for 6G and aims to play a key role. "The smooth introduction of standards for next-generation wireless communications networks is indispensable to boosting Japan's international competitiveness," Japan's Communications Minister, Sanae Takaichi, said at the news conference accompanying the announcement of the 2030 goal.

No doubt, more countries will join the 5G (and 6G) race for international competitiveness. Ironically, IoT has not only spurred the SIFs of the world into the unicorn hunt, but also spawned new SIFs to serve as aggressive policy tools in carving up the digital future by funding its fracturing. What's hopeful is that through the economic independence created by the SIFs, the world may find a new equilibrium and collectively develop a shared digital future.

## MAD to MAP: Peaceful Diplomacy

Just as SIFs can play a role in erecting fences, by favoring domestic champions or staking out global digital domains, so can SIFs assist in building bridges and fostering common interests. Surprisingly, the best example is also between China and the US.

They are major trade partners to each other, and the trade surplus has contributed to a significant part of China's $3 trillion foreign reserve. This enormous holding is managed by two sovereign funds, **CIC** and the relatively less known SAFE (**State Administration of Foreign Exchange,** which does not issue an annual report on its investments like CIC).

Where do they invest the dollars? The majority is parked in nowhere other than the US. The SAFE alone has invested in more than $1 trillion in US Treasury bonds; besides the debt market, they also invested in the broad public market like the Norway fund. CIC manages a diversified portfolio and has more exposure to alternatives assets like PE funds and direct private investments. Still, the majority of the CIC portfolio is in US dollar assets. From time to time, the massive US investments held by China SIFs are referred to as the "nuclear weapon" China has in the financial market.

The logic, argued by some, is that if China dumps the US dollar assets in trillions, US financial markets will be devastated. Even if merely the US government bond holdings are sold off by China, the largest lender to the US government (sometimes China comes second, slightly below Japan SIF's holding of US debt), the yield (borrowing rate) on US government debt will skyrocket, the argument goes, and the US economy will be pushed into a recession. But would the Chinese use that weapon?

This is an important question, because for SIFs' investments into the host nations, both their entries and exits, when large in size, carry profound implications. The reasonable answer is no, because doing so would wound China grievously as well. If the US dollars and economy are ruined, China's national savings held in the same dollars will also disappear. Besides, China will no longer enjoy a trade surplus from its distressed trade partner. The same is true for US taking punitive trade actions against China.

The economic interdependence (see **Figure 10.7**) is so great that any effort by one to inflict pain on the other would do as much harm to the perpetrator as to the intended victim,

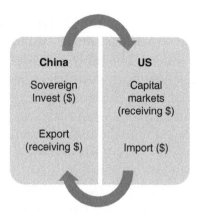

Figure 10.7    **The US–China Circle of Dollar**

which most likely contributed to their phase I trade agreement in February 2020, after a large-scale trade war lasted almost two years.

Japan's trillion-dollar **GPIF,** described earlier in this chapter, wields a similar force in international markets like the Chinese. When the yen dropped against other currencies in the early stages of the coronavirus crisis (contrary to market expectations that, as a safe haven currency, the yen would rise on news of a pandemic), commentators traced the anomaly to the GPIF's program of increasing the international weighting in its portfolio (and hence selling yen to do so, pushing yen further lower when the pandemic normally would be expected to send it higher). While no one accused GPIF of intentionally lowering the yen relative to other currencies (and collaterally maintaining – or even increasing – the competitiveness of Japanese exports), the evidence seems to indicate that, if it wanted to, it could.

The SIFs' holdings of foreign assets as financial tools (weapons) may remind people of the Cold War era of the 20th century, when the Soviet Union and the US faced off with the existential threat of total nuclear war – a vision of nuclear tipped missiles hurtling simultaneously through space and ending with murderous and total destruction of both sides within moments of the first attack. The strategy became known as Mutual Assured Destruction (**MAD**), meaning that each party, by launching a nuclear attack, simply assured its own destruction by the other. This shared understanding of MAD colored the approach of both countries towards conflicts and led to the absence of a nuclear war.

Following the analogy, SIFs can serve as a tool for geopolitical power balancing. This aspect may be of special interest to nations whose economic means exceed their other attributes of power, because their global investments can foster economic independence among countries. In general, the investments that SWFs make in the host state can lead to a re-evaluation by the host state's government of its political ties with the home state. This is especially so as any act of hostility on the host state's part would have to account for the now increased costs of losing the economic partnership it has built with the foreign SIF investments.

**Singapore** has followed this path. As we have seen, both **GIC** and **Temasek** are in the top leagues of SIFs and have demonstrated an ability to grow globally and remain at the forefront of the digital revolution. Their capital power has enhanced the economic clout of Singapore at the regional and global level. As a small, wealthy nation without natural resources in a region historically in China's sphere, Singapore chose to become China's largest foreign investor, and the savvy SIFs constitute prime examples of the ways in which a small state can improve its position vis-à-vis larger powers.

Temasek, for example, had allocated 26% (more than $50 billion) of its portfolio to Chinese investments by 2019. Previous chapters have reviewed its activity (as well as that of GIC) in the key digital economy sector in China, and both are also major investors across many asset classes in China (for example, commercial real estate and infrastructure). Apart from enjoying the financial upside from investing in the world's greatest economic growth story, there are collateral benefits to the pipsqueak city state.

For instance, Temasek's (aptly named) real estate development subsidiary, Ascendas Singbridge, is co-developing a tech city in Guangzhou named (aptly again) China-Singapore Guangzhou Knowledge City. Originally a business-led initiative to build a smart industry park near Guangzhou to attract high-tech industries, in 2018 a Framework Agreement between the Chinese and Singapore governments elevated the project to a State-Level Bilateral Cooperation Project. The project garnered the attention of the US–China Economic and Security Commission 2019 Report to the US Congress as an example of Singapore's policy of growing closer to China through economic ties.

The Singaporean SIFs illustrate the opportunity for states to enhance their economic capabilities compared to those states that challenge them. In addition to cultivating a favorable profile with the dedication of capital, skills, and know-how to China, their investments underline the benefits flowing to the larger economy and, perhaps subtly, draw the host country's attention to the potential economic and related collateral costs of threatening the relationship. One would expect no less savvy an approach by the canny state whose sole natural resource is its well-educated and hard-working population.

In other words, SIFs enter as an equalizer of sorts, allowing for smaller states to obtain an alternative path into gaining more geopolitical power. If we take the fund values to stand for a greater potential to exercise such political functions by the SWFs, it is interesting to note the home countries from which many of these top funds hail from. For example, powerful SIFs like **Mubadala** and **QIA** belong to states like the UAE and Qatar, states historically not known for their political influence on the international stage, but which are now projecting more geopolitical power than before (see **Figure 10.8**). These new global financial players are no longer headquartered in New York Wall Street, the City of London, or central Hong Kong, but rather in Auckland, Dublin, Montreal, Oslo, and Riyadh, as well as more exotic locales like Azerbaijan, Egypt, Kazakhstan, Malaysia, and Oman.

More important than a check and balance against the dominant world powers, SIFs can promote economic cooperation

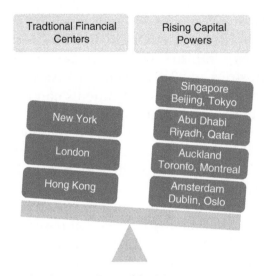

Figure 10.8    **SIFs Projecting New Geopolitical Power**

for mutual assured prosperity (**MAP**). Again, in the US and China example, both economies have benefited greatly from the integrated capital flow. For China, it has enjoyed rapid domestic economic growth; for America, its consumers appreciated cheaper iPhones, reduced mortgage payments (lower interest rates), and a lighter tax burden (abundant foreign capital). The same is true for China and Singapore's deep relationship in trade and investments. That explains the increasing SIF–SIF collaboration in recent years to promote economic development, after they jointly invested in numerous investment transactions together.

The previous chapters have analysed many joint transactions among the SIFs, and in **Chapter 5** we saw many countries purposefully use their own SIFs as a platform to attract foreign funds to develop domestic innovation ecosystems. Of course, MAP is the most apparent where the host and home states have SIFs of their own and invest cross-border in both directions (see **Figure 10.9**). However, such MAP can be found even in unilateral investments. By putting capital into the host state's economy, what the SIF (and the corresponding home state as well) is essentially doing is buying a share in the host state's

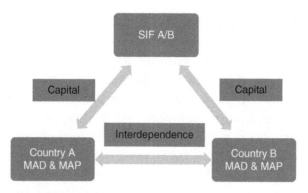

Figure 10.9    **From MAD to MAP**

future. Such investments create more shared interests between both the home and host states, which adds a peace and security dimension to the bilateral relationship.

For example, Saudi Arabia's **PIF** and **Egypt** signed an agreement in 2016 to create a $16 billion investment fund together, without elaborating on each party's contribution. (Egypt set up its sovereign fund in 2018.) PIF is a major funder of NEOM City on the Red Sea which will incorporate portions of Egypt (and Jordan as well) in its master plan (see Chapter 5), allowing Saudi Arabia an important role in the development of the much more populous and culturally influential Arab nation. The NEOM City project gives both countries a mutual stake in the digital and cultural transformation, which could potentially balance the disparity between population and wealth of the two leading Arab countries.

Furthermore, Egypt is advancing its collaboration with other SIFS, particularly in the Gulf. Egypt is reportedly in talks with **Oman**'s sovereign wealth fund to collaborate on investment in a number of sectors in Egypt, including logistics. A $20 billion joint investment fund has already been set up with **Abu Dhabi Developmental Holding Company,** a state-owned enterprise of UAE with a focus on manufacturing, traditional and renewable energy, and technology. **Kuwait** is also being courted for collaboration.

Part of the origin of MAD, **Russia** is now active in SIF-led MAP initiatives. Although differing greatly from Singapore and Middle East – in size, climate, and military power, to name but a few stark differences – Russia appears to be using a similar playbook with its SIFs. **Russian Direct Investment Fund (RDIF)** is a pertinent example. Like Singapore, it developed close investment ties with China, mostly in tech-related fields. As mentioned, RDIF and CIC in 2019 announced plans to establish the Russia–China Technology Investment Fund, and advanced digital technology like AI has been identified as where the joint efforts will focus.

Unlike Singapore's focus on China, RDIF plays a wider field in its efforts. And that is probably because, although RDIF plays the same bridge-building role as Temasek, for example, its strategy serves different goals. Russia is not a small wealthy country trying to achieve a balance with larger powers that preserves its independence. Russia is a large, important, resource-rich nation that seeks to project its power as a counterweight to the other great powers and enhance its standing in the world. As a result, Russia is geographically diverse in its partnerships. RDIF has established joint strategic partnerships with leading international co-investors from more than 15 countries that total more than $40 billion.

In another geopolitically important area, the Middle East, RDIF is active in promoting investment alliance as well. On October 15, 2019, the month following the announcement of the Russia–China Technology Investment Fund, RDIF and **Mubadala,** the UAE's sovereign wealth fund, announced a series of six cooperation agreements as a continuation of their successful long-term investment partnership that dates back to 2013.

According to the announcements, more than 45 investments have been jointly made by RDIF and Mubadala with an aggregate value in excess of $2 billion. Six new cooperation agreements will add to that and extend the cooperation to an array of areas key to the Russian economy. Among them are advanced technologies, AI, healthcare, transport, and logistics (see **Table 10.1**).

Not too far away from Abu Dhabi, RDIF is helping forge closer economic ties between Russia and UAE's neighbor

Table 10.1    RDIF/Mubadala Cooperation Agreements

**Cooperation agreements signed by RDIF and Mubadala October 2019**

**MOU 1 – Artificial Intelligence and National Projects**

RDIF and Mubadala have agreed to explore Russia's national projects and Artificial Intelligence (AI) projects. The parties will jointly implement investment projects in key areas of Russia's five-year strategic development plans.

**MOU 2 – Healthcare cooperation**

RDIF and Mubadala will cooperate to enhance the healthcare infrastructure in Russia. The collaboration will include an exchange of expertise, and give patients from the Russian Federation the opportunity seek treatment and medical care by advanced clinics in the UAE.

**MOU 3 – Industry – The construction of an advanced new pulp mill in Vologda**

RDIF and Mubadala will jointly consider an investment into a new pulp mill construction project with Sveza, one of Russia's leading woodworking companies. The total project size is expected to be up to $2.8 billion and will have a design capacity output of over 1.3 million tons of wood pulp per annum, focusing on Russian and key European and Asian markets.

**MOU 4 – Transport – Expansion of rolling stock fleet for Russian railways**

RDIF and Mubadala are considering a joint investment into NefteTransService (NTS), one of Russia's largest operators of railway rolling stock. The agreement forms part of a consortium, led by RDIF, that is looking to invest $300 million into the expansion of NTS' fleet of rolling stock, strengthening its position in the railway logistics market.

**MOU 5 – Advanced Technologies – Facial Recognition**

RDIF and Mubadala have agreed a partnership with the leading Russian facial recognition technologies developer, NtechLab, a world leader in facial recognition systems based on AI and neural networks. RDIF and Mubadala will support the expansion of NtechLab's business in the Middle East.

**MOU 6 – Logistics – the PLT logistics platform**

RDIF and Mubadala have agreed to expand their investment in the Professional Logistics Technologies (PLT) platform to build new logistics facilities. The parties will invest in the construction of a new class A multi-temperature distribution center and related infrastructure in the Moscow region with a gross leasable area of over 100,000 square meters.

Saudi Arabia through joint ventures with Saudi peers. The deals would flow in the opposite direction: Russia would not host the projects; Saudi Arabia would. In October 2019, RDIF and the Saudi Technology Development and Investment Company (**TAQNIA**), owned by the **PIF,** signed a cooperation agreement for a project to pursue commercial launch services for small spacecraft. RDIF's investment partnership with TAQNIA included staff training and the joint design and development of space technologies for implementing large-scale commercial launch projects.

Under the agreement, TAQNIA and RDIF will coordinate their joint efforts on preparing and investing in the development of technologies for launching small spacecraft into low Earth and solar-synchronous orbits as well as harnessing the potential commercial uses. As we saw in Chapter 4, the former Soviet Union's space launch center lies in Kazakhstan, while mission control sits in Moscow. The proposal would provide an alternative launch site for Russia and, at the same time, further the Saudi goal of fostering its own space tech, as witnessed by its investments in OneWeb and Virgin Galactic described earlier in this book.

In summary, it is no surprise that more sovereign funds are being set up in 2020 and beyond. SIFs have grown in both number and size ever since the Kuwait Investment Authority was founded in 1953. Today, the momentum is stronger than ever. Overall, the SIFs constitute an extremely young community, with Gen Z and Millennials making up the majority of inhabitants. Increasingly, more states are playing with the idea of developing their own SWFs, be it to better utilize their trade surpluses, save wealth from natural resources for future generations, or drive domestic economic growth.

Such proliferation of SIFs will promote economic interdependence, similar to compacts like the European Union (EU), which uses economic cooperation for international peace, security, and prosperity. Through the collaboration among the SIFs, it could be hoped that the US, China, the EU, Japan, and many other parts of the world could reach a new equilibrium to collectively drive the innovation in an increasingly fragmented tech world. That's critical for a shared digital future, because at the core of digital economy is the free flow of trade, capital, talent, know-how, and data.

## Conclusion

As this book concludes, there is no doubt that SIFs – **sovereign wealth funds, public pension funds, state development funds,** and various new forms of **government investment funds –** have become the "super asset owners" in the international monetary and financial system. Far from being a homogenous group of investors, yet nonetheless a discrete investor class, the SIFs hold tremendous power and influence to shape the future direction of the global capital markets and digital economy.

The emergence of SIFs symbolizes a major shift of the world's economic power. For the first time, investment funds from developing countries are playing with OECD financial giants as equals. Furthermore, their investments into high-tech enable them to participate at the cutting-edge of the fourth industrial revolution, challenging traditional innovation powerhouses like the US and Germany. Consequently, new innovation hubs are mushrooming across the globe, and emerging economies are becoming smarter and more competitive. As such, the SIFs will lead to global rebalancing of geopolitical power.

Given both their capital influence and long-term investment horizons, the SIFs are in a unique position to promote the sustainable growth of the future economy. Much of this book serves to push for the normative standpoint that there can be positive economic and political effects that SIFs can uniquely bring about. This book highlights these aspects and bring focus to them, compared to the world's otherwise almost myopic obsession with the negative aspects of SIFs and their threats to national security.

Therefore, we should no longer shy away from the reality that sovereign financing has always been as political as it is economic; instead, we advocate for balanced policy responses among all stakeholders. This book is a merely a starting point for future global dialogue. In the end, it is hoped that we – be we SIF investors, tech unicorns, VC funds, financial firms, policymakers, academics, or the general public – can move towards a more balanced understanding of SIFs in the modern political context, instead of simplistically categorizing them. It is only so that can we move towards an era of greater stability, mutual prosperity, and sustained peace.

> *It is obvious that Nkr 10,000 billion [$1 trillion] is politics, declared Norway's leading candidate for Prime Minister in its 2021 elections, Jonas Gahr Store, when he broke with political consensus recently. True, it is unlikely that SIFs can be devoid of their political nexus, and an increase in transparency only solves part of our dilemma. What is undeniable is the fact that these funds will be available to more states, both small and large, as tools for both economic and political policies in the long run, and the momentum is strong and obvious.*
>
> *This book was written as the coronavirus pandemic gripped the world, a life and death struggle that puts the world of high finance into perspective. But even as the crisis moves human health to the forefront, the sovereign investors had already played their role. You will recall VIR, the biotech unicorn which provided an example of collaboration among ADIA, APFC, and Temasek – SIFs from three disparate continents – in Chapter 3. As we go to press, GSK in April 2020 had just announced its own $250 million investment in VIR to develop a viral antibody treatment for Covid-19.*
>
> *Although the pandemic has pushed more activities online, verifying the investment theme of unicorn hunting, more real-life connectivity is also formed by their global expansion. For evidence, one only needs to look at the NEOM City on the Red Sea. Part of the collaboration between the sovereign funds of Egypt and Saudi Arabia is a literal bridge building exercise: included in the smart city plan, funded by PIF to the tune of $500 million, is an actual bridge to connect Egypt's Sinai with Saudi Arabia's Red Sea coast, joining the two nations, which have no common border, directly for the first time. Until it is completed, the citizens of the futuristic metropolis will have to rely on those flying taxis.*

# Appendix: Table of Abbreviations

## Table of Abbreviations

| Abbreviation | Full Name |
|---|---|
| ABP | Stichting Pensioenfonds ABP (Netherlands) |
| ACIC | Australia's Critical Infrastructure Centre |
| AI | Artificial Intelligence |
| AIIB | Asian Infrastructure Investment Bank |
| AIMCo | Alberta Investment Management Corporation |
| AP6 | Sjatte ap-fonden (Sweden) |
| APFC | Alaska Permanent Fund Corporation |
| APG | APG Group N.V. (Netherlands) |
| BCI | British Columbia Investment Management |
| BDN | Blue Dot Network |
| BIA | Brunei Investment Agency |
| BRI | Belt & Road Initiative |
| CalPERS | California Public Employees Retirement System |
| CDC | Caisse des Depots (France) |
| CDPQ | Caisse de Depot et Placement du Quebec |
| CFIUS | Committee on Foreign Investment in the United States |
| CIC | China Investment Corporation |
| CPPIB | Canadian Pension Plan Investment Board |
| CSC | Commonwealth Superannuation Corporation (Australia) |
| DFC | International Development Finance Corporation (US) |
| DLT | Distributed Ledger Technology |
| DTS | Digital Transformation Strategy |
| ESG | Environmental, social and governance |
| ESSF | Economic and Social Stabilization Fund (Chile) |
| FCC | Federal Communications Commission (US) |
| FII | Fondo Italiano Innovazione |

| Abbreviation | Full Name |
|---|---|
| FIRB | Foreign Investment Review Board (Australia) |
| FIRRMA | Foreign Investment Risk Review Modernization Act |
| FRR | Fond de Regulation des Recettes (Algeria) |
| FSDA | Fundo Soberano de Angola |
| FSI | CDP Equity (f/k/a Fondo Strategico Italiano) |
| GCC | Gulf Cooperation Council |
| GIC | Singapore's GIC Private Limited |
| GP | General Partners |
| GPFG | Norway's Government Pension Fund – Global |
| GPIF | Government Pension Investment Fund Japan |
| HKMA | Hong Kong Monetary Authority |
| HSF | Trinidad and Tobago – Heritage and Stabilization Fund |
| ICT | Information, Communications, Technology |
| INCJ | Innovation Network Corporation Japan |
| IOT | Internet of Things |
| IPO | Initial Public Offering |
| ISIF | Irish Strategic Investment Fund |
| JIC | Japan Investment Corporation |
| KIA | Kuwait Investment Authority |
| KIC | Korean Investment Corporation |
| LIA | Libyan Investment Authority |
| LP | Limited Partner |
| NBIM | Norges Bank Investment Management |
| NIIF | National Infrastructure and Investment Fund (India) |
| NPS | National Pension Service of Korea |
| NSIA | Nigerian Sovereign Investment Authority |
| NWF | National Welfare Fund (Russia) |
| NZ Super | New Zealand Superannuation Fund |
| OIF | Oman Investment Fund |
| OMERS | Ontario Municipal Employees Retirement System |
| OPTrust | OPSEU Pension Trust (Canada) |
| OTPP | Ontario Teachers' Pension Plan |
| PE | Private Equity |
| PIF | Public Investment Fund (Saudi Arabia) |
| PIFSS | Public Institution for Social Security (Kuwait) |
| PII | Personally Identifiable Information |
| PPF | Public Pension Fund |
| PRF | Pension Reserve Fund (Chile) |
| PSP | Public Sector Pension Plan (Canada) |
| QIA | Qatar Investment Authority |
| QIC | Queensland Investment Corporation |
| RCIF | Russian China Investment Fund |
| RDIF | Russian Direct Investment Fund |
| RIF | Rwanda Research and Innovation Fund |

| Abbreviation | Full Name |
| --- | --- |
| SAFE | State Administration of Foreign Exchange (China) |
| SAMA | Saudi Arabian Monetary Agency |
| SDF | Sovereign Development Fund |
| SDG | Sustainable development goals |
| SGRF | State General Reserve Fund (Oman) |
| SIF | Sovereign Investment Fund |
| SK | Samruk-Kaznya (Kazakhstan) |
| SOE | State-Owned Enterprise |
| SOFAZ | State Oil Fund of the Republic of Azerbaijan |
| SWF | Sovereign Wealth Fund |
| SWFI | Sovereign Wealth Fund Institute |
| TID | Critical Technology, Critical Infrastructure, Sensitive Personal Data |
| TRS | Teacher Retirement System of Texas |
| VC | Venture Capital |

# Bibliography

## Chapter 1

Fitzgerald, Drew. "Senators urge $1 billion plan to loosen China's grip on 5G", Wall Street Journal, 14 January 2020. https://www.wsj.com/articles/senators-propose-bill-to-subsidize-u-s-firms-5g-efforts-11579031806

Government Pension Investment Fund. "ESG Report 2018", 2019. https://www.gpif.go.jp/en/investment/190905_Esg_Report.pdf

Hentov, Elliot. "How do sovereign wealth funds invest", State Street Global Advisors, January 2020. https://www.ssga.com/library-content/pdfs/official-institutions-/how-do-sovereign-wealth-funds-invest.pdf

Lahiri, Tripti. "A fund linked to the tech deal Trump just vetoed is an investor in China's national security", Quartz, 14 September 2017. https://qz.com/1077213/trump-has-stopped-an-acquisition-of-lattice-semiconductor-by-canyon-bridge-a-private-equity-fund-with-ties-to-chinese-state-run-firms/

Li, Tao. "How China's 'Big Fund' is helping the country catch up in the global semiconductor race", South China Morning Post, 10 May 2018. https://scmp.com/tech/enterprises/article/2145422/how-chinas-big-fund-helping-country-catch-global-semiconductor-race

Li, Xiang. "PE firm Canyon Bridge shifting focus to Europe", China Daily, 9 February 2018b. https://www.chinadaily.com.cn/a/201802/09/WS5a7d0205a3106e7dcc13bbf1.html

de la Merced, Michael J. "Sovereign Wealth Funds Embrace their Ambitions", 18 October 2018. https://www.nytimes.com/2018/10/08/business/dealbook/sovereign-wealth-funds-embrace-their-ambitions.html

Morozov, Evgeny. "Billion-dollar debts control the future of tech industry", The Guardian, 10 March 2018. https://www.theguardian.com/commentisfree/2018/mar/11/insatiable-global-funds-control-future-of-tech-industry

Prequin. "Prequin Special Report: Sovereign Wealth Funds", August 2018. https://docs.preqin.com/reports/Preqin-Special-Report-Sovereign-Wealth-Funds-August-2018.pdf

Rahadiana, Rieka. "Indonesia Secures $22.8 Billion from U.A.E. for Wealth Fund", Bloomberg, 12 January 2020. https://www.bloomberg

.com/news/articles/2020-01-13/indonesia-snags-22-8-billion-from-uae-for-sovereign-wealth-fund

Reuters. "Goldman Sachs pleads not guilty in Malaysia over 1MDB bond sales: state media", 24 February 2020. https://www.reuters.com/article/us-malaysia-politics-1mdb-goldman/goldman-sachs-pleads-not-guilty-in-malaysia-over-1mdb-bond-sales-state-media-idUSKCN20I0QI

Wall Street Journal. "Citigroup down premarket on Abu Dhabi demands," 16 December 2009. https://blogs.wsj.com/marketbeat/2009/12/16/citigroup-down-premarket-on-abu-dhabi-demands/

## Chapter 2

Alves, Bruno. "What OMERS learnt managing third-party capital", Infrastructure Investor, 23 April 2019. https://www.infrastructureinvestor.com/omers-learnt-managing-third-party-capital/

Canadian Business. "CPPIB looks to cash in on 'disruption' and shifts in technology, demographics." 21 November 2018. https://www.canadianbusiness.com/business-news/cppib-look-to-cash-in-on-disruption-and-shifts-in-technology-demographics/

CBS News. "Airline suspends "nut rage" sister over ad meeting tantrum", 16 April 2018. https://www.cbsnews.com/news/korean-air-nut-rage-sister-emily-cho-water-throwing-ad-meeting-cho-hyun-ah/

Cohan, William D. "VCs have pumped up the value of the 'unicorn' startups", Fortune, 21 January 2016. https://fortune.com/longform/silicon-valley-tech-ipo-market/

Economist. "A vast pension fund is gaining even more financial clout", 19 January 2019. https://www.economist.com/finance-and-economics/2019/01/19/canadas-vast-pension-fund-is-gaining-even-more-financial-clout

Gillers, Heather. "CalPERS Wants to Double Down on Private Equity", Wall Street Journal, 17 March 2019. https://www.wsj.com/articles/calpers-wants-to-double-down-on-private-equity-11552834800

Gonzalez, Guadalupe. "Spotify's CFO: The Traditional IPO Process Hasn't Evolved in Decades –That's 'Moronic'", Inc, 20 June 2019. https://www.inc.com/guadalupe-gonzalez/spotify-cfo-direct-listing-ipo-slack.html

de Leon, Riley. "Airbnb and the Silicon Valley unicorns that may dare to go public in 2020", CNBC, December 23, 2019 https://www.cnbc.com/2019/12/23/airbnb-and-silicon-valley-unicorns-that-may-dare-to-ipo-in-2020.html

Marvin, Rob. "2019: A No Good, Very Bad Year for Unicorn Tech Companies", PCMag, 18 November 2019, https://www.pcmag.com/news/2019-a-no-good-very-bad-year-for-unicorn-tech-companies

Webb, Merryn Somerset. "Proof that the tech-unicorn IPO bubble is bursting", Money Week, 13 September 2019. https://moneyweek.com/515081/proof-that-the-tech-company-unicorn-ipo-bubble-is-bursting

Whyte, Amy. "Norway Blocks Wealth Fund From Investing in Private Equity", institutional investor, 10 April 2018. https://www.institutionalinvestor.com/article/b17q8601nxqmt5/norway-blocks-wealth-fund-from-investing-in-private-equity

Winck, Ben. "The IPO market is rebelling against many of 2019's money-losing unicorns", Business Insider, 2 October 2019. https://markets.businessinsider.com/news/stocks/ipo-market-outlook-trends-why-investors-rebelling-against-unicorns-implications-2019-9-1028570687#reason-1-weak-margins1

Wille, Klaus, Joyce Koh and Yoolim Lee. "How Singapore's wealth fund invests in tech companies", Bloomberg, 22 March 2018. https://www.bloomberg.com/news/articles/2018-03-22/how-singapore-wealth-fund-gic-invests-in-tech-companies-q-a

## Chapter 3

Economist. "The wave of unicorn IPOs reveals Silicon Valley's groupthink", 17 April 2019b. https://www.economist.com/briefing/2019/04/17/the-wave-of-unicorn-ipos-reveals-silicon-valleys-groupthink

Fintech Futures. "Judo Bank breaks Aussie record with $400 million round", 5 August 2019. https://www.fintechfutures.com/2019/08/judo-bank-breaks-aussie-record-with-400m-round/

Melton, Monica. "Babylon Health Gets $2 billion Valuation with New Funding that will help it expand in U.S.", Forbes, 2 August 2019. https://www.forbes.com/sites/monicamelton/2019/08/02/babylon-health-gets-2-billion-valuation-with-new-funding-that-will-help-it-expand-in-us/#7c1d82437a1a

Ontario Teachers' Pension Plan. "Ontario Teachers' to invest in global disruptive technology through new innovation platform", Press Release, 23 April 2019. https://www.otpp.com/news/article/-/article/804527

Rundell, Sarah. "Temasek seeks tomorrow's champions", Top100Funds.com, 12 October 2017. https://www.top1000funds.com/2017/10/temasek-seeks-tomorrows-champions/

Sarkar, Pooja. "Singapore sting: Temasek's game plan for India investments", Forbes India, 12 November 2019. https://www.forbesindia.com/article/boardroom/singapore-sting-temaseks-game-plan-for-india-investments/56081/1

Schipani, Andres. "Nubank Shakes Up Brazil's Banking Industry", Financial Times Special Report Boldness in Business, 30 March 2020. https://www.ft.com/content/c0014ce4-6273-11ea-abcc-910c5b38d9ed

Soo, Zen. "Why sovereign wealth funds are pouring billions into tech firms", SCMP, 6 June 2017, https://scmp.com/business/banking-finance/article/2096993/why-sovereign-wealth-funds-are-buying-more-tech-firms

Soo, Zen. "Excerpts of Q&A with Khazanah Nasional managing director", SCMP, 8 June 2017 https://www.scmp.com/tech/leaders-founders/article/2097400/excerpts-qa-khazanah-nasionalmanaging-director

Wald, Ellen. "Did Saudi Arabia Just Troll Elon Musk's Tesla?", Forbes, 18 September 2018. https://www.forbes.com/sites/ellenrwald/2018/09/18/did-saudi-arabia-just-troll-elon-musks-tesla/#642ad4fc4d7f

Whelan, Robbie and Eliot Brown. "SoftBank is Funding Every Side of a Bruising Startup Battle", Wall Street Journal, 30 January 2020. https://www.wsj.com/articles/softbank-is-funding-every-side-of-latin-americas-bruising-startup-battle-11580398900

Wright, Chris. "Lifting the Lid on Singapore's GIC", Euromoney, 9 May 2019. https://www.euromoney.com/article/b1f9hfdkhkzh7n/asia-sovereign-wealth-funds-lifting-the-lid-on-singapores-gic

# Chapter 4

Abrahams, Jessica. "Uniqlo heads towards full warehouse automation with groundbreaking robot robot that can fold and box clothes", Telegraph, 24 December 2019. https://www.telegraph.co.uk/news/2019/12/24/uniqlo-heads-towards-full-warehouse-automation-groundbreaking/

Global Construction Review. "Plans announced for $86 billion first phase of Kuwait's Silk City", 20 February 2019. http://www.globalconstructionreview.com/news/plans-announced-86bn-first-phase-kuwaits-silk-city/

Kamiya, Marco and Winston Ma, "Sovereign investment funds could be the answer to the SDGs", World Economic Forum, December 2019. https://www.weforum.org/agenda/2019/12/sovereign-wealth-funds-sdgs/

Ma, Winston. "The Digital Silk Road brings the new momentum of Green Transformation for the BRI", World Economic Forum, September 2019. https://www.weforum.org/agenda/2018/09/could-a-digital-silk-road-solve-the-belt-and-roads-sustainability-problem/

Ma, Winston. "The Digital Silk Road for the Next Billion Users", Milken Review, 2018. http://www.milkenreview.org/articles/the-digital-silk-road-for-the-next-billion-users

Miller, Rich. "EdgeCore Launches, Plans $2 Billion in Data Center Development", Data Center Frontier, 14 February 2018. https://datacenterfrontier.com/edgecore-launches-plans-2-billion-in-data-center-development/

Miller, Rich. "Going xScale: Equinix, GIC Partner on Hyperscale Data Centers in Europe", Data Center Frontier, 1 July 2019. https://datacenterfrontier.com/going-xscale-equinix-gic-partner-on-hyperscale-data-centers-in-europe/

Queensland Investment Corporation. "Red Papers: Detailed Thinking from Deep Research, Mobility as a Service", 21 June 2018. https://www.qic.com.au/knowledge-centre/mobility-as-a-service-20180621

United States Department of State. "Blue Dot Network", Last retrieved April 20, 2020 from https://www.state.gov/blue-dot-network/

## Chapter 5

African Business Magazine. "How well are Africa's sovereign wealth funds managed?", July 3, 2018. https://africanbusinessmagazine.com/sectors/finance/how-well-are-africas-sovereign-wealth-funds-managed/

African Union. "The Draft Digital Transformation Strategy for Africa (2020-2030)". https://www.tralac.org/documents/resources/african-union/3013-the-draft-digital-transformation-strategy-for-africa-2020-2030/file.html

Bisson, Peter and Jonathon Tetrault. "A conversation with CDPQ's Michael Sabia", McKinsey Industry Insights, July 2015. https://www.mckinsey.com/industries/financial-services/our-insights/a-conversation-with-cdpqs-michael-sabia

Bright, Jake. "Driving deep into Africa's blossoming tech scene", TechCrunch, 31 May 2019. https://techcrunch.com/2019/05/31/diving-deep-into-africas-blossoming-tech-scene/ accessed on Jan. 19, 2020

Caisse de Depot et placement de Quebec. "Two funds created to support Quebec companies' international growth and business transfer projects", press release, 15 February 2017. https://www.cdpq.com/en/news/pressreleases/two-funds-created-to-support-quebec-companies-international-growth-and-business

Ghosh, Indranil. "Transforming Emerging Economies with Sovereign Development Funds", Emerging Markets Views, 13 February 2019. https://em-views.com/transforming-emerging-economies-with-sovereign-development-funds

Lim, Zhi Jian. "Letter: SWF governance model that works for Singapore", letter to the editor, Financial Times, 20 February 2020. https://www.ft.com/content/421c052e-4ce5-11ea-95a0-43d18ec715f5

Ncube, Mthuli, "Sovereign Wealth Funds and Africa's Unique Challenges", Quantum Global Group, 21 August 2017 http://quantumglobalgroup.com/article/sovereign-wealth-funds-and-africas-unique-challenges/

Patrick, Margot, Gabriele Steinhauser and Patricia Kowsmann. "The $500 Million Bank Heist –and How It Was Foiled", Wall Street Journal, 3 October 2018. https://www.wsj.com/articles/the-500-million-central-bank-heistand-how-it-was-foiled-1538578897

Scheck, Justin, Rory Jones and Summer Said. "A Prince's $500 billion Desert Dream: Flying Cars, Robot Dinosaurs and a Giant Artificial Moon", Wall Street Journal, 25 July 2019. https://www.wsj.com/articles/a-princes-500-billion-desert-dream-flying-cars-robot-dinosaurs-and-a-giant-artificial-moon-11564097568

United Nations Conference on Trade and Development. "UNCTAD Digital Economy Report 2019", 4 September 2019. https://unctad.org/en/PublicationsLibrary/der2019_en.pdf

## Chapter 6

Brown, Eliot. "How Adam Neumann's Over-the-Top Style Built WeWork. This Is Not the Way Everybody Behaves", Wall Street Journal, 19 September 2019. https://www.wsj.com/articles/this-is-not-the-way-everybody-behaves-how-adam-neumanns-over-the-top-style-built-wework-11568823827

Koh, Joyce. "Temasek Will Explore AI and Blockchain Deals", Bloomberg, 21 November 2018. https://www.bloomberg.com/news/articles/2018-11-22/temasek-to-explore-ai-blockchain-deals-with-experimental-pods

McNish, Jacquie. "Quebec's Caisse eyes $1 billion payday on Bombardier train sale", 21 February 2020. https://www.wsj.com/articles/quebecs-caisse-eyes-1-billion-payday-on-bombardier-train-sale-11582286403

Mohamed, Theron. "Softbank wework valuation 5 billion staggering drop", Business Insider, 8 November 2019. https://markets.businessinsider.com/news/stocks/softbank-wework-valuation-5-billion-staggering-drop-2019-11-1028673855

Mubadala. "Mubadala to launch $400 million European tech fund", press release, 13 June 2018. https://www.mubadala.com/en/news/mubadala-launch-400-million-european-tech-fund

Powell, Jamie, "NIO's New Years Day Surprise" Financial Times, 7 January 2020. https://ftalphaville.ft.com/2020/01/06/1578327570000/Nio-s-New-Years-Day-surprise/

Reuters. "WeWork debacle has unicorn investors seeking cover", 13 January 2020b. https://www.reuters.com/article/us-funding-unicorns-analysis/wework-debacle-has-unicorn-investors-seeking-cover-idUSKBN1ZC0ZK

Russell, Jon. "Temasek jumps into China's bike-rental startup war with investment in Mobike", Techcrunch, 20 February 2017. https://techcrunch.com/2017/02/20/temasek-jumps-into-chinas-bike-rental-startup-war-with-investment-in-mobike/

Saigol, Lina and Selin Bucak. "One Canadian Pension Fund Is Betting That 'Cuddly Capital' Can Raise Its Profile in Private Equity", Barron's, 13 January 2020. https://www.barrons.com/articles/canadas-omers-bets-cuddly-capital-can-raise-profile-in-private-equity-51578953912

Sen, Anirban and Jane Lanhee Lee, "China's 'Big Gamble': Lessons From the Bike Sharing Bust May Hang Over Its A.I. Boom", Fortune, 7 December 2019. https://fortune.com/2019/12/06/china-bike-sharing-investors-ai/

## Chapter 7

Ai-CIO. "3 Large Funds Commit $700 Million to Form Capital Constellation", 26 February 2018. https://www.ai-cio.com/news/3-large-funds-commit-700-million-form-capital-constellation/

Aldred, Stephen. "Chasing Temasek, China's CIC explores broader investing role", Reuters, 19 July 2012. https://www.reuters.com/article/us-cic-strategy/chasing-temasek-chinas-cic-explores-broader-investing-role-idUSBRE86I0BW20120719

Caisse de Depot et placement de Quebec. "CDPQ and Generation Investment Management make long term-investment in FNZ", press release 8 October 2018. https://www.cdpq.com/en/news/pressreleases/cdpq-and-generation-investment-management-make-long-term-investment-in-fnz

Hope, Bradley and Jenny Strasburg. "SoftBank's Rajeev Misra used campaign of sabotage to hobble internal rivals", Wall Street Journal, 26 February 2020. https://www.wsj.com/articles/softbanks-rajeev-misra-used-campaign-of-sabotage-to-hobble-internal-rivals-11582743294

Japan Times. "Japan Investment Corp. at risk of becoming another 'zombie' rescue fund after METI intervention" 31 January 2019. https://www.japantimes.co.jp/news/2019/01/31/business/japan-investment-corp-risk-becoming-another-zombie-rescue-fund-metis-intervention/#.Xpx7JVNKhR1

Loizos, Connie. "Unity, whose software powers half of all new mobile games, lands $400 million from Silver Lake", 23 May 2017. https://techcrunch.com/2019/05/09/with-new-raise-unitys-valuation-could-climb-towards-6-billion/

Martin, Matthew. "Saudi Wealth Fund Plans San Francisco Office", Bloomberg, 13 February 2019. https://www.bloomberg.com/news/ articles/2019-02-13/saudi-wealth-fund-plans-san-francisco-office-in- technology-push

McElhaney, Alicia. "After Blowback, Texas Teachers Pauses Its Move to a New Office" Institutional Investor, February 2020. https://www .institutionalinvestor.com/article/b1khm9bk17qchs/After-Blowback- Texas-Teachers-Pauses-Its-Move-to-a-New-Office

Milstead, David. "The price of a pension: Inside CPPIB, the $3-billion-a-year operation that invests your money", The Global and Mail, 7 September 2019. https://www.theglobeandmail.com/ business/article-the-price-of-a-pension-inside-cppib-the-3-billion-a- year-operation/

Misra, Rajeev and Marcelo Claure, "Trouble at the top of SoftBank may threaten its pricey investments", The Real Deal, 8 February 2019. https://therealdeal.com/2019/02/08/trouble-at-the-top-of-softbank- may-threaten-investments/

O'Hear, Steve. "Omers Ventures outs €300M European fund — Q&A with Managing Partner Harry Briggs", Techcrunch, 25 March 2019. https:// techcrunch.com/2019/03/25/omers-ventures-europe/

Pfeuti, Elizabeth. "Where in the World is the Kuwait Investment Office?" Chief Investment Officer, 27 June 2014. https://www.ai-cio.com/news/ where-in-the-world-is-the-kuwait-investment-authority/

Proud, Liam and George Hay. "Vision Fund may be Hotel California for investors", Reuters, 19 June 2019. https://www.reuters.com/article/us- softbank-group-vision-fund-breakingvi/breakingviews-vision-fund-may- be-hotel-california-for-investors-idUSKCN1TK1YL

PYMNTS. "SoftBank's Vision Fund Sequel Fails To Meet Funding Goal", 7 February 2020. https://www.pymnts.com/news/investment-tracker/ 2020/softbank-vision-fund-sequel-fails-meet-funding-goal/

Shieber, Jonathan. "WestSummit Looks Beyond CIC for Newest Fund", PE News, 25 June 2012. https://www.penews.com/articles/westsummit- looks-beyond-cic-20120625

Wickham, Phil and Koichiro Nakamura, "SoftBank's problems aren't so surprising if you understand this one thing about the company", Market Watch, 30 October 2019. https://www.marketwatch.com/story/ softbanks-problems-arent-so-surprising-if-you-understand-this-one- thing-about-the-company-2019-10-30

## Chapter 8

Ferek, Katy Stech. "National Security Regulator to Take Closer Look at Privacy Risks in Foreign Investors' U.S. Deals", Wall Street Journal, 13 February 2020. https://www.wsj.com/articles/national-security-regulator-to-take-closer-look-at-privacy-risks-in-foreign-investors-u-s-deals-11581600600

Hartcher, Peter. "Revealed: why the sale of Ausgrid to Chinese buyers was vetoed", Sydney Morning Herald, 28 May 2018. https://www.smh.com.au/opinion/revealed-why-the-sale-of-ausgrid-to-chinese-buyers-was-vetoed-20180528-p4zhxh.html

Innovation, Science and Economic Development Canada. "Investment Canada Annual Report 2018-2019", 2019. https://www.ic.gc.ca/eic/site/ica-lic.nsf/eng/h_lk81126.html

Musgrave, Paul. "The Slip that Revealed the Real Trump Doctrine", Foreign Policy, 2 May 2019. https://foreignpolicy.com/2019/05/02/the-slip-that-revealed-the-real-trump-doctrine/

Needham, Kirsty. "China's Australia investments fell amid 2018-19 tensions", Reuters, 7 May 2020. https://www.reuters.com/article/australia-china-investment/chinas-australia-investments-fell-amid-2018-19-tensions-data-shows-idUSL4N2CP1M1

Sanger, David. "Japanese Purchase of Chip Maker Cancelled After Objections in US", New York Times, 17 March 1987. https://www.nytimes.com/1987/03/17/business/japanese-purchase-of-chip-maker-canceled-after-objections-in-us.html

Satariano, Adam and Monika Pronczuk. "Europe, Overrun by Foreign Tech Giants Wants to Grow Its Own", 19 February 2020, New York Times. https://www.nytimes.com/2020/02/19/business/europe-digital-economy.html

Scott, Jason. "Australia to Toughen Foreign Investment Laws Amid China Spat", Bloomberg, 4 June 2020. https://www.bloomberg.com/news/articles/2020-06-04/australia-to-boost-foreign-investment-rules-for-sensitive-assets

United States Department of Justice. "Attorney General William Barr delivers the keynote address at the Department of Justice's China Initiative Conference", 6 February 2020. https://www.justice.gov/opa/speech/attorney-general-william-p-barr-delivers-keynote-address-department-justices-china

United States Treasury. "CFIUS Overview". Last retrieved 18 April 2020 from https://home.treasury.gov/policy-issues/international/the-committee-on-foreign-investment-in-the-united-states-cfius/cfius-overview

Zhong, Raymond. "U.S. Blocks a Chinese Deal Amid Rising Tensions Over Technology," New York Times, 23 February 2018. https://www.nytimes.com/2018/02/23/technology/china-microchips-cfius-xcerra.html

## Chapter 9

Agence France-Press. "Germany aims to shield tech firms from foreign takeovers", SCMP, 28 November 2019. https://scmp.com/tech/policy/article/3039814/germany-aims-shield-tech-firms-foreign-takeovers

Business Wire. "Boyd Corporation Announces Agreement to be Acquired by Affiliates of Goldman Sachs from Genstar Capital", 11 July 2018. https://www.businesswire.com/news/home/20180711005888/en/ Boyd-Corporation-Announces-Agreement-Acquired-Affiliates-Goldman

Clark, Harry and Betty Louie. "United States: Grindr And PatientsLikeMe Outcomes Show Non-Cleared Transactions' Exposure To CFIUS Scrutiny, Especially When PII Is Involved", Mondaq, 8 May 2019. https://www.mondaq.com/unitedstates/Government-Public-Sector/ 804096/Grindr-And-PatientsLikeMe-Outcomes-Show-Non-Cleared-Transactions39-Exposure-To-CFIUS-Scrutiny-Especially-When-PII-Is-Involved

Dickman, Steve. "US Crackdown On Foreign Biotech Investment Makes Us Poorer, Not Safer", Forbes, 24 May 2019. https://www.forbes.com/ sites/stevedickman/2019/05/24/us-crackdown-on-foreign-biotech-investment-makes-us-poorer-not-safer/#311dbd558197

Gal, Danit. "The U.S.-China-Israel Technology Triangle", foreignaffairs .com, 30 July 2019. https://www.cfr.org/blog/us-china-israel-technolo gy-triangle

Harris, Mark. "Google and Facebook turn their backs on undersea cable to China", Techcrunch, 6 February 2020. https://techcrunch.com/ 2020/02/06/google-and-facebook-turn-their-backs-on-undersea-cable-to-china/

Jing, Meng. "Your money's not wanted HERE: Chinese-led bid for stake in high-res map maker rejected by US", SCMP, 27 September 2017. https://scmp.com/business/companies/article/2113119/your-moneys-not-wanted-here-chinese-led-bid-stake-high-res-map

Jing, Meng. "Tencent, partners invest in HERE's digital maps to get a leg up on self-driving cars", SCMP, 27 December 2016. https://scmp.com/ business/article/2057446/tencent-partners-invest-heres-digital-maps-get-leg-self-driving-cars

Khan, Mehren. "EU Floats Plan for €100 billion sovereign wealth fund", Financial Times, 23 August 2019 https://www.ft.com/content/ 033057a2-c504-11e9-a8e9-296ca66511c9

Japan Times. "Japan Display bailout plan gets shareholder approval", 26 March 2020. https://www.japantimes.co.jp/news/2020/03/26/ business/corporate-business/japan-display-bailout/

Mercury News. "Fairchild turns down Chinese offer", 17 February 2016. https://www.mercurynews.com/2016/02/17/fairchild-turns-down-chinese-offer/

Newton, Casey. "How Grindr became a national security issue", The Verge, 28 March 2019. https://www.theverge.com/interface/2019/3/ 28/18285274/grindr-national-security-cfius-china-kunlun-military

New York Times. "Really? Is the White House Proposing to Buy Ericsson or Nokia?" 13 February 2020b. https://www.nytimes.com/2020/02/07/business/dealbook/bill-barr-huawei-nokia-ericsson.html

Titcomb, James. "British chip firm Imagination needs support from Chinese owner after royalties from Apple dry up", Telegraph, 12 August 2019. https://www.telegraph.co.uk/technology/2019/08/12/british-chip-firm-imagination-needs-support-chinese-owner-royalties/

Xiang, Li. "PE firm Canyon Bridge shifting focus to Europe", China Daily, 9 February 2018. https://www.chinadaily.com.cn/a/201802/09/WS5a7d0205a3106e7dcc13bbf1.html

U.S.-China Economic and Security Review Commission. "2019 Report to Congress", 14 November 2019. https://www.uscc.gov/annual-report/2019-annual-report

White House. "Executive Order Establishing the Committee for the Assessment of Foreign Participation in the United States Telecommunications Sector", 4 April 2020. https://www.whitehouse.gov/presidential-actions/executive-order-establishing-committee-assessment-foreign-participation-united-states-telecommunications-services-sector/

# Chapter 10

Akhlas, Adrian Wail. "Things you need to know about the government's sovereign wealth fund", The Jakarta Post, 24 January 2020. https://www.thejakartapost.com/news/2020/01/24/things-you-need-to-know-about-governments-sovereign-wealth-fund.html

Bird, Mike. "Japan's Pension Whales May Be Making Waves in Currency Markets", Wall Street Journal, 21 February 2020. https://www.wsj.com/articles/japans-pension-whales-may-be-making-waves-in-currency-markets-11582285660

Burgess, Matthew. "Wildfires are Forcing Aussie Pension Funds to Be More Green", Bloomberg, 13 February 2020. https://www.bloomberg.com/news/articles/2020-02-13/wildfires-are-forcing-aussie-pension-funds-to-be-more-green

Canadian Pension Plan Investment Board. "CPP Investments participates in Waymo's first external investment round", press release, 2 March 2020. https://www.cppinvestments.com/public-media/headlines/2020/cpp-investments-participates-in-waymos-first-external-investment-round

Clark, Simon and Ben Dummet. "Coronavirus Accelerates European Efforts to Block Foreign Takeovers", Wall Street Journal, 10 April 2020. https://www.wsj.com/articles/coronavirus-accelerates-european-efforts-to-block-foreign-takeovers-11586516403

Fetalvero, Nathaniel. "These engineers are the driving force behind Temasek's digital transformation", TechInAsia, 30 April 2019. https://www.techinasia.com/engineers-driving-force-temaseks-digital-transformation

Fink, Larry. "Letter to CEOs", BlackRock press release, 14 January 2020. https://www.blackrock.com/corporate/investor-relations/larry-fink-ceo-letter

Grab. "Grab and Singtel partner for Singapore digital banking licence", press release, 30 December 2019. https://www.grab.com/sg/press/others/grab-and-singtel-partner-for-singapore-digital-banking-licence/

Gross, Anna and Madhumita Mugia. "China and Huawei propose reinvention of the internet", Financial Tismes, 27 March 2020. https://www.ft.com/content/c78be2cf-a1a1-40b1-8ab7-904d7095e0f2

Holter, Mikael. "World's Biggest Wealth Fund Dragged Closer to Dumping Assets", Bloomberg News, 30 March 2020. https://www.bloomberg.com/news/articles/2020-03-30/world-s-biggest-wealth-fund-dragged-closer-to-forced-asset-sales

Japan Time. "Japan to develop strategy for 6G wireless communication networks expected around 2030", 21 January 2020. https://www.japantimes.co.jp/news/2020/01/21/business/tech/japan-strategy-6g-wireless-communication-networks-2030/#.XvTGTChKhPZ

Mandow, Nikki. "NZ Super Fund corrals $13 trillion for live streaming action", Newsroom, 20 August 2019. https://www.newsroom.co.nz/2019/08/20/762606/nz-super-fund-corrals-15tn-for-livestreaming-action

Pullar-Strecker, Tom and Rob Stock. "NZ call for better social media controls gains global traction", Stuff, 1April 2019. https://www.stuff.co.nz/business/111710382/nz-call-for-better-social-media-controls-gains-global-traction

Whineray, Matt. "New Zealand's Sovereign Fund Reckons With a Massacre", Institutional Investor, 24 April 2019. https://www.institutionalinvestor.com/article/b1f3tr9mc41xm0/New-Zealand-s-Sovereign-Fund-Reckons-With-a-Massacre

Tomás, Juan Pedro. "US lawmakers propose $1 billion fund to replace Chinese network gear", RCRWireless, 26 September 2019. https://www.rcrwireless.com/20190926/5g/us-lawmakers-propose-1-billion-fund-replace-huawei-gear

# Index

Page numbers followed by *f* and *t* refer to figures and tables, respectively.

ABP (Stichting Pensioenfonds ABP), 22, 25, 127
Abu Dhabi Developmental Holding Company, 337
Abu Dhabi Investment Authority (ADIA):
    coronavirus pandemic, 76
    direct investments, 20
    financial crisis bailouts, 7, 8*f*, 243
    fund manager, 38
    Megvii Technology, 90–91
    NIIF, 110–111
Accountability, 191–193
ACIC (Australia's Critical Infrastructure Centre), 259
Additionality, 140–146, 143*f*
ADIA, *see* Abu Dhabi Investment Authority
Africa, 150–163, 155*f*, 157*f*
Agenda 2063 (Africa), 157
AI (artificial intelligence), 94, 120, 244–245, 296
AIIB (Asian Infrastructure Investment Bank), 108

AIMCo (Alberta Investment Management Corporation), 211
Airbnb, 52
Akkiraji, Praveen, 232
Alaska, 9
Alaska Permanent Fund, 42
Alaska Permanent Fund Corporation (APFC), 76, 210–211, 234
Alberta Investment Management Corporation (AIMCo), 211
Alibaba, 87, 119–120
AlpInvest, 211–214, 212*f*
Amazon, 72, 318
Angola, 138, 162
Ant Financial, 91–92, 262–263, 284
AP6, 196–197
APFC, *see* Alaska Permanent Fund Corporation
APG Group N.V., 22–23, 39, 127, 212–213, 212*f*, 321
Apple, Inc., 28, 194, 318
Arndt, Raphael, 5
Artificial intelligence, *see* AI

Asian Infrastructure Investment
 Bank (AIIB), 108
Australia, 95–96, 257–259. *See
 also* Future Fund
AustralianSuper, 42
Australia's Critical Infrastructure
 Centre (ACIC), 259

Baldrige, Malcolm, 279
Barr, William, 304, 329
BCI, *see* British Columbia
 Investment Management
 Corporation
BDN (Blue Dot Network),
 106–108, 107*f*
Belt & Road Initiative (BRI),
 124–125, 124*f,* 130
Bezos, Jeff, 26
Billdesk, 96
Biotechnology sector, 76
Bloomberg Business Week, 25
Bloomberg News, 12
Blue Dot Network (BDN),
 106–108, 107*f*
BongoHive, 160
Botswana, 138
Branding, 106
Branson, Richard, 26
Brazil, 95
Brexit, 293
BRI, *see* Belt & Road Initiative
British Columbia Investment
 Management Corporation
 (BCI), 18–19, 25, 322–323
Bush, George W., 246*t*, 250, 261
Byju, 98
ByteDance, 286–287, 287*f*

Caisse de Depot Placement du
 Quebec (CDPQ), 18, 25,
 121–122, 165–166,
 190–191, 317
Caisse des Dépôts (CDC), 168
CalPERS, 25
Canada, 251
Canadian Pension Plan
 Investment Board (CPPIB):
 Alibaba, 87
 co-investments, 18–19
 digital health, 134
 direct investments, 19–20
 global footprint, 98
 infrastructure, 42
 logistics system, 122–123
 overseas offices, 219–220
 Silicon Valley arrival, 85
 sovereign pension funds, 17
Capital Constellation, 234–236,
 234*f*
CARES Act, 8–9
Carnival Cruises, 8
CDP Equity, 167
CDPQ, *see* Caisse de Depot
 Placement du Quebec, 18
CFIUS, *see* Committee on
 Foreign Investment in the
 United States
Chile, 17, 151–152
China, 87–92
 Belt & Road Initiative, 124,
 124*f,* 130
 Digital Silk Road Initiative,
 131
 semiconductors, 29–32
 source of savings, 10–11

China Investment Corp (CIC),
    87
  Alibaba, 87
  Blackstone, 38, 40–41, 192
  "China Factors," 71–72
  digital financial infrastructure,
    133
  establishment, 11
  financial crisis bailouts, 7, 242
  fintech investments, 237, 238*f*
  ISIF, 144
  seeding, 227–228, 228*f*
  US–China relationship, 332
China–Ireland Fund, 144–145,
    146*f*
China National Offshore Oil
    Company (CNOOC),
    251–254, 251*f*
China Venture Capital Fund
    (CVCF), 281
Cho Hyun-ah, 47
Cho Hyun-min, 48
Christchurch massacre, 316
Chuxing, Didi, 90*f*
CIA, 25–26
CIC, *see* China Investment Corp
Citibank, 8*f*
Climate Action 100+, 25
Climate change, 5, 23–25
Cloutier, Roland, 287
CNOOC (China National
    Offshore Oil Company),
    251–254, 251*f*
Co-investing, 18–19, 36, 46*t*, 144,
    237
Cold War, 333
Collective Health, 83

Cologix, 83
Committee on Foreign
    Investment in the United
    States (CFIUS), 245
  Ant Financial/MoneyGram
    transaction, 262–263
  critical technology, 283
  excepted foreign states,
    268*f*
  FIRRMA, 264, 270–272
  German transactions, 290
  history, 246–251, 247*f*, 248*t*
  Lattice/Canyon Bridge Deal,
    280–281
  personally identifiable
    information, 288
  Qualcomm/Broadcom
    transaction, 262
  review process, 264–268
  semiconductor transactions,
    282, 290
  TID focus, 29–30, 30*f*
  transaction reviews, 259–260,
    260*t*, 263*f*
Commonwealth
    Superannuation
    Corporation (CSC), 114
Coronavirus pandemic, 7–9,
    11–12, 76, 77*f*, 100–101,
    333
CPPIB, *see* Canadian Pension
    Plan Investment Board
CRFM (China Reform Fund
    Management Co), 280–282
Critical infrastructure, 278
Critical technology, 277–278,
    283

Cross-border technology
transfer, 139

De Bever, Leo, 210
Decacorn, 69
Delhivery, 123
Development funds, 14–16
DFC, *see* International
Development Finance
Corporation
Digital data:
empowerment, 104–105, 105*f*
Digital economy, 103–104, 104*f*,
277*f*, 330
Digital finacial infrastructure,
132–133
Digital health, 133–134
Digital infrastructure, 158
Digital Kazakhstan, 125
Digital revolution, 25–32
Digital Silk Road Initiative,
131
Digital Transformation Strategy
for Africa (DTS Africa), 158
Direct investing, 112–113
Direct listing (DL), 50–52
Diversification, 233–238
DL (direct listing), 50–52
DP World (Dubai Ports World),
255–257, 256*f*
DTS Africa (Digital
Transformation Strategy
for Africa), 158
Dubai Ports World (DP World),
255–257, 256*f*
Due diligence, 188, 195
Dutch Disease, 9–10

Early stage investing, 196–198,
197*f*
E-commerce, 97–98, 118–121
Economic and Social
Stabilization Fund (ESSF),
11
*The Economist,* 9
Education tech (edtech), 98
Egypt, 165, 337
ESG, 13, 19–25, 314–319
ESSF (Economic and Social
Stabilization Fund), 11
E Umbrella, 181
European Future Fund, 330
European Union, 28–29
Ewing-Chow, Paul, 76

Facebook, 303, 318
Fairchild Semiconductor,
279–280, 280*f*
FCC (Federal Communications
Commission), 30
FDI (foreign direct investment),
243–245
Federal Reserve, 9
FIEX (Foreign Investment), 14
5G, 328*f*, 329–331
50Hertz, 291, 291*f*, 292*f*
Financial crisis:
bailouts, 7–9, 242–244, 243*t*
2008-2009, 7, 14, 242–243
*Financial Times,* 20
Fintech, 94, 96, 147, 319–325
FIRB (Foreign Investment
Review Board), 257–258
FIRPTA (Foreign Investment in
Real Property Tax Act), 83

FIRRMA, *see* Foreign Investment Risk Review Modernization Act
Fiscal stabilization funds, 11–14
5G, 30, 300
Fllomena dos Santos, Jose, 162–163
FOF investments, *see* Fund of funds investments
Ford, Gerald, 246–247
Foreign direct investment (FDI), 243–245
Foreign Investment (FIEX), 14
Foreign Investment in Real Property Tax Act (FIRPTA), 83
Foreign Investment Risk Review Modernization Act (FIRRMA), 264, 268, 287–288, 296
Founder's accounting, 187, 187*f*
France, 168, 293
FRR (Algeria's Fonds des Regulations des Recettes), 150
FSI (Fondo Strategico Italiano), 166–167, 167*f*
Fullerton, Calif., 128–129, 128*f*
Funding, 6–19
  development funds, 14–16
  fiscal stabilization funds, 11–14
  long-term savings fund, 6–11
  public pension funds, 17–19
Fund of funds (FOF) investments, 34–35, 34*f*, 110

Fundo Soberano de Angola, 138, 162
Future Fund, 5, 17
  Canberra Data Centers, 113, 113*f*, 115
  fund manager, 38
  infrastructure, 42
  Silicon Valley arrival, 86

GAAP (Generally Accepted Accounting Principles), 187–188, 187*f*
GCI (Grand Chip Investment GmbH), 289
Generally Accepted Accounting Principles (GAAP), 187–188, 187*f*
General partner (GP) managers, 35–37, 37*f*
Germany, 95, 288–291
Ghana, 152
GIC, 322*f*
  data center FLAP markets, 115–117, 116*f*, 117*t*
  digital finacial infrastructure, 133
  direct investments, 20
  financial crisis bailouts, 7, 8*f*
  fintech, 96, 319–321, 319*f*
  fund manager, 38
  logistics systems, 121–122
  overseas office, 221–222
  real estate, 40
  reorganization, 61
  Silicon Valley arrival, 73–78, 74*t*
GIC Labs, 320

GIC Technology Group, 320
Global downturn, 100–101
Global Strategic Investment
    Alliance (GSIA), 42, 43*t*
Go-Jek, 97
Google, 318
Government of Rwanda, 118
Government Pension
    Investment Fund (GPIF),
    25, 43–45, 317–318, 333
GP (general partner) managers,
    35–37, 37*f*
Grand Chip Investment GmbH
    (GCI), 289
Greenko Holding, 20
Grindr, 275, 284
GSIA (Global Strategic
    Investment Alliance), 42,
    43*t*

Hangzhou, China, 129
Healthcare investments, 153
Healthtech, 94
Hectacorn, 69
HERE, 306–308, 307*f*
Horn, Michelle, 232
Huawei, 28, 327–328
Hub71, 15–16, 149

ICA (Investment Canada Act),
    253–255
ICarbonX/PatientsLikeMe deal,
    284
ICD (Investment Corporation of
    Dubai), 95
IFSWF (International Forum of
    Sovereign Wealth Funds),
    68

INCJ (Innovation Network
    Corporation of Japan),
    297–299
India, 92–93
Indonesia, 15, 164, 317
InfraCredit, 156
Infrastructure:
    critical, 278
    digital finacial, 132–133
    domestic innovation
        ecosystem, 140
    gap, 105–113
    investment approach, 39–42
    network, 113–118
    super investors, 114–115
Initial public offerings (IPOs):
    Alibaba, 87, 88*f*
    decline in, 26
    direct listing vs., 50–52
    JD.com, 87–88, 88*f*
Institutional investors, 5
Intellectual property (IP), 100
Intergenerational funds, 6
International Development
    Finance Corporation
    (DFC), 30, 107, 329
International Forum of
    Sovereign Wealth Funds
    (IFSWF), 68
Internet economy, 276
Internet of Things (IoT), 104,
    132
Investment Canada Act (ICA),
    253–255
Investment Framework, 24
IoT (Internet of Things), 104,
    132

IP (intellectual property), 100
IPOs, *see* Initial public offerings
Ireland Strategic Investment
    Fund (ISIF), 86
Irish Strategic Fund (ISIF), 14,
    25, 138, 140–146, 142*f*,
    143*f*, 145*f*
Israel, 294–295, 294*f*
Italy, 166–168
Ithmar Capital, 154, 169

Japan, 249–250, 269, 296–299,
    331
Japan Display Inc. (JDI),
    296–299, 298*f*
Japan Investment Corporation
    (JIC), 224–226, 297
JD.com, 87–88, 88*f*
JDI (Japan Display Inc.),
    296–299, 298*f*
JIC (Japan Investment
    Corporation), 224–226,
    297
Jiwei, Lou, 72
Jumal Technologies AG, 161

Kaneko, Yasunori, 225–226
Kanters, Patrick, 39
Kazakhstan, 125
Kenya, 16, 156
Kepler Fi, 320
Khazanah, 12, 93
    Alibaba, 87
    domestic development, 165
    logistics system, 122
    offices, 205–206
    Silicon Valley arrival, 76–78

KIA, *see* Kuwait Investment
    Authority
Kiat, Lim Chow, 75
KIC (Korea Investment
    Corporation), 48
Korean Air Lines, 47–49
Kuehne + Nagel, 229
Kuka, 289
Kuwait–China Silk Road Fund,
    131
Kuwait Investment Authority
    (KIA), 7
    co-investments, 19
    financial crisis bailouts, 8*f*,
        243
    fund manager, 38
    overseas office, 207–208
    Silicon Valley arrival, 78

Late stage investing, 186–189,
    189*f*
Lattice/Canyon Bridge Deal,
    280–282, 281*f*
Lee, Aileen, 69
Libyan Investment Authority
    (LIA), 150
Limited partnership (LP)
    investors, 35–36, 35*f*, 37*f*
LiveNation, 8
Logistic systems, 118–126, 120*f*
Long-term savings fund, 6–11
Low, Jho, 21
LP investors, *see* Limited
    partnership investors

Ma, Jack, 62, 233
Machnig, Matthias, 290

MAD (Mutual Assured
  Destruction), 334, 338
Malaysia, 12
Mayer, Kevin, 287
Megvii Technology Inc, 90–91,
  91*f*
Meituan-Dianping, 183–184
Minerals Development Fund,
  156
Mobike, 182–183
Mobile economy, 277*f*
Mobility, 96–97
MoneyGram, 262–263, 284
Morocco, 154–155, 154*f*, 169,
  170*f*
Mubadala, *see* UAE's Mubadala
  Investment Company
Mumtalakat, 129
Musgrave, Paul, 269
Musk, Elon, 26

Namibia, 156
National Pension Service (NPS),
  21, 45–49, 47*t*, 49*t*
National security, 241–273
  about, 245–246
  CFIUS, 246–251, 264–268
  critical infrastructure,
    255–259
  energy security, 251–255
  financial crisis bailouts,
    242–245
  personally identifiable
    information, 285*f*
  semiconductor chips, 279
National security review,
  254–255

NBIM, 316
NBIM (Norges Bank Investment
  Management), 4–5
NEDO (New Energy and
  Industrial Technology
  Development
  Organization), 331
Neom City, 131–132, 148–149
Net benefit review, 253–254
Netherlands, 9–10
Network infrastructure, 113–118
Neumann, Adam, 101, 175
Newcastle United, 8
New Energy and Industrial
  Technology Development
  Organization (NEDO),
  331
New Zealand Superannuation
  Fund (NZ super), 17,
  24–25, 314–316
Nigeria, 16, 154*f*
Nigerian Sovereign Investment
  Authority (NSIA), 16, 17*f*,
  150–156, 152*f*, 160
NIIF (National Investment and
  Infrastructure Fund),
  108–111, 110*f*
NIO, 179–180
Nixon, Richard, 247
Non-conventional venture
  investors, 53*f*, 54
Norges Bank Investment
  Management (NBIM), 4–5
Norway, 4, 12–14, 40, 50
Norway Government Pension
  Fund, 4
Norway's Oil Fund, 12–14, 50

NPRF (National Pensions
    Reserve Fund), 141
NPS, *see* National Pension
    Service
NSIA, *see* Nigerian Sovereign
    Investment Authority
NZ Super, *see* New Zealand
    Superannuation Fund

Obama, Barack, 246*t*, 250,
    260–261, 289
OCP Morocco, 155
Odell, Mats, 197
OIF (Oman Investment Fund),
    200, 202
Ola Cabs, 97
Old Mutual of South Africa, 155
Oman Investment Fund (OIF),
    200, 202
Oman's State General Reserve
    Fund (SGRF), 14, 139–140,
    140*f*
OMERS Ventures, *see* Ontario
    Municipal Employees
    Retirement System
1Malaysia Development Berhad
    (1MDB), 21
One Planet, 23–24, 23*f*
Ontario Municipal Employees
    Retirement System
    (OMERS) Ventures, 20
  early stage investing, 198–199,
    199*f*
  infrastructure, 42–43
  overseas office, 220–221, 221*f*
  Oxford Properties, 214–216,
    215*f*

real estate, 40
Silicon Valley arrival, 84
Ontario Teachers' Pension Plan
    (OTPP), 18–19, 25, 84, 87
OPTrust, 96, 116–117, 196
OSI (Oxford Sciences
    Innovation plc), 200–201,
    201*f*
OTPP, *see* Ontario Teachers'
    Pension Plan
Overseas offices, 207–211
  culture tension, 216–217
  integration, 217*f*
Oxford Properties Group Inc.,
    214–216, 215*f*
Oxford Sciences Innovation plc
    (OSI), 200–201, 201*f*

Pacific Light Cable Network
    (PLCN), 301, 301*f*
Partnerships, 310
Passive active investors, 62*f*
PE (private equity) funds, 34
Pension Reserve Fund, 151–152
Performance benchmarks,
    193–195
Personally identifiable
    information (PII),
    285–286, 285*f*
PGGM, 212–213, 212*f*
PIF, *see* Public Investment Fund
PIFSS (Public Institution for
    Social Security of Kuwait),
    234
PII (personally identifiable
    information), 285–286,
    285*f*

Pine Labs, 96
Platform9, 83
PLCN (Pacific Light Cable
    Network), 301, 301*f*
Policy Bazaar, 96
Political intervention, 172
PPFs, *see* Public pension funds
Private equity (PE) funds, 34
Public Institution for Social
    Security of Kuwait (PIFSS),
    234
Public Investment Fund (PIF):
    digital health, 134
    Egypt agreement, 337
    financial crisis bailouts, 7–8
    fintech, 148
    NEOM City, 317
    Silicon Valley arrival, 78–82
    TAQNIA, 340
    tech focus, 57
    Uber, 63, 178
    Vision Fund, 26–27
Public market, rarity of
    unicorns, 50–54
Public pension funds (PPFs), 2,
    3–4, 3*t*, 17–19. *See also*
    Sovereign investment funds
    (SIFs)
Public Sector Pension (PSP),
    18–19
Pula Fund, 138

Qatar, 40
Qatar Investment Authority
    (QIA), 10
QFPFs (Qualified Foreign
    Pension Fund), 84

QIA (Qatar Investment
    Authority), 10
QIC (Queensland Investment
    Corporation), 42, 114
Q-Telventure, 26
Qualcomm/Broadcom
    transaction, 261–262,
    329–330
Qualified Foreign Pension Fund
    (QFPFs), 84
Queensland Investment
    Corporation (QIC), 42, 114

Razak, Najib, 21
RDIF, *see* Russian Direct
    Investment Fund
Real estate, 39–45
Recursion Pharmaceuticals,
    83
RIF (Rwanda Innovation Fund),
    163
Rokid, 88–89
RPMI Railpen (Railways Pension
    Scheme in UK), 234
Russia, 338
Russian Direct Investment Fund
    (RDIF), 14, 91, 168–169,
    169*f*, 338, 339*t*
Rwanda Innovation Fund (RIF),
    163

Sabia, Michael, 166, 191, 195
SAFE (State Administration of
    Foreign Exchange), 11, 332
Sagan, Carl, 107
Samruk-Kazyna (SK), 125
Samsung, 28

Saudi Arabia, 165. *See also* Public Investment Fund (PIF)
Saudi Aramco, 26
Saudi Technology Development and Investment Company (TAQNIA), 340
Schumer, Chuck, 286
SDFs, *see* Sovereign development funds
Securities and Exchange Commission (SEC), 53–54
Security, national, *see* National security
Seko, Hiroshige, 226
Semiconductor industry, 279–282, 294
SenseTime Group Ltd, 88–89
Sensitive personal data, 278, 287–288
SGRF, *see* Oman's State General Reserve Fund
SIFs, *see* Sovereign investment funds
Silicon Valley, 25, 67, 73, 78–86
Singapore, 165, 243. *See also* GIC; Temasek
Singles' Day, 118–121
Sipahimalani, Rohit, 219
SK (Samruk-Kazyna), 125
Skinner, Kiron, 269
Smart cities, 126–134, 128*f*
Smart City Infrastructure Fund, 127–128
Smithfield Foods, 270–271
Snapdeal, 97

SoftBank Vision Fund, *see* Vision Fund
Sonmez, Zafer, 171
SOPEF (Spain-Oman Private Equity Fund), 14–15
South Africa, 156
South Korea, 20–21
Sovereign development funds (SDFs), 2, 236–237, 236*f*, 341–342
Sovereign investment funds (SIFs):
    active investing, 45–49
    behind-the-scene asset owners, 33–38
    current focus, 100
    functions, 164
    London offices, 206*t*
    office location, 207–211
    real estate to infrastructure, 39–45
    reorganization, 60*f*
    tech investments, 55–64, 68–73
    unicorn engagement, 70–71, 71*f*
Sovereign investors, 1–32
    development, 2
    digital revolution, 25–32
    funds, 6–19
    growth, 19–25
    representative sampling, 66*t*
    trillion-dollar club, 2–6
Sovereign pension funds, 17–18
Sovereign Wealth Fund Institute (SWFI), 3

Sovereign wealth funds (SWFs).
    *See also* Sovereign
    investment funds (SIFs)
    development, 2
    technology innovation, 67
    top five sectors, 67*t*
    top ten, 2–3, 2*t*
Spain, 14
Spotify, 51
State Administration of Foreign
    Exchange (SAFE), 11, 332
StayNTouch/Beijing Shiji
    Group, 285
Stichting Pensioenfonds ABP, *see*
    ABP
Strategic Investment fund of
    Gabon, 163
Sweden, 196–197
SWFI (Sovereign Wealth Fund
    Institute), 3
SWFs, *see* Sovereign wealth funds
Switzerland, 95

TAQNIA (Saudi Technology
    Development and
    Investment Company), 340
Teachers' Innovation Platform
    (TIP), 84
Team building, 59–60
Team Telecom, 301–304
Tech investment programs,
    184–185
Tech investments, 22, 65
    desert hubs, 146–150
    digital revolution, 25–32
    drivers of focus, 55–57
    fractured future, 325–328

objectives, 55*f*
    rethinking going direct,
        305–311
Technology, critical, 277–278,
    283
Tel Aviv, 25
Temasek:
    Alibaba, 87
    challenges, 179–184
    Chinese investments, 334–335
    digital finacial infrastructure,
        133
    digital health, 134
    early stage investing, 196, 200
    financial crisis bailouts, 7, 8*f*
    fintech, 96–97, 323–325, 324*f*
    investment strategy, 22, 22*f*
    overseas offices, 214–220,
        218*t*
    real estate, 41
    regulation, 61
    reorganization, 61
    seeding, 228–229
    SenseTime, 90*f*
    Silicon Valley arrival, 73–78,
        74*t*
    tech investments, 88, 219*t*
Thevenon, David, 232
Thrift Savings Plan, 31
"TID" technologies, 277–278,
    278*f*
TikTok, 286–287
TIP (Teachers' Innovation
    Platform), 84
Tokopedia, 97
Transgrid, 256*f*, 258
Transparency, 13–14

TRS (Teacher Retirement
    System of Texas), 222–224
Trump, Donald, 29, 106, 246*t*,
    248, 259, 261, 280, 282,
    294, 327–328
Turkey Wealth Fund, 171
Twitch, 72

UAE's Mubadala Investment
    Company (Mubadala), 12
  Alphabet investment, 85
  digital health, 134
  early stage investing, 199–200
  fintech, 147–149
  fund manager, 38
  funds, 15
  logistics system, 122
  RDIF partnership, 338–339,
    339*t*
  SenseTime, 90, 90*f*
  Silicon Valley arrival, 82–84
  tech focus, 57
Uber, 63, 178, 178*f*
Unicorns:
  defined, 69–70
  engagement, 62–63
  industrialization, 69
  life cycle of, 185*f*
  rarity in public market, 50–54

United Kingdom, 93–95, 293
US–China relationship,
    294–295, 299–305,
    331–333, 333*f*
US Securities Act (1933),
    53–54

Venture capital (VC) investors,
    58*f*, 68–69, 159, 191–195
Vestager, Margrethe, 299
Vintage year, 236
Vision Fund, 27, 27*f*, 101,
    122–123, 178, 229–233
Von der Leyen, Ursula, 28–29,
    330

*Wall Street Journal*, 68
West Summit, 72, 227–228
WeWork, 62–63, 101, 175–178,
    177*f*, 184, 203

Yellen, Janet, 9
Yellow Peril, 269
Yozma program, 26

Zambia, 160
Zomato, 97
Zuckerberg, Mark,
    62, 286